BUDDHA'S TEACHINGS

BUDDHA'S TEACHINGS

BEING THE

Sutta-Nipāta or Discourse-Collection

EDITED IN THE ORIGINAL PALI TEXT
WITH AN ENGLISH VERSION FACING IT

BY

LORD CHALMERS

G.C.B. Hon. D.Litt., Oxford

Sometime Master of Peterhouse, Cambridge University
Sometime Governor of Ceylon

GYAN

Published by

GYAN

Gyan Publishing House
5, Ansari Road
Daryaganj, New Delhi-110002
Phone: 011-47034999, 9811692060
E-mail: books@gyanbooks.com

Distribution Network
gyanbooks.com
India, USA, Canada, UK, Australia, France

ISBN : 978-81-212-6200-2 (PB)
First Published, 1932

2nd Impression 2022

Printed at: Gyan Press, Delhi.

BUDDHA'S TEACHINGS
Author: Lord Chalmers

BUDDHA'S TEACHINGS

BEING THE

Sutta-Nipāta or Discourse-Collection

EDITED IN THE ORIGINAL PALI TEXT
WITH AN ENGLISH VERSION FACING IT

BY

LORD CHALMERS
G.C.B. Hon. D.Litt., Oxford
Sometime Master of Peterhouse, Cambridge University
Sometime Governor of Ceylon

Πάντα γέλως καὶ πάντα κόνις καὶ πάντα τὸ μηδέν·
πάντα γὰρ ἐξ ἀλόγων ἐστὶ τὰ γινόμενα. — GLYCON

1932

PRAEPOSITO SOCIISQUE
ORIELENSIBUS
ΤΡΟΦΕΙΑ

PREFACE

Some time ago, when reading the Sutta-Nipāta, I was led to the conclusion that, while all verse when translated should receive a metrical rendering, it was particularly desirable to make the attempt here, so as to emphasize in English the historically significant varieties of versification found in the Pāli. In 1928 Professor Lanman suggested that, with a Pāli text on the opposite page (as in the Loeb Classics), my metrical experiment should find a place in the Harvard Oriental Series. This volume is the outcome of his suggestion.

My Pāli text has been based on Fausböll's *editio princeps* of 1885 and on the 'new edition' of 1913 for the Pāli Text Society (by Andersen and Helmer Smith),—as modified by the subsequent P.T.S. editions of the Commentary on the Sutta-Nipāta (Paramatthajotikā II) and of the canonical Niddesa. The conclusion borne in on me was that, apart from minor matters and a very few real divergences of readings, the text of the Sutta-Nipāta (thanks to this distinguished *paramparā* of Danish scholars) was practically now a *textus receptus*; and that, in a volume which is primarily intended for English readers, it was unnecessary to discuss various readings which Pāli scholars can readily investigate in the authorities quoted above. Where I have differed, I have aimed at the restoration, not at the conjectural emendation, of the text.

Nor, in the matter of interpretation of the text, have I thought it desirable to cumber the translation with polemic notes or with a record of others' renderings. I have therefore confined myself to an examination (in the *Introduction*) into the literary evolution of the Sutta-Nipāta, so far as it can be traced to-day, and will let the version speak for itself as a commentary no less than as a rendering.

My conclusion is that, while its materials are by no means all of equal antiquity, there is no older *book* in Buddhist literature than the Sutta-Nipāta, and no earlier corpus of primitive Buddhist doctrine than it contains.

While the presence of the Pāli on the opposite page forbids exuberance in translation, the limitations of metre (and I have sought to make the English follow roughly the Pāli scheme of versification) make it no easy matter—even without rhyme—to compress terse Pāli into a relatively modest compass in English. *Ignoscent experti.*

PETERHOUSE,

18 *February* 1931.

CONTENTS

PAGE

PREFACE vii

INTRODUCTION. xiii

Tabular conspectus of the five main divisions (Vaggas or 'Books')

Book	*Name*	*Suttas*	*Stanzas*	*Fausböll*	*Name in Pali*	
1	Snake Book	12	221	1–221	Uraga vagga	2
2	Short Book	14	183	222–404	Cūla vagga	54
3	Long Book	12	361	405–765	Mahā vagga	98
4	The Octads	16	210	766–975	Aṭṭhaka vagga	184
5	The Way-across	16	174	976–1149	Pārāyana vagga	234

Table of the seventy Suttas or minor divisions

For some Pali sutta-names (marked with a star) there are alternative Pali names. These are given below, at end of page xi.

BOOK 1. THE SNAKE BOOK, OR URAGA VAGGA

Sutta	*Name in Pali*	
1. As Snakes slough outworn skins	Uragasutta	2
2. Dhaniya, the rich herdsman	Dhaniyasutta	4
3. Alone — like the rhinoceros	Khaggavisāṇasutta	10
4. Bhāradvāja, the franklin	Kasi-Bhāradvāja-sutta	20
5. Cunda, the smith	Cundasutta	24
6. The Twelve Failures	Parābhavasutta	26
7. The Wastrel	*Vasalasutta	30
8. Good-will	Mettasutta	36
9. The Himālayan Sprite	*Hemavatasutta	38
10. The Woodland Sprite	Āḷavakasutta	44
11. Disillusion (as to the body)	*Vijayasutta	46
12. The Sage	Munisutta	48

BOOK 2. THE SHORT BOOK, OR CŪLA VAGGA

1. The Three Gems	Ratanasutta	54
2. Carrion	Āmagandhasutta	58
3. Loyalty	Hirisutta	62
4. The Boon of Boons	Mahāmangalasutta	64
5. Inward Growths	Sūcilomasutta	66
6. The Good Life	*Dhammacariyasutta	68
7. Brahminism's Golden Age	Brāhmaṇadhammikasutta	70

Sutta	*Name in Pali*	
8. The Good Ship	*Nāvāsutta	76
9. Right Conduct	Kiṁsīlasutta	78
10. Arise!	Uṭṭhānasutta	78
11. To Rāhula	Rāhulasutta	80
12. Kappa's Destiny	*Vangīsasutta	82
13. The Anchorite's Ideal	*Sammāparibbājaniyasutta	86
14. The Almsman's Life and the Householder's	Dhammikasutta	90

BOOK 3. THE LONG BOOK, OR MAHĀ VAGGA

1. Gotama's Pilgrimage	Pabbajjāsutta	98
2. Gotama's Temptation by Māra	Padhānasutta	100
3. Apt Words	Subhāsitasutta	104
4. Offerings	*Sundarika-Bhāradvājasutta	106
5. Māgha; or Largesse	Māghasutta	114
6. Sabhiya's Questions	Sabhiyasutta	120
7. The Superman	Selasutta	132
8. The Pangs of Grief	Sallasutta	144
9. What is a Brahmin?	Vāseṭṭhasutta	146
10. Slander's Doom	*Kokāliyasutta	156
11. Asita's *Nunc dimittis*	*Nālakasutta	164
12. The Dyads: Origin and Ending of Ills	Dvayatānupassanāsutta	172

BOOK 4. BOOK OF OCTADS, OR AṬṬHAKA VAGGA

1. Prologue: Desires	Kāmasutta	184
2. Octad of the Den	Guhaṭṭhakasutta	184
3. Octad of Malice	Duṭṭhaṭṭhakasutta	186
4. Octad of Purity	Suddhaṭṭhakasutta	188
5. Octad of Perfection	Paramaṭṭhakasutta	192
6. Vita brevis	Jarāsutta	192
7. Lechery	Tissa-Metteyya-sutta	196
8. Warring sects	Pasūrasutta	196
9. Beauty scorned	Māgandiyasutta	200
10. 'Ere dissolution comes'	Purābhedasutta	202
11. Contentions	Kalaha-vivāda-sutta	204
12. Rejoinders	Cūla-viyūha-sutta	210
13. More Rejoinders	Mahā-viyūhasutta	214
14. Without delay	Tuvaṭakasutta	220
15. The Armed Hand	Attadaṇḍasutta	224
16. What Sāriputta asked	*Sāriputtasutta	228

BOOK 5. BOOK OF THE WAY-ACROSS, OR PĀRĀYANA VAGGA

Division			
1. Prologue: Bāvarī and his 16 disciples		Vatthugāthā	234
Answer to	*Sutta*	*Pucchā*	
2. Ajita's question	(1)	Ajitamāṇava-pucchā	242
3. Tissa Metteyya's question	(2)	Tissametteyyamāṇavapucchā	244
4. Puṇṇaka's question	(3)	Puṇṇakamāṇavapucchā	244
5. Mettagū's question	(4)	Mettagūmāṇavapucchā	246
6. Dhotaka's question	(5)	Dhotakamāṇavapucchā	250
7. Upasīva's question	(6)	Upasīvamāṇavapucchā	252
8. Nanda's question	(7)	Nandamāṇavapucchā	254
9. Hemaka's question	(8)	Hemakamāṇavapucchā	256
10. Todeyya's question	(9)	Todeyyamāṇavapucchā	258
11. Kappa's question	(10)	Kappamāṇavapucchā	258
12. Jatukaṇṇī's question	(11)	Jatukaṇṇīmāṇavapucchā	260
13. Bhadrāvudha's question	(12)	Bhadrāvudhamāṇavapucchā	260
14. Udaya's question	(13)	Udayamāṇavapucchā	262
15. Posāla's question	(14)	Posālamāṇavapucchā	264
16. Mogharāja's question	(15)	Mogharājamāṇavapucchā	264
17. Pingiya's question	(16)	Pingiyamāṇavapucchā	266
— Epilogue: lauding Gotama and his Way-across			266

INDEXES

(I) Pali 275

(II) English (by Miss Isaline Horner) 292

Alternative Pali names for Suttas marked above with a star

1.07. Vasala-sutta *or* Aggi(ka)-Bhāradvāja-sutta (cf. 1.4 and 3.4) 30

1.09. Hemavata-sutta *or* Sātāgira-sutta 38

1.11. Vijaya-sutta *or* Kāya-vicchandanika-sutta 46

2.06. Dhammacariya-sutta *or* Kapila-sutta 68

2.08. Nāvā-sutta *or* Dhamma-sutta 76

2.12. Vangīsa-sutta *or* Nigrodha-Kappa-sutta 82

2.13. Sammā-paribbājaniya-sutta *or* Muni-sutta *or* Mahāsamaya-sutta . . 86

3.04. Sundarika-Bhāradvāja-sutta *or* Pūraḷāsa-sutta 106

3.10. Kokāliya-sutta *or* Kokālika-sutta 156

3.11. Nālaka-sutta *or* Moneyya-sutta 164

4.16. Sāriputta-sutta *or* Thera-pañha-sutta. 228

INTRODUCTION

I

The Pāli Canon, as it has come down to us, is divided into three Piṭakas (or 'baskets'), viz.:

I. Vinaya-p°,—containing the detailed Rule with which (in a simpler form) Gotama's bhikkhus (or 'Almsmen') began their corporate life.

II. Sutta-p°,—containing (subsequent) discourses and dialogues, embodying doctrinal Buddhism.

III. Abhidhamma-p°,—containing (still later) scholastic expositions of the Sutta-piṭaka.

The Sutta-Nipāta, which is here translated, contains an ancient, probably the most ancient, part of the Sutta-piṭaka. It belongs to that portion of the Sutta-piṭaka which is named the Khuddaka Nikāya, or 'collection of short' treatises (as distinct from the four long Nikāyas,— called Dīgha, Majjhima, Saṁyutta, and Anguttara).

Of the five Vaggas (or 'books') of the present Sutta-Nipāta, the fifth stands out from its fellows by reason of its purposeful unity. While the Uraga, Mahā, Cūla, and Aṭṭhaka Vaggas consist each of a collection of independent and unconnected poems (sometimes interspersed with prose) called *Suttas*, the Pārāyana aims at a dramatic synthesis. Its prologue and epilogue serve as a setting to the sixteen Questions which elicit Gotama's gradual exposition of the saving 'Way Across',—an exposition which collectively is styled a homily (dhamma-pariyāya) in the prose preface to verse 1124 (cf. v. 1130) and is classified as simply a 'suttanta' (not a Vagga, or 'book' of many suttas) at Paramatthajotikā, II. 163.

Uncertainty still attaches to the sense in which the word 'Sutta' was used in primitive Buddhism. Originally meaning 'a thread', the word has come to denote prose narratives or dialogues concerning the *dhamma*, such as those which, in (e.g.) the Dīgha and Majjhima Nikāyas, characterize the great Sutta-Piṭaka,—in contradistinction to the contents of the Vinaya and Abhidhamma Piṭakas. But this was not the case from the outset. Thus, (*a*) in the Vinaya (II. 95), we find 'Sutta' specifically applied to the canonical Pātimokkha:—'Ubhayāni assa Pātimokkhāni vitthārena svāgatāni honti . . . *suttato* anuvyañjanaso' ('to him have been handed down accurately and in full both Pātimokkhas, Sutta by Sutta and in extenso'). (*b*) At the end of the canonical Sutta Vibhanga's exposition of the Pātimokkha (Vin. IV. 351), there occur the words: 'Ettakaṁ tassa Bhagavato *sutta*-gataṁ *sutta*-pariyāpannaṁ anvaddhamāsaṁ uddesaṁ āgacchati' ('thus much of the Lord's words, as handed down in Suttas and as embodied in Suttas, comes in course of recitation once a fortnight'). And (*c*) at Vinaya, II. 96–7 there is a condemnation of any 'dhamma-kathika', or professed reciter of the Dhamma (not of the Vinaya alone, it will incidentally be noted), who has failed to master not only the Pātimokkha *Suttas* but also the *Sutta*-Vibhanga commentary thereon ('tassa Suttaṁ āgataṁ, no Sutta-vibhango', or—*a fortiori*—'tassa n' eva Suttaṁ āgataṁ no Sutta-vibhango').

While the foregoing quotations prove the use of the term 'Sutta' to include the disciplinary regulations of the young Community, I am not aware of the term being applied in the Canon to isolated apophthegms, which formed the kernel of Gotama's doctrinal teachings. It may well be, I suggest, that the title of 'Sutta' (primarily meaning 'thread' or 'string', cf. Sumangala Vilāsinī, I. 18) was reserved from the outset for any consecutive *thread* of argument or narration (whether of Rule or of Doctrine) continuously *strung* together and coherent.[1]

II

The compilation of the Pāli Canon must have been spread over centuries, and have employed successive generations of ecclesiastical authors and editors before the present Ti-piṭaka was finally evolved. No credence can be extended to the orthodox Buddhist belief that the whole Pali Canon—at least in essentials—was settled in its present form at the First Council (which was held immediately after Gotama's death in (?) 483 B.C.). Originally, there were no 'scriptures', only memories of individual utterances by Gotama, and perhaps by his chief lieutenants,—memories like those which, some five and a half centuries later, formed the basic material of the Christian synoptics. Indeed, it cannot safely be assumed that, *in its present form*, any given 'book' of the Canon dates back to before Asoka's Council held at Patna in (perhaps) 240 B.C.

Composition of course preceded compilation; the date (if ascertainable) of the compilation of a canonical 'book' as a whole does not determine the date of composition of its constituents,—which latter may well be more ancient, in whole or part, than the synthetic book into which they have been incorporated.

[1] At Sumangala Vilāsinī, I. 23, Buddhaghosa defines 'sutta' as denoting 'the two (Sutta-) Vibhangas, the Niddesa, the Khandhakas and Parivāra (of the Vinaya Piṭaka), the Mangala, Ratana, Nālaka, and Tuvaṭaka Suttas in the Sutta-Nipāta, together with all other utterances of the Tathāgata which are styled Suttas.'

He adds, that all those Suttas which contain both prose and verse are also classified as 'geyya'.

It will be noted, and is (I think) significant, that the list starts with the ancient *Commentaries* on (*a*) the Vinaya and (*b*) the Sutta-Nipāta's earliest elements.

In support of the belief now generally accepted that the Pāli Canon was evolved from common material, there is the evidence afforded not only by the constant repetition throughout the great Nikāyas of 'stock passages' (which were as convenient for Eastern recitation as they are wearisome to a Western reader) but also by the frequent incorporation of the same composition, title and all, in more than one canonical book. To take a simple instance from the Sutta-Nipāta:—the Sela and Vāseṭṭha Suttas of our Mahā-vagga recur verbatim under the same titles in the Majjhima Nikāya. Also, the Metta Sutta of our Uraga Vagga, and the Ratana and (Mahā-) Mangala Suttas of our Cūla-vagga, reappear bodily in the canonical Khuddaka Pāṭha. Numerous also are the instances of individual stanzas of the Sutta-Nipāta recurring elsewhere in the Canon;—e.g. verses 45 and 46 are found also in the Majjhima Nikāya (III. 154), and in the Vinaya (I. 350), as well as in the Dhammapada (vv. 328–9).

A special light, however, is thrown on the evolution of our Sutta-Nipāta by the inclusion *in the Canon* of its ancient commentary, called Niddesa (or 'exposition'). Now, this canonical Niddesa is a commentary not on the whole of our 'Sutta-Nipāta' (which it does not name *as such*) but only on its concluding Vaggas (Aṭṭhaka and Pārāyana) and on the Khaggavisāṇa (or 'rhinoceros') Sutta of the Uraga Vagga. The canonical Niddesa, therefore, leaves untouched (i) the whole of the Mahā and Cūla Vaggas, and (ii) eleven out of twelve Suttas of the Uraga Vagga; i.e. it wholly ignores the Sutta-Nipāta's corporate title and two-thirds of its existing contents.

But the Canonical Niddesa is not the sole external authority for the relative age of our Sutta-Nipāta. Further direct (and corroborative) evidence is furnished by the following references to our Sutta-Nipāta in other canonical books, such as the Vinaya and the Saṁyutta and Anguttara Nikāyas,—references, it will be observed, which are specifically restricted to those two Vaggas with which the Niddesa deals. Thus:

(i) Sn. 844 is quoted at Saṁyutta Nikāya, III. 9 and 12:—Vuttaṁ idam Bhagavatā Aṭṭhaka-vaggike Māgandiya-pañhe: 'Okaṁ pahāya . . . kayirā ti'.

(ii) Sn. 1038 is quoted at Saṁyutta Nikāya, II. 47:—Vuttaṁ idaṁ Pārāyane Ajita-pañhe: 'Ye ca . . . mārisâti'.

(iii) Sn. 1042 is quoted at Anguttara Nikāya, III. 399:—Vuttaṁ idaṁ Bhagavatā Pārāyane Metteyya-pañhe: 'Yo ubh' ante . . . accagā ti'.

(iv) Sn. 1048 is quoted at Anguttara Nikāya, I. 133 and II. 45:—Idañ ca pana me taṁ sandhāya bhāsitaṁ Pārāyane Puṇṇaka-pañhe: 'Saṁkhāya . . . brūmīti'.

(v) Sn. 1106–7 is quoted at Anguttara Nikāya, I. 134:—Idañ ca pana me taṁ sandhāya bhāsitaṁ Pārāyane Udaya-pañhe: 'Pahānaṁ . . . pabhedanaṁ'.

(vi) At Vinaya, I. 196[1], Soṇa, being asked by Gotama to show what he knew of the Dhamma, recited the whole contents of the Aṭṭhaka Vagga:—Sabbān' eva Aṭṭhaka-vaggikāni sarena abhāsi.

Hence it may be concluded that, at the date of its composition, the existing Niddesa covered as a commentary the whole of the then existing 'Sutta-Nipāta'; and that, after the composition of the Niddesa commentary, but before the Pāli Canon was fixed, further material was incorporated with the Pārāyana, the Aṭṭhaka Vagga, and the Khaggavisāṇa Sutta to make up the final Sutta-Nipāta as it has come down to us in the Canon. Thus the Pārāyana, the Aṭṭhaka Vagga, and the Khaggavisāṇa are older, as a compilation, not only than the canonical Niddesa which comments on them, but also than (those portions of) the Vinaya and of the two Nikāyas which specifically cite them.

III

But, as has been noted *supra*, authorship precedes editorial compilation; and the ascertained stages of growth of a compiled 'book' by no means settle the relative date of composition of its contents, a question for the solution of which internal evidence must be invoked, for what it is worth.

Internal evidence may be linguistic, metrical, or doctrinal.

Mainly on linguistic grounds, Fausböll (in his Introduction to his translation of the Sutta-Nipāta in vol. x of the *Sacred Books of the East*) originally considered 'the greater part of the Mahāvagga and nearly the whole of the Aṭṭhaka-vagga' as very old', arriving at this conclusion from two reasons, first from the language, and secondly from the contents (the latter perhaps not on sufficient grounds). As regards language, 'we not only find here (he said in 1880) what we meet with in other Pāli poetry, the fuller Vedic forms of nouns and verbs in the plural . . . but also unusual (sometimes old) forms[2] and words. . . . Sometimes we meet also with difficult and irregular constructions, and very condensed expressions. All this (he urged) proves, I think, that these parts of the book are much older than the Suttas in which the language is not only fluent, but of which some verses are even singularly melodious.'

In 1885, however, in the preface to his *editio princeps* of the Pāli text of the Sutta-Nipāta, Fausböll modified the foregoing view,—solely on external

[1] Repeated at Udāna V. 6, with the specific amplification that Soṇa recited (or 'intoned') 'all the sixteen' Aṭṭhakavaggika Suttas.

In the Pāli Text Society's *Journal* for 1896, and in the *Journal Asiatique* for May 1915, will be found important articles by the late Professor Rhys Davids and by M. Sylvain Lévi, respectively, in which the Soṇa episode is traced beyond the Pāli Canon into Buddhist Sanskrit, Chinese, and Thibetan. A common error of these later translations is the confusion of aṭṭha (= eight) with attha (= welfare).

[2] I have adopted a suggestion of Professor Lanman that in (e.g.) verse 29 usabhor iva represents, by wholly regular sandhi, the old nominative termination usabhos. Cf. thambhor iva in v. 214, sāsapor iva in v. 631, haṁsor iva in v. 1134; and cf. also vuttir esā in vv. 81 and 480.

evidence. 'I ought (he said in 1885) to have added' (*sc.* to the Mahā and Aṭṭhaka Vaggas) 'the Pārāyana Vagga. That my then (1880) expressed opinion holds good about the two last-mentioned at least' (*sc.* the Aṭṭhaka Vagga and the Pārāyana), seems to me to be evident from there being a commentary on them, called Niddesa, which has been incorporated in the Buddhist canon and from their having been quoted' (as Trenckner had pointed out) 'in the Nikāyas and in the Vinaya-piṭaka'.

This frank shifting of linguistic judgement in deference to non-linguistic evidence tends to support Max Müller's general opinion (in his 1880 Introduction to the Dhammapada at p. xix of vol. x of the *S.B.E.*):—'Nor is the language, whether Sanskrit or Pāli, a safe guide for fixing dates. . . . This branch of critical scholarship requires to be cultivated far more extensively and accurately before true scholars would venture to fix the date of a Sanskrit or Pāli text on the strength of linguistic evidence alone.'

To pass from language to metre, anuṣṭubh ślokas—represented in my translation by blank verse of five accents—constitute a relatively easy metre and thus would naturally be employed, in later recensions, to pad out old triṣṭubh material, which is metrically more difficult to write. Take for example the Aṭṭhaka Vagga, or 'Book of the Octads',—so called because in four of its initial Suttas (Nos. 2–5) there are *eight* stanzas.[1] Though these four eponymous Suttas are all triṣṭubh 'octads', they are now preceded by a Kāma Sutta of only six stanzas, in anuṣṭubh ślokas, which manifestly forms a late preface to the 'Aṭṭhaka' Vagga as a re-edited whole. So, too, in the Sāriputta Sutta (No. 16) of the same Vagga, the equally edifying ślokas, Nos. 955–62, suggest an editorial preamble to the vigorous triṣṭubhs with which the Aṭṭhaka Vagga ends. In the Mahāvagga also, the triṣṭubh verse No. 728 persists in the Dvayatānupassanā Sutta as an oasis amid scholastic accretions. So, also, the Pārāyana now consists, as regards nearly three quarters of its contents, of mixed prose and anuṣṭubh ślokas, which together form as it were a matrix in which are imbedded triṣṭubhs obviously earlier than the interstitial matter surrounding them.

Instances might be multiplied to support the working hypothesis which I venture to advance for the Sutta-Nipāta, that, while all its prose is late, the longer the metrical line the later is the composition likely to have been. It would, however, be straining this working hypothesis unduly to argue that, though in the Pāli Canon triṣṭubhs are most probably ancient, *therefore* all anuṣṭubh ślokas are necessarily, and in all cases, of late date; for both metres go back to the Ṛg-veda.[2]

[1] The Uraga Vagga is named after its initial Uraga Sutta.

[2] Charpentier has shown (Die Suparṇasage, p. 204 *et seqq.*) that the triṣṭubh is normally used for dialogue in the Vedic hymns and in early narrative poetry, including the Jātaka.

The Pārāyana, which perhaps contains the oldest material in the Sutta-Nipāta and is quoted by name four times in the Nikāyas, calls for special comment. Although the Pārāyana now forms a literary unity, it is made up of divers materials, new and old. Evidently new is:

(*a*) the not wholly relevant prologue, dealing with the curse on Bāvarī (? = Babylonian), and

(*b*) the epilogue,—except the triṣṭubhs (vv. 1133–4 and 1142–6) which would seem to have been originally a sequel to Pingiya's Question and to have been amplified subsequently so as to round off the composite Pārāyana.

As regards its sixteen 'Questions', each is in form a separate dialogue dealing with a separate element of Buddhist doctrine; but not all suggest one and the same date of composition. If, tentatively, a metrical test be applied, the triṣṭubhs of the five Questions 3 to 7 (Puṇṇaka's to Nanda's), and of the three Questions 9, 11, and 12 (Todeyya's, Jatukaṇṇī's, and Bhadrāvudha's), would rank as the earlier elements (and, personally, I think such a conclusion probable),—the remaining 'Questions' having been inserted later, when the earliest matter was being supplemented.

Further, there is the direct historical evidence of Asoka's Bhābrū (or Second Bairāt) Rock Edict, which Vincent Smith (*Asoka*, 3rd edition, 1920) would date from Asoka's 13th regnal year, i.e. 257 B.C. As this early Edict cites among seven passages from the Canon at least three from the Sutta-Nipāta (viz. the Muni-sutta (I. 12), the Nālaka-sutta (III. 11), and the Sāriputta-sutta (IV. 16)), there is thus historical evidence for the existence of these Sutta-Nipāta texts before the Patna Council (? 240 B.C.)

The conclusions indicated by the foregoing observations may be summarized as follows:

(i) The Pārāyana, the Aṭṭhaka Vagga, and the Khaggavisāṇa Sutta are the earliest elements of our present canonical Sutta-Nipāta.

(ii) These earliest elements preceded in date not only their canonical commentary (the Niddesa) but also those portions (at least) of the Vinaya and of the Saṁyutta and Anguttara Nikāyas which specifically quote them.

(iii) The date of compilation by Vaggas, which is later than the date of composition of Suttas, does not necessarily fix the date either of original composition, or of later transformations, of Suttas.

(iv) Metrically, triṣṭubhs suggest the oldest (as prose suggests the latest) elements of our Sutta-Nipāta which, as a composite whole, cannot be dated with any certainty earlier than the final compilation of the Canon.

IV

In accord with the foregoing, internal, linguistic and metrical conclusions, are the following considerations—the first based on the primitive connotation of the word 'buddha', and the second on the unvarnished presentment in the Sutta-Nipāta of events which later on were overlaid by the exuberance of Oriental fantasy.

(i) Whilst the title of 'Sambuddha' (or more fully: 'Bhagavā Arahaṁ Sammā-sambuddho') is restricted to him whom we call 'the Buddha' (or to his apocryphal seven—later twenty-five—forerunners of other æons), and whilst the uncompounded form 'buddha' throughout the Canon usually has the same denotation, there are in the Sutta-Nipāta some half-dozen instances of its use in a more extended sense so as to embrace 'catusacca-buddhā ariyapuggalā' (Pj. II. 374), i.e. 'the Noble ones who are alive to the Four Truths' of Buddhism. These instances of the plural use of buddhā in the Sutta-Nipāta occur, it will be found, in triṣṭubh stanzas, indicated above as the oldest material of this book; and it seems *a priori* probable that what was in Buddhism at first a title open to all bhikkhus of highest 'comprehension' or 'enlightenment' (cf. verse 386 d.), came later to be confined to the Founder alone.

(ii) As against the lavish marvels and wonders which, even in canonical writings (e.g. Majjhima Nikāya, Sutta No. 123), embroider the accounts of Gotama's birth and departure from home, it is with a sense of relief that in the Sutta-Nipāta we find an absence of Nativity prodigies and (in the first two Suttas of the Mahāvagga) a wholesome austerity in the primitive record of his renunciation and of his ascetic quest of Peace. In the Sutta-Nipāta he is simply a well-born Sakyan who left house and home for the higher life and nearly starved himself to death by the implacable rigours of his self-mortifications.

(iii) Notable, too, is the absence from the Sutta-Nipāta of any mention of bhikkhunīs, or Alms*women*, in connexion with the Buddhist saṁgha or community. It may be that this silence (if not, indeed, accidental) reveals a primitive stage in which there existed Almsmen without Almswomen,—a stage earlier than the accepted account of Gotama's (eventual) admission of women to his community at the instance of his aunt, Mahā-pajāpatī.[1] At all events the Sutta-Nipāta restricts itself to Alms*men* alone.

(iv) In the Royal Asiatic Society's Journal for 1898 I advanced the view that the title of 'Tathāgata' indicated one who had won through to the truth (tatha). I point out here that this title—given in v. 236 (as usually) to the Buddha—is, in vv. 237–8, extended (in identical terms) to the dhamma and

[1] See Miss Horner's *Women under primitive Buddhism*, Routledge, 1930.

to the saṁgha. This extension of the title from Gotama to the Doctrine and to the Community excludes from the connotation of tathāgata (as thus extended) those fanciful explanations[1] of Gotama's own career which turn on tathā (=thus), as indicating that Gotama personally followed the exact example, and reproduced the experience, of earlier Buddhas in attaining Buddhahood. As applied here to all three members of the Buddhist Triad alike, tathāgata cannot be restricted in meaning to Gotama's own mental processes and their evolution. These specific processes in time and space, whilst historically untrue of his (subsequent) Community, can have no place in the abstract philosophy of his final Doctrine. The only interpretation of 'tathāgata' which will apply here to dhamma and saṁgha, as well as to the Buddha himself, must be abstract in its nature and not lie in the phenomenal realm of historical sequences. Such an interpretation I find only in deriving the word from *tatha* (=true) and in rendering it in all the three cases alike as 'bringing the Truth'.

But I recognize that the author of vv. 236–8 of the Sutta-Nipāta, in applying the title to dhamma and saṁgha, as well as to 'the Buddha', may simply have failed to understand its meaning.

V

I close this Introduction by adducing two parallels—if, indeed, they are not ultimately one—between Buddhism and Christianity. I premise in advance that there is here no question of one creed borrowing from the other; the relationship goes deeper than that. (In his *Ecclesiastical Polity*, Richard Hooker has affirmed a moral law of divine origin, which is not enshrined in the Bible but is deducible from other sources and derives its sanction from man's rational faculties.)

A. The first of these two parallels relates to what Jeremy Taylor would term 'holy living'. From (e.g.) a 1927 lecture on Ireland and Mediaeval Europe (*Proc. Brit. Acad.* vol. xiii) I quote a Franciscan Exhortation to the clergy of the fifteenth century:

> 'Be not quick to anger, or loud of voice or covetous. Eat not to fulness, be neither niggard nor liar. Delight not in food. Thy side half-bare, half-cold thy bed . . . knowledge, steadfastness, persistence. Silence, humility, chastity, patience. Take not the world's way.'

It would not be difficult to match from the Buddhist scriptures each individual clause and word of this succinct passage, though it would involve citations from several books, and the elimination of otiose matter. For

[1] e.g. Sumangala Vilāsinī, I. 59, et seqq.

brevity's sake I confine myself here to citing from the Sutta-Nipāta the following stanzas of the Mahāmangala Sutta, *infra* (II. 4):

8. 'Tis rev'rent awe, content, prompt gratitude,
and due attendance when the Doctrine 's preached;
9. 'tis patience, courtesy, the company
of Almsmen, timely talks on gospel truth;
10. 'tis strict austerity, a holy life,—

'These', observed Gotama (see p. 12 of the first volume of the Dīgha Nikāya), 'are the trifling matters, the minor details, of mere morality.' And so too in the Christian scheme these stages do not rank higher than the '*remote* preparation by purgation'. 'Holiness *before* Peace' was the dictum of Hurrell Froude,—see Brilioth's *Anglican Revival.*

B. In higher realms than such ἄσκησις or 'training', Saint Augustine's 'proximate preparation' for Contemplation (θεωρία) finds its parallel, I suggest, in the *jhāna* of Buddhism. In the ancient Sutta-Nipāta, *jhāna* ('reverie' or 'meditation') is used in the singular only; in the Nikāyas generally, it has come to be subdivided (e.g. in the 4th Sutta of the Majjhima Nikāya) into the following four stages for eliminating mental process:

1. 'Strenuous effort (says Gotama of himself) won for me perseverance that never flagged; there arose in me mindfulness that knew no distraction, perfect tranquillity of body, steadfastness of mind that never wavered.

'Divested of pleasures of sense, divested of wrong states of consciousness, I entered on, and abode in, the First Jhāna with all its zest and satisfaction—a state bred of inward aloofness but not divorced from observation and reflection.

2. 'As I rose above observation and reflection, I entered on, and abode in, the Second Jhāna with all its zest and satisfaction—a state bred of rapt concentration, above all observation and reflection, a state whereby the heart is focused and tranquillity reigns within.

3. 'By shedding the emotion of zest, I entered on, and abode in, the Third Jhāna, with its poised equanimity—mindful and self-possessed, feeling in my frame the satisfaction of which the Noble say that poise and mindfulness bring abiding satisfaction.

4. 'By putting from me both satisfaction and dissatisfaction, and by shedding the joys and sorrows I used to feel, I entered on, and abode in, the Fourth Jhāna—the state that, knowing neither satisfaction nor dissatisfaction, is the consummate purity of poised equanimity and mindfulness.'

Gotama's four stages lead up to a heart and mind 'steadfast, clarified and purified, clean and cleansed of things impure, tempered and apt for service, stablished and immutable', i.e. to a perfectly tempered instrument for intellectual conquests to be achieved therewith and thereafter.

From Gotama I pass to Augustine of Hippo a thousand years later,—restricting myself here too to the latter's autobiographical records, as marshalled with authority by Dom Cuthbert Butler in his *Western Mysticism*. The *Confessions*, observes the learned Abbot of Downside, are 'the portrayal of an emergence from intellectual error and from moral disorder' by a process 'for the most part intellectual in idea and in language, sometimes being frankly Plotinian'. 'Western mystics (he adds) commonly represent Contemplation' (the older term for mysticism, restored by Dom Cuthbert Butler) 'as attained to by and in absorption in prayer; but for Augustine it seems to have been primarily an intellectual process—informed, indeed, by intense religious warmth, but still primarily intellectual'.

It is after and beyond the 'remote preparation by purgation' that the Christian aspirant proceeds to the Augustinian counterpart of the Buddhist *Jhānas*, viz. the proximate preparation for Contemplation by the processes called 'Recollection' and 'Introversion'. Here 'Recollection' is taken in its primary sense of gathering together and concentrating the mind; it consists—and this is the essential link with the *jhānas*—first in the effort to banish from the mind all images and thoughts of external things, all sense-perceptions and thoughts of 'creatures'; then the reasoning processes of the intellect are silenced, and by this exercise of abstraction a solitude is produced wherein the soul may operate in its most spiritual faculties. This shutting off of all internal things from the mind, and emptying it of distracting thoughts, which is the object of 'Recollection', is the prelude to that entering of the mind into itself that is effected by 'Introversion', which is a concentration of the mind on its own highest or deepest part.

With ultimate outlook we are not here concerned. We are not concerned with Gotama's claim to be able both to recall his own previous existences and to foretell the future lot of his fellow creatures; nor on the other hand are we concerned with St. Augustine's claim to have seen God *in ictu trepidantis aspectus*. Our sole concern here is not with the vision of a Promised Land but only with the climb up Pisgah's slopes by stages so similar as to approximate to identity.

C.

SUTTA-NIPĀTA

TEXT AND TRANSLATION

(Throughout this volume, Pāli citations are from the Pāli Text Society's publications.)

I. URAGAVAGGA

1. Uragasutta

1. Yo uppatitaṁ vineti kodhaṁ, [1]
visataṁ sappavisaṁ va osadhehi,
so bhikkhu jahāti orapāraṁ,
urago jiṇṇam iva tacaṁ purāṇaṁ.

2. Yo rāgam udacchidā asesaṁ [2]
bhisapupphaṁ va saroruhaṁ vigayha,
so bhikkhu jahāti . . . .

3. Yo taṇham udacchidā asesaṁ [3]
saritaṁ sīghasaraṁ visosayitvā,
so bhikkhu . . . .

4. Yo mānam udabbadhī asesaṁ [4]
naḷasetuṁ va sudubbalaṁ mahogho,
so bhikkhu . . . .

5. Yo nâjjhagamā bhavesu sāraṁ [5]
vicinaṁ puppham iva udumbaresu,
so bhikkhu . . . .

6. Yass' antarato na santi kopā [6]
itibhavâbhavatañ ca vītivatto,
so bhikkhu . . . .

7. Yassa vitakkā vidhūpitā [7]
ajjhattaṁ suvikappitā asesā,
so bhikkhu . . . .

8. Yo nâccasārī na paccasārī [8]
sabbam accagamā imaṁ papañcaṁ,
so bhikkhu . . . .

9. Yo nâccasārī na paccasārī [9]
'sabbaṁ vitatham idan' ti ñatvā loke,
so bhikkhu . . . .

10. Yo nâccasārī na paccasārī [10]
'sabbaṁ vitatham idan' ti vītalobho,
so bhikkhu . . . .

BOOK I. THE SNAKE BOOK

Sutta 1. Snakes

As snakes slough outworn skins, [1]
an Almsman sheds belief
in this or after- worlds,
—who curbs his wrath (as herbs
quell vipers' poisoned bite);

—who passion extirpates, [2]
(as divers by the root
pluck out the lotus plant);

—who cravings extirpates [3]
by drying up their flow;

—who sweeps away conceit, [4]
as floods a bridge of reeds;

—who looks for bliss in lives [5]
to come, as little as
for flow'rs on fig-tree boughs;

—whose heart no rancour holds; [6]
who heeds no 'future state';

—whose ev'ry theme of thought [7]
has through the furnace passed
to ordered discipline;

—who hurries not nor lags, [8]
because he 's through this maze;

—who hurries not nor lags, [9]
because he knows this world
'has no reality';

—who hurries not nor lags, [10]
being from wants now freed,
because the world around
'has no reality';

11. Yo nâccasārī na paccasārī [11]
'sabbaṁ vitatham idan' ti vītarāgo,
so bhikkhu . . . .

12. Yo nâccasārī na paccasārī [12]
'sabbaṁ vitatham idan' ti vītadoso,
so bhikkhu . . . .

13. Yo nâccasārī na paccasārī [13]
'sabbaṁ vitatham idan' ti vītamoho,
so bhikkhu . . . .

14. Yassânusayā na santi keci, [14]
mūlā akusalā samūhatāse,
so bhikkhu . . . .

15. Yassa darathajā na santi keci [15]
oraṁ āgamanāya paccayāse,
so bhikkhu . . . .

16. Yassa vanathajā na santi keci [16]
vinibandhāya bhavāya hetukappā,
so bhikkhu . . . .

17. Yo nīvaraṇe pahāya pañca [17]
anīgho tiṇṇakathaṁkatho visallo,
so bhikkhu jahāti orapāraṁ
urago jiṇṇam iva tacaṁ purāṇaṁ.

---

2. Dhaniyasutta

1. Pakkodano duddhakhīro 'ham asmi (*iti Dhaniyo gopo*) [18]
anutīre Mahiyā samānavāso;
channā kuṭi, āhito gini.
Atha ce patthayasī, pavassa, deva.

—who hurries not nor lags, [11]
being from passion freed,
because the world around
'has no reality';

—who hurries not nor lags, [12]
being from blemish freed,
because the world around
'has no reality';

—who hurries not nor lags, [13]
being from error freed,
because the world around
'has no reality';

—whose mind admits no warp; [14]
whose wrongful growths are stubbed;

—who has no fever'd schemes [15]
for getting back to earth;

—who has no undergrowths [16]
to tie him to rebirth;

—who, having shed the five [17]
inward impediments,
abides unharried, sure,
and free from rankling barbs.

Sutta 2. Dhaniya, The Rich Herdsman

Dhaniya: My food is dressed; my kine [18]
are milked; by Máhī's banks
my folk and I abide;
my fire is lit; my roof
will keep the weather out.
—So, an the heavens will,
the storm may burst amain.

2. Akkodhano vigatakhilo 'ham asmi (*iti Bhagavā*) [19]
anutīre Mahiy' ekarattivāso;
vivaṭā kuṭi, nibbuto gini.
Atha ce patthayasī, pavassa, deva.

3. Andhakamakasā na vijjare (*iti Dhaniyo gopo*) [20]
kacche rūḷhatiṇe caranti gāvo
vuṭṭhim pi saheyyuṁ āgataṁ.
Atha ce . . . .

4. Baddhā hi bhisī susaṁkhatā, (*iti Bhagavā*) [21]
tiṇṇo pāragato vineyya oghaṁ;
attho bhisiyā na vijjati.
Atha ce . . . .

5. Gopī mama assavā alolā (*iti Dhaniyo gopo*) [22]
dīgharattaṁ saṁvāsiyā manāpā;
tassā na suṇāmi kiñci pāpaṁ.
Atha ce . . . .

6. Cittaṁ mama assavaṁ vimuttaṁ (*iti Bhagavā*) [23]
dīgharattaṁ paribhāvitaṁ sudantaṁ;
pāpam pana me na vijjati.
Atha ce . . . .

7. Attavetanabhato 'ham asmi (*iti Dhaniyo gopo*) [24]
puttā ca me samāniyā arogā;
tesaṁ na suṇāmi kiñci pāpaṁ.
Atha ce . . . .

The Lord: My mood is blest; my mind [19]
is tilled; by Máhī's banks
one night I stay; my Fires
are quenched; my Roof yawns wide.
—So, an the heavens will,
the storm may burst amain.

Dhaniya: No gnats, no gad-flies here! [20]
Amid the fen's lush grass
my cattle roam at large;
they're proof against the rain!
—So, an the heavens will,
the storm may burst amain.

The Lord: I framed a well-wrought Raft, [21]
which bore me o'er the Flood;
I need no further rafts.
—So, an the heavens will,
the storm may burst amain.

Dhaniya: A staunch and loyal dame [22]
have I, by many years
of comradeship endeared,
of whom I hear naught wrong.
—So, an the heavens will,
the storm may burst amain.

The Lord: A staunch, enfranchised heart [23]
have I, by many years
of discipline subdued;
in me naught wrong persists.
—So, an the heavens will,
the storm may burst amain.

Dhaniya: No hireling's livelihood [24]
is mine;—I keep myself.
Round me are stalwart sons,
of whom I hear naught wrong.
—So, an the heavens will,
the storm may burst amain.

8. Nâhaṁ bhatako 'smi kassaci (*iti Bhagavā*) [25]
nibbiṭṭhena carāmi sabbaloke;
attho bhatiyā na vijjati.
Atha ce ....

9. Atthi vasā, atthi dhenupā, (*iti Dhaniyo gopo*) [26]
godharaṇiyo, paveṇiyo pi atthi,
usabho pi gavampatī ca atthi.
Atha ce ....

10. Na 'tthi vasā, na 'tthi dhenupā, (*iti Bhagavā*) [27]
godharaṇiyo, paveṇiyo pi na 'tthi;
usabho pi gavampatîdha na 'tthi.
Atha ce ....

11. Khīlā nikhātā asampavedhī, (*iti Dhaniyo gopo*) [28]
dāmā muñjamayā navā susaṇṭhānā;
na hi sakkhinti dhenupā pi chettuṁ.
Atha ce ....

12. Usabhor iva chetvā bandhanāni, (*iti Bhagavā*) [29]
nāgo pūtilataṁ va dālayitvā,
nâhaṁ puna upessaṁ gabbhaseyyaṁ.
Atha ce patthayasī, pavassa, deva.

---

13. Ninnañ ca thalañ ca pūrayanto [30]
mahāmegho pāvassi tāvad eva.
Sutvā devassa vassato
imam atthaṁ Dhaniyo abhāsatha:

14. 'Lābhā vata no anappakā, [31]
ye mayaṁ Bhagavantam addasāma!
Saraṇaṁ taṁ upema, cakkhuma!
Satthā no hohi tuvaṁ, mahāmuni!

The Lord: I serve no man for hire; [25]
with what I 'gained' I range
the world, nor need a wage.
—So, an the heavens will,
the storm may burst amain.

Dhaniya: Both cows and sucking calves [26]
have I, with cows in calf
and heifers ripe to breed,
and o'er my kine a bull.
—So, an the heavens will,
the storm may burst amain.

The Lord: No cows nor sucking calves [27]
have I, no cows in calf,
no heifers ripe to breed,
nor bull to rule my kine.
—So, an the heavens will,
the storm may burst amain.

Dhaniya: Stout pales surround my byres; [28]
new ropes secure my kine;
not e'en a calf gets through.
—So, an the heavens will,
the storm may burst amain.

The Lord: Breaking my Bonds in twain, [29]
—with strength as of a bull,
or elephant that snaps
a creeper—nevermore
shall I conception know!
—So, an the heavens will,
the storm may burst amain.

Here, flooding hill and dale, [30]
down poured the rain; and, as
he heard it, Dhaniya
thus hailed these happenings:—

Dhaniya: Great gain is ours to view [31]
the Lord. We come, O seer,
for refuge unto thee;
be thou our teacher, sage!

15. Gopī ca ahañ ca assavā [32]
brahmacariyaṁ Sugate carāmase;
jātimaraṇassa pāragā
dukkhass' antakarā bhavāmase!'

---

16. Nandati puttehi puttimā; (*iti Māro pāpimā*) [33]
gomiko gohi tath' eva nandati;
upadhī hi narassa nandanā;
na hi so nandati yo nirūpadhi.

17. Socati puttehi puttimā; (*iti Bhagavā*) [34]
gomiko gohi tath' eva socati;
upadhī hi narassa socanā;
na hi so socati yo nirūpadhi.

3. Khaggavisāṇasutta

1. Sabbesu bhūtesu nidhāya daṇḍaṁ [35]
aviheṭhayaṁ aññataram pi tesaṁ
na puttam iccheyya kuto sahāyaṁ;
eko care khaggavisāṇakappo.

2. Saṁsaggajātassa bhavanti snehā, [36]
sneh' anvayaṁ dukkham idaṁ pahoti;
ādīnavaṁ snehajaṁ pekkhamāno
eko care khaggavisāṇakappo.

3. Mitte suhajje anukampamāno [37]
hāpeti atthaṁ paṭibaddhacitto;
etaṁ bhayaṁ santhave pekkhamāno
eko care . . . .

4. Vaṁso visālo va yathā visatto [38]
puttesu dāresu ca yā apekhā;
vaṁsākaḷīro va asajjamāno
eko care . . . .

Fain would my dame and I, [32]
follow the Blessed One,
till, birth and death o'erpast,
we make an end of Ills.

Māra: Upon his sons is based [33]
a father's joy,—as on
his herds their owner's joy.
For, man is based on joys,
nor has he any joy
whose life depends on naught.

The Lord: Upon his sons is based [34]
a father's woe,—as on
his herds their owner's woe.
But woes assail not him
whose life depends on Naught.

Sutta 3. The Rhinoceros

Hurt naught that lives; do harm [35]
to none; yearn not for sons
or friends; but live—as lives
th' rhinoceros—alone!

Alone! Companionships [36]
breed fondness; fondness leads
to Ills as consequence;
so mark where fondness ends!

Go forth alone! To live [37]
for friends and comrades means
your own weal sacrificed;
—beware acquaintances!

Alone! A man absorbed [38]
in wife and child is like
a tree with tangled boughs.
Copy the bamboo-shoot,
—which grows up straight and free.

5. Migo araññamhi yathā abandho [39]
yen' icchakaṁ gacchati gocarāya,
viññū naro seritaṁ pekkhamāno
eko care . . . .

6. Āmantanā hoti sahāyamajjhe [40]
vāse ṭhāne gamane cārikāya;
anabhijjhitaṁ seritaṁ pekkhamāno
eko care . . . .

7. Khiḍḍā ratī hoti sahāyamajjhe, [41]
puttesu ca vipulaṁ hoti pemaṁ,
piyavippayogaṁ vijigucchamāno
eko care . . . .

8. Cātuddiso appaṭigho ca hoti [42]
santussamāno itarîtarena,
parissayānaṁ sahitā achambhī
eko care . . . .

9. Dussaṅgahā pabbajitā pi eke, [43]
atho gahaṭṭhā gharam āvasantā;
appossukko paraputtesu hutvā
eko care . . . .

10. Oropayitvā gihivyañjanāni, [44]
saṁsīnapatto yathā koviḷāro,
chetvāna vīro gihibandhanāni
eko care . . . .

11. Sace labhetha nipakaṁ sahāyaṁ [45]
saddhiṁcaraṁ sādhuvihāri' dhīraṁ,
abhibhuyya sabbāni parissayāni,
careyya ten' attamano satīmā.

12. No ce labhetha nipakaṁ sahāyaṁ [46]
saddhiṁcaraṁ sādhuvihāri' dhīraṁ,
rājā va raṭṭhaṁ vijitam pahāya
eko care . . . .

Alone! As wild things—free [39]
to range the woodlands—browse
at pleasure where they will,
the sage seeks liberty.

Alone! For, fellows give [40]
a man no peace,—in hall,
on walks, or tours for alms.
No liberty dwells there.

Alone! Though fellowship [41]
bring mirth, and children joy,
beware the severance
affection's ties entail.

Alone! To all the world [42]
—north, south, and east and west—
be kindly; take what comes;
brave perils manfully.

Alone! Grumbling is rife [43]
with homeless Almsmen, as
in worldlings' homes.—Fret not
o'er sons of other men.

Alone! As trees shed leaves, [44]
discard the layman's garb
and sever dauntlessly
all ties to house and home.

Alone! If fortune grant [45]
a trusty, staunch, true friend,
with him brave dangers, cleave
to him,—with mindfulness.

If fortune grant thee no [46]
such friend, then, like a king
who quits a conquered realm,
go forth and live—alone.

13. Addhā pasaṁsāma sahāyasampadaṁ; [47]
seṭṭhā samā sevitabbā sahāyā;
ete aladdhā anavajjabhojī
eko care ....

14. Disvā suvaṇṇassa pabhassarāni [48]
kammāraputtena suniṭṭhitāni
saṁghaṭṭamānāni duve bhujasmiṁ,
eko care ....

15. 'Evaṁ dutiyena sahā mam' assa [49]
vācâbhilāpo abhisajjanā vā,'—
etaṁ bhayaṁ āyatiṁ pekkhamāno
eko care ....

16. Kāmā hi citrā madhurā manoramā [50]
virūparūpena mathenti cittaṁ;
ādīnavaṁ kāmaguṇesu disvā
eko care ...

17. 'Ītī ca gaṇḍo ca upaddavo ca [51]
rogo ca sallañ ca bhayañ ca m' etaṁ',—
etaṁ bhayaṁ kāmaguṇesu disvā,
eko care ....

18. Sītañ ca uṇhañ ca, khudaṁ, pipāsaṁ, [52]
vātâtape ḍaṁsasiriṁsape ca,
sabbāni p'etāni abhisambhavitvā,
eko care ....

19. Nāgo va yūthāni vivajjayitvā [53]
sañjātakhandho padumī uḷāro
yathâbhirantaṁ vihare araññe,
eko care ....

20. Aṭṭhāna' taṁ saṁgaṇikāratassa [54]
yaṁ phassaye sāmayikaṁ vimuttiṁ.
Ādiccabandhussa vaco nisamma,
eko care ....

Prize comradeship! Choose out [47]
equals, or better men.
But, if such fail, lead thou
a blameless life—alone.

Alone! A lesson learn [48]
from bangles richly wrought,
which clash and jangle if
one wrist wears two at once;

Alone! In company [49]
a squabble may arise
or angry jar; reflect
what troubles thus may come.

With varied winsome charm [50]
pleasures seduce the heart;
their menace recognize
—and go thy way alone.

View pleasure as the plague, [51]
as virus fraught with doom,
as fever's deadly dart;
—and go thy way alone.

Alone! Brave cold and heat, [52]
thirst, hunger, wind and sun,
mosquitos, gnats, and snakes;
o'ercome them one and all.

As some huge elephant, [53]
fair as the lotus, quits
the herd to dwell where'er
he will,—go forth alone.

No boon-companion wins [54]
Release, e'en for a time.
Go forth alone,—as he,
the Sun's great kinsman, taught.

21. Diṭṭhivisūkāni upātivatto [55]
patto niyāmaṁ paṭiladdhamaggo
'uppannañāṇo 'mhi anaññaneyyo',
eko care . . . .

22. Nillolupo nikkuho nippipāso [56]
nimmakkho niddhantakasāvamoho
nirāsayo sabbaloke bhavitvā,
eko care . . . .

23. Pāpaṁ sahāyaṁ parivajjayetha [57]
anatthadassiṁ visame niviṭṭhaṁ,
sayaṁ na seve pasutaṁ pamattaṁ;
eko care . . . .

24. Bahussutaṁ dhammadharaṁ bhajetha [58]
mittaṁ uḷāraṁ paṭibhānavantaṁ;
aññāya atthāni, vineyya kankhaṁ,
eko care . . . .

25. Khiḍḍaṁ ratiṁ kāmasukhañ ca loke [59]
analankaritvā anapekkhamāno,
vibhūsanaṭṭhānā virato, saccavādī,
eko care . . . .

26. Puttañ ca dāraṁ pitarañ ca mātaraṁ [60]
dhanāni dhaññāni ca bandhavāni ca
hitvāna kāmāni yathodhikāni,
eko care . . . .

27. 'Sango eso, parittam ettha sokhyaṁ, [61]
appassādo, dukkham ettha bhiyyo,
gaḷo eso' iti ñatvā mutīmā,
eko care . . . .

28. Sandālayitvāna saṁyojanāni [62]
jālaṁ va bhetvā salil' ambucārī,
aggîva daḍḍhaṁ anivattamāno,
eko care . . . .

Above hypotheses, [55]
in certitude assured,
tread thou the Way alone,
to claim full insight won
and pupilage outgrown.

Alone! *Sans* wants, deceit, [56]
hopes, jealousy! Unsmirched
by fond illusions! Tied
to naught the world can show!

Go forth alone! Discard [57]
evil associates
who prompt no good, whose bent
is wrong. Avoid all such
as chop and change, or flag.

Go forth alone. Secure [58]
a friend of garnered lore,
of shining parts and worth,
to teach thee where Weal dwells
and clear thy mind of doubts.

Alone! Leave jollity, [59]
pleasure and mundane joys;
avoid display; speak truth.

Alone! Quit wife and child; [60]
quit parents, wealth and gear,
and kinsfolk,—all life's joys.

Go forth alone! Be sure [61]
pleasure 's a chain, brief bliss,
short rapture, long-drawn woe,
a baited hook for fools.

Alone! Thy fetters burst, [62]
—as fish the net; be like
the forest fires which ne'er
revisit burnt-out scenes.

29. Okkhittacakkhu, na ca pādalolo, [63]
guttindriyo, rakkhitamānasāno,
anavassuto, apariḍayhamāno,
eko care ....

30. Ohārayitvā gihivyañjanāni, [64]
saṁchinnapatto yathā pārichatto,
kāsāyavattho abhinikkhamitvā,
eko care ....

31. Rasesu gedhaṁ akaraṁ, alolo, [65]
anaññaposī, sapadānacārī,
kule kule appaṭibaddhacitto,
eko care ....

32. Pahāya pañc' āvaraṇāni cetaso [66]
upakkilese vyapanujja sabbe,
anissito, chetvā sinehadosaṁ,
eko care ....

33. Vipiṭṭhikatvāna sukhaṁ dukhañ ca [67]
pubbe va ca somanassadomanassaṁ,
laddhān' upekhaṁ samathaṁ visuddhaṁ,
eko care ....

34. Āraddhaviriyo paramatthapattiyā, [68]
alīnacitto, akusītavutti,
daḷhanikkamo thāmabalûpapanno,
eko care ....

35. Paṭisallāṇaṁ jhānam ariñcamāno, [69]
dhammesu niccaṁ anudhammacārī,
ādīnavaṁ sammasitā bhavesu,
eko care ....

36. Taṇhakkhayaṁ patthayaṁ appamatto [70]
anelamūgo sutavā satīmā
saṁkhātadhammo niyato padhānavā,
eko care ....

Alone! With downcast eyes, [63]
not loitering, keep watch
o'er ev'ry faculty;
keep thoughts in leash; let naught
invade, let naught inflame.

Alone! As trees shed leaves, [64]
discard the layman's garb,
and, clad in orange robes,
relinquish house and home.

Alone! Let dainty fare [65]
seduce thee not. With none
to keep besides thyself,
seek alms from door to door,
making no favourites.

Alone! Divest thyself [66]
of all Five Hindrances;
banish the Lesser Faults;
shed likes and dislikes; live
th' emancipated life.

Alone! Leave weal and woe; [67]
leave whilom joys and griefs;
ensue the holy calm
of poised indifference.

Alone! Strive hard to win [68]
the goal of goals,—with heart
unfetter'd, strenuous,
stout, persevering, staunch.

Alone! To lonely thought [69]
and reverie hold fast;
in all thy mental states
the Doctrine keep, alive
to transmigration's doom.

Alone! Toil on to quench [70]
cravings by watchfulness,
by lore, by mindfulness,
by Doctrine's mastery,
by certitude, and grip.

37. Sīho va saddesu asantasanto, [71]
vāto va jālamhi asajjamāno,
padumaṁ va toyena alippamāno,
eko care....

38. Sīho yathā dāṭhabalī pasayha [72]
rājā migānaṁ abhibhuyyacārī,
sevetha pantāni senāsanāni;
eko care....

39. Mettaṁ upekhaṁ karuṇaṁ vimuttiṁ [73]
āsevamāno muditañ ca kāle,
sabbena lokena avirujjhamāno,
eko care....

40. Rāgañ ca dosañ ca pahāya mohaṁ, [74]
sandālayitvāna saṁyojanāni,
asantasaṁ jīvitasaṁkhayamhi,
eko care....

41. 'Bhajanti sevanti ca kāraṇatthā, [75]
nikkāraṇā dullabhā ajja mittā,
attaṭṭhapaññā asucī manussā,'—
eko care khaggavisāṇakappo.

4. Kasibhāradvājasutta

Evam me sutaṁ. Ekaṁ samayaṁ Bhagavā Magadhesu viharati Dakkhiṇāgirismiṁ Ekanāḷāyaṁ brāhmaṇagāme. Tena kho pana samayena Kasibhāradvājassa brāhmaṇassa pañcamattāni nangalasatāni payuttāni honti vappakāle. Atha kho Bhagavā, pubbaṇhasamayaṁ nivāsetvā pattacīvaraṁ ādāya, yena Kasibhāradvājassa brāhmaṇassa kammanto ten' upasaṁkami. Tena kho pana samayena Kasibhāradvājassa brāhmaṇassa parivesanā vattati. Atha kho Bhagavā yena parivesanā ten' upasaṁkami, upasaṁkamitvā ekamantaṁ aṭṭhāsi. Addasā kho Kasibhāradvājo brāhmaṇo Bhagavantaṁ piṇḍāya ṭhitaṁ, disvāna Bhagavantaṁ etad avoca: Ahaṁ kho, samaṇa, kasāmi ca vapāmi ca, kasitvā ca vapitvā ca bhuñjāmi; tvam pi, samaṇa, kasassu ca vapassu ca, kasitvā ca vapitvā ca bhuñjassûti.

Alone! Be undismayed [71]
(as lions are) by sounds,
uncaged as whistling wind,
unspotted by the world
as lotus by the wave.

Alone! Dwell far aloof, [72]
—as, after spring and kill,
the strong-fanged king of beasts
seeks out a distant lair.

Alone! In season due [73]
practise goodwill, and poise,
pity, and kindliness,
thereby to win Release,
unthwarted by the world.

Alone! Oust passion, hate, [74]
illusion! Burst all bonds!
Face death intrepidly!

Alone! Self-seeking sways [75]
friends nowadays;—few bring
disinterested hearts.
Mankind is foul, but quick
to compass private ends.

Sutta 4. Bhāradvāja, the Franklin

Thus have I heard. Once the Lord was living among the Magadha folk at Dakkhiṇā-giri in the brahmin village of Eka-Nāḷā, at a time when the brahmin Kasi-Bhāradvāja's five hundred ploughs were harnessed for the sowing. In the morning early, duly robed and bowl in hand, the Lord went to where the brahmin was busy, at an hour when a meal was forward; and stood there to one side. Observing him standing there for alms, the brahmin said:—Before I eat, I plough and sow, anchorite; and you too should plough and sow before you eat.

Aham pi kho, brāhmaṇa, kasāmi ca vapāmi ca, kasitvā ca vapitvā ca bhuñjāmîti.

Na kho pana mayaṁ passāma bhoto Gotamassa yugaṁ vā nangalaṁ vā phālaṁ vā pācanaṁ vā balivadde vā; atha ca pana bhavaṁ Gotamo evam āha: Aham pi kho, brāhmaṇa, kasāmi ca vapāmi ca, kasitvā ca vapitvā ca bhuñjāmîti.

Atha kho Kasibhāradvājo brāhmaṇo Bhagavantaṁ gāthāya ajjhabhāsi:

1. Kassako paṭijānāsi, na ca passāma te kasiṁ. [76]
Kasin no pucchito brūhi yathā jānemu te kasiṁ.

2. Saddhā bījaṁ, tapo vuṭṭhi, paññā me yuganangalaṁ, [77]
hirī īsā, mano yottaṁ, sati me phālapācanaṁ.

3. Kāyagutto, vacīgutto, āhāre udare yato, [78]
saccaṁ karomi niddānaṁ, soraccam me pamocanaṁ.

4. Viriyam me dhuradhorayhaṁ, yogakkhemâdhivāhanaṁ [79]
gacchati anivattantaṁ, yattha gantvā na socati.

5. Evam esā kasī kaṭṭhā; sā hoti amatapphalā; [80]
etaṁ kasiṁ kasitvāna sabbadukkhā pamuccatîti.

Atha kho Kasibhāradvājo brāhmaṇo mahatiyā kaṁsapātiyā pāyāsaṁ vaḍḍhetvā Bhagavato upanāmesi: Bhuñjatu bhavaṁ Gotamo pāyāsaṁ, kassako bhavaṁ, yaṁ hi bhavaṁ Gotamo amatapphalaṁ kasiṁ kasatîti

6. Gāthābhigītam me abhojaneyyaṁ; [81]
sampassataṁ, brāhmaṇa, n' esa dhammo;
gāthābhigītaṁ panudanti buddhā.
Dhamme satī, brāhmaṇa, vuttir esā.

7. Aññena ca kevalinaṁ mahesiṁ [82]
khīṇāsavaṁ kukkucavūpasantaṁ
annena pānena upaṭṭhahassu;
khettaṁ hi taṁ puññapekhassa hotîti.

Atha kassa câhaṁ, bho Gotama, imaṁ pāyāsaṁ dammîti?

Na kho 'han taṁ, brāhmaṇa, passāmi sadevake loke samārake sabrahmake sassamaṇabrāhmaṇiyā pajāya sadevamanussāya yassa so pāyāso bhutto sammāpariṇāmaṁ gaccheyya aññatra Tathāgatassa vā Tathāgatasāvakassa

I too, brahmin, do plough and do sow before I eat.

We fail, however, to see the worthy Gotama's yoke, or plough, or ploughshare, or goad, or ox-team,—albeit he asserts that he ploughs and sows before he eats.

Thereupon, the brahmin addressed the Lord in this stanza:

You claim to be a tiller, though we see [76]
none of your tillage. Tell us how you till;
for of your tilling we would fain hear more.

The Lord: My seed is faith; austerity of life [77]
my rain; wisdom my yoke and plough; my pole
is fear to err,—with thought to strap the yoke,
and mindfulness for ploughshare and the goad.

Watchful o'er word and deed, and temperate [78]
in diet, I make insight weed my crop,
nor rest till final bliss is harvested.

Effort is my stout ox, which turns not back [79]
at headlands;—straight to Peace he bears me on,
to that last bourne where anguish is no more.

Thus have I tilled, with Deathlessness for crop. [80]
And whoso tills as I, is freed from Ills.

Hereon, the brahmin served up milk-rice on a great bronze dish and offered it to the Lord, saying—Eat this, Gotama; a tiller indeed art thou, in that thou tillest a crop that is Deathless.

The Lord: I take no chanter's fee. [81]
—Seers countenance it not;
th' Enlighten'd scout such fees;
and while this Doctrine lasts,
this practice must hold good.

Provide with other fare [82]
a sage of holy calm,
consummate, Cankerless;
merit to reap,—sow *there.*

To whom then am I to give this, Gotama?

Brahmin, in the whole wide world of gods, Māras, and Brahmās, I see no one among anchorites and brahmins, gods and men, who could digest this food except a Truth-finder or the disciple of a Truth-finder. So either throw

vā. Tena hi tvaṁ, brāhmaṇa, taṁ pāyāsaṁ appaharite vā chaḍḍehi appāṇake vā udake opilāpehîti.

Atha kho Kasibhāradvājo brāhmaṇo taṁ pāyāsaṁ appāṇake udake opilāpesi. Atha kho so pāyāso udake pakkhitto cicciṭāyati ciṭiciṭāyati sandhūpāyati sampadhūpāyati. Seyyathāpi nāma phālo divasasantatto udake pakkhitto cicciṭāyati ciṭiciṭāyati sandhūpāyati sampadhūpāyati, evam eva so pāyāso udake pakkhitto cicciṭāyati . . . sampadhūpāyati. Atha kho Kasibhāradvājo brāhmaṇo saṁviggo lomahaṭṭhajāto yena Bhagavā ten' upasaṁkami, upasaṁkamitvā Bhagavato pādesu sirasā nipatitvā Bhagavantaṁ etad avoca: Abhikkantaṁ, bho Gotama; abhikkantaṁ, bho Gotama! Seyyathāpi, bho Gotama, nikkujjitaṁ vā ukkujjeyya, paṭicchannaṁ vā vivareyya, mūḷhassa vā maggaṁ ācikkheyya, andhakāre vā telapajjotaṁ dhāreyya: 'cakkhumanto rūpāni dakkhintîti',—evam evaṁ bhotā Gotamena anekapariyāyena dhammo pakāsito. Esâhaṁ bhavantaṁ Gotamaṁ saraṇaṁ gacchāmi dhammañ ca bhikkhusaṁghañ ca; labheyyâhaṁ bhoto Gotamassa santike pabbajjaṁ, labheyyaṁ upasampadan ti. Alattha kho Kasi-Bhāradvājo brāhmaṇo Bhagavato santike pabbajjaṁ, alattha upasampadaṁ. Acirûpasampanno kho pan' āyasmā Bhāradvājo eko vūpakaṭṭho appamatto ātāpī pahitatto viharanto na-cirass' eva yass' atthāya kulaputtā samma-d-eva agārasmā anagāriyaṁ pabbajanti tad anuttaraṁ brahmacariya-pariyosānaṁ diṭṭhe va dhamme sayaṁ abhiññā sacchikatvā upasampajja vihāsi; 'khīṇā jāti, vusitaṁ brahmacariyaṁ, kataṁ karaṇīyaṁ, nâparaṁ itthattāyâti' abbhaññāsi. Aññataro ca kho pan' āyasmā Bhāradvājo arahataṁ ahosi.

5. Cundasutta

1. Pucchāmi Muniṁ pahūtapaññaṁ (*iti Cundo kammāraputto*) [83]
Buddhaṁ dhammassāmiṁ vītataṇhaṁ
dipaduttamaṁ sārathīnaṁ pavaraṁ:
Kati loke samaṇā? Tad ingha brūhi.

2. Caturo samaṇā; na pañcam' atthi. (*Cundâti Bhagavā*) [84]
Te te āvikaromi sakkhipuṭṭho:
—Maggajino, Maggadesako ca,
Magge jīvati, yo ca Maggadūsī.

it away where little grass grows, or else fling it into water where there are no living creatures.

Thereupon, into water where there were no living creatures the brahmin flung that milk-rice,—which hissed and sputtered, smoked and steamed, just like a ploughshare that has lain broiling in the sun.

Aghast, and with every hair on his body standing erect, the brahmin went over to the Lord, and, bowing his head at the Lord's feet, cried:—Wonderful, Gotama; quite wonderful! Just as a man might set upright again what had fallen down, or reveal what had been hidden away, or tell a man who had gone astray which was his way, or bring a lamp into darkness so that those with eyes to see might see the things about them,—even so, in many ways has Gotama made his Doctrine clear! To the reverend Gotama I come for refuge and to his Doctrine and to his Community. Be it mine to receive admission and confirmation at the hands of the Lord! So the brahmin Kasi-Bhāradvāja was admitted and confirmed as an almsman of the Lord. Nor was it long after his confirmation before the Reverend Bhāradvāja, dwelling alone and aloof, strenuous, ardent and purged of self, won after no great time that prize in quest of which young men go forth from home to homelessness as Pilgrims, that prize of prizes which crowns the higher life,—even this did he think out for himself, realize and attain, and in this did he dwell here and now, convinced that for him rebirth was no more, that he had lived the highest life, that his task was done, and that now there was no more left of what he had been. So the Reverend Bhāradvāja was numbered among the Arahats.

Sutta 5. Cunda, the Smith

Cunda: I ask th' Enlightened Sage [83]
of boundless lore, the Lord
of Doctrine, craving-free,
foremost of all mankind,
man's matchless charioteer,—
I ask how many kinds
of anchorites there are?

The Lord: Four kinds there are,—no fifth; [84]
and here in order are
the four: Way-master first;
Way-preacher next; then he
that treads the Way; and fourth
the man that fouls the Way.

3. Kaṁ 'Maggajinaṁ' vadanti buddhā? (*iti Cundo kammāraputto*) [85]
'Maggajjhāyī' kathaṁ atulyo hoti?
'Magge jīvati' me brūhi puṭṭho.
Atha me āvikarohi 'Maggadūsiṁ'.

4. Yo tiṇṇakathaṁkatho visallo, [86]
nibbānâbhirato anānugiddho,
lokassa sadevakassa netā,
tādiṁ 'Maggajinaṁ' vadanti buddhā.

5. 'Paramaṁ, paraman' ti yo 'dha ñatvā [87]
akkhāti vibhajati idh' eva Dhammaṁ,
taṁ kaṁkhacchidaṁ muniṁ anejaṁ
dutiyaṁ bhikkhunam āhu 'Maggadesiṁ'.

6. Yo dhammapade sudesite [88]
magge jīvati saṁyato satīmā
anavajjapadāni sevamāno,
tatiyaṁ bhikkhunam āhu 'Maggajīviṁ'.

7. Chadanaṁ katvāna subbatānaṁ [89]
pakkhandī kuladūsako pagabbho
māyāvī asaṁyato palāpo
patirūpena caraṁ,—sa 'Maggadūsī'.

8. Ete ca paṭivijjhi yo gahaṭṭho [90]
sutavā ariyasāvako sapañño
'sabbe ne tādisā' tī ñatvā,
iti disvā na hāpeti tassa saddhā.
Kathaṁ hi duṭṭhena asampaduṭṭhaṁ
suddhaṁ asuddhena samaṁ kareyya?

6. Parābhavasutta

Evam me sutaṁ. Ekaṁ samayaṁ Bhagavā Sāvatthiyaṁ viharati Jetavane Anāthapiṇḍikassa ārāme. Atha kho aññatarā devatā abhikkantāya rattiyā abhikkantavaṇṇā kevalakappaṁ Jetavanaṁ obhāsetvā yena Bhagavā ten'

Cunda: Whom do th' Enlightened call [85]
Way-master? What inspires
the Way's rapt votary?
Who treads—who fouls—the Way?

The Lord: The man who sheds all doubt [86]
and, free from rankling barbs,
Nirvāna's bliss enjoys;
who, craving nothing, guides
the world of gods and men;
—him seers 'Way-master' call.

'Way-preacher' second ranks [87]
among the Almsmen four.
Convinced perfection 's here,
he preaches and expounds
the Doctrine, solving doubts,
—a sage from cravings purged.

'Way-farer' ranks as third. [88]
The Path, in texts revealed,
he treads in temperance,
in mindfulness, in zeal,
and blamelessness of life.

'Way-fouler' counterfeits [89]
the good, and homes defiles,
—a reckless ruffian,
a base, low cozener.

If taught and grounded well, [90]
the saints' lay-hearer knows
these four divergent types,
with faith not undermined.
For, how could he confuse
impure with pure, or take
a rascal for a saint?

Sutta 6. Failures

Thus have I heard. Once while the Lord was staying at Sāvatthī in Jeta's grove in Anāthapiṇḍika's pleasaunce, as night was passing away, a deity of surpassing beauty came to the Lord, flooding the whole grove with radiance,

upasaṁkami upasaṁkamitvā Bhagavantaṁ abhivādetvā ekamantaṁ aṭṭhāsi. Ekamantaṁ ṭhitā kho sā devatā Bhagavantaṁ gāthāya ajjhabhāsi:

1\. Parābhavantaṁ purisaṁ mayaṁ pucchāma Gotamaṁ, [91]
Bhagavantaṁ puṭṭhuṁ āgamma: Kim parābhavato mukhaṁ?

2\. Suvijāno bhavaṁ hoti, suvijāno parābhavo; [92]
—dhammakāmo bhavaṁ hoti, dhammadessī parābhavo.

3\. Iti h' etaṁ vijānāma; paṭhamo so parābhavo. [93]
Dutiyaṁ Bhagavā brūhi: Kim parābhavato mukhaṁ?

4\. Asant' assa piyā honti; sante na kurute piyaṁ; [94]
asataṁ dhammaṁ roceti;—tam parābhavato mukhaṁ.

5\. Iti h' etaṁ vijānāma; dutiyo so parābhavo. [95]
Tatiyaṁ Bhagavā brūhi: Kim parābhavato mukhaṁ?

6\. Niddāsīlī sabhāsīlī anuṭṭhātā ca yo naro [96]
alaso kodhapaññāṇo;—tam parābhavato mukhaṁ.

7\. Iti h' etaṁ vijānāma; tatiyo so parābhavo. [97]
Catutthaṁ Bhagavā brūhi: Kim parābhavato mukhaṁ?

8\. Yo mātaraṁ vā pitaraṁ vā jiṇṇakaṁ gatayobbanaṁ [98]
pahu santo na bharati;—tam parābhavato mukhaṁ.

9\. Iti h' etaṁ vijānāma; catuttho so parābhavo. [99]
Pañcamaṁ Bhagavā brūhi: Kim parābhavato mukhaṁ?

10\. Yo brāhmaṇaṁ vā samaṇaṁ vā aññaṁ vā pi vaṇibbakaṁ [100]
musāvādena vañceti;—tam parābhavato mukhaṁ.

11\. Iti h' etaṁ vijānāma; pañcamo so parābhavo. [101]
Chaṭṭhamaṁ Bhagavā brūhi: Kim parābhavato mukhaṁ?

12\. Pahūtavitto puriso sahirañño sabhojano [102]
eko bhuñjati sādūni;—tam parābhavato mukhaṁ.

13\. Iti h' etaṁ vijānāma; chaṭṭhamo so parābhavo. [103]
Sattamaṁ Bhagavā brūhi: Kim parābhavato mukhaṁ?

14\. Jātitthaddho dhanatthaddho gottatthaddho ca yo naro [104]
saṁ ñātiṁ atimaññeti;—tam parābhavato mukhaṁ.

15\. Iti h' etaṁ vijānāma; sattamo so parābhavo. [105]
Aṭṭhamaṁ Bhagavā brūhi: Kim parābhavato mukhaṁ?

16\. Itthidhutto surādhutto akkhadhutto ca yo naro [106]
laddhaṁ laddhaṁ vināseti;—tam parābhavato mukhaṁ.

and, after salutation meet, stood to one side, addressing the Lord in these stanzas:—

Concerning him who fails, I come to ask [91]
of Gotama from what that failure springs.

The Lord: Both worth and failure can be quickly seen: [92]
—worth still aspires, but failure hates the light.

The deity: Thus much I see;—first failure stands out plain. [93]
Now tell me whence the second failure comes.

The Lord: The second failure's he who loves the bad, [94]
courts not the good, and favours bad men's creeds.

The deity: Thus much I see;—the second failure's plain. [95]
Now tell me whence the further failures come.

The Lord: Third comes the critic, lazy, indolent, [96]
and sleek; his constant carping marks him out.

Fourth failure's he who, well-to-do himself, [97–8]
supports not aged parents, past their prime.

Fifth failure's he who brahmins guides astray, [99–100]
or anchorites, or other wayfarers.

Sixth comes the wealthy man, with pelf and gear, [101–2]
who keeps his dainties strictly to himself.

He seventh comes whom birth or wealth or clan [103–4]
inflates, till he looks down on kith and kin.

The eighth's the rake who squanders all he gets, [105–6]
fast as it comes, on women, drink, and dice.

17. Iti h' etaṁ vijānāma; aṭṭhamo so parābhavo. [107]
Navamaṁ Bhagavā brūhi: Kim parābhavato mukhaṁ?

18. Sehi dārehi asantuṭṭho vesiyāsu padissati, [108]
dissati paradāresu;—tam parābhavato mukhaṁ.

19. Iti h' etaṁ vijānāma; navamo so parābhavo. [109]
Dasamaṁ Bhagavā brūhi: Kim parābhavato mukhaṁ?

20. Atītayobbano poso āneti timbarutthaniṁ; [110]
tassā issā na supati;—tam parābhavato mukhaṁ.

21. Iti h' etaṁ vijānāma; dasamo so parābhavo. [111]
Ekādasamaṁ Bhagavā brūhi: Kim parābhavato mukhaṁ?

22. Itthisoṇḍiṁ vikiraṇiṁ, purisaṁ vā pi tādisaṁ, [112]
issariyasmiṁ ṭhāpeti;—tam parābhavato mukhaṁ.

23. Iti h' etaṁ vijānāma; ekādasamo so parābhavo. [113]
Dvādasamaṁ Bhagavā brūhi: Kim parābhavato mukhaṁ?

24. Appabhogo mahātaṇho khattiye jāyate kule; [114]
so 'dha rajjaṁ patthayati;—tam parābhavato mukhaṁ.

25. Ete parābhave loke paṇḍito samavekkhiya [115]
ariyo dassanasampanno, sa lokaṁ bhajate sivaṁ.

7. Vasalasutta

Evam me sutaṁ. Ekaṁ samayaṁ Bhagavā Sāvatthiyaṁ viharati Jetavane Anāthapiṇḍikassa ārāme. Atha kho Bhagavā pubbaṇhasamayaṁ nivāsetvā pattacīvaram ādāya Sāvatthiṁ piṇḍāya pāvisi. Tena kho pana samayena Aggikabhāradvājassa brāhmaṇassa nivesane aggi pajjalito hoti, āhutī paggahitā. Atha kho Bhagavā Sāvatthiyaṁ sapadānaṁ piṇḍāya caramāno yena Aggikabhāradvājassa brāhmaṇassa nivesanaṁ ten' upasaṁkami. Addasā kho Aggikabhāradvājo brāhmaṇo Bhagavantaṁ dūrato va āgacchantaṁ disvāna Bhagavantaṁ etad avoca: Tatr' eva, muṇḍaka, tatr' eva, samaṇaka, tatr' eva, vasalaka, tiṭṭhāhîti. Evaṁ vutte Bhagavā Aggikabhāradvājaṁ brāhmaṇaṁ etad avoca: Jānāsi pana tvaṁ, brāhmaṇa, vasalaṁ vā vasalakaraṇe vā dhamme ti?

Na khvâhaṁ, bho Gotama, jānāmi vasalaṁ vā vasalakaraṇe vā dhamme. Sādhu me bhavaṁ Gotamo tathā dhammaṁ desetu yathâhaṁ jāneyyaṁ vasalaṁ vā vasalakaraṇe vā dhamme ti.

Tena hi, brāhmaṇa, suṇāhi, sādhukaṁ manasikarohi; bhāsissāmîti.

Evam bho ti kho Aggikabhāradvājo brāhmaṇo Bhagavato paccassosi.

Ninth comes the lecher who, not satisfied [107–8]
with his own wives, is seen about with whores,
or caught in dalliance with others' wives.

Tenth comes the dotard who, in failing age, [109–10]
a maiden takes to wife, with ripe round breasts,
so fair he cannot sleep for jealousy.

Eleventh failure 's he who puts in charge [111–12]
a drunken, spendthrift rake,—of either sex.

Twelfth comes th' ambitious noble, lacking means, [113–14]
who fondly schemes to get himself made king.

The noble sage, whose penetrating eye [115]
these failures scans, has won the realms of bliss.

Sutta 7. The Wastrel

Thus have I heard. Once while the Lord was staying in Sāvatthī in Jeta's grove in Anāthapiṇḍika's pleasaunce, early one morning, duly robed and bowl in hand, he went into the city for alms, at an hour when there was the sacrificial fire lighted in the dwelling of the brahmin Aggika-Bhāradvāja; and the oblation was elevated. In the course of his house-to-house visitations, the Lord approached the brahmin's dwelling, but was seen some way off by the brahmin, who shouted :—Stop where you are, shaveling! Stop where you are, you wretched anchorite! Stop where you are, wastrel!

Said the Lord to the brahmin :—Do you understand, brahmin, what a 'wastrel' is, or what outlooks make a 'wastrel'?

No, replied the brahmin, I do not understand what a 'wastrel' is or what outlooks make a 'wastrel'. Be so good, Gotama, as to explain it, for my information.

Give ear then, brahmin, and pay attention; I will speak.

Certainly, said the brahmin in assent.

Bhagavā etad avoca:

1. Kodhano upanāhī ca pāpamakkhī ca yo naro [116]
vipannadiṭṭhi māyāvī, taṁ jaññā 'vasalo' iti.

2. Ekajaṁ vā dijaṁ vā pi yo 'dha pāṇaṁ vihiṁsati, [117]
yassa pāṇe dayā na 'tthi, taṁ jaññā 'vasalo' iti.

3. Yo hanti parirundhati gāmāni nigamāni ca [118]
niggāhako samaññāto, taṁ jaññā 'vasalo' iti.

4. Gāme vā yadi vâraññe yaṁ paresaṁ mamāyitaṁ [119]
theyyā adinnaṁ ādiyati, taṁ jaññā 'vasalo' iti.

5. Yo have iṇam ādāya cujjamāno palāyati [120]
'na hi te iṇam atthîti', taṁ jaññā 'vasalo' iti.

6. Yo ve kiñcikkhakamyatā panthasmiṁ vajataṁ janaṁ [121]
hantvā kiñcikkham ādeti, taṁ jaññā 'vasalo' iti.

7. Yo attahetu parahetu dhanahetu ca yo naro [122]
sakkhi puṭṭho musā brūti, taṁ jaññā 'vasalo' iti.

8. Yo ñātīnaṁ sakhānaṁ vā dāresu patidissati [123]
sahasā sampiyena vā, taṁ jaññā 'vasalo' iti.

9. Yo mātaraṁ vā pitaraṁ vā jiṇṇakaṁ gatayobbanaṁ [124]
pahu santo na bharati, taṁ jaññā 'vasalo' iti.

10. Yo mātaraṁ vā pitaraṁ vā bhātaraṁ bhaginiṁ sasuṁ [125]
hanti roseti vācāya, taṁ jaññā 'vasalo' iti.

11. Yo atthaṁ pucchito santo anattham anusāsati, [126]
paṭicchannena manteti, taṁ jaññā 'vasalo' iti.

12. Yo katvā pāpakaṁ kammaṁ 'mā maṁ jaññā' ti icchati, [127]
yo paṭicchannakammanto, taṁ jaññā 'vasalo' iti.

13. Yo ve parakulaṁ gantvā bhutvāna sucibhojanaṁ [128]
āgataṁ na paṭipūjeti, taṁ jaññā 'vasalo' iti.

14. Yo brāhmaṇaṁ vā samaṇaṁ vā aññaṁ vāpi vaṇibbakaṁ [129]
musāvādena vañceti, taṁ jaññā 'vasalo' iti.

15. Yo brāhmaṇaṁ vā samaṇaṁ vā bhattakāle upaṭṭhite [130]
roseti vācā, na ca deti, taṁ jaññā 'vasalo' iti.

16. Asataṁ yo 'dha pabrūti mohena paliguṇṭhito [131]
kiñcikkhaṁ nijigiṁsāno, taṁ jaññā 'vasalo' iti.

17. Yo c' attānaṁ samukkaṁse parañ ca-m-avajānāti, [132]
nihīno sena mānena, taṁ jaññā 'vasalo' iti.

The Lord began:—

Be he as 'wastrel' known, who harbours ire [116]
and rancour, slander, error, and deceit.

The wastrel's he who injures living things [117]
(or beast or bird), and pities naught that lives.

The wastrel harries and beleaguers folk [118]
in town and village,—where he's called a scourge.

The wastrel steals, in village or the waste, [119]
whate'er he covets of another's goods.

The wastrel, pressed to pay up what he owes, [120]
denies a debt is owing and absconds.

The wastrel, coveting some trifle, slays [121]
a peaceful trav'ller for that trifle's sake.

The wastrel bears false witness in a suit, [122]
to help himself or others, or for cash.

By force, or with consent, the wastrel holds [123]
commerce with wives of kinsmen or of friends.

The wastrel's he who, well-to-do himself, [124]
supports not aged parents, past their prime.

The wastrel strikes, and goads with taunts, his sire, [125]
his mother, brother, sister, mother-in-law.

The wastrel, asked for counsel, counsels wrong [126]
and clokes pronouncements in obscurities.

The wastrel hopes his villainies will not [127]
be known as his, and privily proceeds.

The wastrel gladly shares another's feast, [128]
but, when his host calls, offers no return.

The wastrel's he who brahmins guides astray, [129]
or anchorites, or other travellers.

At dinner-time, the wastrel greets with jeers [130]
—not alms—a brahmin or an anchorite.

The wastrel, greedy for a penny fee, [131]
tells fortunes,—in abysmal ignorance.

Debased by overweening arrogance, [132]
the wastrel lauds himself, runs others down.

18. Rosako kadariyo ca pāpiccho maccharī saṭho [133]
ahirako anottāpī, taṁ jaññā 'vasalo' iti.

19. Yo Buddhaṁ paribhāsati atha vā tassa sāvakaṁ, [134]
paribbājaṁ gahaṭṭhaṁ vā, taṁ jaññā 'vasalo' iti.

20. Yo ve anarahā santo arahaṁ paṭijānati, [135]
coro sabrahmake loke, esa kho vasalâdhamo.
—Ete kho 'vasalā' vuttā, mayā vo ye pakāsitā.

---

21. Na jaccā 'vasalo' hoti;—na jaccā hoti brāhmaṇo; [136]
kammanā 'vasalo' hoti, kammanā hoti brāhmaṇo.

22. Tad aminâpi jānātha yathā me 'daṁ nidassanaṁ: [137]
Caṇḍālaputto sopāko Mātango iti vissuto.

23. So yasaṁ paramaṁ patto Mātango yaṁ sudullabhaṁ; [138]
āgañchuṁ tass' upaṭṭhānaṁ khattiyā brāhmaṇā bahū.

24. So devayānam āruyha virajaṁ so mahāpathaṁ [139]
kāmarāgaṁ virājetvā brahmalokūpago ahu;
—na taṁ jāti nivāresi brahmalokûpapattiyā.

25. Ajjhāyakakule jātā brāhmaṇā mantabandhavā [140]
te ca pāpesu kammesu abhiṇham upadissare,

26. diṭṭhe va dhamme gārayhā samparāye ca duggati; [141]
na ne jāti nivāreti duggaccā garahāya vā.

27. Na jaccā 'vasalo' hoti;—na jaccā hoti brāhmaṇo. [142]
Kammanā 'vasalo' hoti, kammanā hoti brāhmaṇo ti.

Evaṁ vutte Aggikabhāradvājo brāhmaṇo Bhagavantaṁ etad avoca:—Abhikkantaṁ, bho Gotama; abhikkantaṁ, bho Gotama! Seyyathāpi, bho Gotama, nikkujjitaṁ vā ukkujjeyya, paṭicchannaṁ vā vivareyya, mūḷhassa vā maggaṁ ācikkheyya, andhakāre vā telapajjotaṁ dhāreyya 'cakkhumanto rūpāni dakkhintīti',—evam evaṁ bhotā Gotamena anekapariyāyena dhammo pakāsito. Esâhaṁ bhavantaṁ Gotamaṁ saraṇaṁ gacchāmi dhammañ ca bhikkhusaṁghañ ca; upāsakaṁ maṁ bhavaṁ Gotamo dhāretu ajjatagge pāṇupetaṁ saraṇaṁ gataṁ.

The wastrel fosters strife, is miserly, [133]
evil of aspirations, stingy, sly,
devoid of conscience, and unscrupulous.

The wastrel's tongue defames th' Enlighten'd One, [134]
or His disciples, mendicant or lay.

Th' unsaintly wastrel, claiming saint to be, [135]
is master-thief of all the universe,
and vilest wastrel of the wastrel crowd.
—All these are wastrels whom I have portrayed.

No *birth* a wastrel—or a Brahmin—makes; [136]
'tis *conduct* wastrels makes,—and Brahmins too.

And here's an illustration proves my case:— [137]
Low, dog-devouring outcastes had a son

—Mātanga named—whose fame preëminent [138]
drew crowds of brahmins and nobility.

Upborne in heaven's chariot, he soared, [139]
from passion purged, along the spotless path
till bliss was won; nor did his lowly birth
deny him entry into paradise!

But there are brahmins born, in runes profound, [140]
whose evil lives proclaim them what they are,

whom men on earth condemn, whom doom awaits; [141]
nor does their brahmin birth forbid, or bar,
their condemnation here, or future doom.

No birth a wastrel—or a Brahmin—makes; [142]
'tis conduct wastrels makes,—and Brahmins too.

Hereupon, the brahmin Aggika-Bhāradvāja said to the Lord:—Wonderful, Gotama; quite wonderful! Just as a man might set upright again what had been cast down, and reveal what had been hidden away, or tell a man who had gone astray which was his way, or bring a lamp into darkness so that those with eyes to see might see the things about them,—even so, in many ways, has Gotama made his Doctrine clear. To the reverend Gotama I come as my refuge, and to his Doctrine, and to his Community. I ask him to accept me as a follower who has found an abiding refuge from this day forth while life lasts.

8. Mettasutta

1. Karaṇīyam atthakusalena [143]
yan taṁ santaṁ padaṁ abhisamecca
sakko uju ca sūjū ca
suvaco c' assa mudū anatimānī,

2. santussako ca subharo ca [144]
appakicco ca sallahukavutti
santindriyo ca nipako ca
appagabbho kulesu ananugiddho;

3. na ca khuddaṁ samācare kiñci [145]
yena viññū pare upavadeyyuṁ.
Sukhino vā khemino hontu
sabbe sattā bhavantu sukhitattā,

4. ye keci pāṇabhūt' atthi [146]
tasā vā thāvarā vā anavasesā
dīghā vā ye mahantā vā
majjhimā rassakā aṇukathūlā,

5. diṭṭhā vā ye vā addiṭṭhā [147]
ye ca dūre vasanti avidūre
bhūtā vā sambhavesī vā,
sabbe sattā bhavantu sukhitattā.

6. Na paro paraṁ nikubbetha, [148]
nâtimaññetha katthaci naṁ kañci,
vyārosanā paṭighasaññā
nâññamaññassa dukkham iccheyya.

7. Mātā yathā niyaṁ puttaṁ [149]
āyusā ekaputtam anurakkhe,
evam pi sabbabhūtesu
mānasam bhāvaye aparimāṇaṁ.

Sutta 8. Goodwill

When Peace is won, th' adept [143]
in welfare needs to prove
an able, upright man,
of gracious speech, kind mood,
devoid of arrogance,

an easy, grateful, guest, [144]
—no busybody; wants
but few; sense-disciplined,
quick-witted, bluster-free,
never importunate;

and let him never stoop [145]
to conduct mean or low,
evoking grave rebuke.
May creatures all abound

in weal and peace; may all [146]
be blessed with peace always;
all creatures weak or strong,
all creatures great and small;

creatures unseen or seen, [147]
dwelling afar or near,
born or awaiting birth,
—may all be blessed with peace!

Let none cajole or flout [148]
his fellows anywhere;
let none wish others harm
in dudgeon or in hate.

Just as with her own life [149]
a mother shields from hurt
her own, her only, child,—
let all-embracing thoughts
for all that lives be thine,

8. Mettañ ca sabbalokasmiṁ [150]
mānasam bhāvaye aparimāṇaṁ
uddham adho ca tiriyañ ca
asambādhaṁ averam asapattaṁ.

---

9. Tiṭṭhaṁ caraṁ nisinno vā [151]
sayāno vā yāvat' assa vigatamiddho
etaṁ satiṁ adhiṭṭheyya,
—'brahmam etaṁ vihāram' idha-m-āhu.

10. Diṭṭhiñ ca anupagamma [152]
sīlavā dassanena sampanno
kāmesu vineyya gedhaṁ,
na hi jātu gabbhaseyyaṁ punar eti.

9. Hemavatasutta

1. Ajja pannaraso uposatho (*iti Sātāgiro yakkho*) [153]
divyā ratti upaṭṭhitā;
anomanāmaṁ Satthāraṁ
handa passāma Gotamaṁ.

2. Kacci mano supaṇihito (*iti Hemavato yakkho*) [154]
sabbabhūtesu tādino?
Kacci iṭṭhe aniṭṭhe ca
saṁkapp' assa vasīkatā?

3. Mano c' assa supaṇihito (*iti Sātāgiro yakkho*) [155]
sabbabhūtesu tādino;
atho iṭṭhe aniṭṭhe ca
saṁkapp' assa vasīkatā.

4. Kacci adinnaṁ nâdiyati? (*iti Hemavato yakkho*) [156]
Kacci pāṇesu saṁyato?
Kacci ārā pamādamhā?
Kacci jhānaṁ na riñcati?

5. Na so adinnaṁ ādiyati, (*iti Sātāgiro yakkho*) [157]
atho pāṇesu saṁyato,
atho ārā pamādamhā
buddho jhānaṁ na riñcati.

—an all-embracing love [150]
for all the universe
in all its heights and depths
and breadth, unstinted love,
unmarred by hate within,
not rousing enmity.

So, as you stand or walk, [151]
or sit, or lie, reflect
with all your might on this;
—'tis deemed 'a state divine'.

Ignoring sophists' views, [152]
the good—with insight filled,
and purged of appetite
for sensuous delights—
shall never see rebirth.

Sutta 9. The Himalayan Sprite

Sātāgira: It's mid-month sabbath, and a lovely night; [153]
—to peerless Gotama let us repair.

Hemavata: Has he his thoughts in full control? Does such [154]
control of thoughts extend to all that lives?
Come fair or foul, can he control his mind?

Sātāgira: He keeps his thoughts in full control, and this [155]
control of thoughts extends to all that lives.
Come fair or foul, he still controls his mind.

Hemavata: Leaves he untouched what is not given him? [156]
Keeps he his hands from harming living things?
Is he remiss in zeal or reverie?

Sātāgira: He leaves untouched what is not given him; [157]
he keeps his hands from harm to living things;
he knows no sloth; he cleaves to reverie.

6. Kacci musā na bhaṇati? (*iti Hemavato yakkho*) [158]
Kacci na khīṇavyappatho?
Kacci vebhūtiyaṁ nâha?
Kacci samphaṁ na bhāsati?

7. Musā ca so na bhaṇati, (*iti Sātāgiro yakkho*) [159]
atho na khīṇavyappatho,
atho vebhūtiyaṁ nâha,
mantā atthaṁ so bhāsati.

8. Kacci na rajjati kāmesu? (*iti Hemavato yakkho*) [160]
Kacci cittaṁ anāvilaṁ?
Kacci mohaṁ atikkanto?
Kacci dhammesu cakkhumā?

9. Na so rajjati kāmesu, (*iti Sātāgiro yakkho*) [161]
atho cittaṁ anāvilam,
sabbamohaṁ atikkanto
buddho dhammesu cakkhumā.

10. Kacci vijjāya sampanno? (*iti Hemavato yakkho*) [162]
Kacci saṁsuddhacāraṇo?
Kacci 'ssa āsavā khīṇā?
Kacci na 'tthi punabbhavo?

11. Vijjāya-m-eva sampanno, (*iti Sātāgiro yakkho*) [163]
atho saṁsuddhacāraṇo;
sabb' assa āsavā khīṇā;
na 'tthi tassa punabbhavo.

11A. Sampannaṁ munino cittaṁ kammanā vyappathena ca [163 A]
vijjācaraṇasampannaṁ dhammato naṁ pasaṁsasi.

11B. Sampannaṁ munino cittaṁ kammanā vyappathena ca [163 B]
vijjācaraṇasampannaṁ dhammato anumodasi.

12. Sampannaṁ munino cittaṁ kammanā vyappathena ca [164]
vijjācaraṇasampannaṁ handa passāma Gotamaṁ.

13. Eṇijaṁghaṁ kisaṁ vīraṁ appāhāraṁ alolupaṁ [165]
muniṁ vanasmiṁ jhāyantaṁ ehi passāma Gotamaṁ.

14. Sīhaṁ v' ekacaraṁ, nāgaṁ kāmesu anapekhinaṁ [166]
upasaṁkamma pucchāma maccupāsā pamocanaṁ.

Hemavata: Tell me; do falsehoods ever cross his lips? [158]
Is he harsh-spoken or calumnious?
Or does his speech bewray frivolity?

Sātāgira: Not so. No falsehoods ever cross his lips; [159]
he 's not harsh-spoken nor calumnious;
his edifying words proclaim him Seer.

Hemavata: Is he unstained by sensuous delights? [160]
Keeps he a heart unmarred? Has he o'ercome
illusion? Has his eye all outlooks gauged?

Sātāgira: Unstained is he by sensuous delights; [161]
he keeps a heart unmarred; illusion he
has overcome and ev'ry outlook gauged.

Hemavata: Say, has he lore? Walks he in purity? [162]
Are Cankers dead? Will he be born no more?

Sātāgira: Yes, he has lore, and walks in purity; [163]
Cankers are dead; he 'll ne'er be born again.

Hemavata: A sage indeed! His mind within is matched [163A & B]
by deed and utterance. Conviction prompts
your praise and gratitude to one who blends
insight and life in one consummate whole.

Sātāgira: Come let us visit this great Gotama. [164]

Hemavata: Yes, let us visit him,—that superman, [165]
lean, self-denying, temperate, the seer
in lonesome forest rapt in reverie.

Seek we this lion lone—this elephant [166]
that heedeth none of pleasure's lures—and ask
the way to gain release from snares of death.

15. Akkhātāraṁ pavattāraṁ sabbadhammāna' pāraguṁ [167]
buddhaṁ verabhayātītaṁ mayaṁ pucchāma Gotamaṁ.

---

16. Kismiṁ loko samuppanno? (*iti Hemavato yakkho*) [168]
Kismiṁ kubbati santhavaṁ?
Kissa loko upādāya?
Kismiṁ loko vihaññati?

17. Chassu loko samuppanno; (*Hemavatâti Bhagavā*) [169]
chassu kubbati santhavaṁ;
channam eva upādāya
chassu loko vihaññati.

18. Kataman taṁ upādānaṁ yattha loko vihaññati? [170]
Niyyānaṁ pucchito brūhi: kathaṁ dukkhā pamuccati?

19. Pañca kāmaguṇā loke manochaṭṭhā paveditā. [171]
Ettha chandaṁ virājetvā evaṁ dukkhā pamuccati.

20. Etaṁ lokassa niyyānaṁ akkhātaṁ vo yathātathaṁ. [172]
Etaṁ vo aham akkhāmi: Evaṁ dukkhā pamuccati.

21. Ko sū 'dha tarati oghaṁ? Ko 'dha tarati aṇṇavaṁ? [173]
Appatiṭṭhe anālambe ko gambhīre na sīdati?

22. Sabbadā sīlasampanno paññavā susamāhito [174]
ajjhattacintī satimā oghaṁ tarati duttaraṁ.

23. Virato kāmasaññāya, sabbasaṁyojanâtigo, [175]
nandībhavaparikkhīṇo,—so gambhīre na sīdati.

---

24. Gambhīrapaññaṁ nipuṇatthadassiṁ [176]
akiñcanaṁ kāmabhave asattaṁ,
—taṁ passatha sabbadhi vippamuttaṁ
dibbe pathe kamamānaṁ mahesiṁ!

25. Anomanāmaṁ nipuṇatthadassiṁ [177]
paññādadaṁ kāmālaye asattaṁ,
—taṁ passatha sabbaviduṁ sumedhaṁ,
ariye pathe kamamānaṁ mahesiṁ!

Sātāgira and Hemavata: Let us together question Gotama, [167]
the great revealer and expounder, who
has gauged all outlooks, won Enlightenment,
and sloughed away transgression's haunting fears.

Hemavata to the Lord: How came the world to be? Whereby [168]
gets it relation? What gives it support?
Say, what assails the world? What brings it low?

The Lord: From six things springs the world, and six [169]
give it relation; six give it support;
six bring the world to final overthrow.

Hemavata: What's this support? What overthrows the world? [170]
Expound Release, and how to end all Ills.

The Lord: Five worldly strands has pleasure; mind makes six. [171]
By scouting pleasure comes the end of Ills;
—just this affords Release from worldly toils; [172]
—just this, I testify, ends mortal Ills.

Hemavata: Who makes a crossing hence o'er Stream and Flood? [173]
Who braves the shoreless, bottomless abyss?

The Lord: Across the raging Flood in safety fares [174]
the virtuous, of comprehending mind,
serene, reflective, watchful evermore.

Th' abyss engulfs not him who—quit of gust [175]
for pleasure, quit of trammels, freed from bonds—
has stifled hankerings for life on life.

Hemavata: Mark, sirs, this mighty sage, [176]
—subtle, profound in lore,
stainless, detached from lusts
and dreams of life to come—
who treads the way divine
in full Deliverance.

Mark, sirs, this mighty sage, [177]
—subtle, as 'peerless' hailed,
giver of lore, immune
from grip of lusts, this seer
who understandeth all
and treads the Noble Way
in full Deliverance.

26. Sudditthaṁ vata no ajja suppabhātaṁ suhuṭṭhitaṁ [178]
yaṁ addasāma Sambuddhaṁ oghatiṇṇam anāsavaṁ.

27. Ime dasasatā yakkhā iddhimanto yasassino [179]
sabbe taṁ saraṇaṁ yanti; tvaṁ no Satthā anuttaro.

28. Te mayaṁ vicarissāma gāmā gāmaṁ nagā nagaṁ, [180]
namassamānā Sambuddhaṁ, dhammassa ca sudhammataṁ.

10. Āḷavakasutta

Evam me sutaṁ. Ekaṁ samayaṁ Bhagavā Āḷaviyaṁ viharati Āḷavakassa yakkhassa bhavane. Atha kho Āḷavako yakkho yena Bhagavā ten' upasaṁkami, upasaṁkamitvā Bhagavantaṁ etad avoca: Nikkhama, samaṇâti. Sādh' āvuso ti Bhagavā nikkhami. Pavisa, samaṇâti. Sādh' āvuso ti Bhagavā pāvisi. Dutiyam pi kho Āḷavako yakkho Bhagavantaṁ etad avoca: Nikkhama . . . pāvisi. Tatiyam pi kho Āḷavako yakkho Bhagavantaṁ etad avoca: Nikkhama . . . pāvisi. Catuttham pi kho Āḷavako yakkho Bhagavantaṁ etad avoca: Nikkhama, samaṇâti. Na khvâhan taṁ, āvuso, nikkhamissāmi; yan te karaṇīyaṁ, taṁ karohîti. Pañhan taṁ, samaṇa, pucchissāmi. Sace me na vyākarissasi, cittaṁ vā te khipissāmi, hadayaṁ vā te phāḷessāmi, pādesu vā gahetvā pāra-Gangāya khipissāmîti.

Na khvâhaṁ taṁ, āvuso, passāmi sadevake loke, sabrahmake, sassamaṇabrāhmaṇiyā pajāya sadevamanussāya yo me cittaṁ vā khipeyya, hadayaṁ vā phāḷeyya, pādesu vā gahetvā pāra-Gangāya khipeyya. Api ca tvaṁ, āvuso, puccha yad ākankhasîti.

Atha kho Āḷavako yakkho Bhagavantaṁ gāthāya ajjhabhāsi:

1. Kiṁ sū 'dha vittaṁ purisassa seṭṭhaṁ? [181]
Kiṁ su suciṇṇaṁ sukham āvahāti?
Kiṁ su have sādutaraṁ rasānaṁ?
Kathaṁjīviṁ jīvitaṁ āhu seṭṭhaṁ?

2. Saddh' īdha vittaṁ purisassa seṭṭhaṁ; [182]
dhammo suciṇṇo sukham āvahāti;
saccaṁ have sādutaraṁ rasānaṁ;
paññājīviṁ jīvitaṁ āhu setthaṁ.

3. Kathaṁ su taratī oghaṁ? Kathaṁ su tarati aṇṇavaṁ? [183]
Kathaṁ su dukkhaṁ acceti? Kathaṁ su parisujjhati?

4. Saddhāya taratī oghaṁ, appamādena aṇṇavaṁ; [184]
viriyena dukkhaṁ acceti, paññāya parisujjhati.

All the Sprites: A gracious sight, a vision glorious, [178]
has dawned on us, whose eyes have seen the Lord
of all Enlightenment, from Cankers purged,
who o'er the Flood has crossed triumphantly.

We thousand Sprites, most potent, far-renowned, [179]
with thee seek refuge, guide beyond compare!

Village to village, hill to hill, we'll laud [180]
the All-Enlighten'd and his matchless creed.

Sutta 10. The Woodland Sprite

Thus have I heard. Once the Lord was staying at Āḷavi in the domain of the Woodland Sprite Āḷavaka, who came to the Lord saying:—Come out, anchorite!

Yes, sir, replied the Lord, as out he came.

Get in again, anchorite, said the Sprite.

Yes, sir, replied the Lord, as in he went.

A second and a third time the same thing happened. But when the Sprite ordered the Lord out for the fourth time, the Lord replied:—No, I will not come out for you, sir. Do what you please.

I will ask you a question, anchorite. If you don't answer me, I will scare you out of your wits, or rive your heart, or fling you by the heels across the Ganges.

Sir, in all the wide world of gods, Māras, and Brahmās, I see no one among anchorites and brahmins, gods or men, who could do to me what you suggest. However, sir, ask what you will.

Hereon, the Sprite Āḷavaka addressed the Lord in these stanzas:—

What forms a man's chief wealth? [181]
What leads men on to weal?
What taste excels the rest?
What life is deemed the best?

The Lord: Faith forms a man's chief wealth; [182]
the Doctrine leads to weal;
the sweetest taste is truth;
a life of wisdom's best.

Āḷavaka: How cross the Surge? How cross the raging Flood? [183]
How shed besetting Ills? How cleanse the heart?

The Lord: The Surge is crossed by faith, the Flood by zeal; [184]
Effort sheds Ills; and Insight cleanses hearts.

5. Kathaṁ su labhate paññaṁ? Kathaṁ su vindate dhanaṁ? [185]
Kathaṁ su kittiṁ pappoti? Kathaṁ mittāni ganthati?
Asmā lokā paraṁ lokaṁ kathaṁ pecca na socati?

6. Saddahāno arahataṁ dhammaṁ nibbānapattiyā [186]
sussūsā labhate paññaṁ appamatto vicakkhaṇo;

7. patirūpakārī dhuravā uṭṭhātā vindate dhanaṁ; [187]
saccena kittiṁ pappoti; dadaṁ mittāni ganthati.

8. Yass' ete caturo dhammā saddhassa gharamesino [188]
—saccaṁ, dhammo, dhiti, cāgo—, sa ve pecca na socati.

9. Ingha aññe pi pucchassu puthū samaṇabrāhmaṇe [189]
yadi saccā damā cāgā khantyā bhiyyo 'dha vijjati.

10. Kathan nu dāni puccheyyaṁ puthū samaṇabrāhmaṇe? [190]
—So 'ham ajja pajānāmi yo attho samparāyiko.

11. Atthāya vata me Buddho vāsāy' Āḷavim āgamā. [191]
—So 'ham ajja pajānāmi yattha dinnaṁ mahapphalaṁ.

12. So ahaṁ vicarissāmi gāmā gāmaṁ purā puraṁ [192]
namassamāno Sambuddhaṁ dhammassa ca sudhammataṁ.

11. Vijayasutta

1. Caraṁ vā yadi vā tiṭṭhaṁ, nisinno uda vā sayaṁ, [193]
sammiñjeti pasāreti,—esā kāyassa iñjanā.

2. Aṭṭhīnahārusaṁyutto tacamaṁsâvalepano [194]
chaviyā kāyo paṭicchanno yathābhūtaṁ na dissati.

3. Antapūro udarapūro yakapeḷassa vatthino [195]
hadayassa papphāsassa vakkassa pihakassa ca

4. siṁghāṇikāya khelassa sedassa ca medassa ca [196]
lohitassa lasikāya pittassa ca vasāya ca.

Āḷavaka: How's Insight gained? And how are Riches found? [185]
How comes renown? What knits affection's ties?
How, after life on earth, shall sorrow cease?

The Lord: Insight is gained by trust that Arahats [186]
hold saving doctrine; next, by diligent
and close attention to their homilies;

he Riches finds whose life is in the right, [187]
who bears his yoke with strenuous resolve.
Through truth there comes renown; affection's ties
are knit by ready generosity.

Equipped with truthfulness and Doctrine sound, [188]
with stedfast heart and openhandedness,
a man shall cease from sorrow after death.

Go ask of brahmins, ask of anchorites, [189]
if aught on earth surpasses truthfulness,
self-mastery, munificence, and ruth.

Āḷavaka: Why should I ask them,—I who grasp to-day [190]
wherein resides true welfare after life?

'Twas well for me there came to Āḷavi [191]
th' Enlighten'd Lord, since I have heard to-day
where gifts bestowed ensure a harvest rich.

Village to village, town to town, I'll laud [192]
the All-Enlighten'd and his matchless creed.

Sutta 11. Disillusion

If—walking, standing, sitting, lying-down— [193]
a man draws in a limb or thrusts it forth,
'tis but a movement of a mortal frame.

Whilst knit by bones and sinews, plaster'd o'er [194]
by flesh and tissues, and encased in skin,
the body does not pass for what it is.

Within, 'tis stuffed with entrails, liver, paunch, [195]
with heart and bladder, kidneys, lungs, and spleen;

'tis stuffed with spittle, snot, and sweat, and blood, [196]
joints' lubricating humours, bile, and fat;

5. Ath' assa navahi sotehi asucī savati sabbadā: [197]
—akkhimhā akkhigūthako, kaṇṇamhā kaṇṇagūthako,

6. siṁghāṇikā ca nāsāto, mukhena vamat' ekadā [198]
pittaṁ, semhañ ca vamati, kāyamhā sedajallikā;

7. ath' assa susiraṁ sīsaṁ matthalungassa pūritaṁ. [199]
subhato naṁ maññati bālo avijjāya purakkhato.

8. Yadā ca so mato seti uddhumāto vinīlako [200]
apaviddho susānasmiṁ, anapekhā honti ñātayo,

9. khādanti naṁ supāṇā ca sigālā ca, vakā kimī [201]
kākā gijjhā ca khādanti, ye c' aññe santi pāṇayo.

10. Sutvāna Buddhavacanaṁ bhikkhu paññāṇavā idha, [202]
—so kho naṁ parijānāti; yathābhūtaṁ hi passati:

11. 'Yathā idaṁ, tathā etaṁ; yathā etaṁ, tathā idam'; [203]
ajjhattañ ca bahiddhā ca kāye chandaṁ virājaye.

12. Chandarāgaviratto so bhikkhu paññāṇavā idha [204]
ajjhagā amataṁ santiṁ nibbānapadam accutaṁ.

13. Dipādako 'yam asuci duggandho parihīrati [205]
nānākuṇapaparipūro vissavanto tato tato.

14. Etādisena kāyena yo maññe uṇṇametave [206]
paraṁ vā avajāneyya,—kim aññatra adassanā?

12. Munisutta

1. Santhavāto bhayaṁ jātaṁ, niketā jāyate rajo. [207]
Aniketam asanthavaṁ :—etaṁ ve munidassanaṁ.

2. Yo jātam ucchijja na ropayeyya, [208]
jāyantaṁ assa nânuppavecche,
tam āhu ekaṁ muninaṁ carantaṁ:—
'Addakkhi so santipadaṁ mahesi'.

3. Saṁkhāya vatthūni pamāya bījaṁ [209]
sineham assa nânuppavecche.
Sa ve munī jātikhayantadassī
takkaṁ pahāya na upeti saṁkhaṁ.

and evermore from its nine apertures [197]
nine several excretions issue forth,

as eyes and ears, with nostrils, mouth, and skin,
exude abroad their foul discharge of filth, [198]

and brains fill up the hollow cranium. [199]
—'A fine thing this!' say fools, by error led.

But, when the livid bloated corpse is flung [200]
out on the charnel-ground, his kin heed not,

while jackals, dogs, wolves, vultures, crows, and worms, [201]
with other living things, devour his flesh.

But th' Almsman, here in Buddha's teaching versed, [202]
—he knows the body, sees its nature clear.

So let the thought—'this corpse was once as you, [203]
and is as you will some day be', dispel
pride in the body from your heart and mind.

For when such pride and passion pass away, [204]
the Almsman, here in Buddha's teaching versed,
wins Deathless peace, Nirvāna's changeless state.

This noisome, two-legged body man parades, [205]
—though inly putrid, though discharging filth.

What is 't but blindness, for *that* body's sake, [206]
to plume one's self or sneer at other men?

Sutta 12. The Sage

From close association perils spring; [207]
a home degrades. Clear-eyed, the sage concludes
to have no home, and no associates.

When ancient growths are dead, [208]
When no fresh growths arise,
the lonely sage is hailed
'a seer who peace beholds'.

Weigh causes; kill off germs, [209]
before affection grows.
Proof then against rebirth,
the sage is lost to ken.

4. Aññāya sabbāni nivesanāni, [210]
anikāmayaṁ aññataram pi tesaṁ,
sa ve munī vītagedho agiddho
nâyūhatī;—pāragato hi hoti.

5. Sabbâbhibhuṁ sabbaviduṁ sumedhaṁ [211]
sabbesu dhammesu anūpalittaṁ
sabbañjahaṁ taṇhakkhaye vimuttaṁ,
—taṁ vâpi dhīrā 'muniṁ' vedayanti.

6. Paññābalaṁ sīlavatûpapannaṁ [212]
samāhitaṁ jhānarataṁ satīmaṁ
sangā pamuttaṁ akhilaṁ anāsavaṁ,
—taṁ vâpi dhīrā 'muniṁ' vedayanti.

7. Ekaṁ carantaṁ muniṁ appamattaṁ [213]
nindāpasaṁsāsu avedhamānaṁ,
sīhaṁ va saddesu asantasantaṁ,
vātaṁ va jālamhi asajjamānaṁ,
padumaṁ va toyena alippamānaṁ,
netāraṁ aññesaṁ anaññaneyyaṁ,
taṁ vâpi—pe—

8. Yo ogahane thambhor ivâbhijāyati, [214]
yasmiṁ pare vācāpariyantaṁ vadanti,
taṁ vītarāgaṁ susamāhitindriyaṁ,
taṁ vâpi . . . .

9. Yo ve ṭhitatto tasaraṁ va ujjuṁ [215]
jigucchati kammehi pāpakehi
vīmaṁsamāno visamaṁ samañ ca,
taṁ vâpi. . . .

10. Yo saṁyatatto na karoti pāpaṁ, [216]
daharo ca majjho ca munī yatatto,
arosaneyyo (so) na roseti kañci,
taṁ vâpi . . . .

11. Yad aggato majjhato sesato vā [217]
piṇḍaṁ labhetha paradattūpajīvī,
nâlan thutun no pi nipaccavādī,
taṁ vâpi . . . .

Alive to errors all, [210]
a prey to none, the Sage
harbours no want, wants naught;
—across the Flood is he.

The wise acclaim as 'Sage' [211]
a conqueror all-wise,
flawless of thought, without
one tie or craving, Freed;

—the thinker wise and good, [212]
thought's watchful votary,
released from ties, and quit
of crassness, Canker-free;

—the Sage who walks aloof, [213]
unmoved by praise or blame,
whom (lion-like) no sounds
dismay, whom (like the wind)
no nets enmesh, who (like
the lotus) sheds whate'er
would tarnish him;—the guide
of others, led by none;

—tranquil, sense-disciplined, [214]
still imperturbable
(no matter what men say)
as is a timber-balk;

—who loathes depravity, [215]
as, shuttle-wise, he moves
onward 'twixt right and wrong,

—the Sage, by self-restraint [216]
through youth and manhood kept
from wrong, who angers none
nor ever anger feels;

—who, careless if his dole [217]
from top or bottom comes,
carps not at what he gets,
nor meagre thanks returns;

12. Muniṁ carantaṁ virataṁ methunasmā, [218]
yo yobbane na upanibajjhate kvaci,
madappamādā virataṁ vippamuttaṁ,
taṁ vâpi . . . .

13. Aññāya lokaṁ paramatthadassiṁ, [219]
oghaṁ samuddaṁ atitariya tādiṁ,
taṁ chinnaganthaṁ asitaṁ anāsavaṁ,
taṁ vâpi dhīrā 'muniṁ' vedayanti.

---

14. Asamā ubho dūravihāravuttino: [220]
gihī dāraposī, amamo ca subbato.
Parapāṇarodhāya gihī asaṁyato;
niccaṁ munī rakkhati pāṇine yato.

15. Sikhī yathā nīlagīvo vihangamo [221]
haṁsassa nôpeti javaṁ kudācanaṁ,
evaṁ gihī nânukaroti bhikkhuno
munino vivittassa vanamhi jhāyato ti.

Uragavaggo paṭhamo

—the Sage who chastely lives, [218]
unsnared by youthful charms,
who ne'er gives way to drink
or riotous excess;

—who comprehends the world, [219]
who sees the supreme good
who, safe across the Flood,
has burst his chains and now
no ties nor Cankers knows;
—him wise men hail as 'Sage'.

Unlike and wide apart they stand [220]
in mode of life and livelihood,
—the layman with a house and home,
and virtue's upright, selfless son.
Heedless, the layman kills and slays;
heedful, the Sage shields life from harm.

For all its crest and neck so blue [221]
the peacock ne'er can match in flight
the swan, nor layman emulate
an Almsman, when in lonesome wilds
the Sage is plunged in Reverie.

End of the Snake Book

II. CŪLAVAGGA

1. Ratanasutta

1. Yānîdha bhūtāni samāgatāni [222]
bhummāni vā yāni va antalikkhe,
sabbe va bhūtā sumanā bhavantu;
atho pi sakkacca suṇantu bhāsitaṁ.

2. Tasmā hi bhūtā nisāmetha sabbe: [223]
mettaṁ karotha mānusiyā pajāya
divā ca ratto ca haranti ye baliṁ.
Tasmā hi ne rakkhatha appamattā.

---

3. Yaṁ kiñci vittaṁ idha vā huraṁ vā [224]
saggesu vā yaṁ ratanaṁ paṇītaṁ,
na no samaṁ atthi tathāgatena.
Idam pi Buddhe ratanaṁ paṇītaṁ.
Etena saccena suvatthi hotu!

4. Khayaṁ virāgaṁ amataṁ paṇītaṁ [225]
yad ajjhagā Sakyamunī samāhito,
na tena Dhammena sam' atthi kiñci.
Idam pi Dhamme ratanaṁ paṇītam.
Etena saccena suvatthi hotu!

5. Yam Buddhaseṭṭho parivaṇṇayī suciṁ [226]
('samādhim ānantarikañ' ñam āhu),
samādhinā tena samo na vijjati.
Idam pi Dhamme ratanaṁ paṇītaṁ.
Etena saccena suvatthi hotu!

6. Ye puggalā aṭṭha satam pasatthā [227]
(cattāri etāni yugāni honti),
te dakkhiṇeyyā Sugatassa sāvakā;
etesu dinnāni mahapphalāni.
Idam pi Saṁghe ratanaṁ paṇītaṁ.
Etena saccena suvatthi hotu!

II. THE SHORT BOOK

Sutta 1. The Three Gems

May denizens of earth [222]
and sky assembled here,
may beings all, rejoice
and hearken unto me.

List, beings all, and show [223]
goodwill to men, who bring
oblations night and day.
So shield mankind from harm.

No wealth in earth or skies, [224]
no gem divine, can vie
with Him who found the Truth.
This gem the Buddha holds;
—and may that truth bless all!

The perfect Peace He preached [225]
—our Sage's Deathless Peace—
can find no match elsewhere.
This gem the Doctrine holds;
—and may that truth bless all!

'Rapt contemplation's meed', [226]
which matchless Buddha praised,
can find no match elsewhere.
This gem the Doctrine holds;
—and may that truth bless all!

His faithful followers, [227]
Conversion's eightfold ranks
(four Paths, four Fruits, in all),
deserve oblations; gifts
to them yield rich returns.
This gem the Order holds;
—and may that truth bless all!

7. Ye suppayuttā manasā daḷhena [228]
nikkāmino Gotamasāsanamhi,
te pattipattā amataṁ vigayha,
laddhā mudhā nibbutiṁ bhuñjamānā.
Idam pi Saṁghe ratanaṁ paṇītaṁ.
Etena saccena suvatthi hotu!

8. Yath' Indakhīlo paṭhaviṁ sito siyā [229]
catubbhi vātehi asampakampiyo,
tathûpamaṁ sappurisaṁ vadāmi,
yo ariyasaccāni avecca passati.
Idam pi Saṁghe ratanaṁ paṇītaṁ.
Etena saccena suvatthi hotu!

9. Ye ariyasaccāni vibhāvayanti [230]
gambhīrapaññena sudesitāni,
kiñcâpi te honti bhusappamattā,
na te bhavaṁ aṭṭhamaṁ ādiyanti.
Idam pi Saṁghe ratanaṁ paṇītaṁ.
Etena saccena suvatthi hotu!

10. Sahā v' assa dassanasampadāya, [231]
tayas su dhammā jahitā bhavanti:—
sakkāyadiṭṭhi vicikicchitañ ca
sīlabbataṁ vâpi yad atthi kiñci;
catūh' apāyehi ca vippamutto
cha câbhiṭhānāni abhabbo kātuṁ.
Idam pi Saṁghe ratanaṁ paṇītaṁ.
Etena saccena suvatthi hotu!

11. Kiñcâpi so kammaṁ karoti pāpakaṁ [232]
kāyena vācā uda cetasā vā,
abhabbo so tassa paṭicchādāya;
—abhabbatā diṭṭhapadassa vuttā.
Idam pi Saṁghe ratanaṁ paṇītaṁ.
Etena saccena suvatthi hotu!

12. Vanappagumbe yathā phusitagge [233]
gimhānamāse paṭhamasmiṁ gimhe,
tathûpamaṁ Dhammavaraṁ adesayi
nibbānagāmiṁ parama-ṁ-hitāya.
Idam pi Buddhe ratanaṁ paṇītaṁ.
Etena saccena suvatthi hotu!

And they whose stedfast hearts, [228]
by lusts unswayed, are set
on Gotama's behests,
—these win their goal; these taste
a bliss right cheaply earned.
This gem the Order holds;
—and may that truth bless all!

As Indra's deep-sunk balk [229]
defies all winds that blow,
so stedfast stand the good
who grasp the Noble Truths.
This gem the Order holds;
—and may that truth bless all!

All who absorb those Truths [230]
which our deep thinker preached,
though they backslide, shall see
not more than seven births.
This gem the Order holds;
—and may that truth bless all!

And when full vision comes, [231]
three outlooks pass away:—
doubt, personality,
and ritual. Thus freed
from dread of hell and doom,
man cannot perpetrate
the six dire, deadly sins.
This gem the Order holds;
—and may that truth bless all!

And if one should transgress [232]
in word or deed or thought,
he cannot cloke his fault,
since he has 'seen the light'.
This gem the Order holds;
—and may that truth bless all!

As when in spring the brake [233]
is gay with flow'r and leaf,
this best of gospels lights
the way Nirvāna-ward.
This gem the Buddha holds;
—and may that truth bless all!

13. Varo varaññū varado varāharo [234]
anuttaro Dhammavaraṁ adesayi.
Idam pi Buddhe ratanaṁ paṇītaṁ.
Etena saccena suvatthi hotu!

14. 'Khīṇaṁ purāṇaṁ, navaṁ na 'tthi sambhavaṁ', [235]
virattacittā āyatike bhavasmiṁ
te khīṇabījā avirūḷhichandā
nibbanti dhīrā yathâyam padīpo.
Idam pi Saṁghe ratanaṁ paṇītaṁ.
Etena saccena suvatthi hotu!

---

15. Yānîdha bhūtāni samāgatāni [236]
bhummāni vā yāni va antalikkhe,
tathāgataṁ devamanussapūjitaṁ
Buddhaṁ namassāma; suvatthi hotu!

16. Yānîdha bhūtāni samāgatāni [237]
bhummāni vā yāni va antalikkhe,
tathāgataṁ devamanussapūjitaṁ
Dhammaṁ namassāma; suvatthi hotu!

17. Yānîdha bhūtāni samāgatāni [238]
bhummāni vā yāni va antalikkhe,
tathāgataṁ devamanussapūjitaṁ
Saṁghaṁ namassāma; suvatthi hotu!

2. Āmagandhasutta

1. Sāmākacingulakacīnakāni [239]
pattapphalaṁ mūlapphalaṁ gavipphalaṁ
dhammena laddhaṁ sata-m-asamānā
na kāmakāmā alikaṁ bhaṇanti.

2. Yad asamāno sukataṁ suniṭṭhitaṁ [240]
parehi dinnaṁ payataṁ paṇītaṁ
sālīnam annaṁ paribhuñjamāno,
so bhuñjatī, Kassapa, āmagandhaṁ.

He is—He knows—He gives— [234]
the best; His Doctrine 's best.
This gem the Buddha holds;
—and may that truth bless all!

'The old is dead; no fresh [235]
growths rise', cry saints, who, quit
of germs and hopes, reject
all life to come and pass
away like lamps unfed.
This gem the Order holds;
—and may that truth bless all!

Praise, denizens of earth [236]
and skies, praise, beings all,
the Buddha, dear to gods
and men,—who brings the Truth;
—and may a blessing come!

Praise, denizens of earth [237]
and skies, praise, beings all,
the Doctrine, dear to gods
and men,—which brings the Truth;
—and may a blessing come!

Praise, denizens of earth [238]
and skies, praise, beings all,
the Order, dear to gods
and men,—which brings the Truth:
—and may a blessing come!

Sutta 2. Carrion

A brahmin: The millet-grain, palm-nuts, [239]
pulse, bulbs, and wilding shoots,
—this diet, rightly got,
ne'er prompts the good to lie.

'Tis eating carrion [240]
to touch a host's rich fare,
well-dressed and delicate!

3. 'Na āmagandho mama kappatîti' [241]
icc-eva tvaṁ bhāsasi, Brahmabandhu,
sālīnam annaṁ paribhuñjamāno
sakuntamaṁsehi susaṁkhatehi.
Pucchāmi taṁ, Kassapa, etam atthaṁ:
Kathappakāro tava āmagandho?

4. Pāṇātipāto vadhachedabandhanaṁ [242]
theyyaṁ musāvādo nikatī vañcanāni ca
ajjhenakujjaṁ paradārasevanā,
—es' āmagandho, na hi maṁsabhojanaṁ.

5. Ye idha kāmesu asaṁyatā janā [243]
rasesu giddhā asucīkamissitā
natthikadiṭṭhī visamā durannayā,
—es' āmagandho, na hi maṁsabhojanaṁ.

6. Ye lūkhasā dāruṇā piṭṭhimaṁsikā [244]
mittadduno nikkaruṇâtimānino
adānasīlā, na ca denti kassaci,
—es' āmagandho—pe—

7. Kodho mado thambho paccupaṭṭhāpanā [245]
māyā usuyyā bhassasamussayo ca
mānātimāno ca asabbhi santhavo,
—es' āmagandho . . . .

8. Ye pāpasīlā iṇaghātasūcakā [246]
vohārakūṭā idha pāṭirūpikā
narâdhamā ye 'dha karonti kibbisaṁ,
—es' āmagandho . . . .

9. Ye idha pāṇesu asaṁyatā janā [247]
paresam ādāya vihesam uyyutā
dussīlaluddā pharusā anādarā,
—es' āmagandho . . . .

10. Etesu giddhā, viruddhâtipātino [248]
nicc' uyyutā pecca tamaṁ vajanti ye,
patanti sattā nirayaṁ avaṁsirā,
—es' āmagandho . . . .

Though you (a brahmin!) say [241]
you touch no carrion,
you eat choice dishes made
with flesh of birds.—I ask
what you term 'carrion'.

Kassapa (a former Buddha): Killing and maiming, stripes, [242]
bonds, theft, lies, fraud, deceit,
adultery,—not meats,
but these, are carrion.

Pursuit of pleasure, lust [243]
for guzzling, life unclean,
blatant dissent,—not meats,
but these, are carrion.

Backbiting, cruelty, [244]
betrayals, ruthless pride,
mean stinginess,—not meats,
but these, are carrion.

Anger, conceit, revolt, [245]
guile, envy, bluster, pride,
low company,—not meats,
but these, are carrion.

Base living, slander, fraud, [246]
cheating, the trickster's wiles,
foul infamies,—not meats,
but these, are carrion.

The lust to kill and hurt [247]
and rob, the evil trade
of hunters fierce,—not meats,
but these, are carrion.

This rage to slay and steal, [248]
these crimes, are fraught with doom
and end in hell;—not meats,
but these, are carrion.

11. Na macchamaṁsaṁ nânāsakattaṁ, [249]
na naggiyaṁ muṇḍiyaṁ jaṭājallaṁ
kharâjināni vā,
nâggihuttass' upasevanā va yā,
ye vā pi loke amarā bahū tapā,
mantâhutī yañña-m-utûpasevanā
sodhenti maccaṁ avitiṇṇakankhaṁ.

12. Sotesu gutto vijitindriyo care [250]
dhamme ṭhito ajjavamaddave rato
sangātigo sabbadukkhappahīno
na lippati diṭṭhasutesu dhīro.

---

13. Icc' etam attham Bhagavā punappunaṁ [251]
akkhāsi; taṁ vedayi mantapāragū.
Citrāhi gāthāhi Muni-ppakāsayi
nirāmagandho asito durannayo.

14. Sutvāna Buddhassa subhāsitam padaṁ [252]
nirāmagandhaṁ sabbadukkhâpanūdanaṁ,
nīcamano vandi Tathāgatassa;
tatth' eva pabbajjam arocayittha.

3. Hirisutta

1. Hirin tarantaṁ vijigucchamānaṁ, [253]
'sakhâham asmi' iti bhāsamānaṁ,
sayhāni kammāni anādiyantaṁ,
'N' eso maman' ti iti naṁ vijaññā.

2. Ananvayaṁ piyaṁ vācaṁ yo mittesu pakubbati, [254]
'Akarontaṁ bhāsamānaṁ' parijānanti paṇḍitā.

No abstinence from meat [249]
and fish, no nudity,
no top-knots, shaven crowns,
no grime or garb of pelt,
no cult of sacred fire,
no stark austerities
to purchase future bliss,
no runes, burnt-off'rings, rites,
—can cleanse the man who doubts.

Control thy senses, rule [250]
thy powers, hold to Truth,
be kind. The saint who leaves
all ties and vanquishes
all Ills, is stained by naught
he either sees or hears.

What thus the Lord set forth, [251]
the brahmin realized,
as, verse by verse, he heard
th' unswerving mystic Sage,
all 'carrion' above.

Hearing the Buddha preach [252]
these lofty, saving truths,
denouncing 'carrion'
and sweeping Ills away,
the brahmin meekly knelt
and asked to be enrolled
an Almsman then and there.

Sutta 3. Loyalty

Renounce dishonest men [253]
who flout their plighted word
and, though they pose as friends,
perform not what they might.

When glozing protestations end in naught, [254]
then sage observers style it 'words, not deeds'.

3. Na so mitto yo sadā appamatto [255]
bhedāsaṁkī randham evânupassī;
yasmiṁ ca seti urasîva putto,
sa ve mitto yo parehi abhejjo.

4. Pāmujjakaraṇaṁ ṭhānaṁ pasaṁsāvahanaṁ sukhaṁ [256]
phalānisaṁso bhāveti vahanto porisaṁ dhuraṁ.

5. Pavivekarasam pītvā rasaṁ upasamassa ca [257]
niddaro hoti nippāpo dhammapītirasaṁ pivaṁ.

4. Mahāmangalasutta

Evam me sutaṁ. Ekaṁ samayaṁ Bhagavā Sāvatthiyaṁ viharati Jetavane Anāthapiṇḍikassa ārāme. Atha kho aññatarā devatā abhikkantāya rattiyā abhikkantavaṇṇā kevalakappaṁ Jetavanaṁ obhāsetvā yena Bhagavā ten' upasaṁkami, upasaṁkamitvā Bhagavantaṁ abhivādetvā ekamantaṁ aṭṭhāsi. Ekamantaṁ ṭhitā kho sā devatā Bhagavantaṁ gāthāya ajjhabhāsi:—

1. Bahū devā manussā ca mangalāni acintayuṁ, [258]
ākankhamānā sotthānaṁ:—brūhi mangalam uttamaṁ.

---

2. Asevanā ca bālānaṁ, paṇḍitānañ ca sevanā, [259]
pūjā ca pūjanīyānaṁ;—etam mangalam uttamaṁ.

3. Patirūpadesavāso ca, pubbe ca katapuññatā, [260]
attasammāpaṇidhi ca;—etam mangalam uttamaṁ.

4. Bāhusaccañ ca sippañ ca vinayo ca susikkhito [261]
subhāsitā ca yā vacā;—etam mangalam uttamaṁ.

5. Mātāpitu upaṭṭhānaṁ, puttadārassa sangaho, [262]
anākulā ca kammantā;—etam mangalam uttamaṁ.

6. Dānañ ca dhammacariyā ca, ñātakānañ ca sangaho, [263]
anavajjāni kammāni;—etam mangalam uttamaṁ.

7. Ārati virati pāpā majjapānā ca saṁyamo, [264]
appamādo ca dhammesu;—etam mangalam uttamaṁ.

No friend is he whose eye [255]
is ever on the watch
to spy shortcomings out,
—against a future breach.
But if you rest secure,
like babe on mother's breast,
you have a friend indeed,
whom none can rob you of.

Whoso, while shouldering man's common lot, [256]
has reaped a harvest blest, accomplishes
a happy life and well-earned meed of praise.

But he who, in aloofness, tastes true Peace, [257]
puts haunting dread away, and wickedness,
and quaffs those draughts of bliss the Doctrine gives.

Sutta 4. The Boon of Boons

Thus have I heard. Once while the Lord was staying at Sāvatthī in Jeta's grove in Anāthapiṇḍika's pleasaunce, a certain deity of surpassing beauty illumined the whole grove as night was on the wane, and, coming to the Lord, stood to one side after meet salutations, addressing the Lord in the following stanzas:—

In quest of weal, full many gods and men [258]
have ponder'd over fortune's choicest boons.
Tell me, I pray, what boon stands out supreme.

The Lord: 'Tis shunning fools, consorting with the wise, [259]
and heartfelt worship of the worshipful;

'tis life in scenes befitting spent, a past [260]
of garner'd goodness, aspiration high;

'tis lore profound and skill, obedience [261]
to rules prescribed, and well-weighed utterance;

'tis ministry to parents, tender care [262]
for wife and child, an undistracting trade;

'tis largesse, pious living, tender care [263]
for kith and kin, conduct beyond reproach;

'tis shunning and eschewing wickedness, [264]
forswearing drink, keeping right states of mind;

8. Gāravo ca nivāto ca santuṭṭhī ca kataññutā [265]
kālena dhammasavanaṁ;—etam mangalam uttamaṁ.

9. Khantī ca sovacassatā samaṇānañ ca dassanaṁ [266]
kālena dhammasākacchā;—etam mangalam uttamaṁ.

10. Tapo ca brahmacariyā ca, ariyasaccāna' dassanaṁ, [267]
nibbānasacchikiriyā ca;—etam mangalam uttamaṁ.

11. Phuṭṭhassa lokadhammehi cittaṁ yassa na kampati [268]
asokaṁ virajaṁ khemaṁ;—etam mangalam uttamaṁ.

12. Etādisāni katvāna sabbattha-m-aparājitā [269]
sabbattha sotthiṁ gacchanti;—taṁ tesaṁ mangalam uttamaṁ.

5. Sūcilomasutta

Evam me sutaṁ. Ekaṁ samayaṁ Bhagavā Gayāyaṁ viharati Ṭaṁkitamañce Sūcilomassa yakkhassa bhavane. Tena kho pana samayena Kharo ca yakkho Sūcilomo ca yakkho Bhagavato avidūre atikkamanti. Atha kho Kharo yakkho Sūcilomaṁ yakkhaṁ etad avoca: Eso samaṇo ti.

N' eso samaṇo; samaṇako eso. Yāva jānāmi yadi vā so samaṇo yadi vā samaṇako ti.

Atha kho Sūcilomo yakkho yena Bhagavā ten' upasaṁkami, upasaṁkamitvā Bhagavato kāyaṁ upanāmesi. Atha kho Bhagavā kāyaṁ apanāmesi. Atha kho Sūcilomo yakkho Bhagavantaṁ etad avoca: Bhāyasi maṁ, samaṇâti.

Na khvâhan taṁ, āvuso, bhāyāmi; api ca kho te samphasso pāpako ti.

Pañhaṁ taṁ, samaṇa, pucchissāmi. Sace me na vyākarissasi, cittaṁ vā te khipissāmi, hadayaṁ vā te phāḷessāmi, pādesu vā gahetvā pāra-Gangāya khipissāmîti.

Na khvâhan taṁ, āvuso, passāmi sadevake loke samārake sabrahmake sassamaṇabrāhmaṇiyā pajāya sadevamanussāya yo me cittaṁ vā khipeyya, hadayaṁ vā phāḷeyya, pādesu vā gahetvā pāra-Gangāya khipeyya. Api ca tvaṁ, āvuso, puccha yad ākankhasîti.

Atha kho Sūcilomo yakkho Bhagavantaṁ gāthāya ajjhabhāsi:—

1. Rāgo ca doso ca kutonidānā? [270]
Aratī ratī lomahaṁso kutojā?
Kuto samuṭṭhāya mano vitakkā,
kumārakā vaṁkam iv', ossajanti?

2. 'Rāgo ca doso ca itonidānā; [271]
aratī ratī lomahaṁso itojā;
ito samuṭṭhāya mano vitakkā,
kumārakā vaṁkam iv', ossajanti.

'tis rev'rent awe, content, prompt gratitude, [265]
and due attendance when the Doctrine's preached;

'tis patience, courtesy, the company [266]
of Almsmen, timely talks on gospel truth;

'tis strict austerity, a holy life, [267]
the Noble Truths seen clear, Nirvāna won;

a heart untouched by wordly things, a heart [268]
from sorrow freed, th' unspotted heart at Peace.

—To them who live that life, defeat ne'er comes, [269]
but always weal;—this 'boon of boons' is theirs!

Sutta 5. Inward Growths

Thus have I heard. Once, while the Lord was staying at Gayā near Stone-Couch in the domain of the sprite Sūciloma, the sprites Khara and Sūciloma were passing close by the Lord.

That's an anchorite, said Khara.

No, it is not, answered Sūciloma;—though he looks anchoritish. Wait till I make sure whether he is a real anchorite or only looks like one.

Accordingly, the sprite, with bristles like needles, went and brushed up against the Lord,—who drew back.

You're afraid of me, anchorite, said the sprite.

No, said the Lord; I am not afraid of you; but contact with you is unpleasant.

I will ask you a question, anchorite; if you do not answer it, I'll scare you out of your wits, or rive your heart, or fling you by the heels across the Ganges.

Sir, replied the Lord, in all the wide world of gods, Māras, and Brahmās, I see no one among anchorites and brahmins, gods or men, who could do to me what you suggest. However, sir, ask what you will.

Hereupon, the sprite Sūciloma addressed the Lord in these stanzas:—

Whence spring ill-will and lusts? [270]
Whence likes, dislikes, and dread?
Whence thoughts which plague the mind
as boys a captive crow?

The Lord: '*Self*' breeds ill-will and lusts, [271]
dislikes and likes and dread,
and thoughts which plague the mind
as boys a captive crow.

3. Snehajā attasambhūtā nigrodhassêva khandhajā, [272]
puthū visattā kāmesu māluvā va vitatā vane.

4. Ye naṁ pajānanti yatonidānaṁ, [273]
te naṁ vinodenti (suṇohi yakkha!);
te duttaraṁ ogham imaṁ taranti
atiṇṇapubbaṁ apunabbhavāya.

6. Dhammacariyasutta

1. Dhammacariyaṁ brahmacariyaṁ, etad āhu vasuttamaṁ. [274]
Pabbajito pi ce hoti agārasmā anagāriyaṁ,

2. so ce mukharajātiko vihesâbhirato mago, [275]
jīvitan tassa pāpiyo, rajaṁ vaḍḍheti attano.

3. Kalahâbhirato bhikkhu mohadhammena āvaṭo [276]
akkhātam pi na jānāti Dhammaṁ Buddhena desitaṁ.

4. Vihesaṁ bhāvitattānaṁ avijjāya purakkhato [277]
saṁkilesaṁ na jānāti maggaṁ nirayagāminaṁ.

5. Vinipātaṁ samāpanno, gabbhā gabbhaṁ, tamā tamaṁ, [278]
sa ve tādisako bhikkhu pecca dukkhaṁ nigacchati.

6. Gūthakūpo yathā assa sampuṇṇo gaṇavassiko, [279]
yo evarūpo assa; dubbisodho hi sangaṇo.

7. Yaṁ evarūpaṁ jānātha, bhikkhavo, gehanissitaṁ [280]
pāpicchaṁ pāpasaṁkappaṁ pāpa-ācāragocaraṁ,

8. sabbe samaggā hutvāna abhinibbijjayātha naṁ, [281]
kāraṇḍavaṁ niddhamatha, kasambuṁ apakassatha;

9. tato palāpe vāhetha assamaṇe samaṇamānine, [282]
niddhamitvāna pāpicche pāpa-ācāragocare,

10. suddhā suddhehi saṁvāsaṁ kappayavho patissatā; [283]
tato samaggā nipakā dukkhass' antaṁ karissatha.

Like banyan saplings, these are inward growths [272]
by 'Self' begotten, craving's progeny,
which spread abroad a tangled growth of lusts,
like creepers rank that overgrow the woods.

All such as know their source, [273]
dispel the brood (give ear!)
and cross life's Flood at last,
to know rebirth no more.

Sutta 6. The Good Life

The good, the holy life is hailed 'supreme'! [274]
Though one goes forth from home to homelessness,

but shows himself harsh-tongued, and brutishly [275]
delights to harry others, then his life
is evil and he waxes fouler still.

The wrangling Almsman, in blank folly pent, [276]
misses the Doctrine which the Buddha preached.

By ignorance impelled to harry saints, [277]
he fails to see his guilt leads straight to hell.

Passed now to doom—to birth on birth always, [278]
darkness succeeding darkness—, this life o'er
that Almsman goes to dree his weird of woe.

E'en as a jakes chock-full through years of use, [279]
that man would be;—since guilt is hard to cleanse.

Almsmen, if such a parasite ye find, [280]
of evil wants and aims, of evil life,

let all with one accord him shun, as chaff [281]
him winnow out, as refuse cast away.

So, cart away, like empty husks, those frauds [282]
who pose as Almsmen, being vile at heart.

Be pure, and only with the pure consort; [283]
and ye, in concord sage, shall end all Ills.

7. Brāhmaṇadhammikasutta

Evam me sutaṁ. Ekaṁ samayaṁ Bhagavā Sāvatthiyaṁ viharati Jetavane Anāthapiṇḍikassa ārāme. Atha kho sambahulā Kosalakā brāhmaṇamahāsālā jiṇṇā vuddhā mahallakā addhagatā vayo anuppattā yena Bhagavā ten' upasaṁkamiṁsu, upasaṁkamitvā Bhagavatā saddhiṁ sammodiṁsu, sammodanīyaṁ kathaṁ sāraṇīyaṁ vītisāretvā ekamantaṁ nisīdiṁsu. Ekamantaṁ nisinnā kho te brāhmaṇamahāsālā Bhagavantaṁ etad avocuṁ: Sandissanti nu kho, bho Gotama, etarahi brāhmaṇā porāṇānaṁ brāhmaṇānaṁ brāhmaṇadhamme ti?

Na kho, brāhmaṇā, sandissanti etarahi brāhmaṇā porāṇānaṁ brāhmaṇānaṁ brāhmaṇadhamme ti.

Sādhu no bhavaṁ Gotamo porāṇānaṁ brāhmaṇānaṁ brāhmaṇadhammaṁ bhāsatu, sace bhoto Gotamassa agarûti.

Tena hi, brāhmaṇā, suṇātha sādhukaṁ manasikarotha, bhāsissāmîti.

Evam bho ti kho te brāhmaṇamahāsālā Bhagavato paccassosuṁ. Bhagavā etad avoca:—

1. Isayo pubbakā āsuṁ saṁyatattā tapassino; [284]
pañca kāmaguṇe hitvā atta-d-attham acārisuṁ.

2. Na pasū brāhmaṇān' āsuṁ, na hiraññaṁ, na dhāniyaṁ; [285]
sajjhāyadhanadhaññâsuṁ, brahmaṁ nidhim apālayuṁ.

3. Yaṁ tesaṁ pakataṁ āsi dvārabhattaṁ upaṭṭhitaṁ [286]
saddhāpakatam esānaṁ dātave tad amaññisuṁ.

4. Nānārattehi vatthehi sayaneh' āvasathehi ca [287]
phitā janapadā raṭṭhā te namassiṁsu brāhmaṇe.

5. Avajjhā brāhmaṇā āsuṁ ajeyyā dhammarakkhitā; [288]
na ne koci nivāresi kuladvāresu sabbaso.

6. Aṭṭhacattārīsaṁ vassāni komārabrahmacariyaṁ cariṁsu te; [289]
vijjācaraṇapariyiṭṭhiṁ acaruṁ brāhmaṇā pure.

7. Na brāhmaṇā aññam agamuṁ, na pi bhariyaṁ kiṇiṁsu te; [290]
sampiyen' eva saṁvāsaṁ sangantvā samarocayuṁ.

8. Aññatra tamhā samayā utuveramaṇiṁ pati [291]
antarā methunaṁ dhammaṁ nâssu gacchanti brāhmaṇā.

Sutta 7. Brahminism's Golden Age

Thus have I heard. Once while the Lord was staying at Sāvatthī in Jeta's grove in Anāthapiṇḍika's pleasaunce, there came to him a number of Kosalan brahmins of great wealth—broken and old, aged and stricken in years, drawing to their life's close—who, after courteous salutations, took their seats to one side, saying: Are the brahmins of to-day in accord, Gotama, with the brahminic outlook of the brahmins of old?

No, brahmins; they are not.

If it is agreeable to you, sir, please tell us what was the brahminic outlook of the brahmins of old.

Give ear then and hearken; I will tell you.

Certainly, sir, answered they in assent.

The Lord began:—

In self-control and strict austerity [284]
the ancient sages dwelt; the fivefold strands
of pleasure they renounced, themselves to save.

No herds had brahmins then, no gold or pelf; [285]
their wealth was holy lore and holy life.

They deemed the common scraps outside folks' doors [286]
to be faith's offering for brahmin needs.

The rich of country sides and realms at large [287]
great court and homage to these brahmins paid
with garments dyed and couches and abodes.

Inviolate, invincible were they, [288]
shielded from harm by holiness of life;
and on a brahmin no man closed his doors.

For eight and forty years as celibates [289]
the early brahmins lived, in quest devout
of ken and vision and of holy life.

For wives these brahmins sought no other caste, [290]
and never purchased brides; 'twas their delight
to pass their wedded lives in bonds of love.

'Twas only when a period was o'er, [291]
that brahmins knew their wives,—and not between.

9. Brahmacariyañ ca sīlañ ca ajjavaṁ maddavaṁ tapaṁ [292]
soraccaṁ avihiṁsañ ca khantiñ câpi avaṇṇayuṁ.

10. Yo nesaṁ paramo āsi brahmā daḷhaparakkamo, [293]
sa vâpi methunaṁ dhammaṁ supinante pi nâgamā.

11. Tassa vattaṁ anusikkhantā idh' eke viññujātikā [294]
brahmacariyañ ca sīlañ ca khantiñ câpi avaṇṇayuṁ.

12. Taṇḍulaṁ sayanaṁ vatthaṁ sappitelañ ca yāciya [295]
dhammena samudānetvā tato yaññam akappayuṁ;
upaṭṭhitasmiṁ yaññasmiṁ nâssu gāvo haniṁsu te.

13. 'Yathā mātā pitā bhātā aññe vâpi ca ñātakā, [296]
gāvo no paramā mittā, yāsu jāyanti osadhā,

14. annadā baladā c' etā vaṇṇadā sukhadā tathā,' [297]
—etam atthavasaṁ ñatvā nâssu gāvo haniṁsu te.

15. Sukhumālā mahākāyā vaṇṇavanto yasassino [298]
brāhmaṇā sehi dhammehi kiccâkiccesu ussukā,
yāva loke avattiṁsu sukham edhittha ayam pajā.

16. Tesaṁ āsi vipallāso. Disvāna aṇuto aṇuṁ [299]
rājino ca viyākāraṁ, nariyo ca samalankatā,

17. rathe c' ājaññasaṁyutte sukate, cittasibbane, [300]
nivesane, nivese ca vibhatte bhāgaso mite,

18. gomaṇḍalaparibbūḷhaṁ, nārīvaragaṇâyutaṁ, [301]
uḷāraṁ mānusaṁ bhogaṁ abhijjhāyiṁsu brāhmaṇā.

19. Te tattha mante ganthetvā Okkākaṁ tad' upāgamuṁ: [302]
—Pahūtadhanadhañño si;
yajassu, bahu te vittaṁ; yajassu, bahu te dhanaṁ!

20. Tato ca rājā saṁyatto brāhmaṇehi rathesabho, [303]
assamedhaṁ purisamedhaṁ sammāpāsaṁ
vājapeyyaṁ niraggaḷaṁ,—
ete yāge yajitvāna brāhmaṇānaṁ adā dhanaṁ,

21. —gāvo, sayanañ ca, vatthañ ca, nariyo ca samalankatā, [304]
rathe c' ājaññasaṁyutte sukate, cittasibbane,

22. nivesanāni rammāni suvibhattāni bhāgaso [305]
nānādhaññassa pūretvā brāhmaṇānaṁ adā dhanaṁ.

Brahmins prized holy living, rectitude, [292]
meek kindly gentleness, austerities,
patient forbearance, tender mercy, ruth.

The pattern brahmin—steadfast, resolute— [293]
not e'en in dreams had carnal intercourse.

By his example, wisdom's sons were brought [294]
to prize forbearance, virtue, holy life.

They asked but rice, beds, garments, ghee, and oil; [295]
and with such gifts they made their offerings;
—no cows were slaughter'd for their sacrifice.

Holding that cows,—like parents, brothers, kin— [296]
were their best friends, the source of healthful things,

of food, well-being, goodliness, and strength, [297]
—grateful for this, they never slaughter'd cows.

Tall, goodly, debonair, and famous men [298]
were brahmins then, inspired by zeal to grow
to their own standards high of right and wrong;
and, while these lived on earth, mankind fared well.

Then came corruption. Bit by bit, they saw [299]
the monarch's splendour, women richly dight,

steeds yoked to chariots, gay coverlets, [300]
stately abodes, and chamber'd palaces,

girt round with crowded byres, and graced with troops [301]
of women fair to view;—vast mundane wealth
those brahmins saw, and, seeing, coveted.

Thereon, they framed these verses and they sought [302]
Okkāka;—'King', said they, 'abounding wealth
is thine and substance; offer sacrifice!
great store, great wealth hast thou; make sacrifice!'

Thereon the king, that doughty charioteer, [303]
won o'er by brahmins, offered sacrifice
of horses, human victims, and the rest;
and, at the close, to brahmins largesse gave

of kine, beds, garments, women richly dight, [304]
steeds yoked to chariots, gay coverlets,

stately abodes, and chambered palaces, [305]
filled full of gear.—The king this largesse gave.

23. Te ca tattha dhanaṁ laddhā sannidhiṁ samarocayuṁ; [306]
tesaṁ icchāvatiṇṇānaṁ bhiyyo taṇhā pavaḍḍhatha.
Te tattha mante ganthetvā Okkākaṁ puna-m-upāgamuṁ:

24. 'Yathā āpo ca paṭhavī ca hiraññadhanadhāniyaṁ, [307]
evaṁ gāvo manussānaṁ; parikkhāro so hi pāṇinaṁ.
Yajassu, bahu te vittaṁ; yajassu, bahu te dhanaṁ!

25. Tato ca rājā saṁyatto brāhmaṇehi rathesabho [308]
'nekā satasahassiyo gāvo yaññe aghātayi.

26. Na pādā na visāṇena nâssu hiṁsanti kenaci [309]
gāvo eḷakasamānā soratā kumbhadūhanā,
—tā visāṇe gahetvāna rājā satthen' aghātayi.

27. Tato ca devā pitaro Indo asura-rakkhasā [310]
'Adhammo' iti pakkanduṁ yaṁ satthaṁ nipatī gave.

28. Tayo rogā pure āsuṁ:—icchā, anasanañ, jarā; [311]
pasūnañ ca samārambhā aṭṭhānavuti-m-āgamuṁ.

29. Eso adhammo daṇḍānaṁ okkanto purāṇo ahū, [312]
adūsikāyo haññanti, dhammā dhaṁsenti yājakā,

30. —evam eso aṇudhammo porāṇo viññugarahito; [313]
yattha edisakaṁ passati, yājakaṁ garahatī jano.

31. Evaṁ dhamme viyāpanne vibhinnā sudda-vessikā, [314]
puthu vibhinnā khattiyā, pati' bhariyā 'vamaññatha.

32. Khattiyā Brahmabandhū ca ye c' aññe gottarakkhitā [315]
jātivādaṁ niraṁkatvā kāmānaṁ vasam upāgamun ti.

Evaṁ vutte te brāhmaṇamahāsālā Bhagavantaṁ etad avocuṁ: Abhikkantaṁ, bho Gotama; abhikkantaṁ, bho Gotama! Seyyathā pi, bho Gotama, nikkujjitaṁ vā ukkujjeyya, paṭicchannaṁ vā vivareyya, mūḷhassa vā maggaṁ ācikkheyya, andhakāre vā telapajjotaṁ dhāreyya 'cakkhumanto rūpāni dakkhintîti', evam evaṁ bhotā Gotamena anekapariyāyena dhammo pakāsito. Ete mayaṁ bhavantaṁ Gotamaṁ saraṇaṁ gacchāma dhammañ ca bhikkhusaṁghañ ca; upāsake no bhavaṁ Gotamo dhāretu ajjatagge pāṇupetaṁ saraṇaṁ gate.

But largesse fired their passion more to get; [306]
their craving grew and grew. Once more they sought
Okkāka, with these verses newly framed:—

'As earth and water, gold and silver, so [307]
are cows a primal requisite of man.
Great store, great wealth is thine; make sacrifice!'

Thereon the king, that doughty charioteer, [308]
won o'er by brahmins, for the sacrifice
doomed cows by hundred-thousands to the knife.

—The cows that do no hurt with horn or hoof, [309]
yes, gentle lamblike cows that fill the pail,
he bade be taken by the horn and slain.

''Tis wrong! 'tis wrong!' arose th' united wail [310]
of Brahmās, Indra, Titans, ogres too,
as cows were butcher'd for the sacrifice.

Diseases, which of yore were only three [311]
—desires, and hunger, and senility—
with cattle-killing rose to ninety-eight!

'Of old began this outrage; harmless cows [312]
are slain by guilty sacrificers' hands':—

thus, thus, the wise condemn this ancient guilt, [313]
and folk condemn the sacrificers' crime.

When right thus perished, straightway discord split [314]
farmers and serfs, and split the nobles' ranks,
while wives looked down upon their lords with scorn;

nobles and 'Brahmā's kin', with folk of rank, [315]
flouting their birthright, fell a prey to lusts.

Hereupon, those brahmins of great wealth said to the Lord:—Wonderful, Gotama! quite wonderful! Just as a man might set upright again what had been cast down, or reveal what had been hidden away, or tell a man who had gone astray which was his way, or bring a lamp into the dark so that those with eyes to see might see the things about them,—even so in many ways has Gotama made his Doctrine clear. We come to the reverend Gotama as our refuge, and to his Doctrine and to his Community. We ask him to accept us as followers who have found an abiding refuge from this day forth while life lasts.

8. Nāvāsutta

1. Yasmā hi Dhammaṁ puriso vijaññā, [316]
Indaṁ va naṁ devatā pūjayeyya;
so pūjito tasmiṁ pasannacitto
bahussuto pātukaroti Dhammaṁ.

2. Tad aṭṭhikatvāna nisamma dhīro [317]
dhammânudhammaṁ paṭipajjamāno
viññū vibhāvī nipuṇo ca hoti,
yo tādisaṁ bhajati appamatto.

3. Khuddañ ca bālaṁ upasevamāno [318]
anāgatatthañ ca usūyakañ ca
idh' eva Dhammaṁ avibhāvayitvā
avitiṇṇakankho maraṇaṁ upeti.

4. Yathā naro āpagaṁ otaritvā [319]
mahodikaṁ salilaṁ sīghasotaṁ,
so vuyhamāno anusotagāmī
—kiṁ so pare sakkhati tārayetuṁ?

5. Tath' eva Dhammaṁ avibhāvayitvā, [320]
bahussutānaṁ anisāmay' atthaṁ,
sayaṁ ajānaṁ avitiṇṇakankho
—kiṁ so pare sakkhati nijjhapetuṁ?

6. Yathā pi nāvaṁ daḷhaṁ āruhitvā [321]
phiyen' arittena samangibhūto,
so tāraye tattha bahū pi aññe
tatr' ūpāyaññū kusalo mutīmā;

7. —evam pi yo vedagu bhāvitatto [322]
bahussuto hoti avedhadhammo,
so kho pare nijjhapaye pajānaṁ
sotâvadhānūpanisūpapanne.

8. Tasmā have sappurisaṁ bhajetha [323]
medhāvinañ c' eva bahussutañ ca;
aññāya atthaṁ paṭipajjamāno
viññātadhammo so sukhaṁ labhethâti.

Sutta 8. The Good Ship

As gods their homage pay [316]
to Indra, pay thou thine
to him who teaches thee.
Well-pleased thereby, thy sage
will make the Doctrine plain.

When earnest study guides [317]
along the way ordained,
the leal disciple comes,
through converse with his sage,
to grasp, to see, to know.

But with a sorry dolt, [318]
who fails to win the goal,
yet envies those who do,
the student misses Truth
and dies with doubts still rife.

As one whom th' headlong rush [319]
of some vast stream in spate
whirls willy-nilly down,
—can he help others o'er?

So he who grasps not Truth [320]
and heeds not learning's voice,
a doubter, knowing nought,
—can he gain others o'er?

As on a good stout ship, [321]
equipped with helm and oar,
a man expert and skilled
can ferry many o'er;

—so he who knows, who's trained, [322]
deep student, calmly sure,
by his full knowledge wins
hearers who're ripe to learn.

So pick a good and wise [323]
and learned teacher; tread
the path of Truth he shows,
till insight bring thee bliss.

9. Kiṁsīlasutta

1. Kiṁsīlo, kiṁsamācāro, kāni kammāni brūhayaṁ [324]
naro sammāniviṭṭh' assa uttamatthañ ca pāpuṇe?

2. Vaddhāpacāyī anusuyyako siyā, [325]
kālaññu c' assa garūnaṁ dassanāya
dhammiṁ kathaṁ erayitaṁ khaṇaññū
suṇeyya sakkacca subhāsitāni.

3. Kālena gacche garūnaṁ sakāsaṁ [326]
thambhaṁ nirankatvā nivātavuttī
atthaṁ dhammaṁ saṁyamaṁ brahmacariyaṁ
anussare c' eva samācare ca.

4. Dhammārāmo Dhammarato [327]
Dhamme ṭhito Dhammavinicchayaññū
n' evâcare Dhammasandosavādaṁ,
tacchehi niyyetha subhāsitehi.

5. Hassaṁ jappaṁ paridevaṁ padosaṁ [328]
māyākataṁ kuhanaṁ giddhimānaṁ
sārambhakakkassakasāvamucchaṁ
hitvā care vītamado ṭhitatto.

6. Viññātasārāni subhāsitāni, [329]
sutañ ca viññātaṁ samādhisāraṁ,
na tassa paññā ca sutañ ca vaḍḍhati
yo sāhaso hoti naro pamatto.

7. Dhamme ca ye ariyapavedite ratā [330]
anuttarā te vacasā manasā kammanā ca,
te santisoraccasamādhisaṇṭhitā
sutassa paññāya ca sāram ajjhagū

10. Uṭṭhānasutta

1. Uṭṭhahatha! nisīdatha! Ko attho supitena vo? [331]
Āturānaṁ hi kā niddā sallaviddhāna' ruppataṁ?

Sutta 9. Right Conduct

Sāriputta: What conduct, code, or scheme of things to do, [324]
will make man sure, and bring the highest good?

The Lord: Revere and envy not [325]
thine Elders; go to them
at seasons due; betimes
attend their homilies
and hear their weighty words.

Betimes thine Elders seek [326]
with meek humility;
weigh, follow, what they teach
of Doctrine, self-control,
the higher life, and Weal.

Be Doctrine thy delight [327]
and joy; in it stand fast;
plumb, plumb its depths; eschew
unworthy, vapid talk;
be Truth thy lofty theme.

Quit merry japes, laments, [328]
deceit and fraud, greed, pride,
brawls, taunts, the triple taint,
—quit, quit them each and all
and live self-poised, serene.

An exhortation's crown [329]
is comprehension, merged
in concentration rapt.
No growth in ken and lore
attends remiss self-will.

But they who find their joy [330]
in Buddha's Doctrine, shine
in word and thought and deed.
Full ken and lore reward
the meek, th' intent, the calm.

Sutta 10. Arise!

Arise! Sit up! Of what avail is sleep? [331]
What slumbers visit sick men writhing sore
beneath the barbèd arrow's rankling smart?

2. Uṭṭhahatha! nisīdatha! Daḷhaṁ sikkhatha santiyā, [332]
mā vo pamatte viññāya maccurājā amohayittha vasānuge.

3. Yāya devā manussā ca sitā tiṭṭhanti atthikā, [333]
tarath' etaṁ visattikaṁ, khaṇo ve mā upaccagā.
Khaṇâtītā hi socanti nirayamhi samappitā.

4. Pamādo rajo, pamādā pamādânupatito rajo. [334]
Appamādena vijjāya abbūḷhe sallam attano.

11. Rāhulasutta

1. 'Kacci abhiṇhasaṁvāsā nâvajānāsi paṇḍitam? [335]
Ukkādhāro manussānaṁ kacci apacito tayā?'

2. 'Nâhaṁ abhiṇhasaṁvāsā avajānāmi paṇḍitaṁ; [336]
ukkādharo manussānaṁ niccaṁ apacito mayā'.

---

3. Pañca kāmaguṇe hitvā piyarūpe manorame, [337]
saddhāya gharā nikkhamma dukkhass' antakaro bhava.

4. Mitte bhajassu kalyāṇe pantañ ca sayanāsanam [338]
vivittaṁ appanigghosaṁ; mattaññū hohi bhojane,

5. cīvare piṇḍapāte ca paccaye sayanāsane; [339]
etesu taṇhaṁ mā 'kāsi, mā lokaṁ punar āgami.

6. Saṁvuto pātimokkhasmiṁ indriyesu ca pañcasu; [340]
satī kāyagatā ty-atthu; nibbidābahulo bhava.

7. Nimittaṁ parivajjehi subhaṁ rāgūpasaṁhitaṁ, [341]
asubhāya cittaṁ bhāvehi, ekaggaṁ susamāhitaṁ,

8. animittañ ca bhāvehi, mānânusayam ujjaha: [342]
tato mānâbhisamayā upasanto carissasîti.

Itthaṁ sudaṁ Bhagavā āyasmantaṁ Rāhulaṁ imāhi gāthāhi abhiṇhaṁ ovadati.

Arise! Sit up! Strive hard for inward Peace; [332]
let not Death's monarch, finding you remiss,
snare and befool you as his thralls and dupes.

O'ercome the toils which trap both gods and men. [333]
Let not the moment idly pass; for, they
who let it slip, repine—too late—in hell.

Sloth is defilement; hard aheel of sloth [334]
defilement comes; by zeal and knowledge pluck
the barbèd arrow from your rankling wound.

Sutta 11. To Rāhula

The Lord: Does constant dwelling with thy teacher leave [335]
thee scornful? Dost thou inly honour him
who bears aloft the torch that lights mankind?

Rāhula: No constant dwelling with my teacher leaves [336]
me scornful; always do I honour him
who bears aloft the torch which lights mankind.

The Lord: Leave pleasure's fivefold strands,—so sweet, so dear; [337]
and, led by Faith, leave home, to end all Ills.

Choose worthy friends; a distant lodging seek, [338]
remote and quiet; sparing be in food

and raiment, alms, the requisites, and bed. [339]
Crave not for these, lest back to earth thou come.

Obey the code; control thy senses five; [340]
watch well thy body; grow to loathe the world.

Forsake the gay appearances of things, [341]
where passion reigns. In things austere, not gay,
school thou thy heart to fixity and calm.

Foster what harbours no appearances. [342]
Discard all trend to pride; pride comprehend
and thou shalt go thy way serene and calm.

It was in this wise that, in these stanzas, the Lord again and again exhorted the reverend Rāhula.

12. Vangīsasutta

Evam me sutaṁ. Ekaṁ samayaṁ Bhagavā Āḷaviyaṁ viharati, Aggāḷave cetiye. Tena kho pana samayena āyasmato Vangīsassa upajjhāyo Nigrodhakappo nāma thero Aggāḷave cetiye aciraparinibbuto hoti. Atha kho āyasmato Vangīsassa rahogatassa paṭisallīnassa evaṁ cetaso parivitakko udapādi:—Parinibbuto nu kho me upajjhāyo? udāhu no parinibbuto ti? Atha kho āyasmā Vangīso sāyaṇhasamayaṁ paṭisallānā vuṭṭhito yena Bhagavā ten' upasaṁkami, upasaṁkamitvā Bhagavantaṁ abhivādetvā ekamantaṁ nisīdi. Ekamantaṁ nisinno kho āyasmā Vangīso Bhagavantaṁ etad avoca:—Idha mayhaṁ, bhante, rahogatassa paṭisallīnassa evaṁ cetaso parivitakko udapādi 'Parinibbuto nu kho me upajjhāyo? udāhu no parinibbuto ti?' Atha kho āyasmā Vangīso uṭṭhāyâsanā ekaṁsaṁ cīvaraṁ katvā yena Bhagavā ten' añjalim paṇāmetvā Bhagavantaṁ gāthāya ajjhabhāsi:

1. Pucchāma Satthāraṁ anomapaññaṁ [343]
diṭṭhe va dhamme yo vicikicchānaṁ chettā:
Aggāḷave kālam akāsi bhikkhu
ñāto yasassī abhinibbutatto.

2. Nigrodhakappo iti tassa nāmaṁ [344]
tayā kataṁ, Bhagavā, brāhmaṇassa;
so taṁ namassaṁ acari mutyapekho
āraddhaviriyo daḷhadhammadassī.

3. Taṁ sāvakaṁ, Sakka, mayam pi sabbe [345]
aññātuṁ icchāma, samantacakkhu;
samavaṭṭhitā no savanāya sotā;
—tuvan no Satthā, tvam anuttaro si.

4. Chind' eva no vicikicchaṁ; brūhi m' etaṁ:— [346]
parinibbutaṁ vedaya, bhūripañña,
majjhe va no bhāsa, samantacakkhu,
Sakko va devānaṁ sahassanetto.

5. Ye keci ganthā idha mohamaggā [347]
aññāṇapakkhā vicikicchaṭhānā
Tathāgataṁ patvā na te bhavanti;
—cakkhuṁ hi etaṁ paramaṁ narānaṁ.

Sutta 12. Kappa's Destiny

Thus have I heard. Once while the Lord was staying in the Agg-Āḷava shrine in Āḷavi, there had passed away at the shrine, not long before, the Elder Nigrodha-Kappa, who had been the director of the reverend Vangīsa; and Vangīsa in his private meditations speculated whether his old director had, or had not, passed utterly away. Rising from these meditations at eventide, the reverend Vangīsa betook him to the Lord, and, taking his seat to one side after due salutations, told the Lord of his speculations about his old director. Then, rising up from his seat, with his right shoulder respectfully bared, and with his folded palms extended towards the Lord, the reverend Vangīsa addressed him in these stanzas:—

Teacher beyond compare, [343]
who solvest here and now
all doubts, we come to ask
about an Almsman famed
who died in placid calm.

As 'Banyan-Kappa' thou [344]
didst name that brahmin, Lord,
(so leal to thee) who sought
Release with tireless zeal
and unrelaxing grip.

All-seeing Sákyán, [345]
reveal thy servant's lot.
Teacher without a peer,
we long to learn of thee;

resolve our doubts; declare [346]
if he has ceased to be!
O thou, who seest all,
speak out among us here
as speaks among the gods
Sakka the thousand-eyed.

Deluding bondages, [347]
—th' allies of ignorance,
the harbourers of doubt—
vanish before the Lord,
whose gaze transcends man's sight.

6. No ce hi jātu puriso kilese [348]
(vāto yathā abbhaghanaṁ) vihāne,
tamo v' assa nivuto sabbaloko,
na jotimanto pi narā tapeyyuṁ.

7. Dhīrā ca pajjotakarā bhavanti. [349]
Taṁ taṁ ahaṁ, Vīra, tath' eva maññe,
vipassinaṁ jānam upāgamamha,
parisāsu no āvikarohi Kappaṁ!

8. Khippaṁ giraṁ eraya vagguvagguṁ [350]
haṁsā va paggayha saṇiṁ nikūja
bindussarena suvikappitena;
sabbe va te ujugatā suṇāma.

9. Pahīnajātimaraṇaṁ asesaṁ [351]
niggayha dhonaṁ vadessāmi dhammaṁ.
Na kāmakāro hi puthujjanānaṁ;
saṁkheyyakāro ca Tathāgatānaṁ.

10. Sampannaveyyākaraṇaṁ tava-y-idaṁ [352]
samujjupaññassa samuggahītaṁ.
Ayam añjalī pacchimo suppaṇāmito;
mā mohayi jānam, anomapañña.

11. Parovaraṁ ariyadhammaṁ viditvā, [353]
mā mohayi jānam, anomaviriya;
vāriṁ yathā ghammani ghammatatto
vācâbhikankhāmi. Sutaṁ pavassa!

12. Yadatthiyaṁ brahmacariyaṁ acāri [354]
Kappāyano, kacci 'ssa taṁ amoghaṁ?
Nibbāyi so? ādu sa-upādi-seso?
Yathā vimutto ahu, taṁ suṇāma!

If One dispelled not vice, [348]
as wind the clouds, a pall
of darkness would enshroud
the world entire; not e'en
the Sons of Light could shine.

The wise illumine. Sure [349]
that thou art wise and can'st
illumine, we, who know
thy scope, beg thee to tell
this conclave Kappa's lot.

Haste then to lift thy voice [350]
so sweet, and, like a swan
with outstretched neck, ring out
in strains melodious;
—apt audience are we.

Yes; He who's cleansed and done [351]
with birth and death, will tell!
'Tis not to please the crowd
I ask this; but to learn
the verdict of Truth's Lords.

Thy comprehension holds [352]
the power to make all clear.
Once more, with claspèd hands,
we pray thee, matchless sage,
to leave us not astray.

O thou, whose vision spans [353]
all truth! Untiring sage,
O leave us not astray!
As folk in summer heat
for water pine, pine I
to hear thy words flow forth.

Did Kappa's higher life [354]
prove fruitless in the end?
Has all he was quite gone?
Or does some part survive?
Say, what Release was his?

13. 'Acchecchi taṇhaṁ idha nāmarūpe. (*ti Bhagavā*) [355]
Kaṇhassa sotaṁ dīgharattânusayitaṁ
atāri jātimaraṇaṁ asesaṁ.'
—Icc' abravī Bhagavā pañcaseṭṭho.

14. Esa sutvā pasīdāmi vaco te, isisattama; [356]
'Amoghaṁ kira' me puṭṭhaṁ; na maṁ vañcesi Brāhmaṇo.

15. Yathāvādī tathākārī ahū Buddhassa sāvako; [357]
acchidā Maccuno jālaṁ tataṁ māyāvino daḷhaṁ.

16. Addasa, Bhagavā, ādiṁ upādānassa Kappiyo; [358]
accagā vata Kappāyano maccudheyyaṁ suduttaraṁ.

13. Sammāparibbājaniyasutta

1. Pucchāmi Muniṁ pahūtapaññaṁ [359]
tiṇṇam pāragataṁ parinibbutaṁ ṭhitattaṁ:—
Nikkhamma gharā, panujja kāme,
kathaṁ bhikkhu sammā so loke paribbajeyya?

---

2. Yassa mangalā samūhatā (*ti Bhagavā*) [360]
uppādā supinā ca lakkhaṇā ca,
sa mangaladosavippahīno
sammā so loke paribbajeyya.

3. Rāgaṁ vinayetha mānusesu [361]
dibbesu kāmesu câpi bhikkhu,
atikkamma bhavaṁ samecca Dhammaṁ
sammā so loke paribbajeyya.

4. Vipiṭṭhikatvā pesuṇāni, [362]
kodhaṁ kadariyaṁ jaheyya bhikkhu,
anurodhavirodhavippahīno
sammā so—pe—

5. Hitvāna piyañ c' eva appiyañ ca [363]
anupādāya anissito kuhiñci,
saṁyojaniyehi vippamutto
sammā so . . . .

The Lord: On earth he shed the craze [355]
for 'personality';
across dark Māra's stream,
he's safe from birth and death.
(Said He who taught the Five.)

Vangisa: Seventh in line of Seers, I hail thy words! [356]
For, when I asked if Kappa's life had proved
no failure, Brahmin, thou hast spoken out!

So then, thy henchman's words and deeds conformed; [357]
he burst false Māra's wide-spread net so strong.

Lord! Kappa found whence transmigration springs, [358]
and passed beyond fell Māra's grisly realms!

Sutta 13. The Anchorite's Ideal

A Questioner: Deep sage, who, safe 'Across', [359]
art spent, consummate, sure,
—declare how th' Almsman here,
who quits his house and home
and pleasure's path forsakes,
best proves true anchorite?

The Lord: Best anchorite is he [360]
who heeds not omens, dreams,
portents, or prodigies;
who sets no store by luck;

whom passion cannot tempt [361]
with joys of men or gods,
because rebirth is quenched,
because the Truth is won;

who resolutely turns [362]
his back on calumny
and wrath and selfishness,
till love and hate are dead;

who bans dislikes and likes, [363]
whom nought sustains, whom nought
supports, whom nought enchains;

6. Na so upadhīsu sāram eti [364]
ādānesu vineyya chandarāgaṁ,
so anissito anaññaneyyo
sammā so loke paribbajeyya

7. Vacasā manasā ca kammanā ca [365]
aviruddho sammā viditvā Dhammam,
nibbānapadâbhipatthayāno
sammā so . . . .

8. Yo 'vandati man' ti na uṇṇameyya, [366]
akkuṭṭho pi na sandhiyetha bhikkhu,
laddhā parabhojanaṁ na majje,
sammā so . . . .

9. Lobhañ ca bhavañ ca vippahāya [367]
virato chedanabandhanāto bhikkhu,
so tiṇṇakathaṁkatho visallo
sammā so . . . .

10. Sāruppam attano viditvā [368]
na ca bhikkhu hiṁseyya kañci loke,
yathātathiyaṁ viditvāna Dhammaṁ,
sammā so . . . .

11. Yassânusayā na santi keci, [369]
mūlā akusalā samūhatāse,
so nirāsayo anāsayāno
sammā so . . . .

12. Āsavakhīṇo pahīnamāno [370]
sabbaṁ rāgapathaṁ upātivatto
danto parinibbuto ṭhitatto
sammā so . . . .

13. Saddho sutavā niyāmadassī [371]
vaggagatesu na vaggasāri dhīro
lobhaṁ dosaṁ vineyya paṭighaṁ
sammā so . . . .

who never sets his hopes [364]
on mundane things, nor lives
for pelf, whom naught upholds,
who follows no man's lead;

whom words nor thoughts nor deeds [365]
distract from grasping Truth;
who for Nirvāna yearns;

whom homage ne'er inflates [366]
nor scoffs depress, nor feasts
of honour can elate;

who casts out covetise [367]
and lust for life to come;
who harbours no desire
to chain or maim; whose doubts,
with inward barbs, are gone;

whom sense of duty keeps [368]
from harming anyone,
because his eyes have seen
the Doctrine's verities;

whom wrong proclivities [369]
lead not astray because
their harmful roots are gone;
who nothing needs nor seeks;

whose Cankers are destroyed; [370]
who casts forth pride, and quells
all passion,—schooled and sure;
who, being quick, is dead;

whom Faith and Lore have led [371]
to find salvation's road;
whom sects can ne'er pervert;
whom no resentment moves,
nor hate, nor covetise;

14. Saṁsuddhajino, vivattacchaddo, [372]
dhammesu vasī, pāragū, anejo,
saṁkhāranirodhañāṇakusalo,
sammā so loke paribbajeyya.

15. Atītesu anāgatesu câpi [373]
kappâtīto aticca suddhipañño
sabbāyatanehi vippamutto,
sammā so . . . .

16. Aññāya padaṁ samecca Dhammaṁ [374]
vivaṭaṁ disvāna pahānam āsavānaṁ
sabbûpadhīnaṁ parikkhayā,
sammā so loke paribbajeyya.

17. 'Addhā hi, Bhagavā, tath'eva etaṁ; [375]
—yo so evaṁvihārī danto bhikkhu
sabbasaṁyojaniye ca vītivatto
sammā so loke paribbajeyya.'

14. Dhammikasutta

Evam me sutaṁ. Ekaṁ samayaṁ Bhagavā Sāvatthiyaṁ viharati Jetavane Anāthapiṇḍikassa ārāme. Atha kho Dhammiko upāsako pañcahi upāsakasatehi saddhiṁ yena Bhagavā ten' upasaṁkami, upasaṁkamitvā Bhagavantaṁ abhivādetvā ekamantaṁ nisīdi. Ekamantaṁ nisinno kho Dhammiko upāsako Bhagavantaṁ gāthāhi ajjhabhāsi:—

1. Pucchāmi taṁ, Gotama bhūripañña:— [376]
Kathaṁkaro sāvako sādhu hoti:
yo vā agārā anāgāram eti?
agārino vā pan'·upāsakāse?

2. Tuvaṁ hi lokassa sadevakassa [377]
gatiṁ pajānāsi parāyanañ ca;
na t'atthi tulyo, nipuṇatthadassī;
tuvaṁ hi Buddhaṁ pavaraṁ vadanti.

3. Sabbaṁ tuvaṁ ñāṇam avecca, Dhammaṁ [378]
pakāsesi satte anukampamāno,
vivattacchaddo 'si, samantacakkhu,
virocasi vimalo sabbaloke.

whom purity has crowned [372]
with victory; who strips
the veil from things, and knows
all outlooks, mast'ring all,
wantless, and fully skilled
to quench each Plastic Force;

who outgrows time—to come, [373]
or past—by purity
and insight, with Release
from all that springs from sense;

who knows the path and grasps [374]
the Doctrine, seeing clear
how he may Cankers oust
by sapping mundane ties;
—best anchorite is he.

The Questioner: 'Tis surely so, O Lord! [375]
The Almsman schooled to live
like this, who bursts all bonds,
is best of anchorites.

Sutta 14. Dhammika's Enquiry

Thus have I heard. Once while the Lord was staying at Sāvatthī in Jeta's grove in Anāthapiṇḍika's pleasaunce, there came to him, with five hundred other lay-followers, the lay-follower Dhammika, who, after due salutations, took his seat to one side and addressed the Lord in the following stanzas:—

Dhammika: What conduct, Gotama, [376]
perfects, as followers,
both those that homeless are
and those that dwell in homes?

For, thou know'st well the lot [377]
and goal of gods and men,
—thou matchless judge of Weal,
'Buddha most excellent'!

In pity (knowledge won) [378]
thou did'st reveal the Truth
and unveil all, pure seer,
to flood the world with light.

4. Āgañchi te santike nāgarājā, [379]
Erāvaṇo nāma, 'Jino' ti sutvā;
so pi tayā mantayitvâjjhagamā
'sādhûti' sutvāna patītarūpo.

5. Rājā pi taṁ Vessavaṇo Kuvero [380]
upeti, Dhammaṁ paripucchamāno;
tassâpi tvaṁ pucchito brūsi, dhīra;
so câpi sutvāna patītarūpo.

6. Ye kec' ime titthiyā vādasīlā [381]
(Ājīvikā vā yadi vā Nigaṇṭhā),
paññāya taṁ nâtitaranti sabbe
—ṭhito vajantaṁ viya sīghagāmiṁ.

7. Ye kec' ime brāhmaṇā vādasīlā [382]
vuddhā câpi brāhmaṇā santi keci,
sabbe tayi atthabaddhā bhavanti,
—ye vâpi c' aññe vādino maññamānā.

8. Ayaṁ hi Dhammo nipuṇo sukho ca, [383]
yo 'yaṁ tayā, Bhagavā, suppavutto,
tam eva sabbe sussūsamānā;
tvan no vada pucchito, Buddhaseṭṭha.

9. Sabbe c' ime bhikkhavo sannisinnā, [384]
upāsakā câpi, tath' eva sotuṁ
suṇantu Dhammaṁ vimalenânubuddhaṁ
subhāsitaṁ, Vāsavassêva devā.

---

10. Suṇātha me, bhikkhavo, sāvayāmi vo [385]
Dhammaṁ dhutaṁ, tañ ca dharātha sabbe,
iriyāpathaṁ pabbajitânulomikam;
sevetha naṁ atthadassī mutīmā.

11. Na ve vikāle vicareyya bhikkhu, [386]
gāmañ ca piṇḍāya careyya kāle;
akālacāriṁ hi sajanti sangā;
—tasmā vikāle na caranti buddhā.

12. Rūpā ca saddā ca rasā ca gandhā [387]
phassā ca ye sammadayanti satte,
etesu dhammesu vineyya chandaṁ
kālena so pavise pātarāsaṁ.

News of 'a Conqueror' [379]
drew Indra's elephant
(of elephants the king),
who joyed to hear thy talk.

Came too the fairies' king, [380]
thy Doctrine to explore.
Such answers thou didst give
as he rejoiced to hear.

Trained Jains and Mendicants [381]
all failed to vanquish thee,
—as they who stand stock-still
catch not the fleet of foot.

Trained brahmins, ripe in years, [382]
—with others keen to air
their point of view—are led
t' embrace thy saving Truth.

For, 'tis thy saving Truth,— [383]
subtile, but preached so well—
for which all yearn. Vouchsafe,
an answer, Lord, to us!

Let th' Almsmen seated round [384]
with these lay followers
learn from thy lips (as gods
hearken to Indra's words)
thy Lore immaculate!

The Lord: Give ear, ye Almsmen! Hear, [385]
and keep, the rules prescribed:—
Let seekers after Weal,
behave as anchorites.

Go not thy round when noon [386]
is past; betimes seek alms.
Snares greet th' untimely guest;
th' enlighten'd time their rounds.

Before thou seek'st thy meal, [387]
clear thou thy mind of zest
for forms, sounds, odours, taste,
and touch,—which turn men's heads.

13. Piṇḍañ ca bhikkhu samayena laddhā [388]
eko paṭikkamma raho nisīde
ajjhattacintī; na mano bahiddhā
nicchāraye sangahītattabhāvo.

14. Sace pi so sallape sāvakena [389]
aññena vā kenaci bhikkhunā vā,
Dhammaṁ paṇītaṁ tam udāhareyya,
na pesuṇaṁ, no pi parūpavādaṁ.

15. Vādaṁ hi eke paṭiseniyanti. [390]
Na te pasaṁsāma parittapaññe;
tato tato ne pasajanti sangā,
cittaṁ hi te tattha gamenti dūre.

16. Piṇḍaṁ vihāraṁ sayanāsanañ ca [391]
āpañ ca saṁghāṭirajûpavāhanaṁ
sutvāna Dhammaṁ Sugatena desitaṁ
saṁkhāya seve varapaññasāvako.

17. Tasmā hi piṇḍe sayanâsane ca [392]
āpe ca saṁghāṭirajûpavāhane,
etesu dhammesu anūpalitto
bhikkhu, yathā pokkhare vāribindu.

---

18. Gahaṭṭhavattaṁ pana vo vadāmi, [393]
yathākaro sāvako sādhu hoti.
—Na h' eso labbhā sapariggahena
phassetuṁ yo kevalo bhikkhudhammo.

19. Pāṇaṁ na hane, na ca ghātayeyya, [394]
na cânujaññā hanataṁ paresaṁ,
sabbesu bhūtesu nidhāya daṇḍaṁ
ye thāvarā ye ca tasanti loke.

20. Tato adinnaṁ parivajjayeyya [395]
kiñci kvacī sāvako bujjhamāno;
na hāraye, harataṁ nânujaññā;
sabbaṁ adinnaṁ parivajjayeyya.

21. Abrahmacariyaṁ parivajjayeyya, [396]
angārakāsuṁ jalitaṁ va, viññū;
asambhuṇanto pana brahmacariyaṁ
parassa dāraṁ na atikkameyya.

Thine alms received, return [388]
alone, to sit apart
and think,—with fixèd mind
that never strays abroad.

In talk with pious folk [389]
or Almsmen, let thy theme
the Doctrine's virtues be,
—not spite, not finding fault.

If men assail, let us [390]
not heed these shallow pates,
who cling to this or that
as vagrant minds dictate.

Let wisdom's son, who heard [391]
his Lord, treat alms, cell, bed,
water and rinsings, just
as means, and nothing more.

Such reason'd use will leave [392]
an Almsman as unstained
as lotus-leaf,—whereon
no drop of water rests.

To conduct which perfects [393]
lay-followers I pass.
(For, marriage these forbids
to grow to Almsmen's scope.)

Slay not, nor doom to death, [394]
nor sanction slaughter. Do
no violence to aught
that lives,—or strong or weak.

No layman, wittingly, [395]
should thieve, or order theft,
or sanction any theft;
—take but what others give.

And shun incontinence [396]
as 'twere a pit of fire,
or, failing continence,
debauch no wedded wife.

22. Sabhaggato vā parisaggato vā [397]
ekassa v' eko na musā bhaṇeyya,
na bhāṇaye, bhaṇataṁ nânujaññā;
sabbaṁ abhūtaṁ parivajjayeyya.

23. Majjañ ca pānaṁ na samācareyya [398]
—Dhammaṁ imaṁ rocaye yo gahaṭṭho—
na pāyaye, pipataṁ nânujaññā,
ummādanantaṁ iti naṁ viditvā.

24. Madā hi pāpāni karonti bālā, [399]
kāronti c' aññe pi jane pamatte;
etaṁ apuññāyatanaṁ vivajjaye
ummādanaṁ mohanaṁ bālakantaṁ.

25. "Pāṇam na hane, na câdinnaṁ ādiye, [400]
musā na bhāse, na ca majjapo siyā,
abrahmacariyā virameyya methunā,
rattiṁ na bhuñjeyya vikālabhojanaṁ,

26. mālaṁ na dhāre, na ca gandham ācare, [401]
mañce chamāyaṁ va sayetha santhate".
—Etaṁ hi aṭṭhangikam āh' uposathaṁ
Buddhena dukkhantagunā pakāsitaṁ.

27. Tato ca pakkhass' upavass' uposathaṁ [402]
—'cātuddasiṁ pañcadasiṁ aṭṭhamiṁ'—
pāṭihāriyapakkhañ ca pasannamānaso
aṭṭhangupetaṁ susamattarūpaṁ.

28. Tato ca pāto upavutthuposatho [403]
annena pānena ca bhikkhusaṁghaṁ
pasannacitto anumodamāno
yathârahaṁ saṁvibhajetha viññū.

29. Dhammena mātāpitaro bhareyya, [404]
payojaye dhammikaṁ so vaṇijjam;
—etaṁ gihī vattayaṁ appamatto
Sayampabhe nāma upeti deve ti.

Cūlavaggo dutiyo

In conclaves, courts, or talk, [397]
let him not lie; let him
not prompt or sanction lies;
—let him renounce untruth.

Layman, observe this law:— [398]
Shun drink; make no man drink;
sanction no drinking. Mark
how drink to madness leads.

Through drink fools sin, and egg [399]
lax brethren on to sin.
So flee this maddening vice,
this folly, bliss of fools.

"Slay not, nor steal, nor lie; [400]
from strong drink keep away;
refrain from lechery;
touch not wrong meals o' nights;

eschew both scents and wreaths; [401]
spread on the ground thy bed."
(These eightfold sabbath-rules
the saving Buddha framed.)

So make thy sabbath vows [402]
as week succeeds to week,
and keep with pious hearts
this eightfold festival.

At morn, these vows performed, [403]
with pious, thankful heart
be wise and of thy means
give Almsmen food and drink.

Cherish thy parents well; [404]
follow a righteous trade.
—Thus shall the layman staunch
reach realms of light above.

End of the Short Book

III. MAHĀVAGGA

1. Pabbajjāsutta

1. Pabbajjaṁ kittayissāmi, yathā pabbaji Cakkhumā, [405]
yathā vimaṁsamāno so pabbajjaṁ samarocayi.

2. 'Sambādho 'yaṁ gharāvāso, rajass' āyatanaṁ' iti, [406]
'Abbhokāso ca pabbajjā',—iti disvāna pabbaji.

3. Pabbajitvāna kāyena pāpakammaṁ vivajjayi, [407]
vacīduccaritaṁ hitvā ājīvaṁ parisodhayi.

4. Agamā Rājagahaṁ Buddho Magadhānaṁ Giribbajaṁ [408]
piṇḍāya abhihāresi ākiṇṇavaralakkhaṇo.

5. Tam addasā Bimbisāro pāsādasmiṁ patiṭṭhito; [409]
disvā lakkhaṇasampannaṁ, imam atthaṁ abhāsatha:—

6. 'Imaṁ, bhonto, nisāmetha. Abhirūpo, brahā, suci, [410]
caraṇena c'eva sampanno, yugamattañ ca pekkhati

7. okkhittacakkhu satimā; nâyaṁ nīcakulā-m-iva. [411]
Rājadūtā vidhāvantu, kuhiṁ bhikkhu gamissati.'

8. Te pesitā rājadūtā piṭṭhito anubandhisuṁ:— [412]
'Kuhiṁ gamissati bhikkhu? Katthavāso bhavissati?'

9. Sapadānañ caramāno, guttadvāro, susaṁvuto, [413]
khippaṁ pattaṁ apūresi sampajāno patissato.

10. Sa piṇḍacāraṁ caritvā, nikkhamma nagarā, muni [414]
Paṇḍavaṁ abhihāresi: 'Etthavāso bhavissati'.

11. Disvāna vāsûpagataṁ tato dūtā upāvisuṁ, [415]
eko ca dūto āgantvā rājino paṭivedayi:

12. 'Esa bhikkhu, mahārāja, Paṇḍavassa puratthato [416]
nisinno vyagghusabho va sīho va girigabbhare.'

III. THE LONG BOOK

Sutta 1. Gotama's Pilgrimage

My tongue shall tell his going forth from home, [405]
shall tell how he, our Seer, left house and home
for Pilgrimage, and why he chose that life.

Because he saw 'a hole and corner life' [406]
was all a house and home could give, the Lord
went forth from home, embracing homelessness.

A Pilgrim now, he shunned all evil deeds [407]
and lived his life aright, with blameless lips.

To Rājagáha come, th' Enlighten'd One, [408]
by high distinction stamped, in quest of alms
entered the hill-girt gorge of Mágadhá.

As from his royal palace he looked down, [409]
King Bimbisāra thus addressed his court:—

'Mark, sirs, that man, so handsome, tall, and calm, [410]
of goodly gait, with gaze a plough's length on,

with eyes on earth downcast, of set intent! [411]
He comes, methinks, of no mean humble stock.
Let servants speed to track that Almsman down.'

So royal servants tracked the Almsman's steps [412]
to find where he would go and where would stay.

With senses' portals guarded, self-controll'd, [413]
from house to house he duly went for alms
and quickly filled his bowl,—mindful, alert.

His round for alms now o'er, from out the town [414]
our sage departed, climbing Páṇḍavá
to find a lodging on its craggy heights.

Marking his lodging down, the messengers [415]
drew near, while one went back who told the king:—

'Like puissant tiger, or a lion, sire, [416]
within a cavern on the eastward crags
of rugged Paṇḍava, your Almsman sits.'

13. Sutvāna dūtavacanaṁ bhaddayānena khattiyo [417]
taramānarūpo niyyāsi yena Paṇḍavapabbato.

14. Sa yānabhūmiṁ yāyitvā yānā oruyha khattiyo [418]
pattiko upasaṁkamma āsajja naṁ upāvisi.

15. Nisajja rājā sammodi kathaṁ sārāṇiyaṁ tato [419]
kathaṁ so vītisāretvā imam atthaṁ abhāsatha:—

16. 'Yuvā ca daharo câsi paṭhamuppattiko susu [420]
vaṇṇārohena sampanno, jātimā viya khattiyo

17. sobhayanto anīkaggaṁ nāgasaṁghapurakkhato. [421]
Dadāmi bhoge, bhuñjassu, jātiñ c' akkhāhi pucchito.'

18. 'Ujū janapado, rāja, Himavantassa passato [422]
dhanaviriyena sampanno, Kosalesu niketino,

19. Ādiccā nāma gottena, Sākiyā nāma jātiyā; [423]
tamhā kulā pabbajito [rāja] na kāme abhipatthayaṁ,

20. kāmesv ādīnavaṁ disvā, nekkhammaṁ daṭṭhu khemato, [424]
padhānāya gamissāmi; ettha me rañjati mano' ti.

2. Padhānasutta

1. Tam maṁ padhānapahitattaṁ, nadiṁ Nerañjaram pati, [425]
viparakkamma jhāyantaṁ yogakkhemassa pattiyā,

2. Namucī karuṇaṁ vācaṁ bhāsamāno upāgami:— [426]
'Kiso tvam asi dubbaṇṇo; santike maraṇan tava.

3. Sahassabhāgo maraṇassa, ekaṁso tava jīvitaṁ. [427]
Jīva, bho! Jīvitaṁ seyyo;—jīvaṁ puññāni kāhasi.

4. Carato ca te brahmacariyaṁ, aggihuttañ ca jūhato, [428]
pahūtaṁ cīyate puññaṁ.—Kiṁ padhānena kāhasi?

5. Duggo maggo padhānāya, dukkaro durabhisambhavo.' [429]
—Imā gāthā bhaṇaṁ Māro aṭṭhā Buddhassa santike.

Hearing the news, with speed the noble prince [417]
drove forth from town towards Mount Paṇḍava;

and when no further he could ride, on foot [418]
the monarch made his way till him he reached.

Then, seated, after courteous exchange [419]
of seemly greetings, thus the monarch spoke:

'Thou 'rt young,—a stripling still in early bloom! [420]
Thy goodly mien bespeaks a gallant prince

his host arraying, elephants in van. [421]
Lo! Here I offer wealth to spend thereon,
and ask thee to disclose thy lineage.'

The Lord: Flanking Himálaya, in Kósalá, [422]
yonder extends a land both rich and brave.

By lineage 'the Kinsmen of the Sun' [423]
are we, and Sākiyans by family.
—Such was the stock I left behind me, sire,
having no appetite for pleasure's toys.

Alive to all the perils pleasure brings, [424]
and finding in Renunciation peace,
I'll struggle onward.—Thus my mind finds bliss.

Sutta 2. Gotama's Struggle

As, purged of self by struggles stern, I sat [425]
in Reverie beside Neráñjará,
resolved to win by insight perfect peace,

came Māra, breathing words of ruth, to say [426]
how lean and ill I looked, how nigh to death.

'Death owns' (said he) 'a thousand parts of thee, [427]
and life can claim but one. Hold fast to life!
Life 's best; for, living, thou 'lt store merit up.

If thou wilt lead a pious life and tend [428]
the fires of sacrifice, much merit will
accrue. By struggles what wilt thou achieve?

Rough is the road, the struggle desperate.' [429]
(Thus Māra, standing by the Buddha's side.)

6. Taṁ tathā-vādinaṁ Māraṁ Bhagavā etad abravi:— [430]
Pamattabandhu pāpima, yen' atthena idhâgato,

7. aṇumattena pi puññena attho mayhaṁ na vijjati. [431]
Yesañ ca attho puññānaṁ, te Māro vattum arahati.

8. Atthi saddhā, tato viriyaṁ, paññā ca mama vijjati! [432]
Evaṁ maṁ pahitattaṁ [pi] kiṁ jīvaṁ anupucchasi?

9. Nadīnam api sotāni ayaṁ vāto visosaye, [433]
kiñ ca me pahitattassa lohitaṁ n' upasussaye?

10. Lohite sussamānamhi pittaṁ semhañ ca sussati; [434]
maṁsesu khīyamānesu bhiyyo cittaṁ pasīdati,
bhiyyo sati ca paññā ca samādhi mama tiṭṭhati.

11. Tassa mêvaṁ viharato, pattassa uttamavedanaṁ, [435]
kāmesu nâpekkhate cittaṁ.—Passa sattassa suddhataṁ!

12. Kāmā te paṭhamā senā, dutiyā arati vuccati, [436]
tatiyā khuppipāsā te, catutthī taṇhā pavuccati,

13. pañcamī thīnamiddhan te, chaṭṭhā bhīrū pavuccati, [437]
sattamī vicikicchā te, makkho thambho te aṭṭhamo,

14. lābho siloko sakkāro micchāladdho ca yo yaso, [438]
yo c' attānaṁ samukkaṁse pare ca avajānati;

15. —esā, Namuci, te senā Kaṇhassâbhippahāraṇī; [439]
na naṁ asūro jināti, jetvā ca labhate sukhaṁ.

16. Esa muñjaṁ parihare? Dhi-r-atthu idha jīvitaṁ! [440]
Sangāme me mataṁ seyyo, yañce jīve parājito!

17. Pagāḷhā ettha na dissanti eke samaṇabrāhmaṇā [441]
tañ ca maggaṁ na jānanti yena gacchanti subbatā.

18. Samantā dhajiniṁ disvā yuttaṁ Māraṁ savāhanaṁ [442]
yuddhāya paccuggacchāmi. Mā maṁ ṭhānā acāvayi.

19. Yaṁ te taṁ na-ppasahati senaṁ loko sadevako, [443]
taṁ te paññāya vecchāmi, āmaṁ pattaṁ va asmanā.

To Māra's words the Lord made answer thus:— [430]
The Lord: Thou Evil One! Thou congener of sloth!

I lack no peddling rudiments like these; [431]
no jot of suchlike 'merit' profits me!
Māra should speak to those who 'merit' lack.

Seeing that faith and energy and lore [432]
have purged all Self away, why talk of 'life'?

The wind dries rivers up;—shall this my blood [433]
still course when Self is dead, when Self has gone?

While blood is drying up, the humours too [434]
dry up; and with decay of flesh my mind
grows calmer; stronger grows its watchfulness,
its garner'd Lore, its concentration rapt.

As thus I dwell, who 've braved and borne pain's worst, [435]
my heart for pleasure feels no zest at all.
Behold then, Māra, how a man is cleansed.

Pleasures of sense compose thy foremost ranks; [436]
dislikes thy second; thirst and hunger form
thy third array; cravings come fourth; the fifth

is sloth and torpor; sixth faintheartedness; [437]
doubts make the seventh; th' eighth,—pretence, hard heart,

and pelf, repute, the pride of place, with fame [438]
ill-gotten, scorn of others, praise of self.

Black Māra, such is thine attacking force, [439]
which only heroes overcome in fight,
and in their conquest find abiding Weal.

Shall I cry craven? Nay; a pest on life! [440]
I'd sooner die than brook defeat—and live.

(Engulfed in this world's bogs, some anchorites [441]
and brahmins wholly sink from sight and view,
and never come to know the path saints tread.)

Seeing this host arrayed, with Māra there [442]
riding his elephant of war, I go
to fight him. May he never beat me back!

Thy hosts—which neither men nor gods can rout— [443]
with Lore I'll crush, as pebbles smash a bowl.

20. Vasiṁkaritvā saṁkappaṁ satiñ ca sûpatiṭṭhitaṁ [444]
raṭṭhā raṭṭhaṁ vicarissaṁ sāvake vinayaṁ puthu.

21. Ty-appamattā pahitattā mama sāsanakārakā [445]
akāmassa, te gamissanti yattha gantvā na socare.

---

22. "Satta vassāni Bhagavantaṁ anubandhiṁ padā padaṁ, [446]
otāraṁ nâdhigacchissaṁ Sambuddhassa satīmato.

23. Medavaṇṇaṁ va pāsāṇaṁ vāyaso anupariyagā: [447]
'Ap' ettha mudu vindema, api assādanā siyā?'

24. Aladdhā tattha assādaṁ vāyas' etto apakkami. [448]
—Kāko va selaṁ āsajja nibbijjâpema Gotamaṁ."

25. Tassa sokaparetassa vīṇā kacchā abhassatha; [449]
tato so dummano yakkho tatth' ev' antaradhāyatha.

3. Subhāsitasutta

Evam me sutaṁ. Ekaṁ samayaṁ Bhagavā Sāvatthiyaṁ viharati Jetavane —pe—Bhagavā etad avoca:—Catūhi, bhikkhave, angehi samannāgatā vācā subhāsitā hoti na dubbhāsitā, anavajjā ca ananuvajjā ca viññūnaṁ. Katamehi catūhi? Idha, bhikkhave, bhikkhu subhāsitañ ñeva bhāsati no dubbhāsitaṁ, Dhammañ ñeva bhāsati no adhammaṁ, piyañ ñeva bhāsati no appiyaṁ, saccañ ñeva bhāsati no alikaṁ. Imehi kho, bhikkhave, catūhi angehi samannāgatā vācā subhāsitā hoti no dubbhāsitā, anavajjā ca ananuvajjā ca viññūnan ti.

Idam avoca Bhagavā; idaṁ vatvā Sugato athâparaṁ etad avoca Satthā:—

1. Subhāsitaṁ uttamam āhu santo; [450]
dhammaṁ bhaṇe nâdhammaṁ,—tam dutiyaṁ;
piyaṁ bhaṇe nâppiyaṁ,—taṁ tatiyaṁ;
saccaṁ bhaṇe nâlikaṁ,—taṁ catutthan ti.

Atha kho āyasmā Vangīso uṭṭhāyâsanā ekaṁsaṁ cīvaraṁ katvā yena Bhagavā ten' añjaliṁ paṇāmetvā Bhagavantaṁ etad avoca: 'Paṭibhāti maṁ, Sugatâti.' 'Paṭibhātu taṁ, Vangīsâti' Bhagavā avoca. Atha kho āyasmā Vangīso Bhagavantaṁ sammukhā sāruppāhi gāthāhi abhitthavi:—

2. Tam eva vācaṁ bhāseyya yāy' attānaṁ na tāpaye, [451]
pare ca na vihiṁseyya;—sā ve vācā subhāsitā.

3. Piyavācam eva bhāseyya, yā vācā patinanditā, [452]
yaṁ anādāya pāpāni paresaṁ bhāsate piyaṁ.

As Captain of my thoughts, with set resolve, [444]
from realm to realm I'll find me followers

zealous and purged of Self, whom loyalty [445]
to my commandments and their lust-free Lord,
shall bring where sorrows find no place at all.

Māra: 'For seven years I might keep dogging him, [446]
yet with the watchful Buddha get no chance!

To see if it was soft and good to eat, [447]
a crow hopped round a stone that looked like fat;

but, disappointed, flew away again. [448]
—In like disgust I give up Gotama!'

The Lord: In grief, the sprite then let his lute slip down, [449]
as, sick at heart, he vanished out of sight.

Sutta 3. Apt words

Thus have I heard. Once while staying at Sāvatthī in Jeta's grove (*&c.*), the Lord spoke as follows:—There are four respects which characterize words apt and not inapt, words irreproachable and beyond reproach from the discerning. And what are the four? Take the case, Almsmen, of an Almsman who always speaks aptly and never inaptly, whose discourse is of the Doctrine only and not of vain matters, whose words are always kindly and never unkind, always truthful and never false. These four respects characterize apt speech. Thus spoke the Lord; and when the Blessed One had thus spoken, he, as Master, went on to say:—

Apt speech the good rank first, [450]
and, second, Doctrine's themes,
the third is kindly speech,
and fourth is truthfulness.

Here the reverend Vangīsa rose from his seat and, with his right shoulder bared and with folded palms outstretched, said to the Lord that a thought had struck him. Being bidden to express it, Vangīsa extolled the Lord to his face in suitable verses, saying:—

Speak thou what neither breeds thyself remorse [451]
nor hurts another.—Suchlike speech is apt.

Speak only kindly words, welcome to hear; [452]
avoid all railing; kindly be thy words.

4. 'Saccaṁ ve amatā vācā', esa dhammo sanantano; [453]
'sacce atthe ca Dhamme ca', āhu, 'santo patiṭṭhitā'.

5. Yaṁ Buddho bhāsati vācaṁ khemaṁ nibbānapattiyā, [454]
dukkhass' antakiriyāya,—sā ve vācānam uttamā.

4. Sundarikabhāradvājasutta

Evam me sutaṁ. Ekaṁ samayaṁ Bhagavā Kosalesu viharati Sundarikāya nadiyā tīre. Tena kho pana samayena Sundarikabhāradvājo brāhmaṇo Sundarikāya nadiyā tīre aggiṁ juhati aggihuttaṁ paricarati. Atha kho Sundarikabhāradvājo brāhmaṇo aggiṁ juhitvā aggihuttaṁ paricaritvā uṭṭhāyâsanā samantā catuddisā anuvilokesi: Ko nu kho imaṁ havyasesaṁ bhuñjeyyâti? Addasā kho Sundarikabhāradvājo brāhmaṇo Bhagavantaṁ avidūre aññatarasmiṁ rukkhamūle sasīsaṁ pārutaṁ nisinnaṁ, disvāna vāmena hatthena havyasesaṁ gahetvā dakkhiṇena hatthena kamaṇḍaluṁ gahetvā yena Bhagavā ten' upasaṁkami. Atha kho Bhagavā Sundarikabhāradvājassa brāhmaṇassa padasaddena sīsaṁ vivari. Atha kho Sundarikabhāradvājo brāhmaṇo 'Muṇḍo ayaṁ bhavaṁ! Muṇḍako ayaṁ bhavan ti', tato va puna nivattitukāmo ahosi. Atha kho Sundarikabhāradvājassa brāhmaṇassa etad ahosi: Muṇḍā pi hi idh' ekacce brāhmaṇā bhavanti; yan nūnâhaṁ upasaṁkamitvā jātiṁ puccheyyan ti?

Atha kho Sundarikabhāradvājo brāhmaṇo yena Bhagavā ten' upasaṁkami, upasaṁkamitvā Bhagavantam etad avoca: Kiṁjacco bhavan ti?

Atha kho Bhagavā Sundarikabhāradvājaṁ brāhmaṇaṁ gāthāhi ajjhabhāsi:—

1. Na brāhmaṇo no 'mhi, na rājaputto, [455]
na vessāyano, uda koci no 'mhi.
Gottaṁ pariññāya puthujjanānaṁ
akiñcano manta carāmi loke.

2. Saṁghāṭivāsī agiho carāmi [456]
nivuttakeso abhinibbutatto,
alippamāno idha mānavehi.
Akalla' maṁ pucchasi gotta-pañhaṁ.

3. 'Pucchanti ve, bho, brāhmaṇā brāhmaṇehi saha: Brahmaṇo no [457]
bhavan ti?'
'Brāhmaṇo [hi] ce tvaṁ brūsi, mañ ca brūsi abrāhmaṇaṁ,
taṁ taṁ Sāvittiṁ pucchāmi tipadaṁ catuvīsat-akkharaṁ.'

'Truth is Nirvāna's speech' (the adage runs); [453]
truth, weal, and Doctrine (so 'tis said) make saints.

The Buddha's words of peace, which show the way [454]
to win Nirvāna and to end all Ill,
rank far above all other spoken words.

Sutta 4. Offerings

Thus have I heard. Once while the Lord was staying among the Kosalans on the banks of the river Sundarikā, the brahmin Sundarika-Bhāradvāja was busy there with fire offerings and with ministering to the sacrificial fire; and when all was over and done, he rose up and was looking round in all the four directions to find on whom to bestow what remained over from his sacrifice, when he became aware of the Lord seated close by at the foot of a tree, enveloped—head and all—in his cloak. So, taking in his left hand the remains from the sacrifice and the waterpot in his right hand, the brahmin moved towards the Lord. At the sound of the brahmin's approaching footsteps, the Lord uncovered his head. 'Why, it's only a shaveling, a wretched shaveling!'—said the brahmin to himself and he was minded to turn back. But he bethought him that there were some brahmins too who shaved their heads, and that he might ask the Lord about his descent. So the brahmin came up and asked the Lord what he was by birth.

The Lord: No brahmin I, no prince, [455]
no farmer, or aught else.
All worldly ranks I know,
but, knowing, go my ways
as—simply nobody.

Homeless, in Pilgrim garb, [456]
with shaven crown, I go
my way alone, serene.
—To ask my birth is vain.

The Brahmin: Nay, sir; when brahmins meet they never fail to ask if 'tis a brahmin they address.

The Lord: If you deny to me the brahminhood [457]
you claim, I ask you then of Sāvittī,
with clauses three, two dozen syllables.

4. 'Kiṁ nissitā isayo manujā khattiyā brāhmaṇā devatānaṁ yaññaṁ akappayiṁsu puthū idha loke?' [458]

'Ya-d-antagū vedagū yaññakāle
yassâhutiṁ labhe, tass' ijjhe ti brūmi.'

5. 'Addhā hi tassa hutam ijjhe (*ti brāhmaṇo*) [459]
yaṁ tādisaṁ vedaguṁ addasāma;
tumhâdisānaṁ hi adassanena
añño jano bhuñjati pūraḷāsaṁ.'

6. 'Tasmātiha tvaṁ, brāhmaṇa, atthena atthiko upasaṁkamma puccha.

Santaṁ vidhūmaṁ anighaṁ nirāsaṁ [460]
appev' idha abhivinde sumedhaṁ.'

7. 'Yaññe ratâhaṁ, bho Gotama, yaññaṁ yiṭṭhukāmo nâhaṁ pajānāmi, anusāsatu maṁ bhavaṁ; [461]
yattha hutaṁ ijjhate, brūhi me taṁ.'

'Tena hi tvaṁ, brāhmaṇa, odahassu sotaṁ, Dhammaṁ te desessāmi:—

8. Mā jātiṁ puccha, caraṇañ ca puccha. [462]
Kaṭṭhā have jāyati jātavedo;
nīcākulīno pi munī dhitīmā
ājāniyo hoti hirīnisedho,

9. saccena danto, damasā upeto, [463]
vedantagū, vusitabrahmacariyo;
kālena tamhi havyaṁ pavecche,
yo brāhmaṇo puññapekho yajetha.

10. Ye kāme hitvā agihā caranti, [464]
susaṁyatattā tasaraṁ va ujju
kālena tesu havyaṁ pavecche
yo brāhmaṇo puññapekho yajetha.

The Brahmin: What moved so many sages—brahmins, nobles, and others —to make oblations to deities here on earth? [458]

The Lord: If saints partake (say I),
the donor 's thereby blest.

The Brahmin: A blessing sure is mine [459]
who find a saint in thee.
Had I not found thy like,
my cake had gone elsewhere.

The Lord: Well, brahmin, since you are in quest of Weal, draw near and question me.

You'll find in me a sage [460]
good, taint-less, want-less, calm.

The Brahmin: My delight, Gotama, is in offerings; I am anxious to make offerings; but know not how.
Pray, teach me, sir,— [461]
what offerings will bless.

The Lord: Hearken, then, brahmin; and I will expound the Doctrine to you:—

Judge not by birth, but life. [462]
As any chips feed fire,
mean birth may breed a sage
noble and staunch and true.

Let brahmins 'merit' seek [463]
by offerings where truth
and self-control hold sway,
with lore and holy life;

and where the homeless, dead [464]
to pleasure, temperate,
press—shuttle-wise—straight on;

11. Ye vītarāgā susamāhitindriyā [465]
cando va Rāhugahaṇā pamuttā,
kālena tesu—pe—

12. Asajjamānā vicaranti loke [466]
sadā satā, hitvā mamāyitāni,
kālena tesu . . . .

13. Yo kāme hitvā abhibhuyyacārī, [467]
yo vedi jātimaraṇassa antaṁ
parinibbuto udakarahado va sīto,
Tathāgato arahati pūraḷāsaṁ.

14. Samo samehi, visamehi dūre, [468]
Tathāgato hoti anantapañño;
anūpalitto idha vā huraṁ vā,
Tathāgato arahati pūraḷāsaṁ.

15. Yamhi na māyā vasati na māno, [469]
yo vītalobho amamo nirāso,
panuṇṇakodho abhinibbutatto,
so Brāhmaṇo sokamalaṁ ahāsi;
Tathāgato—pe—

16. Nivesanaṁ yo manaso ahāsi, [470]
pariggahā yassa na santi keci,
anupādiyāno idha vā huraṁ vā,
Tathāgato . . . .

17. Samāhito yo udatāri oghaṁ [471]
Dhammañ ca ñāsi paramāya diṭṭhiyā,
khīṇāsavo, antimadehadhārī,
Tathāgato . . . .

18. Bhavāsavā yassa vacī kharā ca [472]
vidhūpitā, atthagatā, na santi,
sa vedagū sabbadhi vippamutto,
Tathāgato . . . .

19. Sangātigo, yassa na santi sangā, [473]
yo mānasattesu amānasatto,
dukkhaṁ pariññāya sakhettavatthuṁ,
Tathāgato . . . .

20. Āsaṁ anissāya, vivekadassī, [474]
paravediyaṁ diṭṭhim upātivatto,
ārammaṇā yassa na santi keci,
Tathāgato . . . .

and where the passion-free [465]
in peace have found Release,
—like moons from Rāhu's jaws;

and where th' emancipate [466]
in ceaseless vigilance
move, calling nothing theirs.

Victor by quelling lusts, [467]
Ender of birth and death,
calm, cool as is a lake,
Truth's Finder claims your gifts;

to former Buddhas peer, [468]
remote from lesser men,
stainless, of boundless Lore;

who, void of guile and pride, [469]
cares not to get or have,
true Brahmin, wrathless, spent;

whose mind, from errors freed, [470]
retains no hankerings,
who clings to naught at all;

who stoutly crossed the Flood, [471]
whose vision saw the Truth,
whose Cankers now are gone,
whom clay shall clothe no more;

the sage of full Release, [472]
from whom the lust to live
(and biting tongue) have gone
and left no smould'ring trace;

who, bursting ties, is free, [473]
who, pride-less 'mong the proud,
has plumbed Ill's cause and range;

who, craving nothing, soars [474]
to heights no others knew,
with naught to cause rebirth;

21. Parovarā yassa samecca dhammā [475]
vidhūpitā, atthagatā, na santi;
santo, upādānakhaye vimutto,
Tathāgato . . . .

22. Saṁyojanaṁjātikhayantadassī [476]
yo 'pānudi rāgapathaṁ asesaṁ,
suddho niddoso vimalo akāco,
Tathāgato . . . .

23. Yo attanā 'Attānaṁ' nânupassati, [477]
samāhito ujjugato ṭhitatto,
sa ve anejo akhilo akankho,
Tathāgato . . . .

24. Mohantarā yassa na santi keci, [478]
sabbesu dhammesu ca ñāṇadassī,
sarīrañ ca antimaṁ dhāreti,
patto Sambodhiṁ anuttaraṁ sivaṁ
(ettāvatā yakkhassa suddhi),
—Tathāgato arahati pūraḷāsaṁ.'

25. 'Hutañ ca mayhaṁ hutam atthu saccaṁ, [479]
yaṁ tādisaṁ vedagunaṁ alatthaṁ.

Brahmā hi sakkhi! Patigaṇhātu me Bhagavā, bhuñjatu me Bhagavā, pūraḷāsam!'

26. 'Gāthābhigītaṁ me abhojaneyyam. [480]
Sampassataṁ, brāhmaṇa, n' esa dhammo;
gāthābhigītaṁ panudanti buddhā;
Dhamme sati, brāhmaṇa, vuttir esā.

27. Aññena ca kevalinaṁ mahesim, [481]
khīṇāsavaṁ kukkucavūpasantaṁ
annena pānena upaṭṭhahassu;
khettaṁ hi taṁ puññapekhassa hoti.'

28. 'Sādhâhaṁ, Bhagavā, tathā vijaññaṁ [482]
yo dakkhiṇaṁ bhuñjeyya mādisassa,
yaṁ yaññakāle pariyesamāno,
pappuyya tava sāsanaṁ.'

29. 'Sārambhā yassa vigatā, cittaṁ yassa anāvilaṁ, [483]
vippamutto ca kāmehi, thīnaṁ yassa panūditaṁ,

beneath whose gaze all 'creeds', [475]
consumed to ashes, die;
who, being spent, is freed;

who saw how bonds and birth [476]
could be destroyed and cease;
who—passion swept away—
is cleansed, unmarred, and pure;

who finds no inward 'Self'; [477]
who—fixed, unswerving, sure—
is schooled, craves not, nor doubts;

he who with mind unwarped [478]
fathoms each mental state,
whose body is his last,
who in Enlightenment
won bliss which crowns the pure;
—Truth's Finder claims your gifts.

The Brahmin: May mine prove off'ring true, [479]
who find a sage like thee.

Brahmā be witness! Lord, vouchsafe to take my cake.

The Lord: I touch no chanter's fee! [480]
Seers countenance it not;
th' enlighten'd scout such fees;
and while the Doctrine lasts,
this practice must obtain.

Provide with other fare [481]
a sage of holy peace,
consummate, Canker-less.
—Merit to reap, sow *there*!

The Brahmin: Who, Lord, should have my cake? [482]
Whom would'st thou bid me seek,
at time of sacrifice,
to eat a cake of mine?

The Lord: Seek him who 's done with strife, unmarred of heart, [483]
lust-free, and roused from crass stolidity;

30. sīmantānaṁ vinetāraṁ, jātimaraṇakovidaṁ, [484]
muniṁ moneyyasampannaṁ, tādisaṁ yaññam āgataṁ

31. bhakuṭiṁ vinayitvāna pañjalikā namassatha, [485]
pūjetha annapānena;—evaṁ ijjhanti dakkhiṇā.'

32. 'Buddho bhavaṁ arahati pūraḷāsaṁ, puññakkhettam anuttaraṁ, [486]
āyāgo sabbalokassa; bhoto dinnaṁ mahapphalan ti.'

Atha kho Sundarikabhāradvājo brāhmaṇo Bhagavantaṁ etad avoca: Abhikkantaṁ . . . (&c. as at page 24) . . . arahataṁ ahosi.

5. Māghasutta

Evam me sutaṁ. Ekaṁ samayaṁ Bhagavā Rājagahe viharati Gijjhakūṭe pabbate. Atha kho Mągho māṇavo yena Bhagavā ten' upasaṁkami, upasaṁkamitvā Bhagavatā saddhiṁ sammodi, sammodanīyaṁ kathaṁ sārāṇīyaṁ vītisāretvā ekamantaṁ nisīdi. Ekamantaṁ nisinno kho Māgho māṇavo Bhagantaṁ etad avoca:—Ahaṁ hi, bho Gotama, dāyako dānapati vadaññū yācayogo; dhammena bhoge pariyesāmi; dhammena bhoge pariyesitvā, dhammaladdhehi bhogehi dhammâdhigatehi ekassa pi dadāmi, dvinnam pi dadāmi, tiṇṇam pi dadāmi, catunnam pi dadāmi, pañcannam pi dadāmi, channam pi dadāmi, sattannam pi dadāmi, aṭṭhannam pi dadāmi, navannam pi dadāmi, dasannam pi dadāmi, vīsāya pi dadāmi, tiṁsāya pi dadāmi, cattārīsāya pi dadāmi, paññāsāya pi dadāmi, satassa pi dadāmi, bhiyyo pi dadāmi. Kaccâhaṁ, bho Gotama, evaṁ dadanto, evaṁ yajanto, bahuṁ puññaṁ pasavāmîti?

Taggha tvaṁ, māṇava, evaṁ dadanto evaṁ yajanto bahuṁ puññaṁ pasavasi. Yo kho, māṇava, dāyako dānapati . . . ekassa pi dadāti—pe—satassa pi dadāti, bhiyyo pi dadāti, bahuṁ so puññaṁ pasavatîti.

Atha kho Māgho māṇavo Bhagavantaṁ gāthāya ajjhabhāsi:—

1. Pucchām' aham bho Gotamaṁ vadaññuṁ (*iti Māgho māṇavo*) [487]
kāsāyavāsim agihaṁ carantaṁ:—
Yo yācayogo dānapatī gahaṭṭho
puññatthiko yajati puññapekho
dadaṁ paresaṁ idha annapānaṁ,
—kathaṁ hutaṁ yajamānassa sujjhe?

who teaches folk the bounds of rectitude [484]
and, versed in birth and death, is 'perfect sage'.
When such a one draws near the sacrifice,

scorn not but welcome him; entreat him well. [485]
'Tis thus that offerings a blessing bring.

The Brahmin: Th' Enlighten'd Lord is chief recipient; [486]
for, he is merit's richest field, a shrine
for all the world's oblations;—gifts to him
bring forth abundant fruit in rich return!

Wonderful, Gotama; quite wonderful! Just as a man might set upright again . . . (*&c., as at p. 25*) . . . Sundarika-Bhāradvāja was numbered among the Arahats.

Sutta 5. Largesse

Thus have I heard. Once while the Lord was staying near Rājagaha at Vulture's Peak, a young brahmin named Māgha came to him and after courteous greetings took his seat to one side, saying to the Lord:—I am generous, Gotama, accessible and openhanded. I seek my substance aright, and from what I thus get and obtain I give away to a single individual, or to two or more recipients—up to a hundred or more. Now tell me, Gotama, do I by all these doles and oblations store up much merit?

Certainly you do, young brahmin; so would anyone who is generous, accessible and openhearted,—seeking his substance aright and, from what he has thus got and obtained, giving away to a single individual, or to two or more recipients, up to a hundred or more.

Thereupon, Māgha addressed the Lord in these stanzas:—

Māgha: Skilled judge of men's requests, [487]
who goest, yellow-robed,
thy homeless way,—I ask
thee, Gotama, to whom
should open-handed folk,
who merit seek, do well
to offer food and drink?

2. Yo yācayogo dānapatī gahaṭṭho (*Māghâti Bhagavā*) [488]
puññatthiko yajati puññapekho
dadaṁ paresaṁ idha annapānaṁ,
ārādhaye dakkhiṇeyyehi tādi.

3. Yo yācayogo dānapatī gahaṭṭho (*iti Māgho māṇavo*) [489]
puññatthiko yajati puññapekho
dadaṁ paresaṁ idha annapānaṁ,
—akkhāhi me, Bhagavā, "dakkhiṇeyye"?

4. Ye ve asattā vicaranti loke, [490]
akiñcanā kevalino yatattā,
kālena tesu havyaṁ pavecche
yo brāhmaṇo puññapekho yajetha.

5. Ye sabbasaṁyojanabandhanacchidā, [491]
dantā vimuttā anighā nirāsā,
kālena tesu havyaṁ pavecche
yo brāhmaṇo puññapekho yajetha.

6. Ye sabbasaṁyojanavippamuttā, [492]
dantā vimuttā anighā nirāsā,
kālena—pe—

7. Rāgañ ca dosañ ca pahāya mohaṁ [493]
khīṇāsavā vusitabrahmacariyā,
kālena . . . .

8. Yesu na māyā vasatī, na māno, [494]
ye vītalobhā amamā nirāsā,
kālena . . . .

9. Ye ve na taṇhāsu upātipannā, [495]
vitareyya oghaṁ, amamā caranti
kālena . . . .

10. Yesaṁ taṇhā na 'tthi kuhiñci loke, [496]
bhavâbhavāya idha vā huraṁ vā,
kālena . . . .

11. Ye kāme hitvā agihā caranti, [497]
susaṁyatattā, tasaraṁ va ujju,
kālena . . . .

The Lord: Success will crown their gifts [488]
if he who takes has worth.

Māgha: In what consists that worth? [489]

The Lord: When 'merit' is the aim, [490]
let brahmins give to saints
who walk in self-control,
without belongings, freed;

—to those who, bursting Bonds, [491]
are schooled, free, want-less, calm;

—to those who, loosed from Bonds, [492]
are schooled, free, want-less, calm;

—to those, from passion, hate, [493]
and error purged, who live
th' uncanker'd, holy life;

—to those in whom no guile [494]
nor pride abides; who care
neither to get nor have;

—to those who—cravings quelled— [495]
unburthened cross the Flood;

—to those who nowise crave [496]
a future term of life,
on earth or anywhere;

—to those who, rid of lusts, [497]
pursue their homeless way
straight onward, shuttle-wise,
in perfect self-control;

12. Ye vītarāgā susamāhitindriyā, [498]
cando va Rāhugahaṇā pamuttā,
kālena ....

13. Samitāvino vītarāgā akopā [499]
yesaṁ gatī na 'tthi idha vippahāya,
kālena ....

14. Jahetvā jātimaraṇam asesaṁ, [500]
kathaṁkathaṁ sabbaṁ upātivattā,
kālena ....

15. Ye attadīpā vicaranti loke, [501]
akiñcanā sabbadhi vippamuttā,
kālena ....

16. Ye h' ettha jānanti yathātathā idaṁ: [502]
'Ayam antimā, na 'tthi punabbhavo' ti,
kālena ....

17. Yo vedagū jhānarato satīmā, [503]
sambodhipatto, saraṇaṁ bahunnaṁ,
kālena tamhi havyaṁ pavecche,
yo brāhmaṇo puññapekho yajetha.

18. Addhā amoghā mama pucchanā ahu; [504]
akkhāsi me Bhagavā "dakkhiṇeyye".
Tvaṁ h' ettha jānāsi yathātathā idaṁ,
tathā hi te vidito esa dhammo.

19. Yo yācayogo dānapatī gahaṭṭho (*iti Māgho māṇavo*) [505]
puññatthiko yajati puññapekho
dadaṁ paresaṁ idha annapānaṁ,
—akkhāhi me, Bhagavā, "yaññasampadaṁ".

20. 'Yajassu; yajamāno, Māghâ, (*ti Bhagavā*) [506]
sabbattha ca vippasādehi cittaṁ;
ārammaṇaṁ yajamānassa yañño,
ettha patiṭṭhāya jahāti dosaṁ.

21. So vītarāgo, pavineyya dosaṁ, [507]
mettaṁ cittaṁ bhāvayaṁ appamāṇaṁ,
rattiṁdivaṁ satataṁ appamatto
sabbā disā pharate appamaññaṁ.'

—to those, to passion dead, [498]
with pow'rs in leash, Released
(like moons from Rāhu's jaws),

at peace, meek, passionless, [499]
who've barred all further births,

who've done with birth and death, [500]
and overcome all doubts;

—to those who're their own light, [501]
unburthened, wholly freed;

—to those who realize:— [502]
'This life's my last! my last!'

—to Him, the watchful seer, [503]
whose Lore and Reveries
won him Enlightenment
to shelter multitudes;
—on Him let brahmins gifts
bestow, who merit seek.

Māgha: Not vainly did I ask. [504]
For now the Lord (who knows
and clearly sees it all)
has shown to whom to give.

When open-handed folk [505]
who merit seek to win,
bestow their food and drink
on others as a gift,
—does that a 'blessing' bring?

The Lord: In giving, purge thy heart, [506]
till giving fills thy thought
and Blemishes depart.

Thus, shalt thou,—calm, benign, [507]
zealous by night and day—
breed limitless goodwill
embracing all the worlds.

22. Ko sujjhati?—muccati?—bajjhatī ca? [508]
Ken' attanā gacchati Brahmalokaṁ?
Ajānato me, Muni, brūhi puṭṭho!
(Bhagavā hi me sakkhi, Brahm' ajja diṭṭho;
tvaṁ hi no Brahmasamo ti saccaṁ!)
Kathaṁ upapajjati Brahmalokaṁ, jutīmā?

23. Yo yajati tividhaṁ yaññasampadaṁ [509]
(*Māghâti Bhagavā*)
ārādhaye dakkhiṇeyyehi tādi,
evaṁ yajitvā sammā yācayogo
upapajjati Brahmalokan ti brūmîti.

Evaṁ vutte Māgho māṇavo Bhagavantaṁ etad avoca: 'Abhikkantaṁ bho Gotama—pe—ajjatagge pāṇupetaṁ saraṇaṁ gatan ti.'

6. Sabhiyasutta

Evam me sutaṁ. Ekaṁ samayaṁ Bhagavā Rājagahe viharati Veḷuvane Kalandakanivāpe. Tena kho pana samayena Sabhiyassa paribbājakassa purāṇasālohitāya devatāya pañhā uddiṭṭhā honti:—'Yo te, Sabhiya, samaṇo vā brāhmaṇo vā ime pañhe puṭṭho vyākaroti, tassa santike brahmacariyaṁ careyyāsîti.' Atha kho Sabhiyo paribbājako, tassā devatāya santike te pañhe uggahetvā, ye te samaṇabrāhmaṇā saṁghino gaṇino gaṇācariyā ñātā yasassino titthakarā sādhusammatā bahujanassa, seyyathîdaṁ: Pūraṇo Kassapo, Makkhali Gosālo, Ajito Kesakambali, Pakudho Kaccāyano, Sañjayo Belaṭṭhiputto, Nigaṇṭho Nātaputto,—te upasaṁkamitvā te pañhe pucchati. Te Sabhiyena paribbājakena pañhe puṭṭhā na sampāyanti; asampāyantā kopañ ca dosañ ca appaccayañ ca pātukaronti; api ca Sabhiyaṁ yeva paribbājakaṁ paṭipucchanti. Atha kho Sabhiyassa paribbājakassa etad ahosi:—'Ye kho te bhonto samaṇabrāhmaṇā saṁghino gaṇino gaṇācariyā ñātā yasassino titthakarā sādhusammatā bahujanassa, seyyathîdaṁ: Pūraṇo Kassapo—pe—Nigaṇṭho Nātaputto, te mayā pañhe puṭṭhā na sampāyanti; asampāyantā kopañ ca dosañ ca appaccayañ ca pātukaronti; api ca maṁ yev' ettha paṭipucchanti. Yan nūnâhaṁ hīnāy' āvattitvā kāme paribhuñjeyyan ti?'

Atha kho Sabhiyassa paribbājakassa etad ahosi:—'Ayam pi samaṇo Gotamo saṁghī c' eva gaṇī ca gaṇācariyo ca ñāto yasassī titthakaro sādhusammato bahujanassa. Yan nūnâhaṁ samaṇaṁ Gotamaṁ upasaṁkamitvā ime pañhe puccheyyan ti?'

Atha kho Sabhiyassa paribbājakassa etad ahosi:—Ye pi kho te bhonto samaṇabrāhmaṇā jiṇṇā vuddhā mahallakā addhagatā vayo anuppattā therā

Māgha: Who 's cleansed, or freed, or bound? [508]
Whereby can one secure
passage to Bráhmā's realms?
I know not; tell me, Sage,
—thou Bráhmā manifest!
I vow thee Bráhmā's peer!
How, Lord of light, can man
pass hence to Bráhmā's realms?

The Lord: Let him whose gifts are graced [509]
by gifts' three virtues, find
recipients of worth;
—Such openhandedness
admits to Bráhmā's realms.

Hereon, the young brahmin Māgha said to the Lord:—Wonderful, Gotama, quite wonderful! Just as a man might set upright again . . . (*&c., as at p. 35*) . . . from this day forth while life lasts.

Sutta 6. Sabhiya's Questions

Thus have I heard. Once while the Lord was staying at Rājagaha in the Bamboo grove where the squirrels were fed, a certain deity who in life on earth had been a relation of Sabhiya the Wanderer, propounded certain questions, with the injunction to Sabhiya to follow any anchorite or brahmin who could answer them. After learning these questions from the deity, Sabhiya betook him to anchorites and brahmins who had confraternities and schools, and were known and famed as heads of schools and founders of saving creeds and were held in high popular repute,—such as Pūraṇa Kassapa, Makkhali Gosāla, Ajita Kesa-Kambali, Pakudha Kaccāyana, Sañjaya Belaṭṭhi-putta, and Nāta-putta the Jain; and to each of these six he put those questions. But not one of them could furnish the answers; each and all of them, on being questioned by Sabhiya, showed temper and irritation and resentment, and put counter-questions of their own to Sabhiya, till he was tempted to abandon the higher life for a life of pleasure.

But the thought came to him that, over and above these six, there was the anchorite Gotama, who equally had a confraternity and a school of his own, and was known and famed as the head of a school and the founder of a saving creed, and was held in high popular repute. Why not ask Gotama?

Then followed the thought that all those personages whom he had already asked without success, were old and venerable men of long standing as

rattaññū cirapabbajitā saṁghino gaṇino . . . maṁ yev' ettha paṭipucchanti. Kiṁ pana me samaṇo Gotamo ime pañhe puṭṭho vyākarissati? Samaṇo hi Gotamo daharo c' eva jātiyā navo ca pabbajjāyâti.'

Atha kho Sabhiyassa paribbājakassa etad ahosi:—'Samaṇo kho daharo ti na uññātabbo, na paribhotabbo; daharo pi ce samaṇo hoti, so ca hoti mahiddhiko mahānubhāvo. Yan nūnâhaṁ samaṇaṁ Gotamaṁ upasaṁkamitvā ime pañhe puccheyyan ti?'

Atha kho Sabhiyo paribbājako yena Rājagahaṁ tena cārikaṁ pakkāmi, anupubbena cārikaṁ caramāno yena Rājagahaṁ, Veḷuvanaṁ, Kalandakanivāpo, yena Bhagavā ten' upasaṁkami, upasaṁkamitvā Bhagavatā saddhiṁ sammodi, sammodanīyaṁ kathaṁ sārāṇīyaṁ vītisāretvā ekamantaṁ nisīdi. Ekamantaṁ nisinno kho Sabhiyo paribbājako Bhagavantaṁ gāthāya ajjhabhāsi:—

1. Kaṁkhī vecikicchī āgamaṁ (*iti Sabhiyo*) [510]
pañhe pucchituṁ abhikaṁkhamāno;
tes' antakaro bhavāhi me, pañhe me puṭṭho
anupubbaṁ anudhammaṁ vyākarohi me.

2. Dūrato āgato si (*Sabhiyâti Bhagavā*) [511]
pañhe pucchituṁ abhikaṁkhamāno;
—tes' antakaro bhavāmi te, pañhe te puṭṭho
anupubbaṁ anudhammaṁ vyākaromi te.

3. Puccha maṁ, Sabhiya, pañhaṁ yaṁ kiñci manas' icchasi, [512]
tassa tass' eva pañhassa ahaṁ antaṁ karomi te ti.

Atha kho Sabhiyassa paribbājakassa etad ahosi:—'Acchariyaṁ vata bho; abbhutaṁ vata bho! yaṁ vatâhaṁ aññesu samaṇabrāhmaṇesu okāsamattam pi nâlatthaṁ, tam me idaṁ samaṇena Gotamena okāsakammaṁ katan ti', attamano pamodito udaggo pītisomanassajāto Bhagavantaṁ pañhaṁ pucchi:—

4. Kiṁpattinaṁ āhu 'bhikkhunaṁ?' (*iti Sabhiyo*) [513]
'Soratаṁ' kena? Kathañ ca 'dantam' āhu?
'Buddho' ti kathaṁ pavuccati?
Puṭṭho me, Bhagavā, vyākarohi.

5. Pajjena katena attanā (*Sabhiyâti Bhagavā*) [514]
parinibbānagato vitiṇṇakaṁkho,
vibhavañ ca bhavañ ca vippahāya,
vusitavā khīṇapunabbhavo,—sa "bhikkhu".

anchorites, and that, as they had all failed to answer the questions, how could answers be expected from Gotama,—who was so junior in years and had only become an anchorite so recently?

But here came the thought to Sabhiya that an anchorite was not to be despised and scorned on grounds of youth, and that if a young man became an anchorite, he attained great potency and powers. So why not ask Gotama the questions?

Thereupon, Sabhiya the Wanderer set out on an alms-pilgrimage to Rājagaha and at last found the Lord in the Bamboo grove where the squirrels were fed and, after courteous greetings sat down to one side, addressing the Lord in these stanzas:—

Sabhiya: Doubt and perplexity [510]
bring me with questions here;
I pray you make all clear;
expound their full import
as I put each in turn.

The Lord: Thou comest from afar [511]
with questionings; and I
will answer each in turn
and show its full import.

So ask me what thou wilt [512]
and I will answer it.

Thought Sabhiya to himself:—It is wonderful, it is marvellous, how the anchorite Gotama has accorded me the hearing which all those other anchorites and brahmins refused me! So in gladness and joy, the elated and jubilant Sabhiya asked the Lord the following question:—

What stamps 'the Almsman true'? [513]
What makes him 'meek' and 'schooled'?
What marks 'Enlightenment'?
Answer me, Lord, I pray.

The Lord: The 'Almsman true' is he [514]
who treads his chosen path
up to Nirvāna, quit
of doubts, not troubling if
life closes or runs on,
—the man who greatly lived
and now hath slain rebirth.

6. Sabbattha upekhako satīmā, [515]
na so hiṁsati kañci sabbaloke,
tiṇṇo samaṇo anāvilo,
ussadā yassa na santi, "sorato" so.

7. Yass' indriyāni bhāvitāni, [516]
ajjhattaṁ bahiddhā ca sabbaloke;
nibbijjha imaṁ parañ ca lokaṁ
kālaṁ kaṁkhati bhāvito, sa "danto".

8. Kappāni viceyya kevalāni, [517]
saṁsāraṁ dubhayaṁ cutûpapātaṁ,
vigatarajaṁ ananganaṁ visuddhaṁ,
pattaṁ jātikkhayaṁ,—tam āhu "buddhan" ti.

Atha kho Sabhiyo paribbājako Bhagavato bhāsitaṁ abhinanditvā anumoditvā attamano pamodito udaggo pītisomanassajāto Bhagavantaṁ uttariṁ pañhaṁ apucchi:—

9. Kiṁpattinaṁ āhu "brāhmaṇaṁ"? (*iti Sabhiyo*) [518]
"samaṇaṁ" kena? kathañ ca "nhātako" ti?
"nāgo" ti kathaṁ pavuccati?
—Puṭṭho me, Bhagavā, vyākarohi.

10. Bāhetvā sabbapāpakāni, (*Sabhiyâti Bhagavā*) [519]
vimalo sādhusamāhito ṭhitatto,
saṁsāram aticca kevalī so
asito tādi pavuccate "brahmā".

11. Samitāvi, pahāya puññapāpaṁ, [520]
virajo, ñatvā imaṁ parañ ca lokaṁ,
jātimaraṇaṁ upātivatto,
"samaṇo" tādi pavuccate tathattā.

The man of watchful poise [515]
who harms no living thing,
the stainless anchorite
—beyond life's Flood, devoid
of arrogance,—is 'meek'.

He 's 'schooled' who drills each thought [516]
—self-bred or from without—,
whom scrutiny of this
and other worlds has taught
calmly to wait death's call.

'Enlightenment' is his [517]
whose piercing eye surveys
all ages, and perceives
how creatures come and go
to tramp their dismal round;
who—spotless, stainless, pure—
has done with birth and death.

Thereon, in gladness and joy at the Lord's words, the elated and jubilant Sabhiya asked his next question:—

What stamps a 'Brahmin', Lord? [518]
—an 'Anchorite'?—a 'Saint'?
What makes a 'Paragon'?
Answer me, Lord, I pray.

The Lord: 'Brahmin' is he who—quit [519]
of evil, stedfast, rapt—
has left rebirth behind
for calm, consummate Peace.

True 'Anchorite' is he [520]
who, finding anchorage
beyond works good or bad,
by faultlessness has plumbed
both this and other worlds,
and vanquished birth and death.

12. Ninhāya sabbapāpakāni, [521]
ajjhattaṁ bahiddhā ca sabbaloke,
devamanussesu kappiyesu
kappaṁ n' eti, tam āhu "nhātako" ti.

13. Āguṁ na karoti kiñci loke, [522]
sabbasaṁyoge visajja bandhanāni
sabbattha na sajjati vimutto,
—"nāgo" tādi pavuccate tathattā ti.

Atha kho Sabhiyo paribbājako—pe—Bhagavantaṁ uttariṁ pañhaṁ apucchi:—

14. Kaṁ "khettajinaṁ" vadanti buddhā? (*iti Sabhiyo*) [523]
"kusalaṁ" kena? kathañ ca "paṇḍito" ti?
"muni" nāma kathaṁ pavuccati?
—Puṭṭho me, Bhagavā, vyākarohi.

15. Khettāni viceyya kevalāni (*Sabhiyâti Bhagavā*) [524]
divyaṁ mānusakañ ca brahmakhettaṁ
sabbakhettamūlabandhanā pamutto,
"khettajino" tādi pavuccate tathattā.

16. Kosāni viceyya kevalāni [525]
dibbaṁ mānusakañ ca brahmakosaṁ,
sabbakosamūlabandhanā pamutto,
"kusalo" tādi pavuccati tathattā.

17. Dubhayāni viceyya paṇḍarāni [526]
ajjhattaṁ bahiddhā ca suddhipañño,
kaṇhasukkaṁ upātivatto,
"paṇḍito" tādi pavuccate tathattā.

18. Asatañ ca satañ ca ñatvā dhammaṁ [527]
ajjhattaṁ bahiddhā ca sabbaloke,
devamanussehi pūjiyo so,
sangaṁ jālaṁ aticca,—so "munîti".

The 'Saint' has washed away [521]
all evil, inly bred
or from without; no more
he'll enter time—like gods
and men, the brood of time.

He who lives guiltless here, [522]
who, bursting bonds and ties,
hugs naught, but wins Release,
—is therefore 'Paragon'.

Hereupon, in gladness and joy at the Lord's words, the elated and jubilant Sabhiya asked his next question:—

Whom do th' enlighten'd term [523]
'field's conqueror'? What makes
a 'skilled' man?—what a 'sage'?
and what proclaims the 'seer'?
Answer me, Lord, I pray.

The Lord: When thought on fields to grow [524]
bliss—human or divine—
uproots all zest for fields,
a man has 'conquer'd fields'.

When thought on barns to store [525]
bliss—human or divine—
uproots all zest for barns,
a man attains to 'skill'.

When thought on senses' range [526]
(internal or without)
has left conviction clear
—above all hopes or fears—,
that makes a man a 'sage'.

A 'seer' is he who knows [527]
all outlooks good or bad,
selfbred or from without;
whom gods and men revere;
who bursts all ties and snares.

Atha kho Sabhiyo paribbājako—pe—Bhagavantaṁ uttariṁ pañhaṁ apucchi:—

19. Kiṁpattinaṁ āhu "vedagum"? (*iti Sabhiyo*) [528]
"Anuviditam" kena? kathañ ca "viriyavā" ti?
"Ājāniyo" kin ti nāma hoti?
—Puṭṭho me, Bhagavā, vyākarohi.

20. Vedāni viceyya kevalāni (*Sabhiyâti Bhagavā*) [529]
samaṇānaṁ yāni p' atthi brāhmaṇānaṁ
sabbavedanāsu vītarāgo
sabbaṁ vedam aticca,—"vedagū" so.

21. Anuvicca papañca-nāmarūpaṁ, [530]
ajjhattaṁ bahiddhā ca rogamūlaṁ,
sabbarogamūlabandhanā pamutto,
"anuvidito" tādi pavuccate tathattā.

22. Virato idha sabbapāpakehi, [531]
nirayadukkham aticca, viriyavāso,
so "viriyavā" padhānavā
dhīro tādi pavuccate tathattā.

23. Yass' assu lūtāni bandhanāni [532]
ajjhattam bahiddhā ca sangamūlaṁ,
sabbasangamūlabandhanā pamutto,
"ājāniyo" tādi pavuccate tathattā ti.

Atha kho Sabhiyo paribbājako—pe—Bhagavantaṁ uttariṁ pañhaṁ apucchi:—

24. Kiṁpattinaṃ āhu "sottiyaṁ" (*iti Sabhiyo*) [533]
"ariyaṁ" kena? Kathañ ca "caraṇavā" ti?
"Paribbājako" kin ti nāma hoti?
Puṭṭho me, Bhagavā, vyākarohi.

25. Sutvā sabbadhammaṁ abhiññāya loke (*Sabhiyâti Bhagavā*) [534]
sāvajjânavajjaṁ yad atthi kiñci
abhibhuṁ, akathaṁkathiṁ, vimuttaṁ,
anighaṁ, sabbadhi-m-āhu "sottiyo" ti.

Hereon, in gladness and joy at the Lord's words, the elated and jubilant Sabhiya asked his next question:—

What stamps 'th' adept in lore'? [528]
What makes him 'come to know'?
How gets he 'zeal'? And what
is termed a 'scion', Lord?
Answer me, Lord, I pray.

The Lord: He who surveying lore [529]
(brahmins' and anchorites'),
and, losing zest for things
of sense, outgrows all lore,
—'tis he is 'lore's adept'.

He who detects the curse [530]
of 'personality'
(disease's root!), and plucks
out all that bound him fast,
—'tis he has 'come to know'.

He who, eschewing wrong, [531]
prevails o'er pains of hell,
shews 'zeal' by battling on
in staunch persistency.

He who snaps bonds within [532]
and stubs all roots without,
till he is free from roots
and bonds,—a 'scion' is.

Hereon in gladness and joy at the Lord's words, the elated and jubilant Sabhiya put his next question:—

What stamps man 'Erudite'? [533]
What makes him 'Noble'?—What
'Upright'?—What 'Anchorite'?
Answer me, Lord, I pray.

The Lord: He who has learned and plumbed [534]
all outlooks, till—beyond
all praise and blame—doubts pass,
and with Release comes calm,
—he's wholly 'Erudite'.

26. Chetvā āsavāni, ālayāni [535]
vidvā, so na upeti gabbhaseyyaṁ;
saññaṁ tividhaṁ panujja pankaṁ
kappan n' eti, tam āhu "ariyo" ti.

27. Yo idha caraṇesu pattipatto [536]
kusalo sabbadā ajāni Dhammaṁ,
sabbattha na sajjati, vimutto,
paṭighā yassa na santi, "caraṇavā" so.

28. Dukkhavepakkaṁ yad atthi kammaṁ [537]
uddhaṁ adho ca tiriyañ câpi majjhe
paribbājayitvā pariññacārī
māyaṁ mānam atho pi lobhakodhaṁ
pariyantam akāsi nāmarūpaṁ,
tam "paribbājakam" āhu pattipattan ti.'

Atha kho Sabhiyo paribbājako Bhagavato bhāsitaṁ abhinanditvā anumoditvā attamano pamodito udaggo pītisomanassajāto uṭṭhāyâsanā ekaṁsaṁ uttarāsangaṁ karitvā yena Bhagavā ten' añjalim paṇāmetvā Bhagavantaṁ sammukhā sāruppāhi gāthāhi abhitthavi:—

29. Yāni ca tīṇi yāni ca saṭṭhi [538]
samaṇappavādasitāni, bhūripañña,
saññakkhara-saññanissitāni
osaraṇāni vineyya oghatam' agā.

30. Antagū si pāragū si dukkhassa! [539]
Arahā si! Khīṇāsavaṁ taṁ maññe!
Jutimā mutimā pahūtapañño,
dukkhass' antakara, atāresi maṁ!

31. Yaṁ me kankhitam aññāsi, [540]
vicikicchaṁ maṁ atāresi, namo te!
Muni monapathesu pattipatta,
akhila Ādiccabandhu, sorato si!

32. Yā me kaṁkhā pure āsi, taṁ me vyākāsi, cakkhumā. [541]
Addhā Munī si Sambuddho; na 'tthi nīvaraṇā tava.

33. Upāyāsā ca te sabbe viddhastā vinaḷīkatā; [542]
sītibhūto damappatto dhitimā saccanikkamo.

34. Tassa te Nāganāgassa, Mahāvīrassa, bhāsato [543]
sabbe devā anumodanti ubho Nārada-Pabbatā.

He who tracks Cankers down [535]
and hacks them out, to know
rebirth no more but sweep
aside, as filth, all things
of sense and banish Time,
—'tis he is 'Noble' styled.

He who on earth walks sure, [536]
with skill to grasp the Truth,
—ensnared, repelled, by nought,
but free,—'Upright' is he.

The pilgrim who discerns [537]
what acts have Ills for fruit,
and, comprehending, sloughs
guile, pride of life, wants, wrath,
and personality,
—is perfect 'Anchorite'.

Hereon, in gladness at the Lord's words, the elated and jubilant Sabhiya rose up from his seat and, with his right shoulder bared, stretched forth his folded palms towards the Lord, as he addressed him to his face in stanzas fit:—

Great sage, who didst reject [538]
the sense-based sophistries
of three and sixty sects,
thou soarest o'er life's gloom!

Ending, transcending, Ills, [539]
Cankerless Arahat,
thy insight, light, and lore
have brought me safe 'Across'!

For marking my distress, [540]
for freeing me from doubt,
I laud thee, sage benign,
consummate master-mind,
great Kinsman of the Sun!

The doubts I had are solved by thee, O Seer, [541]
O All-Enlighten'd sage immaculate!

With ev'ry perturbation rooted up, [542]
unfever'd, tranquil, strong in Truth art thou!

Great Victor! Paragon! Thy words rejoice [543]
all gods, all Nāradás, all Pábbatás.

35. Namo te, purisājañña! Namo te, purisuttama! [544]
Sadevakasmiṁ lokasmiṁ na 'tthi te paṭipuggalo.

36. Tuvaṁ Buddho; tuvaṁ Satthā; tuvaṁ Mārâbhibhū Muni; [545]
tuvaṁ anusaye chetvā tiṇṇo tāres' imaṁ pajaṁ.

37. Upadhī te samatikkantā; āsavā te padālitā; [546]
sīho 'si anupādāno pahīnabhayabheravo.

38. Puṇḍarīkaṁ yathā vaggu toye na upalippati, [547]
evaṁ puññe ca pāpe ca ubhaye tvaṁ na lippasi!
—Pāde, vīra, pasārehi. Sabhiyo vandati Satthuno ti.

Atha kho Sabhiyo paribbājako Bhagavato pādesu sirasā nipatitvā, Bhagavantaṁ etad avoca:—Abhikkantaṁ, bhante,—pe—dhammañ ca bhikkhusaṁghañ ca. Labheyyâhaṁ, bhante, Bhagavato santike pabbajjaṁ, labheyyaṁ upasampadan ti.

Yo kho, Sabhiya, aññatitthiyapubbo imasmiṁ Dhammavinaye ākaṁkhati pabbajjaṁ ākaṁkhati upasampadaṁ, so cattaro māse parivasati, catunnaṁ māsānaṁ accayena āraddhacittā bhikkhū pabbājenti upasampādenti bhikkhubhāvāya. Api ca m' ettha puggalavemattatā viditā ti.

Sace, bhante, aññatitthiyapubbā imasmiṁ Dhammavinaye ākaṁkhantā pabbajjaṁ ākaṁkhantā upasampadaṁ cattāro māse parivasanti, catunnaṁ māsānaṁ accayena āraddhacittā bhikkhū pabbājenti upasampādenti bhikkhubhāvāya,—ahaṁ cattāri vassāni parivasissāmi; catunnaṁ vassānaṁ accayena āraddhacittā bhikkhū pabbājentu upasampādentu bhikkhubhāvāyâ ti.

Alattha kho Sabhiyo Bhagavato santike pabbajjaṁ, alattha upasampadaṁ—pe—aññataro kho pan' āyasmā Sabhiyo arahataṁ ahosi.

7. Selasutta

Evam me sutaṁ. Ekaṁ samayaṁ Bhagavā Ang-uttarāpesu cārikañ caramāno mahatā bhikkhusaṁghena saddhiṁ aḍḍhateḷasehi bhikkhusatehi yena Āpaṇaṁ nāma Anguttarāpānaṁ nigamo tad avasari. Assosi kho Keniyo jaṭilo:—Samaṇo khalu, bho, Gotamo Sakyaputto Sakyakulā pabbajito Anguttarāpesu cārikaṁ caramāno mahatā bhikkhusaṁghena saddhiṁ aḍḍhateḷasehi bhikkhusatehi Āpaṇaṁ anuppatto; taṁ kho pana bhavantaṁ Gotamaṁ evaṁ kalyāṇo kittisaddo abbhuggato 'Iti pi so Bhagavā arahaṁ Sammāsambuddho vijjācaraṇasampanno sugato lokavidū anuttaro purisadammasārathi satthā devamanussānaṁ Buddho Bhagavā; so imaṁ lokaṁ sadevakaṁ samārakaṁ

I hail thee noblest, foremost of mankind; [544]
nor earth nor heaven holds thy counterpart!

Enlighten'd Master! Over Māra's hosts [545]
triumphant! Sage, who, wrong propensities
uprooting, for thyself salvation found
and taught mankind to find salvation too!

Thou hast surmounted all that breeds rebirth [546]
and extirpated Canker-growths within!
With naught to bind thee thrall to life, thou 'rt free
as forest lion from all fears and dread.

E'en as a lotus fair to water gives [547]
no lodgment, thou by good and bad alike
art unaffected. Stretch thou forth thy feet,
O Victor. I salute my Master's feet!

Hereon, Sabhiya the Wanderer, bowing his head in homage at the Lord's feet, said:—It is wonderful, sir (*&c., as at p. 25*) confirmation as an Almsman with the Lord!

'Sabhiya, a former sectary of another school who seeks admission and confirmation in this Doctrine and Rule, first resides for four months, at the close of which period proved Almsmen admit and confirm him as an Almsman. I recognize a distinction between persons in this case.'

'If, sir, former sectaries of other schools have first to undergo a four months' probation before enrolment here, then I will reside for four years, at the close of which period let proved Almsmen admit and confirm me as an Almsman.'

So Sabhiya the Wanderer received admission and confirmation as an Almsman at the hands of the Lord. Nor was it long thereafter before the reverend Sabhiya, dwelling alone and aloof (*&c., as at p. 25*) was numbered among the Arahats.

Sutta 7. The Superman

Thus have I heard. Once when the Lord was on an alms-pilgrimage in the Anga country north of the Ganges, with a great train of Almsmen, numbering twelve hundred and fifty, he sojourned in the Anga township of Āpaṇa across the river.

It came to the ears of Keniya of the matted-hair that the anchorite Gotama, a Sakyan who had gone forth from home to homelessness as a Pilgrim, was reported to have arrived at Āpaṇa with this great train in the course of an alms-pilgrimage. Such, according to report, was the high repute noised

sabrahmakaṁ sassamaṇabrāhmaṇiṁ pajaṁ sadevamanussaṁ sayaṁ abhiññā sacchikatvā pavedeti; so Dhammaṁ deseti ādikalyāṇaṁ majjhe kalyāṇaṁ pariyosānakalyāṇaṁ sâttham savyañjanaṁ; kevalaparipuṇṇaṁ parisuddhaṁ brahmacariyaṁ pakāseti; sādhu kho pana tathārūpānaṁ arahataṁ dassanaṁ hotîti'.

Atha kho Keniyo jaṭilo yena Bhagavā ten' upasaṁkami, upasaṁkamitvā Bhagavatā saddhiṁ sammodi, sammodanīyam kathaṁ sārāṇīyaṁ vītisāretvā ekamantaṁ nisīdi. Ekamantaṁ nisinnaṁ kho Keniyaṁ jaṭilaṁ Bhagavā dhammiyā kathāya sandassesi samādapesi samuttejesi sampahaṁsesi. Atha kho Keniyo jaṭilo Bhagavatā dhammiyā kathāya sandassito samādapito samuttejito sampahaṁsito Bhagavantaṁ etad avoca:—Adhivāsetu me bhavaṁ Gotamo svātanāya bhattaṁ saddhiṁ bhikkhusaṁghenâti. Evaṁ vutte, Bhagavā Keniyaṁ jaṭilaṁ etad avoca: Mahā kho, Keniya, bhikkhusaṁgho, aḍḍhateḷasāni bhikkhusatāni; tvañ ca kho brāhmaṇesu abhippasanno ti. Dutiyam pi kho Keniyo jaṭilo Bhagavantaṁ etad avoca: Kiñcāpi, bho Gotama, mahā bhikkhusaṁgho aḍḍhateḷasāni bhikkhusatāni ahañ ca brāhmaṇesu abhippasanno, adhivāsetu me bhavaṁ Gotamo . . . bhikkhusaṁghenâti. Dutiyam pi kho Bhagavā Keniyaṁ jaṭilam etad avoca: Mahā kho . . . abhippasanno ti. Tatiyam pi kho Keniyo jaṭilo Bhagavantaṁ etad avoca: Kiñcāpi, bho Gotama, . . . adhivāsetv-eva me bhavaṁ Gotamo . . . bhikkhusaṁghenâti.

Adhivāsesi Bhagavā tuṇhībhāvena.

Atha kho Keniyo jaṭilo, Bhagavato adhivāsanaṁ viditvā, utthāyâsanā yena sako assamo ten' upasaṁkami, upasaṁkamitvā mittâmacce ñātisālohite āmantesi:—Suṇantu me bhonto mittâmaccā ñātisālohitā. Samaṇo me Gotamo nimantito svātanāya bhattaṁ saddhiṁ bhikkhusaṁghena. Yena me kāyaveyyāvaṭikaṁ kareyyāthâti.

Evaṁ bho ti kho Keniyassa jaṭilassa mittâmaccā ñātisālohitā Keniyassa jaṭilassa paṭissutvā app-ekacce uddhanāni khaṇanti, app-ekacce kaṭṭhāni phāḷenti, app-ekacce bhājanāni dhovanti, app-ekacce udakamaṇikaṁ patiṭṭhāpenti, app-ekacce āsanāni paññāpenti; Keniyo pana jaṭilo sāmaṁ yeva maṇḍalamāḷaṁ paṭiyādeti.

Tena kho pana samayena Selo brāhmaṇo Āpaṇe paṭivasati, tiṇṇam vedānaṁ pāragū, sanighaṇḍukeṭubhānaṁ sâkkharappabhedānaṁ; itihāsapañcamānaṁ padako veyyākaraṇo; lokāyatamahāpurisalakkhaṇesu anavayo; tīṇi māṇavakasatāni mante vāceti. Tena kho pana samayena Keniyo jaṭilo Sele brāhmaṇe abhippasanno hoti.

Atha kho Selo brāhmaṇo tīhi māṇavakasatehi parivuto janghāvihāraṁ anucankamamāno anuvicaramāno yena Keniyassa jaṭilassa assamo ten' upasaṁkami. Addasā kho Selo brāhmaṇo Keniyassamiye jaṭile app-ekacce uddhanāni khaṇante—pe—app-ekacce āsanāni paññāpente, Keniyaṁ pana jaṭilaṁ sāmaṁ yeva maṇḍalamāḷaṁ paṭiyādentaṁ; disvāna Keniyaṁ jaṭilaṁ etad avoca: Kin nu kho bhoto Keniyassa āvāho vā bhavissati, vivāho vā bhavissati,

abroad concerning this Gotama that he was said to be:—'The Lord, Arahat All-Enlightened, walking by knowledge, blessed, understanding all worlds, the matchless tamer of the human heart, teacher of gods and men, the Lord Buddha; this universe—with its gods, its Māras, its Brahmās, its anchorites and brahmins, embracing all deities and mankind—all this he has discerned and realized for himself and makes known to others; he preaches a Doctrine which is so fair in its outset, its middle, and its close, with both text and import; he propounds a higher life that is wholly complete and pure;—it is good to go and visit men of worth like him.'

So Keniya came to the Lord and, seating himself after greetings, was by the Lord instructed, roused, fired, and cheered onwards with a doctrinal discourse, at the close of which Keniya invited the Lord, with his Community, to take to-morrow's meal with him. Said the Lord:—There are no less than twelve hundred and fifty Almsmen with me;—and you are an adherent of the brahmins, Keniya!

A second time did Keniya tender his invitation, saying this made no difference; and a second time did he receive the same answer. But when the invitation was repeated for the third time, with the words: 'You have only to assent', the Lord, by his silence, accepted it. Then Keniya got up and went off to his own hermitage, where he told his friends and kinsfolk who was coming, and asked them to help. Readily enough, they set to work, some digging earth-ovens, some splitting firewood, some scouring pans, and others setting out water-jars, and placing seats ready,—while Keniya with his own hands prepared a round pavilion.

Now at that time there was living at Āpaṇa the brahmin Sela, who was versed in all three Vedas, was accomplished in ritual with the glosses thereon, in phonetics, and in etymology, as also in legends, which he could recite and explain; and he was not unversed in the world's duration and in the signs that mark a Superman; he had three hundred young brahmins to whom he taught the runes. At this time, moreover, Keniya of the matted-hair was an adherent of this brahmin Sela.

Accompanied by his three hundred pupils, the brahmin came in the course of a stroll to Keniya's hermitage and saw all Keniya's adherents busy with their several tasks, while Keniya with his own hands was preparing a round pavilion. At the sight, the brahmin said to Keniya:—What is all this? Is it a wedding-feast for a bridegroom or for a bride? Or is there a great oblation afoot? Or have you invited to a repast to-morrow Seniya Bimbisāra, king of Magadha, with all his host?

Said Keniya: It is no wedding-feast, Sela; nor is the king coming with all

mahāyañño vā paccupaṭṭhito, rājā vā Māgadho, Seniyo Bimbisāro, nimantito svātanāya saddhiṁ balakāyenâti?

Na me, Sela, āvāho bhavissati, na pi vivāho bhavissati, na pi rājā Māgadho, Seniyo Bimbisāro, nimantito svātanāya saddhiṁ balakāyena. Api ca kho me mahāyañño paccupaṭṭhito atthi. Samaṇo Gotamo Sakyaputto Sakyakulā pabbajito Anguttarāpesu cārikaṁ caramāno mahatā bhikkhusaṁghena saddhiṁ aḍḍhateḷasehi bhikkhusatehi Āpaṇaṁ anuppatto. Taṁ kho pana bhavantaṁ Gotamaṁ—pe—Buddho Bhagavā ti;—so me nimantito svātanāya saddhiṁ bhikkhusaṁghenâti.

'Buddho' ti, bho Keniya, vadesi?

'Buddho' ti, bho Sela, vadāmi.

'Buddho' ti, bho Keniya, vadesi?

'Buddho' ti, bho Sela, vadāmi.

Atha kho Selassa brāhmaṇassa etad ahosi:—Ghoso pi kho eso dullabho lokasmiṁ yadidaṁ 'Buddho' ti. Āgatāni kho pana asmākaṁ mantesu dvattiṁsa Mahāpurisa-lakkhaṇāni, yehi samannāgatassa Mahāpurisassa dve va gatiyo bhavanti, anaññā. Sace agāraṁ ajjhāvasati, rājā hoti cakkavattī dhammiko dhammarājā cāturanto vijitāvī janapadatthāvariyapatto sattaratanasamannāgato; tass' imāni satta ratanāni bhavanti, seyyathīdaṁ: cakkaratanaṁ, hatthiratanaṁ, assaratanaṁ, maṇiratanaṁ, itthiratanaṁ, gahapatiratanaṁ, pariṇāyakaratanaṁ eva sattamaṁ; parosahassaṁ kho pan' assa puttā bhavanti—sūrā vīrangarūpā parasenappamaddanā. So imaṁ paṭhaviṁ sāgarapariyantaṁ, adaṇḍena asatthena, dhammena abhivijiya ajjhāvasati. Sace kho panâgarasmā anagāriyaṁ pabbajati, arahaṁ hoti Sammāsambuddho loke vivattacchaddo.—Kahaṁ pana, bho Keniya, etarahi so bhavaṁ Gotamo viharati, arahaṁ Sammāsambuddho ti?

Evaṁ vutte, Keniyo jaṭilo dakkhiṇaṁ bāhaṁ paggahetvā Selaṁ brāhmaṇaṁ etad avoca: Yen' esā, bho Sela, nīlavanarājī ti.

Atha kho Selo brāhmaṇo tīhi māṇavakasatehi saddhiṁ yena Bhagavā ten' upasaṁkami. Atha kho Selo brāhmaṇo te māṇavake āmantesi:—Appasaddā bhonto āgacchantu pade padaṁ nikkhipantā,—durāsadā hi te Bhagavanto, sīhā va ekacarā; yadā câhaṁ, bho, samaṇena Gotamena saddhiṁ manteyyaṁ, mā me bhonto antarantarākathaṁ opātetha; kathāpariyosānaṁ me bhavanto āgamentûti. Atha kho Selo brāhmaṇo yena Bhagavā ten' upasaṁkami, upasaṁkamitvā Bhagavatā saddhiṁ sammodi, sammodanīyaṁ kathaṁ sārāṇīyaṁ vītisāretvā ekamantaṁ nisīdi. Ekamantaṁ nisinno kho Selo brāhmaṇo Bhagavato kāye dvattiṁsa Mahāpurisa-lakkhaṇāni samannesi. Addasā kho Selo brāhmaṇo Bhagavato kāye dvattiṁsa Mahāpurisa-lakkhaṇāni yebhuyyena ṭhapetvā dve;—dvīsu Mahāpurisa-lakkhaṇesu kaṁkhati vicikicchati nâdhimuccati na sampasīdati,—kosohite ca vatthaguyhe pahūtajivhatāya ca.

Atha kho Bhagavato etad ahosi: Passati kho me ayaṁ Selo brāhmaṇo dvattiṁsa Mahāpurisa-lakkhaṇāni yebhuyyena ṭhapetvā dve; dvīsu Mahā-

his host; but I have got a great oblation afoot. For the anchorite Gotama, who left his Sakyan home to be a Pilgrim, has arrived at Āpaṇa in the course of an alms-pilgrimage, with twelve hundred and fifty Almsmen in his train. Now, such, according to report, is the high repute noised abroad concerning this Gotama that he is said to be . . . (*&c., as p. 135*) . . . the Lord Buddha. He it is who has been invited for to-morrow, he and his Community.

Do you say 'Buddha', Keniya?

Yes, I do, Sela.

Do you really say 'Buddha'?

Yes, I do, Sela.

Thought the brahmin to himself:—Rarely indeed is the title of 'Buddha' heard in the world. In our runes there have been handed down the two and thirty marks of a Superman, for whom, if he bears those marks, there awaits one of two careers and no third. Should he live a home life, he becomes Emperor over the four quarters of the earth, righteous in himself and ruling righteously, victorious abroad, enforcing law and order at home, and possessing the Seven Jewels, to wit,—wheel, elephant, charger, gem, queen-consort, treasurer, and counsellor. More than a thousand sons has he, heroes of might who trample down the enemy's host before them. Over all this earth to the shores of ocean he extends his sway by sheer righteousness alone and not by cudgel or sword. But, if, instead, he goes forth from home to homelessness as a Pilgrim, he becomes the Arahat All-Enlightened who lifts the veil from the world.

Said Sela aloud:—Where, Keniya, is Gotama now staying, this Arahat All-Enlightened?

In answer, Keniya stretched out his right arm and said:—Yonder, Sela, in that stretch of dark trees.

Then the brahmin proceeded to the Lord, attended by his three hundred young brahmins, to whom he gave the following instructions:—Move forward in silence, noiselessly in one another's footsteps; for, these Lords are hard of access, like solitary lions. And, while I am conferring with the anchorite Gotama, keep silent till my talk with him is over, and do not interrupt.

Arrived in the Lord's presence, the brahmin, seating himself after courteous greetings, scanned the Lord's body for the two and thirty marks of a Superman; and in time observed them all save two, namely the privities hidden in a sheath and the big tongue, concerning which two he was in doubt and perplexity, not feeling certain or sure.

Realizing precisely the brahmin's uncertainty of mind, the Lord put forth such a manifestation of psychic power that Sela could see the Lord's privities

purisa-lakkhaṇesu kaṁkhati vicikicchati nâdhimuccati na sampasīdati, kosohite ca vatthaguyhe pahūtajivhatāya câti. Atha kho Bhagavā tathārūpaṁ iddhâbhisaṁkhāraṁ abhisaṁkhāsi yathā addasa Selo brāhmaṇo Bhagavato kosohitaṁ vatthaguyhaṁ. Atha kho Bhagavā jivhaṁ ninnāmetvā ubho pi kaṇṇasotāni anumasi paṭimasi, ubho pi nāsikasotāni anumasi paṭimasi, kevalam pi nalāṭamaṇḍalaṁ jivhāya chādesi. Atha kho Selassa brāhmaṇassa etad ahosi: Samannāgato kho samaṇo Gotamo dvattiṁsa Mahāpurisalakkhaṇehi paripuṇṇehi, no aparipuṇṇehi. No ca kho naṁ jānāmi 'Buddho vā no vā'. Sutaṁ kho pana mêtaṁ brāhmaṇānaṁ vuddhānaṁ mahallakānaṁ ācariyapācariyānaṁ bhāsamānānaṁ: 'Ye te bhavanti arahanto Sammāsambuddhā, te sake vaṇṇe bhaññamāne attānaṁ pātūkarontîti; yannūnâhaṁ samaṇaṁ Gotamaṁ sammukhā sāruppāhi gāthāhi abhitthaveyyan ti?' Atha kho Selo brāhmaṇo Bhagavantaṁ sammukhā sāruppāhi gāthāhi abhitthavi:—

1. Paripuṇṇakāyo suruci sujāto cārudassano [548]
suvaṇṇavaṇṇo 'si, Bhagavā, susukkadāṭho 'si, viriyavā.

2. Narassa hi sujātassa ye bhavanti viyañjanā [549]
sabbe te tava kāyasmiṁ Mahāpurisa-lakkhaṇā.

3. Pasannanetto, sumukho, brahā, uju, patāpavā, [550]
majjhe samaṇasaṁghassa, ādicco va, virocasi

4. kalyāṇadassano bhikkhu, kañcanasannibhattaco. [551]
Kin te samaṇabhāvena evaṁ uttamavaṇṇino?

5. Rājā arahasi bhavituṁ cakkavatti rathesabho, [552]
cāturanto vijitāvī Jambusaṇḍassa issaro.

6. Khattiyā bhojarājāno anuyuttā bhavantu te! [553]
rājâbhirājā, manujindo, rajjaṁ kārehi, Gotama!

7. Rājâham asmi, Selâti, dhammarājā anuttaro, [554]
dhammena cakkaṁ vattemi, cakkaṁ appativattiyaṁ.

8. Sambuddho paṭijānāsi 'dhammarājā anuttaro [555]
dhammena cakkaṁ vattemi' iti bhāsasi, Gotama.

9. Ko nu senāpatī bhoto sāvako Satthu-d-anvayo? [556]
Ko te imaṁ anuvatteti dhammacakkaṁ pavattitaṁ?

within their sheath; and then, putting forth his tongue, he passed it up and down over the orifices of both ears and of both nostrils, and covered with it the whole expanse of his forehead.

Quite sure now about the presence of the two and thirty marks, Sela still did not know whether he possessed Enlightenment or not. But he remembered hearing from old and aged brahmins, teachers of teachers, that those who become Arahats All-Enlightened, reveal themselves when their praises are sung in their presence; and so he made up his mind to extol the Lord to his face in the following stanzas of eulogy:—

Perfect in body, goodly, Lord, art thou, [548]
well-grown, well-liking, golden-hued, with teeth
agleam with lustre; vigour fills thy frame;

thy body's full perfection manifests [549]
each single sign that marks a Superman.

Clear-eyed and handsome, tall, upright, art thou, [550]
effulgent as a sun among thy train,

—so debonair, so golden-hued! Why waste [551]
thy beauty's prime as homeless anchorite?

As world-wide monarch thou should'st ride in state; [552]
and Ind from sea to sea should own thy sway.

Proud princes should thy village-headmen be! [553]
Rule thou mankind as sov'ran king of kings.

The Lord: Know, Sela, know that king indeed am I, [554]
—the peerless king of utter righteousness.
In righteousness my sov'ran Wheel of Truth
I roll, that nevermore shall backwards turn.

Sela: If All-Enlighten'd thou dost claim to be, [555]
the peerless king of utter righteousness,
rolling in righteousness thy sov'ran Wheel,

—who ranks as Captain, next to thee, to keep [556]
thy Wheel still rolling onward in its course?

10. Mayā pavattitaṁ cakkaṁ (*Selâti Bhagavā*) [557]
dhammacakkaṁ anuttaraṁ
Sāriputto anuvatteti anujāto Tathāgataṁ.

11. Abhiññeyyaṁ abhiññātaṁ, bhāvetabbañ ca bhāvitaṁ, [558]
pahātabbaṁ pahīnam me. Tasmā Buddho 'smi, brāhmaṇa.

12. Vinayassu mayī kaṁkhaṁ; adhimuccassu, brāhmaṇa; [559]
dullabhaṁ dassanaṁ hoti Sambuddhānaṁ abhiṇhaso.

13. Yesaṁ vo dullabho loke pātubhāvo abhiṇhaso, [560]
so 'haṁ, brāhmaṇa, Sambuddho, sallakatto anuttaro.

14. Brahmabhūto atitulo Mārasenappamaddano [561]
sabbâmitte vasīkatvā modāmi akutobhayo.

15. 'Imaṁ, bhonto, nisāmetha, yathā bhāsati cakkhumā, [562]
sallakatto, mahāvīro,—sīho va nadatī vane.

16. Brahmabhūtaṁ atitulaṁ Mārasenappamaddanaṁ [563]
ko disvā na-ppasīdeyya,—api kaṇhâbhijātiko?

17. Yo maṁ icchati anvetu; yo vā n' icchati, gacchatu. [564]
Idhâhaṁ pabbajissāmi varapaññassa santike.'

18. 'Etañ ce ruccati bhoto Sammāsambuddhasāsanaṁ, [565]
mayam pi pabbajissāma varapaññassa santike.'

19. 'Brāhmaṇā tisatā ime yācanti pañjalīkatā: [566]
brahmacariyaṁ carissāma, Bhagavā, tava santike.'

20. 'Svākkhātaṁ brahmacariyaṁ (*Selâti Bhagavā*) [567]
sandiṭṭhikam akālikaṁ
yattha amoghā pabbajjā appamattassa sikkhato' ti.

Alattha kho Selo brāhmaṇo sapariso Bhagavato santike pabbajjaṁ, alattha upasampadaṁ.

Atha kho Keniyo jaṭilo tassā rattiyā accayena sake assame paṇītaṁ khādaniyaṁ bhojaniyaṁ paṭiyādāpetva Bhagavato kālaṁ ārocāpesi: Kālo, bho Gotama; niṭṭhitaṁ bhattan ti. Atha kho Bhagavā pubbaṇhasamayaṁ nivāsetvā pattacīvaraṁ ādāya yena Keniyassa jaṭilassa assamo ten' upasaṁkami, upasaṁkamitvā paññatte āsane nisīdi saddhiṁ bhikkhusaṁghena. Atha kho Keniyo jaṭilo Buddhapamukhaṁ bhikkhusaṁghaṁ paṇītena khādaniyena

The Lord: 'Tis Sāriputta, whom I bred and reared, [557]
who keeps my Wheel still rolling on its course.

What mind should know, I know; I am what man [558]
should be, and quit of all man should renounce;
—'tis thus that, brahmin, Buddhahood is mine.

All doubts of me dispel; place trust in me. [559]
—To see a Buddha is a boon most rare;

but that rare boon thou may'st behold in me, [560]
who All-Enlighten'd am, of Healers chief,

perfect and peerless, routing Māra's hosts, [561]
all foes subduing;—fear clouds not my bliss.

Sela: Sirs, mark him! Mark how lion-like he speaks, [562]
—this Seer, this Healer, this great Conqueror.

Lives there a man so base as not to trust [563]
at sight fell Māra's matchless conqueror?

Let who will, follow; let the rest depart; [564]
—be mine the Pilgrimage with Wisdom's Lord!

Sela's pupils: If you the All-Enlighten'd take as guide, [565]
ours too be Pilgrimage with Wisdom's Lord.

Sela: Three hundred brahmins, Lord, with outstretched hands [566]
here pray to lead the higher life with thee.

The Lord: That life, so fully preached, is here and now, [567]
yet outside Time. No barren Pilgrimage
is his who lives that life persistently.

So the brahmin Sela and all his following were admitted to the Lord's Community, and confirmed therein.

Now, when night passed away, an excellent meal was prepared in his hermitage by Keniya, who sent to tell the Lord when everything was ready. Then the Lord, early that morning, duly robed and bowl in hand, proceeded to Keniya's hermitage and there sat down on the seat placed for him, accompanied by his train of Almsmen. With his own hands Keniya served the Lord and his Almsmen with that excellent meal without stint till all had

bhojaniyena sahatthā santappesi sampavāresi. Atha kho Keniyo jaṭilo Bhagavantaṁ bhuttāviṁ onītapattapāṇiṁ upagantvā aññataraṁ nīcaṁ āsanaṁ gahetvā ekamantaṁ nisīdi. Ekamantaṁ nisinnaṁ kho Keniyaṁ jaṭilaṁ Bhagavā imāhi gāthāhi anumodi:—

21. Aggihuttamukhā yaññā; Sāvittī chandaso mukhaṁ; [568]
rājā mukhaṁ manussānaṁ; nadīnaṁ sāgaro mukhaṁ;

22. nakkhattānaṁ mukhaṁ cando; ādicco tapataṁ mukhaṁ; [569]
—puññaṁ ākaṁkhamānānaṁ saṁgho ve yajataṁ mukhan ti.

Atha kho Bhagavā Keniyaṁ jaṭilaṁ imāhi gāthāhi anumoditvā, uṭṭhāyâsanā pakkāmi.

Atha kho āyasmā Selo sapariso, eko vūpakaṭṭho appamatto ātāpī pahitatto viharanto, nacirass' eva . . . [*&c. as page 24*] . . . abbhaññāsi. Aññataro ca kho pan' āyasmā Selo sapariso arahataṁ ahosi.

Atha kho āyasmā Selo sapariso yena Bhagavā ten' upasaṁkami, upasaṁkamitvā ekaṁsaṁ cīvaraṁ katvā yena Bhagavā ten' añjalim paṇāmetvā Bhagavantaṁ gāthāhi ajjhabhāsi:

23. Yan taṁ saraṇaṁ āgamha ito aṭṭhami, cakkhumā, [570]
sattarattena Bhagavā dant' amha tava Sāsane.

24. Tuvaṁ Buddho; tuvaṁ Satthā; tuvaṁ Mārâbhibhū Muni; [571]
tuvaṁ anusaye chetvā tiṇṇo tāres' imaṁ pajaṁ.

25. Upadhī te samatikkantā; āsavā te padālitā; [572]
sīho 'si anupādāno pahīnabhayabheravo.

26. Bhikkhavo tisatā ime tiṭṭhanti pañjalīkatā: [573]
—Pāde, vīra, pasārehi, Nāgā vandantu Satthuno ti.

had their fill. When the Lord had eaten and had removed his hands from his alms-bowl, Keniya went to him and, taking a low seat, sat down to one side, and, so seated, was thanked by the Lord in these stanzas:—

In largesse, fire-oblations take first rank; [568]
of Vedic metres Sāvitrī is first;
the king ranks first 'mong men, the sea 'mong streams;

the moon ranks first among the lamps of night; [569]
and first of luminaries ranks the sun.
—For those who merit seek by charities,
gifts to the Order profit most of all.

Having thanked Keniya of the matted-hair in these stanzas, the Lord arose and departed.

Dwelling alone and aloof, strenuous, ardent, and purged of Self, the reverend Sela, with his following, was not long before he won the prize in quest of which young men go forth from home to homelessness as Pilgrims, that prize of prizes which crowns the higher life;—even this did he think out for himself, realize, and attain, and in this did he dwell here and now, convinced that for him rebirth was no more, that he had lived the highest life, that his task was done, and that now there was nothing left of what he once had been. And the reverend Sela, with his following, was numbered among the Arahats.

Then he came with his following to the Lord, and, with his right shoulder respectfully bared and with his folded palms outstretched, addressed the Lord in these stanzas:—

We who a week ago sought refuge, seer, [570]
with thee, re-moulded by thy Doctrine come.

Enlighten'd Master, Sage, o'er Māra's hosts [571]
triumphant! Thou who, wrong propensities
uprooting, for thyself salvation found
and taught mankind to find salvation too!

Thou hast surmounted all that breeds rebirth, [572]
and extirpated Canker-growths within.
With naught to bind thee thrall to life, thou 'rt free
as forest lion from all fears or dread.

Three hundred Almsmen, Lord, with outstretched hands [573]
pray thee, great Victor, forth to stretch thy feet
that these, thy saints, may bow before them here!

(*Note.*—This Sutta recurs verbatim as Sutta No. 92 of the Majjhima Nikāya. Cf. also Vin. i. 245.)

8. Sallasutta

1. Animittam anaññātaṁ maccānaṁ idha jīvitaṁ [574]
kasirañ ca parittañ ca, tañ ca dukkhena saṁyutaṁ.

2. Na hi so upakkamo hoti yena jātā na miyyare; [575]
jaram pi patvā maraṇaṁ; evaṁdhammā hi pāṇino.

3. Phalānam iva pakkānaṁ pāto papatato bhayaṁ, [576]
evaṁ jātānaṁ maccānaṁ niccaṁ maraṇato bhayaṁ.

4. Yathā pi kumbhakārassa katā mattikabhājanā [577]
sabbe bhedanapariyantā, evaṁ maccāna' jīvitaṁ.

5. Daharā ca mahantā ca, ye bālā ye ca paṇḍitā, [578]
sabbe maccuvasaṁ yanti, sabbe maccuparāyanā.

6. Tesaṁ maccuparetānaṁ gacchataṁ paralokato [579]
na pitā tāyate puttaṁ, ñātī vā pana ñātake.

7. Pekkhataṁ yeva ñātīnaṁ passa lālapataṁ puthu [580]
ekameko va maccānaṁ, go vajjho viya niyyati.

8. Evam abbhāhato loko maccunā ca jarāya ca; [581]
—tasmā dhīrā na socanti viditvā lokapariyāyaṁ.

9. Yassa maggaṁ na jānāsi, āgatassa gatassa vā, [582]
ubho ante asampassaṁ niratthaṁ paridevasi.

10. Paridevayamāno ce kañcid atthaṁ udabbahe [583]
sammūḷho hiṁsam attānaṁ, kayira c'enaṁ vicakkhaṇo.

11. Na hi ruṇṇena sokena santiṁ pappoti cetaso, [584]
bhiyy' ass' uppajjate dukkhaṁ, sarīraṁ upahaññati,

12. Kiso vivaṇṇo bhavati hiṁsaṁ attānam attanā; [585]
na tena petā pālenti; niratthā paridevanā.

13. Sokaṁ appajahaṁ jantu bhiyyo dukkhaṁ nigacchati, [586]
anutthunanto kālakataṁ sokassa vasam anvagū.

14. Aññe pi passa gamine yathākammûpage nare [587]
maccuno vasam āgamma, phandante v' idha pāṇine.

15. Yena yena hi maññanti, tato taṁ hoti aññathā; [588]
—etādiso vinābhāvo; passa lokassa pariyāyaṁ.

16. Api ce vassasataṁ jīve, bhiyyo vā pana, māṇavo [589]
ñātisaṁghā vinā hoti; jahāti idha jīvitaṁ.

17. Tasmā arahato sutvā vineyya paridevitaṁ, [590]
petaṁ kālakataṁ disvā: 'na so labbhā mayā' iti.

Sutta 8. The Pangs of Grief

Men cannot calculate, men cannot gauge, [574]
this life's brief troublous span, by woes beset.

By no device can what is born not die, [575]
or length of days annul life's primal law.

Like ripen'd fruits which threaten soon to drop, [576]
the constant threat of death dogs man from birth.

As ev'ry earthen jar the potter shapes [577]
will broken be, so shows the life of man.

Grown men and younglings, wise and simple,—all [578]
are thralls of death, all death's predestin'd prey.

When they in death depart, no sire can save [579]
his son, nor kith save kin, from passing hence.

Mark how—while kin stand round with loud laments— [580]
like kine to slaughter, men are hauled away.

Since death and sure decay assail the world, [581]
the wise, who know its laws, forbear to grieve.

Ye vainly weep, ye vainly wail, your dead, [582]
whose 'Whence' and 'Whither' both elude your ken.

If wailing eased the mourner's self-made pangs, [583]
then, and then only, let the wise wail too.

No; peace of mind comes not by grief and tears, [584]
—which do but add to pain and bring men low.

Though self-sought pangs leave mourners pale and wan, [585]
they succour not the dead;—laments are vain.

By hugging sorrow man to greater pain [586]
proceeds; his mourning leaves him sorrow's slave.

Mark, too, how others, when their hour has come [587]
to dree their mortal weird, in death's grip writhe.

Whate'er men plan, things turn out otherwise; [588]
and so with human loss;—'tis nature's way.

What though life last a hundred years,—or more! [589]
—Bereft of kin, man yields his life at last.

Therefore, give ear to saints;—weep not; reflect, [590]
at sight of death, thou can'st not 'bring him back'.

18. Yathā saraṇaṁ ādittaṁ vārinā parinibbaye, [591]
evam pi dhīro sappañño paṇḍito kusalo naro
khippam uppatitaṁ sokaṁ, vāto tūlaṁ va, dhaṁsaye

19. paridevaṁ pajappañ ca domanassañ ca attano. [592]
Attano sukham esāno abbahe sallam attano.

20. Abbūḷhasallo asito santiṁ pappuyya cetaso [593]
sabbasokaṁ atikkanto asoko hoti nibbuto.

9. Vāseṭṭhasutta

Evam me sutaṁ. Ekaṁ samayaṁ Bhagavā Icchānaṁkale viharati Icchānaṁkalavanasaṇḍe. Tena kho pana samayena sambahulā abhiññātā abhiññātā brāhmaṇamahāsālā Icchānaṁkale paṭivasanti, seyyathîdam: Caṁkī brāhmaṇo, Tārukkho brāhmaṇo, Pokkharasāti brāhmaṇo, Jāṇussoṇi brāhmaṇo, Todeyya-brāhmaṇo, aññe ca abhiññātā abhiññātā brāhmaṇamahāsālā. Atha kho Vāseṭṭha-Bhāradvājānaṁ māṇavānaṁ janghāvihāraṁ anucaṁkamamānānaṁ anuvicaramānānaṁ ayaṁ antarākathā udapādi:—Kathaṁ, bho, brāhmaṇo hotîti? Bhāradvājo māṇavo evam āha:—Yato kho, bho ubhato sujāto hoti mātito ca pitito ca saṁsuddhagahaṇiko yāva sattamā pitāmahayugā, akkhitto anupakkuṭṭho jātivādena, ettāvatā kho, bho, brāhmaṇo hotîti. Vāseṭṭho māṇavo evam āha:—Yato kho, bho, sīlavā ca hoti vatasampanno ca, ettāvatā kho, bho, brāhmaṇo hotîti. N' eva kho asakkhi Bhāradvājo māṇavo Vāseṭṭhaṁ māṇavaṁ saññāpetuṁ, na pana asakkhi Vāseṭṭho māṇavo Bhāradvājaṁ māṇavaṁ saññāpetuṁ. Atha kho Vāseṭṭho māṇavo Bhāradvājaṁ māṇavaṁ āmantesi: Ayaṁ kho, Bhāradvāja, samaṇo Gotamo Sakyaputto Sakyakulā pabbajito Icchānaṁkale viharati Icchānaṁkalavanasaṇḍe. Taṁ kho pana bhavantaṁ Gotamaṁ evaṁ-kalyāṇo kittisaddo abbhuggato—pe—Buddho Bhagavā ti. Āyāma, bho Bhāradvāja, yena samaṇo Gotamo ten' upasaṁkamissāma, upasaṁkamitvā samaṇaṁ Gotamaṁ etam atthaṁ pucchissāma; yathā no samaṇo Gotamo vyākarissati, tathā naṁ dhāressāmâti. Evaṁ bho ti kho Bhāradvājo māṇavo Vāseṭṭhassa māṇavassa paccassosi.

Atha kho Vāseṭṭha-Bhāradvājā māṇavā yena Bhagavā ten' upasaṁkamiṁsu, upasaṁkamitvā Bhagavatā saddhiṁ sammodiṁsu, sammodanīyaṁ kathaṁ sārāṇīyaṁ vītisāretvā ekamantaṁ nisīdiṁsu. Ekamantaṁ nisinno kho Vāseṭṭho māṇavo Bhagavantaṁ gāthāhi ajjhabhāsi:—

1. Anuññāta-patiññātā tevijjā mayam asm' ubho, [594]
—ahaṁ Pokkharasātissa, Tārukkhassâyaṁ māṇavo.

2. Tevijjānaṁ yad akkhātaṁ, tatra kevalino 'smase, [595]
padak' asma veyyākaraṇā jappe ācariyasādisā.

As with their house on fire, men quench the flames [591]
with water, let the stedfast sage be quick
(as wind wafts cotton-down) to banish grief,

wails, cravings, pangs. For his own weal, let him [592]
pluck out the shafts he plants in his own breast.

Those shafts pluck'd out, at ease, with heart at rest, [593]
he grieves not, but, o'ercoming grief, finds Peace.

Sutta 9. What is a Brahmin?

Thus have I heard. Once when the Lord was staying at Icchānankala, in the forests there, a large number of very well-known and wealthy brahmins were also at Icchānankala,—such as Cankī, Tārukkha, Pokkharasāti, Jāṇussoṇi, and Todeyya, with other very well-known and wealthy brahmins.

Now, as the young brahmins Vāseṭṭha and Bhāradvāja were walking and strolling up and down, they fell to discussing what makes a brahmin.

Bhāradvāja maintained that what made a brahmin was pure descent on both sides right back for seven successive generations of forbears, with no break or blemish in his lineage; whereas Vāseṭṭha contended that it was virtue and moral conduct which made a brahmin.

As neither could convince the other, Vāseṭṭha proposed, and Bhāradvāja agreed, to refer the matter to 'the anchorite Gotama', who was now staying in the forests of Icchānankala, and of whom the high repute noised abroad was that he was said to be:—'The Lord, Arahat All-Enlightened . . . (*&c., as at p. 135*) . . . the Lord Buddha.' Let us go to the anchorite Gotama, my good Bhāradvāja, said Vāseṭṭha; and, when we have found him, let us lay the matter before him and accept whatever he shall decide.

So be it, replied Bhāradvāja.

So together the two young brahmins went to the Lord, and, when they were seated after courteous greetings, Vāseṭṭha addressed the Lord in the following stanzas:—

Pokkhárasắti's pupil I; my friend [594]
had Tắrukkhá for master; both of us
in Threefold Lore have passed and so profess;

in all the Threefold Lore adepts are we, [595]
in text and import, each his master's peer.

3. Tesan no jātivādasmiṁ vivādo atthi, Gotama; [596]
'Jātiyā brāhmaṇo hoti' Bhāradvājo iti bhāsati,
ahañ ca 'kammanā' brūmi:—Evaṁ jānāhi, cakkhuma.

4. Te na sakkoma saṁyattuṁ aññamaññaṁ mayaṁ ubho; [597]
bhavantaṁ puṭṭhuṁ āgamhā, 'Sambuddhaṁ' iti vissutaṁ.

5. Candaṁ yathā khayātītaṁ pecca pañjalikā janā [598]
vandamanā namassanti, evaṁ lokasmiṁ Gotamaṁ.

6. Cakkhuṁ loke samuppannaṁ mayaṁ pucchāma Gotamaṁ: [599]
—Jātiyā brāhmaṇo hoti? udāhu bhavati kammanā?
Ajānataṁ no pabrūhi yathā jānemu 'brāhmaṇam'.

7. Tesaṁ vo 'haṁ vyakkhissaṁ anupubbaṁ yathātathaṁ [600]
(*Vāseṭṭhâti Bhagavā*)
jātivibhangaṁ pāṇānaṁ; aññamaññā hi jātiyo.

8. Tiṇarukkhe pi jānātha, na câpi paṭijānare, [601]
lingaṁ jātimayaṁ tesaṁ; aññamaññā hi jātiyo.

9. Tato kīṭe patange ca yāva kunthakipillike; [602]
lingaṁ jātimayaṁ tesaṁ; aññamaññā hi jātiyo.

10. Catuppade pi jānātha khuddake ca mahallake [603]
lingaṁ—pe—

11. Pādūdare pi jānātha urage dīghapiṭṭhike; [604]
lingaṁ—pe—

12. Tato macche pi jānātha odake vārigocare; [605]
lingaṁ—pe—

13. Tato pakkhī pi jānātha pattayāne vihangame; [606]
lingaṁ—pe—

14. Yathā etāsu jātisu lingaṁ jātimayaṁ puthu, [607]
evaṁ na 'tthi manussesu lingaṁ jātimayaṁ puthu.

15. Na kesehi, na sīsena, na kaṇṇehi, nâkkhihi, [608]
na mukhena, na nāsāya na oṭṭhehi bhamūhi vā,

16. na gīvāya, na aṁsehi, n' udarena, na piṭṭhiyā, [609]
na soṇiyā, na urasā, na sambādhe, na methune,

17. na hatthehi, na pādehi, n' angulīhi nakhehi vā, [610]
na janghāhi, na ūrūhi, na vaṇṇena sarena vā,
—lingaṁ jātimayaṁ n' eva yathā aññāsu jātisu.

On birth we differ. Bhāradvāja says [596]
'tis 'birth' that makes a brahmin; I say 'life'.
'Tis thus we stand, O thou who seest all.

Agree we cannot, so an answer crave [597]
from thee, for high Enlightenment renown'd.

For, as with hands in adoration raised [598]
men hail the crescent moon, the world hails thee!

Of Gotama, who brought the seeing Eye, [599]
we ask if *birth* or *life* the 'Brahmin' makes.
Tell us; we know not, but would fain feel sure.

The Lord: Types manifold of divers living things [600]
in order'd sequence I must first unfold,
to show how nature stamps them diverse breeds.

Regard the grass and trees, which ne'er proclaim, [601]
but prove, how nature stamps them diverse breeds.

Pass next to insects, pass from moths to ants; [602]
and see how nature stamps them diverse breeds.

regard four-footed creatures, great and small; [603]
and see how nature stamps them diverse breeds.

regard the snakes whose length on belly goes; [604]
and see how nature stamps them diverse breeds.

pass now to fish that dwell in water's depths; [605]
and see how nature stamps them diverse breeds.

then pass to birds that wing their airy way; [606]
—all show how nature stamps them diverse breeds.

While these thus widely differ, men alone [607]
show not that nature stamps them diverse breeds.

They differ not in hair, head, ears, or eyes, [608]
in mouth or nostrils, not in eyebrows, lips,

throat, shoulders, belly, buttocks, back, or chest, [609]
nor in the parts of shame, female or male,

nor yet in hands or feet, in fingers, nails, [610]
in calves or thighs; in hue, or sound of voice;
—naught shows men stamped by nature diverse breeds;

18. Paccattaṁ sasarīresu manussesv etaṁ na vijjati; [611]
vokārañ ca manussesu samaññāya pavuccati.

19. Yo hi koci manussesu gorakkhaṁ upajīvati, [612]
evaṁ, Vāseṭṭha, jānāhi: 'Kassako' so, na brāhmaṇo.

20. Yo hi koci manussesu puthusippena jīvati, [613]
evaṁ, Vāseṭṭha, jānāhi: 'Sippiko' so, na brāhmaṇo.

21. Yo hi koci manussesu vohāraṁ upajīvati, [614]
evaṁ, Vāseṭṭha, jānāhi: 'Vāṇijo' so, na brāhmaṇo.

22. Yo hi koci manussesu parapessena jīvati, [615]
evaṁ, Vāseṭṭha, jānāhi: 'Pessiko' so, na brāhmaṇo.

23. Yo hi koci manussesu adinnaṁ upajīvati, [616]
evaṁ, Vāseṭṭha, jānāhi: 'Coro' eso, na brāhmaṇo.

24. Yo hi koci manussesu issatthaṁ upajīvati, [617]
evaṁ, Vāseṭṭha, jānāhi: 'Yodhâjīvo', na brāhmaṇo.

25. Yo hi koci manussesu porohiccena jīvati, [618]
evaṁ, Vāseṭṭha, jānāhi: 'Yājako' so, na brāhmaṇo.

26. Yo hi koci manussesu gāmaṁ raṭṭhañ ca bhuñjati, [619]
evaṁ, Vāseṭṭha, jānāhi: 'Rājā' eso, na brāhmaṇo.

27. Na câhaṁ 'Brāhmaṇaṁ' brūmi yonijaṁ mattisambhavaṁ; [620]
'Bhovādi' nāma so hoti, sa ve hoti sakiñcano;
—akiñcanaṁ, anādānaṁ, tam ahaṁ brūmi 'Brāhmaṇaṁ'.

28. Sabbasaṁyojanaṁ chetvā yo ve na paritassati, [621]
sangâtigaṁ, visaṁyuttaṁ,—tam ahaṁ brūmi 'Brāhmaṇaṁ'.

29. Chetvā nandhiṁ varattañ ca sandānaṁ sahanukkamaṁ [622]
ukkhittapalighaṁ buddhaṁ,—tam ahaṁ brūmi 'Brāhmaṇaṁ'.

30. Akkosaṁ vadhabandhañ ca aduṭṭho yo titikkhati, [623]
khantībalaṁ balānīkaṁ,—tam ....

31. Akkodhanaṁ vatavantaṁ sīlavantaṁ anussadaṁ [624]
dantaṁ antimasārīraṁ,—tam ....

32. Vāri pokkharapatte va, āragge-r-iva sāsapo, [625]
yo na lippati kāmesu, tam ....

33. Yo dukkhassa pajānāti idh' eva khayam attano, [626]
pannabhāraṁ visaṁyuttaṁ,—tam ....

nature's diversities leave man untouched; [611]
—except in names, no difference exists.

The man that lives by keeping herds of cows, [612]
—know him as farmer, not as brahmin true.

The man that lives by divers handicrafts, [613]
—know him as tradesman, not as brahmin true.

The man that lives by selling merchandise, [614]
—know him as merchant, not as brahmin true.

The man that lives by service done for hire, [615]
—know him as hireling, not as brahmin true.

The man that lives by taking things not his, [616]
—know him as robber, not as brahmin true.

The man that lives by warlike sword and bow, [617]
—know him as soldier, not as brahmin true.

The man that lives by sacrificial rites, [618]
—know him as chaplain, not as brahmin true.

The man whom realms and broad domains support, [619]
—know him as monarch, not as brahmin true.

Not birth, not parentage, a 'Brahmin' makes; [620]
—birth fosters hauteur, fosters worldliness.
Th' unworldly, trammel-free, is 'Brahmin' true.

True 'Brahmin' call I him who, shackle-free, [621]
by bonds and ties untroubled, lives his life;

—whom yoke and harness, straps and pin, no more [622]
can hamper, since Enlightenment is his;

—who, guiltless, bears abuse and stripes and chains, [623]
with patient meekness armed, in meekness strong;

—who, wrathless, meekly dutiful, and good, [624]
in stainless self-control wears his last clay;

—in whom low pleasure finds no resting-place, [625]
—as off the lotus-leaf the raindrop rolls,
nor rests the mustard-seed on needle's point;

—who knows that, here and now, all Ill is o'er; [626]
whose pack is off his shoulders; who is freed;

34. Gambhīrapaññaṁ medhāviṁ maggâmaggassa kovidaṁ [627]
uttamatthaṁ anuppattaṁ,—tam . . . .

35. Asaṁsaṭṭhaṁ gahaṭṭhehi anāgārehi cûbhayaṁ [628]
anokasāriṁ appicchaṁ,—tam . . . .

36. Nidhāya daṇḍaṁ bhūtesu, tasesu thāvaresu ca, [629]
yo na hanti, na ghāteti,—tam . . . .

37. Aviruddhaṁ viruddhesu, attadaṇḍesu nibbutaṁ, [630]
sâdānesu anādānaṁ,—tam . . . .

38. Yassa rāgo ca doso ca, māno makkho ca, pātito [631]
sāsapor iva āraggā,—tam . . . .

39. Akakkasaṁ viññapaniṁ giraṁ saccaṁ udīraye [632]
yāya nâbhisaje kañci,—tam . . . .

40. Yo ca dīghaṁ va rassaṁ vā aṇuṁthūlaṁ subhâsubhaṁ [633]
loke adinnaṁ nâdiyati,—tam . . . .

41. Āsā yassa na vijjanti, asmiṁ loke paramhi ca, [634]
nirāsayaṁ, visaṁyuttaṁ,—tam . . . .

42. Yassâlayā na vijjanti—aññāya akathaṁkathī— [635]
amatogadhaṁ anuppattaṁ,—tam . . . .

43. Yo 'dha puññañ ca pāpañ ca ubho sangaṁ upaccagā, [636]
asokaṁ virajaṁ suddhaṁ,—tam . . . .

44. Candam va vimalaṁ suddhaṁ vippasannaṁ anāvilaṁ [637]
nandībhavaparikkhīṇaṁ,—tam . . . .

45. Yo imaṁ palipathaṁ duggaṁ saṁsāraṁ moham accagā [638]
tiṇṇo pāragato jhāyī, anejo akathaṁkathī,
anupādāya nibbuto,—tam . . . .

46. Yo 'dha kāme pahatvāna anāgāro paribbaje, [639]
kāmabhavaparikkhīṇaṁ,—tam . . . .

47. Yo 'dha taṇhaṁ pahatvāna anāgāro paribbaje, [640]
taṇhābhavaparikkhīṇaṁ,—tam . . . .

48. Hitvā mānusakaṁ yogaṁ, dibbaṁ yogaṁ upaccagā, [641]
sabbayogavisaṁyuttaṁ,—tam . . . .

49. Hitvā ratiñ ca aratiñ ca, sītibhūtaṁ nirūpadhiṁ, [642]
sabbalokâbhibhuṁ vīraṁ,—tam . . . .

—whose Lore is deep, whose wit is quick, who knows [627]
right paths from wrong, whose feet have reached the goal;

—who mixes not with lay, or homeless, folk; [628]
who has no habitation, scanty wants;

—who shows no violence to weak or strong, [629]
nor kills nor orders death of aught that lives;

—who, raging not when others rage, and calm [630]
'midst turbulence, discards what others clutch;

—from whom lusts, hate, and pride, and spite are fled [631]
—as from the needle's tip the mustard-seed;

—whose gentle, helpful, utterances preach [632]
the Truth, but never wound the list'ner's ear;

—who takes—ungiven—nothing great or small, [633]
or fine or coarse, or fair or foul to view;

—who yearns for nothing here or after death; [634]
without a longing and without a tie;

—who, craving naught, and purged by vision clear [635]
from haunting doubts, has plunged in Deathlessness;

—who, having passed beyond 'works'—good and bad— [636]
is freed from sorrow, inly cleansed, and pure;

—who, calm and pure as is the spotless moon, [637]
has now no longings left to live again;

—who, safe across th' engulfing bogs and sloughs [638]
of rebirth's round and error's trackless maze,
doubt-free on th' Other Shore, in Reverie,
has 'passed away', because life's stuff is spent;

—who, quitting pleasures for the Pilgrim's way, [639]
deems it no pleasure now to live anew;

—who, quitting cravings for the Pilgrim's way, [640]
has now no craving left to live anew;

—who, casting off his human yoke, transcends [641]
all yokes divine,—from ev'ry yoke unyoked;

—who, casting off dislikes and likes, abides [642]
calm and unfever'd, quit of what feeds life,
—hero triumphant o'er the universe;

50. Cutiṁ yo vedi sattānaṁ upapattiñ ca sabbaso [643]
asattaṁ sugataṁ buddhaṁ,—tam . . . .

51. Yassa gatiṁ na jānanti devā gandhabbamānusā, [644]
khīṇāsavaṁ arahantaṁ,—tam . . . .

52. Yassa pure ca pacchā ca majjhe ca na 'tthi kiñcanaṁ, [645]
akiñcanaṁ anādānaṁ,—tam . . . .

53. Usabhaṁ pavaraṁ vīraṁ mahesiṁ vijitāvinaṁ [646]
anejaṁ nahātakaṁ buddhaṁ,—tam . . . .

54. Pubbenivāsaṁ yo vedi, saggâpāyañ ca passati, [647]
atho jātikkhayaṁ patto,—tam ahaṁ brūmi 'Brāhmaṇam'.

---

55. Samaññā h' esā lokasmiṁ nāmagottaṁ pakappitaṁ, [648]
sammuccā samudāgataṁ tattha tattha pakappitaṁ,

56. dīgharattam anusayitaṁ diṭṭhigatam ajānataṁ; [649]
ajānantā no pabrūvanti:—'Jātiyā hoti brāhmaṇo'.

57. Na jaccā 'Brāhmaṇo' hoti, na jaccā hoti abrāhmaṇo; [650]
—kammanā 'Brāhmaṇo' hoti; kammanā hoti abrāhmaṇo.

58. Kassako kammanā hoti; sippiko hoti kammanā; [651]
vāṇijo kammanā hoti; pessiko hoti kammanā;

59. coro pi kammanā hoti; yodhâjīvo pi kammanā; [652]
yājako kammanā hoti; rājā pi hoti kammanā.

60. Evam etaṁ yathābhūtaṁ kammaṁ passanti paṇḍitā, [653]
paṭiccasamuppādadasā, kammavipākakovidā:—

61. Kammanā vattatī loko, kammanā vattatī pajā; [654]
kammanibandhanā sattā, rathass' āṇîva yāyato.

62. Tapena, brahmacariyena, saṁyamena, damena ca, [655]
—etena 'Brāhmaṇo' hoti; etaṁ brāhmaṇam uttamaṁ.

63. Tīhi vijjāhi sampanno, santo, khīṇapunabbhavo [656]
(evaṁ, Vāseṭṭha, jānāhi), Brahmā, Sakko, vijānataṁ.

Evaṁ vutte, Vāseṭṭha-Bhāradvājā māṇavā Bhagavantaṁ etad avocuṁ:—Abhikkantaṁ, bho Gotama,—pe—ete mayaṁ bhavantaṁ Gotamaṁ saraṇaṁ gacchāma, dhammañ ca, bhikkhusaṁghañ ca; upāsake no bhavaṁ Gotamo dhāretu ajjatagge pāṇupete saraṇâgate ti.

—who knows whence creatures come and whither pass, [643]
—from all attachments freed, Enlighten'd, blest;

—whose bourn no gods, no men, no quire on high, [644]
can tell,—the Arahat from Cankers purged;

—whose present, future, past, are swept and clean; [645]
who harbours naught, and hankers after naught;

—who 's first in prowess, hero, victor, sage, [646]
th' unruffled Lord of All-Enlightenment;

—within whose ken are lives he lived long since; [647]
whose vision takes in paradise and hell;
for whom rebirth is dead. *He*'s 'Brahmin true'.

By general consent men's names and clans [648]
as useful designations current passed;

'twas long ere time evolved the novel view, [649]
till then unknown, that birth a 'Brahmin' makes.

—Birth neither Brahmin, nor non-Brahmin, makes; [650]
'tis life and conduct moulds the Brahmin true.

Their lives mould farmers, tradesmen, merchants, serfs; [651]

their lives mould robbers, soldiers, chaplains, kings. [652]

'Tis thus the wise life's causal outcome see, [653]
discern what went before, what follows thence.

Their past decides how men shall fare,—like carts [654]
that needs must travel in the linchpin's wake.

'Tis self-denial, holy life, control, [655]
which make my Brahmin's perfect Brahminhood.

He who has won the Threefold Lore, the Saint [656]
who ne'er shall see rebirth,—*He* Bráhmā is
(to them that know) and Sakka manifest.

Hereupon, the young brahmins Vāseṭṭha and Bhāradvāja said to the Lord:—Wonderful, Gotama; quite wonderful! . . . (*&c., as at p. 25*) . . . accept us as disciples who have found an abiding refuge, from this day forth whilst life shall last.

(*Note.*—This Sutta recurs verbatim as Sutta No. 98 of the Majjhima Nikāya.)

10. Kokāliyasutta

Evam me sutaṁ. Ekaṁ samayaṁ Bhagavā Sāvatthiyaṁ viharati Jetavane Anāthapiṇḍikassa ārāme. Atha kho Kokāliyo bhikkhu yena Bhagavā ten' upasaṁkami, upasaṁkamitvā Bhagavantaṁ abhivādetvā ekamantaṁ nisīdi. Ekamantaṁ nisinno kho Kokāliyo bhikkhu Bhagavantaṁ etad avoca:—Pāpicchā, bhante, Sāriputta-Moggallānā, pāpikānaṁ icchānaṁ vasaṁgatā ti.

Evaṁ vutte Bhagavā Kokāliyaṁ bhikkhuṁ etad avoca:—Mā h' evaṁ, Kokāliya; mā h' evaṁ, Kokāliya; pasādehi, Kokāliya, Sāriputta-Moggallānesu cittaṁ; pesalā Sāriputta-Moggallānā ti.

Dutiyam pi kho Kokāliyo bhikkhu Bhagavantaṁ etad avoca: Kiñcāpi me, bhante, Bhagavā saddhāyiko paccayiko, atha kho pāpicchā va Sāriputta-Moggallānā, pāpikānaṁ icchānaṁ vasaṁgatā ti.

Dutiyam pi kho Bhagavā Kokāliyaṁ bhikkhuṁ etad avoca: Mā h 'evaṁ ... pesalā Sāriputta-Moggallānā ti.

Tatiyaṁ pi kho Kokāliyo bhikkhu Bhagavantaṁ etad avoca: Kiñcāpi me, bhante, Bhagavā ... vasaṁgatā ti.

Tatiyam pi kho Bhagavā Kokāliyaṁ bhikkhuṁ etad avoca: Mā h' evaṁ ... pesalā Sāriputta-Moggallānā ti.

Atha kho Kokāliyo bhikkhu uṭṭhāyâsanā Bhagavantaṁ abhivādetvā padakkhiṇaṁ katvā pakkāmi. Acirapakkantassa ca Kokāliyassa bhikkhuno sāsapamattīhi piḷakāhi sabbo kāyo phuṭo ahosi, sāsapamattiyo hutvā muggamattiyo ahesuṁ, muggamattiyo hutvā kaḷāyamattiyo ahesuṁ, kaḷāyamattiyo hutvā kolaṭṭhimattiyo ahesuṁ, kolaṭṭhimattiyo hutvā kolamattiyo ahesuṁ, kolamattiyo hutvā āmalakamattiyo ahesuṁ, āmalakamattiyo hutvā beḷuvasalāṭukamattiyo ahesuṁ, beḷuvasalāṭukamattiyo hutvā billimattiyo ahesuṁ, billimattiyo hutvā pabhijjiṁsu, pubbañ ca lohitañ ca paggharimsu. Atha kho Kokāliyo bhikkhu ten' eva ābādhena kālam akāsi; kālakato ca Kokāliyo bhikkhu Padumanirayaṁ upapajji Sāriputta-Moggallānesu cittaṁ āghātetvā.

Atha kho Brahmā Sahampati abhikkantāya rattiyā abhikkantavaṇṇo kevalakappaṁ Jetavanaṁ obhāsetvā yena Bhagavā ten' upasaṁkami, upasaṁkamitvā Bhagavantaṁ abhivādetvā ekamantaṁ aṭṭhāsi. Ekamantaṁ ṭhito kho Brahmā Sahampati Bhagavantaṁ etad avoca:—Kokāliyo, bhante, bhikkhu kālakato; kālakato ca, bhante, Kokāliyo bhikkhu Padumanirayaṁ upapanno Sāriputta-Moggallānesu cittaṁ āghātetvā ti. Idam avoca Brahmā Sahampati, idaṁ vatvā Bhagavantaṁ abhivādetvā padakkhiṇaṁ katvā tatth' ev' antaradhāyi.

Atha kho Bhagavā tassā rattiyā accayena bhikkhū āmantesi:—Imaṁ, bhikkhave, rattiṁ Brahmā Sahampati abhikkantāya rattiyā—pe—idam avoca Brahmā Sahampati, idaṁ vatvā maṁ abhivādetvā padakkhiṇaṁ katvā tatth' ev' antaradhāyîti.

Sutta 10. Slander's doom

Thus have I heard. Once while the Lord was staying at Sāvatthī in Jeta's grove in Anāthapiṇḍika's pleasaunce, the Almsman Kokāliya came to the Lord and after salutations took his seat to one side, saying to the Lord:—Sāriputta and Moggallāna, sir, harbour evil desires and are fallen a prey to evil desires.

To this the Lord made answer:—Nay, Kokāliya; do not entertain this feeling against Sāriputta and Moggallāna,—who are good men.

The second time, Kokāliya said:—Although the Lord personally inspires me with trust and confidence, yet Sāriputta and Moggallāna do harbour evil desires and are fallen a prey to evil desires.

A second time the Lord repeated his answer.

A third time Kokāliya made his charge and received the same answer.

Then the Almsman Kokāliya rose up and departed, after saluting the Lord with deep reverence. He had not been gone long before pustules the size of a mustard-seed broke out all over his body, pustules which grew and grew to the size first of a lentil, then of a chick-pea, then of a jujube's kernel, then of a jujube, then of a myrobalan, then of a vilva fruit, and then of a quince;—then they broke, exuding pus and blood. That disease killed the Almsman Kokāliya, who passed hence to the Paduma Purgatory, all because he hardened his heart against Sāriputta and Moggallāna.

As night was waning, Brahmā Sahampati—in surpassing splendour, which flooded the whole of Jeta's grove with radiance—drew nigh to the Lord, saluted him and stood to one side, saying:—'Sir, the Almsman Kokāliya is dead and has passed to the Paduma Purgatory, all because he hardened his heart against Sāriputta and Moggallāna.' So saying, Brahmā Sahampati saluted the Lord with deep reverence and vanished.

When the night had gone, the Lord, addressing the Almsmen, told them of Brahmā Sahampati's visit and of his report of Kokāliya's death and rebirth in the Paduma Purgatory, all because of his animosity against Sāriputta and

Evaṁ vutte aññataro bhikkhu Bhagavantaṁ etad avoca:—Kīvadīghaṁ nu kho, bhante, Padume niraye āyuppamāṇan ti?

Dīghaṁ kho, bhikkhu, Padume niraye āyuppamāṇaṁ; taṁ na sukaraṁ saṁkhātuṁ 'ettakāni vassāni' iti vā, 'ettakāni vassasatāni' iti vā, 'ettakāni vassasahassāni' iti vā, 'ettakāni vassasatasahassāni' iti vā ti.

Sakkā pana, bhante, upamā kātun ti?

Sakkā bhikkhûti, Bhagavā avoca:—Seyyathâpi, bhikkhu, vīsatikhāriko Kosalako tilavāho, tato puriso vassasatassa vassasatassa accayena ekam ekaṁ tilaṁ uddhareyya;—khippataraṁ kho so, bhikkhu, vīsatikhāriko Kosalako tilavāho iminā upakkamena parikkhayaṁ pariyādānaṁ gaccheyya, na tveva eko Abbudo nirayo. Seyyathâpi, bhikkhu, vīsati Abbudā nirayā, evam eko Nirabbudo nirayo; seyyathâpi, bhikkhu, vīsati Nirabbudā nirayā, evam eko Ababo nirayo; seyyathâpi, bhikkhu, vīsati Ababā nirayā, evam eko Ahaho nirayo; seyyathâpi, bhikkhu, vīsati Ahahā nirayā, evam eko Aṭaṭo nirayo; seyyathâpi, bhikkhu, vīsati Aṭaṭā nirayā, evam eko Kumudo nirayo; seyyathâpi, bhikkhu, vīsati Kumudā nirayā, evam eko Sogandhiko nirayo; seyyathâpi, bhikkhu, vīsati Sogandhikā nirayā, evam eko Uppalako nirayo; seyyathâpi, bhikkhu, vīsati Uppalakā nirayā, evam eko Puṇḍarīko nirayo; seyyathâpi, bhikkhu, vīsati Puṇḍarīkā nirayā, evam eko Padumo nirayo. Padumaṁ kho pana, bhikkhu, nirayaṁ Kokāliyo bhikkhu upapanno Sāriputta-Moggallānesu cittaṁ āghātetvā ti.

Idam avoca Bhagavā; idaṁ vatvā Sugato athâparaṁ etad avoca Satthā:—

1. Purisassa hi jātassa kuṭhārī jāyate mukhe [657]
yāya chindati attānaṁ bālo dubbhāsitaṁ bhaṇaṁ.

2. Yo nindiyaṁ pasaṁsati, taṁ vā nindati yo pasaṁsiyo, [658]
vicināti mukhena so kaliṁ, kalinā tena sukhaṁ na vindati.

3. Appamatto ayaṁ kali, [659]
yo akkhesu dhanaparājayo
sabbassâpi sahâpi attanā;
ayam eva mahattaro kali
yo sugatesu manaṁ padosaye.

4. Sataṁ sahassānaṁ Nirabbudānaṁ, [660]
chattiṁsa ca pañca ca Abbudāni
yaṁ ariyagarahī nirayaṁ upeti
vācaṁ manañ ca paṇidhāya pāpakaṁ.

5. Abhūtavādī nirayaṁ upeti, [661]
yo vā pi katvā 'Na karomi' cc āha;
ubho pi te pecca samā bhavanti
nihīnakammā manujā parattha.

Moggallāna. Thereupon, a certain Almsman asked the Lord how long a term of durance had to be spent in the Paduma Purgatory.

A term so long, answered the Lord, that it is not easy to express it in years, or in hundreds, or thousands, or even hundreds of thousands of years.

Could you give some idea of its duration, sir?

Yes, Almsman, answered the Lord. Imagine a Kosalan cartload of twenty measures of sesamum seed, and suppose that at the close of every century one single seed at a time were removed. Well, by this method, the cartload would be exhausted sooner than the term in a One-æon Purgatory,—a score of which last one Nirabbuda Purgatory, and a score of these one Ababa Purgatory, and a score of these one Ahaha Purgatory, and a score of these one Aṭaṭa Purgatory, and a score of these one Kumuda Purgatory, a score of these one Sogandhika Purgatory, a score of these one Uppalaka Purgatory, a score of these one Puṇḍarīka Purgatory,—a score of which last one Paduma Purgatory. Now it was to Paduma that the Almsman Kokāliya passed hence, all because he hardened his heart against Sāriputta and Moggallāna.

Thus spake the Lord; and when the Blessed One had thus spoken, he went on, as Teacher, to say:—

In each man's mouth at birth there grows an axe, [657]
wherewith fools gash themselves by speaking ill.

The tongue which lauds blameworthy folk, or blames [658]
the laudable, ne'er wins felicity.

A trifling doom it is to lose [659]
one's all, and liberty, at dice;
a doom far greater is a heart
at enmity with blessed saints.

An evil tongue, an evil mind, [660]
condemn to hell whoso maligns
the saintly, till full tale is told
of æons spent in Paduma.

False witness leads, like perjury, [661]
to hell; one equal doom awaits
both villainies when this life ends.

6. Yo appaduṭṭhassa narassa dussati [662]
suddhassa posassa ananganassa,
tam eva bālaṁ pacceti pāpaṁ,
—sukhumo rajo paṭivātaṁ va khitto.

7. Yo lobhaguṇe anuyutto [663]
so vacasā paribhāsati aññe
assaddho kadariyo avadaññū
macchari pesuṇiyasmiṁ anuyutto.

8. Mukhadugga, vibhūta-m-anariya, [664]
bhūnahu, pāpaka, dukkatakāri,
purisanta, kali, avajāta,
mā bahu bhāṇ' idha; nerayiko 'si.

9. Rajam ākirasi ahitāya, [665]
sante garahasi kibbisakāri;
bahūni ca duccaritāni caritvā
gañchisi kho papataṁ cirarattaṁ.

10. Na hi nassati kassaci kammaṁ. [666]
Eti ha taṁ, labhat' eva suvāmī;
dukkhaṁ mando paraloke
attani passati kibbisakāri.

11. Ayosaṁku-samāhata-ṭṭhānaṁ [667]
tiṇhadhāraṁ ayasūlam upeti;
atha tatta' ayoguḷasannibhaṁ
bhojanaṁ atthi tathā patirūpaṁ.

12. Na hi vaggu vadanti vadantā; [668]
nâbhijavanti; na tāṇam upenti,
angāre santhate senti,
aggini-samaṁ jalitaṁ pavisanti.

13. Jālena ca onahiyānā [669]
tattha hananti ayomayakūṭehi.
Andhaṁ va timisaṁ āyanti,
taṁ vitataṁ hi yathā mahikāyo.

14. Atha lohamayaṁ pana kumbhiṁ [670]
aggini-samaṁ jalitaṁ pavisanti;
paccanti hi tāsu cirarattaṁ,
aggini-samāsu samuppilavāso.

If wrong be done to meek and pure [662]
and good, the wickedness and guilt
recoils—like dust that 's flung up-wind—
upon the fool who did that wrong.

Reviling goes with covetise, [663]
—with unbelief and stinginess,
with churlishness and avarice,
and acrimonious calumny.

O foul-mouthed, false, ignoble wretch! [664]
Black-hearted, blighting villain, vile,
degraded, infamous! Forbear
to vent words here, thou spawn of hell!

Thou flingest mud malignantly, [665]
decrying virtue, child of sin!
But, after thy career of guilt,
limbo shall be thine age-long doom!

For, no man's deeds are blotted out; [666]
each deed comes home; the doer finds
it waiting him; in worlds to come
the purblind dree their weird of woe.

They pass to where with pegs of steel [667]
they 're trussed; to ease their hunger's pangs,
they 're fed (meet nutriment for such!)
with red-hot balls of flaming steel.

No words of cheer reach these; no zest [668]
impels them forward; shelter 's none;
their bed is embers, their abode
one sheer expanse of blazing fire.

Hell's warders fling a net o'er them, [669]
and with steel hammers pound them sore.
To blinding, murky realms they go,
realms vast as earth's wide-flung expanse.

The Brazen Cauldron's molten fires, [670]
receive them next, in torrid foam
to seethe, as up and down they bob.

15. Atha pubbalohitamisse [671]
tattha kiṁ paccati kibbisakārī.
Yaṁ yan disataṁ adhiseti,
tattha kilissati samphusamāno.

16. Puḷavâvasathe salilasmiṁ [672]
tattha kiṁ paccati kibbisakārī.
Gantuṁ na hi tīram ap' atthi;
sabbasamā hi samantakapallā.

17. Asipattavanaṁ pana tiṇhaṁ [673]
taṁ pavisanti samacchidagattā;
jivhaṁ baḷisena gahetvā
ārajayārajayā vihananti.

18. Atha Vetaraṇiṁ pana duggaṁ [674]
tiṇhadhāraṁ khuradhāraṁ upenti;
tattha mandā papatanti
pāpakarā pāpāni karitvā.

19. Khādanti hi tattha rudante [675]
sāmā sabalā kākoḷagaṇā ca
soṇā sigālā paṭigijjhā,
kulalā vāyasā ca vitudanti.

20. Kicchā vatâyaṁ idha vutti [676]
yaṁ jano passati kibbisakārī.
Tasmā idha jīvitasese
kiccakaro siyā naro, na pamajje.

---

21. Te gaṇitā vidūhi tilavāhā [677]
ye Padume niraye upanītā;
nahutāni hi koṭiyo pañca bhavanti,
dvādasa koṭisatāni pun' aññā.

22. Yāva-dukkhā nirayā idha vuttā, [678]
tattha pi tāva-ciraṁ vasitabbaṁ.
Tasmā sucipesalasādhuguṇesu
vācaṁ manaṁ satataṁ parirakkhe.

Then in a brew of blood and pus [671]
the malefactor 's put to stew;
turn where he may, on ev'ry side
he wallows still in filth and slime.

In water next which teems with worms [672]
the malefactor stews afresh.
He cannot land; he's vaulted in
beneath that limbo's domed expanse.

They enter next the Sword-leaf Wood, [673]
wherein their limbs are lopped away.
The wardens hook them by the tongue
and slash them sore with whirling strokes.

The Caustic Stream, Vetáraṇī,— [674]
whose waters rive and rip,—comes next;
and purblind evil-doers plunge
therein, because of evil done.

They howl as they a banquet make [675]
for hungry ravens, jackals, dogs,
and vultures dusky-hued or pied,
while stabbed by beaks of kites and crows.

This woeful doom awaits in hell [676]
the malefactor! So while yet
men live on earth, let them fulfil
their duties here unflinchingly.

The experts calculate [677]
the term in Paduma
which represents the loads
of seeds of sesamum
to be five myriads
twelve hundred crores of years.

Such are the griding pains [678]
and such the term in hell!
—Wherefore in purity
and love and virtue keep
both mind and tongue alway.

11. Nālakasutta

1. Ānandajāte tidasagaṇe patīte [679]
Sakkañ ca Indaṁ sucivasane ca deve
dussaṁ gahetvā atiriva thomayante
Asito isi addasa divāvihāre.

2. Disvāna deve muditamane udagge [680]
cittiṁ karitvā idam avocâsi tattha:
'Kiṁ devasaṁgho atiriva kallarūpo?
Dussaṁ gahetvā bhamayatha kiṁ paṭicca?

3. Yadā pi āsi asurehi sangamo, [681]
jayo surānaṁ, asurā parājitā,
tadā pi n' etādiso lomahaṁsano.
Kim abbhutaṁ daṭṭhu marū pamoditā?

4. Seḷanti gāyanti ca vādayanti ca [682]
bhujāni poṭhenti ca naccayanti ca.
Pucchāmi vo 'haṁ, Merumuddhavāsine;
dhunātha me saṁsayaṁ khippa, mārisā.'

5. 'So Bodhisatto ratanavaro atulyo [683]
manussaloke hitasukhatāya jāto
Sakyāna' gāme janapade Lumbhineyye!
—Ten' amha tuṭṭhā atiriva kallarūpā.

6. So sabbasattuttamo aggapuggalo [684]
narâsabho sabbapajānam uttamo
vattessati cakkaṁ Isivhaye vane,
nadaṁ va sīho balavā migâdhibhū.'

7. Taṁ saddaṁ sutvā turitam avaṁsari so, [685]
Suddhodanassa tada bhavanaṁ upāgami.
Nisajja tattha idam avocâsi Sakye:
Kuhiṁ kumāro? aham api daṭṭhukāmo.

8. Tato kumāraṁ, jalitam iva suvaṇṇaṁ [686]
ukkāmukhe va sukusalasampahaṭṭhaṁ
daddallamānaṁ siriyā anomavaṇṇaṁ
dassesu' puttaṁ Asitavhayassa Sakyā.

9. Disvā kumāraṁ, sikhim iva pajjalantaṁ, 687]
tārāsabhaṁ va nabhasigamaṁ visuddhaṁ,
suriyaṁ tapantaṁ saradar iv' abbhamuttaṁ,
ānandajāto vipulam alattha pītiṁ.

Sutta 11. Asita's Nunc Dimittis

At noontide Asita the Sage [679]
beheld the joyous Thrice-ten gods
and Sakka-Indra at their head,
waving their spotless robes in glee.

Asita: At sight of their triumphant joy, [680]
he reverently spoke these words:—
What gladdens thus th' assembled gods?
Say why ye wave your garments so.

Not even when the war with fiends [681]
crushed fiends and gave gods victory,
was such excitement shown as now.
What marvel cheers the gods to-day?

They shout and sing to music's strains; [682]
they toss their arms and dance around.
Ye denizens of Meru's peaks,
quick! tell me why; dispel my doubts.

Deities: 'The future Buddha, pearl of pearls, [683]
for peace and weal is born as man,
a Sákyán in Lumbinī.
—And thence our jubilation springs.

This matchless being, chief of men, [684]
hero, supreme o'er beings all,
as with a kingly lion's roar
in Sages' Wood shall start Truth's Wheel.'

When Asita heard this, straight down he went [685]
till he drew nigh Suddhódana's abode,
and, seated there, addressed the Sákyáns:—
Where is the prince? I too would gaze on him.

Thereon, to Asita, that swarthy sage, [686]
the Sákyans shewed the newborn babe, who shone
with golden sheen, like gold by craftsmen wrought,
fresh from the furnace, and exceeding fair.

In joy and zest abounding, Asita [687]
beheld th' effulgent babe,—bright as a flame,
pure as the riding moon, and radiant
as shines the sun in cloudless autumn skies.

10\. Anekasākhañ ca sahassamaṇḍalaṁ [688]
chattaṁ marū dhārayuṁ antalikkhe,
suvaṇṇadaṇḍā vītipatanti cāmarā;
na dissare cāmarachattagāhakā.

11\. Disvā jaṭī Kaṇhasirivhayo isi, [689]
suvaṇṇanekkhaṁ viya paṇḍukambale,
setañ ca chattaṁ dhariyanta' muddhani,
udaggacitto sumano paṭiggahe.

12\. Paṭiggahetvā pana Sakyapungavaṁ [690]
jigiṁsako lakkhaṇamantapāragū
pasannacitto giraṁ abbhudīrayi:—
'Anuttarâyaṁ, dipadānam uttamo'.

13\. Ath' attano gamanaṁ anussaranto [691]
akalyarūpo gaḷayati assukāni.
Disvāna Sakyā isiṁ avocuṁ rudantaṁ:—
'No ce kumāre bhavissati antarāyo?'

14\. Disvāna Sakye isi-m-avoca akalye:— [692]
'Nâhaṁ kumāre ahitam anussarāmi,
na câpi-m-assa bhavissati antarāyo,
na orakâyam. Adhimanasā bhavātha.

15\. Sambodhiyaggaṁ phusissatâyaṁ kumāro; [693]
so dhammacakkaṁ paramavisuddhadassī
vattessatâyaṁ bahujanahitânukampī;
vitthārik' assa bhavissati brahmacariyaṁ.

16\. Mamañ ca āyu na ciraṁ idhâvaseso, [694]
ath' antarā me bhavissati kālakiriyā.
So 'haṁ na sussaṁ asamadhurassa Dhammaṁ;
ten' amhi aṭṭo vyasanagato aghāvī.'

17\. So Sākiyānaṁ vipula' janetvā pītiṁ [695]
antepuramhā niragama brahmacārī.
—So bhāgineyyaṁ sayaṁ anukampamāno
samādapesi asamadhurassa Dhamme:—

18\. " 'Buddho' ti ghosaṁ yada parato suṇāsi [696]
'sambodhipatto vicarati Dhammamaggaṁ',
gantvāna tattha samayaṁ paripucchiyāno
carassu tasmiṁ Bhagavati brahmacariyaṁ."

A canopy aloft the gods [688]
upheld, with ribs of gold to spread
the thousand widths of its expanse,
while fans were waved on wands of gold;
—yet none could see who held, or waved.

Beneath that canopy so white [689]
there lay—like gold on samite laid—
the babe, whom that swart anchorite,
with matted locks, took up with joy.

He took him up; and when his gaze [690]
found marks and signs his lore knew well,
he lifted up his voice and cried:—
'He has no peer! He's mankind's best!'

Here, rising thoughts of his approaching end [691]
reduced the sage to tears, whereat alarmed
the Sákyans asked the weeping sage to say
if danger would beset the new-born child.

Seeing the Sákyans so disquieted, [692]
the sage made answer thus:—No harm to him
can I foresee; no danger threatens him;
no common clay is he;—give heed to me.

To All-Enlightenment this child shall grow; [693]
in Utter Holiness, by pity moved,
Truth's Wheel a-rolling he shall set, and spread
his Saving Rule abroad both far and wide.

But few are my remaining days of life, [694]
and meantime death will end my dwindling span,
nor shall I hear his weighty Doctrine preached.
'Tis only this that saddens me the while.

Cheering the Sákyans with his heart'ning words [695]
the sage from out the precincts passed, to lead
the Higher Life. By pity moved, he bade
his sister's son embrace the matchless Truth:—

"Nephew (said he), when, later, thou shalt hear [696]
that: 'Th' All-Enlighten'd Buddha treads the Path
his Doctrine shows',—go, seek him out, explore
his gospel, lead the higher life with Him."

19. Tenânusiṭṭho hitamanasena tādinā [697]
anāgate paramavisuddhadassinā
so Nālako upacitapuññasañcayo
'Jinam' patikkhaṁ parivasi rakkhitindriyo.

20. Sutvāna ghosaṁ 'Jinavaracakkavattane' [698]
gantvāna disvā isinisabhaṁ pasanno
moneyyaseṭṭhaṁ munipavaraṁ apucchi,
samāgate Asitavhayassa sāsane.

(*Vatthugāthā niṭṭhitā.*)

21. "Aññātam etaṁ vacanaṁ Asitassa yathātathaṁ, [699]
taṁ taṁ, Gotama, pucchāma sabbadhammāna' pāraguṁ:—

22. Anagāriy' upetassa bhikkhācariyaṁ jigiṁsato, [700]
Muni, pabrūhi me puṭṭho moneyyaṁ uttamaṁ padaṁ."

23. Moneyyan te upaññissaṁ (*ti Bhagavā*) [701]
dukkaraṁ durabhisambhavaṁ.
Handa te naṁ pavakkhāmi:—
'Santhambhassu, daḷho bhava'.

24. Samānabhāgaṁ kubbetha gāme akkuṭṭhavanditaṁ; [702]
manopadosaṁ rakkheyya; santo anuṇṇato care.

25. Uccāvacā niccharanti dāye aggisikhûpamā; [703]
nariyo muniṁ palobhenti;—tā su taṁ mā palobhayuṁ.

26. Virato methunā dhammā, hitvā kāme parovare, [704]
aviruddho asāratto pāṇesu tasathāvare,

27. 'yathā ahaṁ tathā ete, yathā ete tathā ahaṁ' [705]
attānaṁ upamaṁ katvā na haneyya na ghātaye.

28. Hitvā icchañ ca lobhañ ca, yattha satto puthujjano, [706]
cakkhumā paṭipajjeyya; tareyya narakaṁ imaṁ.

29. Ūnûdaro mitāhāro appicch' assa alolupo; [707]
sa ve icchāya nicchāto, aniccho hoti nibbuto.

Thus counsell'd by that kindly, helpful saint [697]
(the destined heir of utter holiness)
this Nālaka lived on, in affluence
of garner'd merit, keeping watch o'er Sense,
till He, the future 'Conqueror', should come.

But when news came 'a Conqueror has set [698]
his Wheel of Truth a-rolling', straight he sought,
and found Him,—found Him and, believing, asked
that prince of seers (since now the time once set
by Asita had come):—'What makes "a Sage"?'

(*End of the Introductory verses.*)

Nālaka: What Asita foretold (said Nālaka) [699]
has turned out true! So tell me, Gotama,
(whose mind has fathom'd ev'ry mental state)—

when home is left to lead the Almsman's life, [700]
expound, o Sage, a sage's perfect way.

The Lord: Learn then that perfect way (the Lord replied), [701]
'Tis hard to compass, hard to tread; but still
its secret I'll impart:—'Stand firm; stand fast!'

Come praise, come blame,—still take it all as one. [702]
Let neither mar thine equanimity;
let blame perturb thee not, nor praise inflate.

Though lone the wood, sense-objects great and small [703]
spring up, e'en there, like sudden tongues of fire;
yea, women tempt the solitary sage;
see thou to it that women tempt not thee!

Rejecting carnal joys, to pleasure dead, [704]
with naught that lives to crib or cabin thee

take pattern from thyself; Forbear to slay [705]
—with thine or other's hand—the strong or weak;
but say: These are as I am, I as they!

By shedding all desires and covetise, [706]
pick thine appointed way where fools stick fast.
Let insight guide thee through this hell on earth.

With empty belly, diet spare, few wants, [707]
live temperate. When once desires are quelled,
their passing ushers in the calm of Peace.

30. Sa piṇḍacāraṁ caritvā vanantam abhihāraye [708]
upaṭṭhito rukkhamūlasmiṁ āsanûpagato muni.

31. Sa jhānapasuto dhīro vanante ramito siyā, [709]
jhāyetha rukkhamūlasmiṁ attānam abhitosayaṁ.

32. Tato ratyā vivasane gāmantaṁ abhihāraye; [710]
avhānaṁ nâbhinandeyya abhihārañ ca gāmato.

33. Na muni gāmam āgamma kulesu sahasā care, [711]
ghāsesanaṁ chinnakatho na vācam payutaṁ bhaṇe.

34. 'Alatthaṁ yad, idaṁ sādhu; nâlatthaṁ, kusalām iti'; [712]
ubhayen' eva so tādī rukkhaṁ va upanivattati.

35. Sa pattapāṇī vicaranto, amūgo mūgasammato, [713]
appaṁ dānaṁ na hīḷeyya, dātāraṁ nâvajāniya.

36. Uccāvacā hi paṭipadā Samaṇena pakāsitā, [714]
na pāraṁ diguṇaṁ yanti, na idaṁ ekaguṇaṁ mutaṁ.

37. Yassa ca visatā na 'tthi chinnasotassa bhikkhuno, [715]
kiccâkiccapahīnassa pariḷāho na vijjati.

38. Moneyyan te upaññissaṁ:— (*ti Bhagavā*) [716]
Khuradhārûpamo bhave,
jivhāya tāluṁ āhacca
udare saṁyato siyā,

39. alīnacitto ca siyā, [717]
na câpi bahu cintaye,
nirāmagandho asito
brahmacariyaparāyano.

40. Ekâsanassa sikkhetha, [718]
Samaṇûpāsanassa ca.
Ekattaṁ monam akkhātaṁ.
Eko ce abhiramissasi,

41. atha bhāsihi dasa disā. [719]
Sutvā dhīrānaṁ nigghosaṁ jhāyīnaṁ kāmacāginaṁ
tato hiriñ ca saddhañ ca bhiyyo kubbetha māmako.

42. Tan nadīhi vijānātha sobbhesu padaresu ca: [720]
—saṇantā yanti kussubbhā, tuṇhī yāti mahôdadhi.

Thine alms-round o'er, within thy wood repair [708]
and take thy seat beneath a spreading tree.

There, in those dear recesses, find thy bliss [709]
beneath thy tree in lonely Reverie.

At morn thy village seek, but take no joy [710]
in invitations or in lavish gifts;

race not from door to door; in quest of alms [711]
seal thou thy lips and proffer no request.

'*They gave;*—'twas well! *Refused was I;*—'tis well!' [712]
—thus minded seek, in either case, thy tree.

As—seeming dumb, but nowise dumb at all— [713]
thou goest bowl in hand, disdain no gift
however humble, nor the giver scorn.

My Rule embraces all things great and small; [714]
its single path alone conducts to Peace;
but never once can senses Peace discern.

But when an Almsman, from this welter freed, [715]
has shed his cravings, old anxieties
about behaviour cease; distress departs.

Learn then this perfect way (the Lord went on); [716]
—be like the razor safe within its sheath;
clap tongue to palate, master appetite;

alert of mind, keep random thoughts at bay; [717]
be redolent of virtue, quit of ties,
absorbed in nothing save the Higher Life;

live like true anchorite alone, aloof; [718]
remember: 'Wisdom in Detachment lies'.
And, if in solitude thou takest joy,
north, south, and east, and west thy fame shall spread. [719]

And when thou hearest eulogies of those
who steadfast prove, woo Reverie, and shun
pleasures of sense, let this but stimulate
thy faith and meekness, follower of mine.

From rivers, cataracts, and deeps learn this: [720]
'Loud roar the cataracts; the deeps are dumb'.

43. Yad ūnakaṁ, taṁ saṇati; yaṁ pūraṁ, santam eva taṁ; [721]
aḍḍhakumbhûpamo bālo; rahado pūro va paṇḍito.

44. Yaṁ Samaṇo bahu bhāsati upetaṁ atthasaṁhitaṁ, [722]
jānaṁ so Dhammaṁ deseti, jānaṁ so bahu bhāsati.

45. Yo ca jānaṁ saṁyatatto, jānaṁ na bahu bhāsati, [723]
sa muni monam arahati, sa muni monam ajjhagā ti.

12. Dvayatānupassanāsutta

Evam me sutaṁ. Ekaṁ samayaṁ Bhagavā Sāvatthiyaṁ viharati Pubbârame Migāramātu pāsāde. Tena kho pana samayena Bhagavā tadahuposathe, pannarase puṇṇāya puṇṇamāya rattiyā bhikkhusaṁghaparivuto abbhokāse nisinno hoti. Atha kho Bhagavā tuṇhībhūtaṁ tuṇhībhūtaṁ bhikkhusaṁghaṁ anuviloketvā bhikkhū āmantesi:—Ye te, bhikkhave, kusalā dhammā ariyā niyyānikā sambodhagāmino, tesaṁ vo, bhikkhave, kusalānaṁ dhammānaṁ ariyānaṁ niyyānikānaṁ sambodhagāmīnaṁ kā upanisā savanāyâti?—iti ce, bhikkhave, pucchitāro assu, te evam assu vacanīyā: Yāvad eva dvayatānaṁ dhammānaṁ yathābhūtaṁ ñāṇāyâti. Kiñ ca dvayataṁ vadetha?—"Idaṁ dukkhaṁ, ayaṁ dukkhasamudayo" ti—ayam ekânupassanā; "Ayaṁ dukkhanirodho, ayam dukkhanirodhagāminī paṭipadā ti"—ayaṁ dutiyânupassanā. Evaṁ sammādvayatânupassino kho, bhikkhave, bhikkhuno appamattassa ātāpino pahitattassa viharato dvinnaṁ phalānaṁ aññataraṁ phalaṁ pāṭikaṁkhaṁ,—diṭṭhe va dhamme aññā; sati vā upādisese anāgāmitā ti.

Idam avoca Bhagavā, idaṁ vatvā Sugato, athâparaṁ etad avoca Satthā:—

1. Ye dukkhaṁ na-ppajānanti atho dukkhassa sambhavaṁ, [724]
yattha ca sabbaso dukkhaṁ asesaṁ uparujjhati,
tañ ca Maggaṁ na jānanti dukkhûpasamagāminaṁ,

2. cetovimuttihīnā te atho paññāvimuttiyā; [725]
abhabbā te antakiriyāya; te ve jātijarûpagā.

3. Ye ca dukkhaṁ pajānanti atho dukkhassa sambhavaṁ, [726]
yattha ca sabbaso dukkhaṁ asesaṁ uparujjhati,
tañ ca Maggaṁ pajānanti dukkhûpasamagāminaṁ,

4. cetovimuttisampannā atho paññāvimuttiyā; [727]
bhabbā te antakiriyāya; na te jātijarûpagā.

Yes; emptiness is loud, but fullness, calm; [721]
the fool's a half-filled crock; the sage, a lake.

Whene'er the Anchorite holds forth, his words [722]
are apposite and fraught with deep import;
with knowledge he expounds the Doctrine's gist,
and from the amplitude of knowledge speaks.

But he whose knowledge goes with self-control, [723]
the sage who, though he knows, eschews much speech,
'tis he has wisdom won,—and wisdom found.

Sutta 12. Pairs to grasp

Thus have I heard. Once while the Lord was staying at Sāvatthī in the Old Pleasaunce in the palace of Migāra's Mother, he was sitting out, on the mid-month sabbath evening, among the Almsmen. Observing the Community of Almsmen around him to be wholly silent, the Lord addressed them, saying:—If you are asked, Almsmen, wherefore you listen to righteous, noble, saving, and all-enlightening homilies, your answer should be that you do so in order to comprehend to the full just a single pair of ideas. When asked to what pair you allude, you will reply that the first conception is Ill and its origin, and that the second is Ill's cessation and the path leading to that Cessation. For, if an Almsman fully grasps these two ideas, and if his life is earnest, ardent, and purged of Self, then you may anticipate for him one or other of two results,—either Illumination here and now, or else, if his stuff of existence be not wholly spent, no subsequent return to earth.

Thus spoke the Lord; and when he, the Blessed One, had thus spoken, he went on, as Master, to say:—

For, those who know not Ill and how Ill grows, [724]
who neither know how Ill is stilled and quenched
nor know the Way to lay all Ill to rest,

—those miss Release, alike of heart and mind; [725]
they cannot end it all and reach the goal;
they tramp the round of birth, decay, and death.

But they who know both Ill and how Ill grows, [726]
and also know how Ill is stilled and quenched
and know the Way that lays all Ill to rest;

—these win Release of heart, Release of mind; [727]
these surely end it all and reach the goal;
these nevermore shall know decay and birth.

Siyā aññena pi pariyāyena sammādvayatânupassanā ti?—iti ce, bhikkhave, pucchitāro assu, 'siyā' ti 'ssu vacanīyā. Kathañ ca siyā?—'Yaṁ kiñci dukkhaṁ sambhoti, sabbaṁ upadhipaccayā' ti—ayam ekânupassanā; 'Upadhīnan tveva asesavirāganirodhā na 'tthi dukkhassa sambhavo' ti,—ayaṁ dutiyânupassanā. Evaṁ sammā—pe—athâparaṁ etad avoca Satthā:—

5. Upadhīnidānā pabhavanti dukkhā [728]
ye keci lokasmiṁ anekarūpā.
Yo ve avidvā upadhiṁ karoti,
punappunaṁ dukkham upeti mando.
Tasmā pajānaṁ upadhiṁ na kayirā
dukkhassa jātippabhavânupassī ti.

Siyā aññena pi pariyāyena sammādvayatânupassanā ti?—iti ce, bhikkhave, pucchitāro assu, 'siyā' ti 'ssu vacanīyā. Kathañ ca siyā?—'Yaṁ kiñci dukkhaṁ sambhoti, sabbaṁ avijjāpaccayā' ti—ayam ekânupassanā; 'Avijjāya tveva asesavirāganirodhā na 'tthi dukkhassa sambhavo' ti,—ayaṁ dutiyânupassanā. Evaṁ sammā—pe—athâparaṁ etad avoca Satthā:—

6. Jātimaraṇasaṁsāraṁ ye vajanti punappunaṁ [729]
itthabhāv-aññathābhāvaṁ avijjāy' eva sā gati.

7. Avijjā h' ayaṁ mahāmoho, yen' idaṁ saṁsitaṁ ciraṁ; [730]
vijjāgatā ca ye sattā, nâgacchanti punabbhavan ti.

Siyā aññena pi . . . Kathañ ca siyā?—'Yaṁ kiñci dukkhaṁ sambhoti, sabbaṁ saṁkhārapaccayā' ti—ayam ekânupassanā; 'Saṁkhārānan tveva asesavirāganirodhā na 'tthi dukkhassa sambhavo' ti—ayaṁ dutiyânupassanā. Evaṁ sammā—pe—athâparaṁ etad avoca Satthā:—

8. Yaṁ kiñci dukkhaṁ sambhoti, sabbaṁ saṁkhārapaccayā; [731]
saṁkhārānaṁ nirodhena na 'tthi dukkhassa sambhavo.

9. Etam ādīnavaṁ ñatvā: 'Dukkhaṁ saṁkhārapaccayā', [732]
sabbasaṁkhārasamathā, saññānaṁ uparodhanā,
—evaṁ dukkhakkhayo hoti;—etaṁ ñatvā yathātathaṁ

10. sammaddasā, vedaguno, samma-d-aññāya, paṇḍitā, [733]
abhibhuyya Mārasaṁyogaṁ, nâgacchanti punabbhavan ti.

If you are asked whether there be yet another mode of grasping the two ideas, and in what way, you will reply that the first conception is, that all Ill which comes about is consequent on the Stuff of Existence, whilst the second is that, by the utter and passionless destruction of this underlying stuff, Ill cannot come about. For, if an Almsman fully grasps these two ideas . . . (*&c., as above*) . . . went on, as Master, to say:—

Life's Stuff breeds ev'ry Ill, [728]
—breeds all the Ills there are.
The dolt who witlessly
creates this stuff, piles Ill
on Ill. Create it not,
since thence all Ills are born.

If you are asked whether there be yet another mode of grasping the two ideas, and in what way, you will reply that the first conception is, that all Ill which comes about is consequent on Ignorance, whilst the second is that, by the utter and passionless destruction of Ignorance, Ill cannot come about. For, if an Almsman fully grasps these two ideas . . . (*&c., as above*) . . ., went on, as Master, to say:—

'Tis Ignorance entails the dreary round [729]
—now here, now there—of countless births and deaths.

'Tis Ignorance tricks purblind dolts to trudge [730]
th' inexorable round from life to life;
—but no hereafter waits for him who *knows*.

If you are asked . . . (*similar paragraph about*) Plastic Forces . . . went on, as Master, to say:—

All growths of Ill from Plastic Forces spring; [731]
if Plastic Forces cease, no Ill can grow.

Aware that Plastic Forces breed all Ill, [732]
and clear that Ill's destruction comes about
by stilling each and ev'ry Plastic Force
and breaking down perceptions utterly,

the wise—clear-eyed, equipped with Lore, who *know*— [733]
o'ercoming Māra's yoke, face birth no more.

Siyā aññena pi . . . Kathañ ca siyā?—'Yaṁ kiñci dukkhaṁ sambhoti, sabbaṁ viññāṇapaccayā' ti,—ayam ekânupassanā; 'Viññāṇassa tveva asesavirāganirodhā na 'tthi dukkhassa sambhavo' ti,—ayaṁ dutiyânupassanā. Evaṁ sammā—pe—athâparaṁ etad avoca Satthā:—

11. Yaṁ kiñci dukkhaṁ sambhoti, sabbaṁ viññāṇapaccayā; [734]
viññāṇassa nirodhena na 'tthi dukkhassa sambhavo.

12. Etam ādīnavaṁ ñatvā: 'Dukkhaṁ viññaṇapaccayā', [735]
viññāṇûpasamā bhikkhu nicchāto parinibbuto ti.

Siyā aññena pi . . . Kathañ ca siyā?—'Yaṁ kiñci dukkhaṁ sambhoti, sabbaṁ phassapaccayā' ti—ayam ekânupassanā; 'Phassassa tveva asesavirāganirodhā na 'tthi dukkhassa sambhavo' ti,—ayaṁ dutiyânupassanā. Evaṁ sammā—pe—athâparaṁ etad avoca Satthā:—

13. Tesaṁ phassaparetānaṁ bhavasotânusārinaṁ [736]
kummaggapaṭipannānaṁ ārā saṁyojanakkhayo.

14. Ye ca phassaṁ pariññāya, aññāya upasame ratā, [737]
te ve phassâbhisamayā nicchātā parinibbutā ti.

Siyā aññena pi . . . Kathañ ca siya?—'Yaṁ kiñci dukkhaṁ sambhoti, sabbaṁ vedanāpaccayā' ti,—ayam ekânupassanā; 'Vedanānaṁ tveva asesavirāganirodhā na 'tthi dukkhassa sambhavo' ti,—ayaṁ dutiyânupassanā. Evaṁ sammā—pe—athâparaṁ etad avoca Satthā:—

15. Sukhaṁ vā yadi vā dukkhaṁ adukkhamasukhaṁ saha, [738]
ajjhattañ ca bahiddhā ca yaṁ kiñci atthi veditaṁ,

16. —etaṁ 'dukkhan' ti ñatvāna mosadhammaṁ palokinaṁ [739]
phussa phussa vayaṁ passaṁ, evaṁ tattha vijānāti
vedanānaṁ khayā bhikkhu nicchāto parinibbuto.

Siyā aññena pi . . . Kathañ ca siyā?—'Yaṁ kiñci dukkhaṁ sambhoti, sabbaṁ taṇhāpaccayā' ti,—ayam ekânupassanā; 'Taṇhāya tveva asesavirāganirodhā na 'tthi dukkhassa sambhavo' ti,—ayaṁ dutiyânupassanā. Evaṁ sammā—pe—athâparaṁ etad avoca Satthā:—

17. Taṇhādutiyo puriso, dīgham addhāna' saṁsaraṁ, [740]
itthabhāv-aññathābhāvaṁ saṁsāraṁ nâtivattati.

18. Etam ādīnavaṁ ñatvā: Taṇhā dukkhassa sambhavaṁ, [741]
vītataṇho anādāno sato bhikkhu paribbaje ti.

If you are asked . . . (*similar paragraph about*) Consciousness . . . went on, as Master, to say:—

All growths of Ill from Consciousness arise; [734]
no Ills can grow, if Consciousness be stilled.

Aware that Consciousness begets all Ills, [735]
and clear that Ill's destruction comes about
by stilling Consciousness, the Almsman, quit
of Consciousness, finds everlasting Peace.

If you are asked . . . (*similar paragraph about*) Contact (between a sense and its object in perception) . . . went on, as Master, to say:—

Far, far, from bursting bonds are Contact's thralls, [736]
who drift along life's swirling stream, astray.

But they who Contact comprehend and know, [737]
who fathom all that Contact means,—these, quit
of Contact, find the everlasting Peace.

If you are asked . . . (*similar paragraph about*) Feelings . . . went on, as Master, to say:—

All Feelings, inly bred or from without, [738]
—with pain or pleasure, or with neither, fraught—

the Almsman knows as Ills,—vain fleeting things [739]
that come and go. From Feelings cleansed, he finds,
when feelings die, the everlasting Peace.

If you are asked . . . (*similar paragraph about*) Cravings . . . went on, as Master, to say:—

Wedded to Cravings, man perforce must pass [740]
from life to life, must trudge now here, now there,
yet never ends rebirth's exacting round.

Aware that Ills are Cravings' progeny, [741]
quell Cravings; clutch at nothing; watchful be,
O Almsman, as you go your homeless way.

Siyā aññena pi . . . Kathañ ca siyā?—'Yaṁ kiñci dukkhaṁ sambhoti, sabbaṁ upādānapaccayā' ti,—ayam ekânupassanā; 'Upādānānan tveva asesavirāganirodhā na 'tthi dukkhassa sambhavo' ti,—ayam dutiyânupassanā. Evaṁ sammā—pe—athâparaṁ etad avoca Satthā:—

19. Upādānapaccayā bhavo; bhūto dukkhaṁ nigacchati; [742]
jātassa maraṇaṁ hoti; eso dukkhassa sambhavo.

20. Tasmā upādānakkhayā samma-d-aññāya paṇḍitā [743]
jātikkhayaṁ abhiññāya nâgacchanti punabbhavan ti.

Siyā aññena pi . . . Kathañ ca siyā?—'Yaṁ kiñci dukkhaṁ sambhoti, sabbaṁ ārambhapaccayā' ti,—ayam ekânupassanā; 'Ārambhānan tveva asesavirāganirodhā na 'tthi dukkhassa sambhavo' ti,—ayaṁ dutiyânupassanā. Evaṁ sammā—pe—athâparaṁ etad avoca Satthā:—

21. Yaṁ kiñci dukkhaṁ sambhoti, sabbaṁ ārambhapaccayā; [744]
ārambhānaṁ nirodhena na 'tthi dukkhassa sambhavo.

22. Etam ādīnavaṁ ñatvā: 'Dukkhaṁ ārambhapaccayā', [745]
sabbārambhaṁ paṭinissajja anārambhe vimuttino

23. ucchinnabhavataṇhassa santacittassa bhikkhuno [746]
vitiṇṇo jātisaṁsāro; na 'tthi tassa punabbhavo ti.

Siyā aññena pi . . . Kathañ ca siyā?—'Yaṁ kiñci dukkhaṁ sambhoti, sabbaṁ āhārapaccayā' ti,—ayam ekânupassanā; 'Āhārānan tveva asesavirāganirodhā na 'tthi dukkhassa sambhavo' ti,—ayaṁ dutiyânupassanā. Evaṁ sammā—pe—athâparaṁ etad avoca Satthā:—

24. Yaṁ kiñci dukkhaṁ sambhoti, sabbaṁ āhārapaccayā; [747]
āhārānaṁ nirodhena na 'tthi dukkhassa sambhavo.

25. Etam ādīnavaṁ ñatvā: 'Dukkhaṁ āhārapaccayā', [748]
sabbāhāraṁ pariññāya sabbāhāram anissito,

26. ārogyaṁ samma-d-aññāya āsavānaṁ parikkhayā [749]
saṁkhāya sevī dhammaṭṭho saṁkhaṁ na upeti vedagū ti.

Siyā aññena pi . . . Kathañ ca siyā?—'Yaṁ kiñci dukkhaṁ sambhoti, sabbaṁ iñjitapaccayā' ti,—ayam ekânupassanā; 'Iñjitānan tveva asesavirāganirodhā na 'tthi dukkhassa sambhavo' ti,—ayaṁ dutiyânupassanā. Evam sammā—pe—athâparaṁ etad avoca Satthā:—

27. Yaṁ kiñci dukkhaṁ sambhoti, sabbaṁ iñjitapaccayā; [750]
iñjitānaṁ nirodhena na 'tthi dukkhassa sambhavo.

If you are asked . . . (*similar paragraph about*) Life's Fuel . . . went on, as Master, to say:—

Life's Fuel feeds existence; what exists [742]
meets Ills; what 's born must die; and so springs Ill.

The wise, who see that Fuel's stoppage stops [743]
rebirth, are saved by insight from rebirth.

If you are asked . . . (*similar paragraph about*) toiling and moiling (at good works for 'merit's sake') . . . went on, as Master, to say:—

All growths of Ill from quest of 'merit' spring; [744]
if 'merit's' quest be stopped, no Ill can grow.

Marking how 'merit's' baleful quest breeds Ills, [745]
the Almsman who discards it all and wins

Release, who craves no more for life renewed [746]
but garners peace of heart, has passsed beyond
rebirth and ne'er again shall be reborn.

If you are asked . . . (*similar paragraph about*) Sustenance . . . went on, as Master, to say:—

All growths of Ill from Sustenance proceed; [747]
if Sustenance be stopped, no Ills can grow.

Marking how baleful Sustenance breeds Ill, [748]
—plumb, comprehend, forswear all Sustenance!

Know inward Health by casting Cankers out; [749]
walk circumspectly; keep the faith; for, so,
by Lore the sage transcends the scheme of things.

If you are asked . . . (*similar paragraph about*) Waverings . . . went on, as Master, to say:—

All growths of Ill from Waverings proceed; [750]
if Waverings be stilled, no Ills can grow.

28. Etam ādīnavaṁ ñatvā: 'Dukkhaṁ iñjitapaccayā', [751]
tasmā ejaṁ ossajja, saṁkhāre uparundhiya,
anejo anupādāno sato bhikkhu paribbaje ti.

Siyā aññena pi . . . Kathañ ca siyā?—'Nissitassa calitaṁ hotîti',—ayam ekânupassanā; 'Anissito na calatîti',—ayaṁ dutiyânupassanā. Evaṁ sammā —pe—athâparaṁ etad avoca Satthā:—

29. Anissito na calati; nissito ca upādiyaṁ [752]
itthabhāvaññathābhāvaṁ saṁsāraṁ nâtivattati.

30. Etam ādīnavaṁ ñatvā: 'Nissayesu mahabbhayaṁ', [753]
anissito anupādāno sato bhikkhu paribbaje ti.

Siyā aññena pi . . . Kathañ ca siyā?—'Rūpehi, bhikkhave, āruppā santatarā' ti,—ayam ekânupassanā; 'Āruppehi nirodho santataro' ti,—ayaṁ dutiyânupassanā. Evaṁ sammā—pe—athâparaṁ etad avoca Satthā:—

31. Ye ca rūpûpagā sattā ye ca āruppavāsino, [754]
nirodhaṁ appajānantā āgantāro punabbhavaṁ.

32. Ye ca rūpe pariññāya arūpesu susaṇṭhitā, [755]
nirodhe ye vimuccanti, te janā maccuhāyino ti.

Siyā aññena pi . . . Kathañ ca siya?—Yaṁ, bhikkhave, sadevakassa lokassa samārakassa sabrahmakassa sassamaṇabrāhmiṇiyā pajāya sadevamanussāya: 'Idaṁ saccan' ti upanijjhāyitaṁ, tadam ariyānaṁ: 'Etaṁ musā' ti yathābhūtaṁ sammappaññāya suddiṭṭhaṁ,—ayam ekânupassanā; 'Yaṁ, bhikkhave, sadevakassa—pe—sadevamanussāya: "Idaṁ musā" ti upanijjhāyitaṁ, tadam ariyānaṁ: "Etaṁ saccan" ti yathābhūtaṁ sammappaññāya suddiṭṭhaṁ', ayaṁ dutiyânupassanā. Evaṁ sammā—pe—athâparaṁ etad avoca Satthā:—

33. Anattani attamānaṁ passa lokaṁ sadevakaṁ [756]
niviṭṭhaṁ nāmarūpasmiṁ 'Idaṁ saccan' ti maññati.

34. Yena yena hi maññanti, tato taṁ hoti aññathā; [757]
taṁ hi tassa musā hoti, mosadhammaṁ hi ittaraṁ.

35. Amosadhammaṁ nibbānaṁ;—tad ariyā saccato vidū, [758]
te ve saccâbhisamayā nicchātā parinibbutā ti.

Marking how baleful Waverings breed Ills, [751]
banish distraction; quench each plastic force.
Still unperturbed, still passionless, alert,
and watchful, Almsman, go your homeless way.

If you are asked . . . (*similar paragraph about*) Quaking . . . went on, as Master, to say:—

No Quakings trouble independent minds; [752]
but thralls must tramp life's rounds, now here now there.

Marking how baleful thraldom fosters Ills, [753]
in independence, Almsman, unattached,
alert, and watchful, go your homeless way.

If you are asked whether there is yet another way of grasping the two ideas, and in what way, you will reply that the first conception is that the Formless is calmer than what has Form, whilst the second is that Cessation is calmer than the Formless. For, if an Almsman fully grasps these two ideas . . . (*&c., as above*) . . . went on, as Master, to say:—

The denizens of Form and Formless worlds [754]
blind to Cessation, face rebirth anew.

But they who, versed in Form and Formlessness, [755]
have in Cessation found Deliverance,
in triumph leave behind them Death's domain.

If you are asked whether there is yet another mode of grasping the two ideas, and in what way, you will reply that, first, what the world at large deems Truth has been rightly viewed as falsehood by the Noble through their consummate comprehension, whilst, secondly, the Noble hail as Truth what the world accounts falsehood. For, if an Almsman fully grasps these two ideas . . . (*&c., as above*) . . . went on, as Master, to say:—

How pride of Self (where Self is none) inflates [756]
the world of gods and men! How sure they feel
of personality's undoubted truth!

Picture it as they will, it's all a lie! [757]
—A lie because all fleeting things are false.

No lie 's Nirvana! This the Noble know, [758]
—they whom from hankerings the Noble Truths
have freed, and crowned with everlasting Peace.

Siyā aññena pi pariyāyena sammādvayatânupassanā ti?—Iti ce, bhikkhave, pucchitāro assu, 'siyā' ti 'ssu vacanīyā. Kathañ ca siyā?—Yaṁ, bhikkhave, sadevakassa—pe—sadevamanussāya 'Idaṁ sukhan' ti upanijjhāyitaṁ, tadam ariyānaṁ 'Etaṁ dukkhan' ti yathābhūtaṁ sammappaññāya suddiṭṭhaṁ;—ayam ekânupassanā; Yaṁ, bhikkhave, sadevakassa—pe—sadevamanussāya 'Idam dukkhan' ti upanijjhāyitaṁ, tadam ariyānaṁ 'Etaṁ sukhan' ti yathāpaññāya suddiṭṭhaṁ;—ayaṁ dutiyânupassanā. Evaṁ sammādvayatânupassino kho, bhikkhave, bhikkhuno appamattassa ātāpino pahitattassa viharato dvinnaṁ phalānaṁ aññataraṁ phalaṁ pāṭikaṁkhaṁ,—diṭṭhe va dhamme aññā; sati vā upādisese anāgāmitā ti.

Idam avoca Bhagavā, idaṁ vatvā Sugato athâparaṁ etad avoca Satthā:—

36. Rūpā saddā rasā gandhā phassā dhammā ca kevalā [759]
iṭṭhā kantā manāpā ca, yāvat' 'atthîti' vuccati.

37. Sadevakassa lokassa ete vo sukhasammatā; [760]
yattha c' ete nirujjhanti, taṁ nesaṁ dukkhasammataṁ.

38. 'Sukhan' ti diṭṭhaṁ ariyehi sakkāyass' uparodhanaṁ; [761]
paccanīkam idaṁ hoti sabbalokena passataṁ.

39. Yam pare 'sukhato' āhu, tad ariyā āhu 'dukkhato'; [762]
yam pare 'dukkhato' āhu, tad ariyā 'sukhato' vidū.
—Passa dhammaṁ durājānaṁ; sampamūḷh' ettha aviddasū.

40. Nivutānaṁ tamo hoti, andhakāro apassataṁ; [763]
satañ ca vivaṭaṁ hoti, āloko passatām iva;
santike na vijānanti magā Dhammass' akovidā.

41. Bhavarāgaparetehi bhavasotânusārihi [764]
Māradheyyânupannehi nâyaṁ Dhammo susambudho.

42. Ko nu, aññatra-m-ariyehi, padaṁ sambuddhuṁ arahati, [765]
yaṁ padaṁ samma-d-aññāya parinibbanti anāsavā ti?

Idam avoca Bhagavā. Attamanā te bhikkhū Bhagavato bhāsitaṁ abhinanduṁ. Imasmiṁ kho pana veyyākaraṇasmiṁ bhaññamāne saṭṭhimattānaṁ bhikkhūnaṁ anupādāya āsavehi cittāni vimucciṁsu.

Mahāvaggo tatiyo

If you are asked whether there is yet another mode of grasping the two ideas, and in what way, you will reply that, first, what the world at large deems Weal has been rightly viewed as Ill by the Noble through their consummate comprehension, whilst, secondly, the Noble hail as Weal what the world accounts Ill. For, if an Almsman fully grasps these two ideas, and if his life is earnest, ardent, and purged of Self, then you may anticipate for him one or other of two results,—either Illumination here and now, or else—if his stuff of existence be not wholly spent—no subsequent return to earth.

Thus spake the Lord; and when he, the Blessed One, had thus spoken, he went on, as Master, to say:—

Forms, sounds, tastes, smell, touch, thoughts—please, charm, and cheer, [759]
whilst deemed t' exist and have reality.

The world accounts them boons, them hails as Weal. [760]
But when they pass away, they 're ranked as Ills!

The Noble rank as Weal the utter rout [761]
of personality;—on this the Seer
joins issue with the purblind world at large.

The Noble count as 'Ill' the worldling's 'Weal'; [762]
the worldling's 'Ill' the Noble hail as 'Weal'.
—This puzzling thought perplexes empty pates.

Behind the veil is gloom; th' unseeing dwell [763]
in utter darkness. All is clear as day
to virtue's eye, but hid—though nigh at hand—
from brutish strangers to the Doctrine's truth.

This Truth eludes the ken of those who pine [764]
for life's continuance, who drift along
life's swirling stream in Māra's deadly grip.

Who, save the Noble, has a right to know [765]
how, Cankerless, men pass away—to Peace?

Thus spoke the Lord. Glad at heart, those Almsmen rejoiced in what the Lord had said. During this exposition, the hearts of some three score Almsmen were delivered from Cankers once for all.

End of the Long Book

IV. AṬṬHAKAVAGGA

1. Kāmasutta

1. Kāmaṁ kāmayamānassa tassa ce taṁ samijjhati, [766]
addhā pītimano hoti laddhā macco yad icchati.

2. Tassa ce kāmayānassa chandajātassa jantuno [767]
te kāmā parihāyanti, sallaviddho va ruppati.

3. Yo kāme parivajjeti—sappassêva padā siro—, [768]
so imaṁ visattikaṁ loke sato samativattati.

4. Khettaṁ vatthuṁ hiraññaṁ vā gavâssaṁ dāsaporisaṁ [769]
thiyo bandhū puthū kāme yo naro anugijjhati,

5. abalā va naṁ balīyanti, maddante naṁ parissayā; [770]
tato naṁ dukkhaṁ anveti, nāvaṁ bhinnam ivôdakaṁ.

6. Tasmā jantu sadā sato kāmāni parivajjaye; [771]
te pahāya tare oghaṁ, nāvaṁ sitvā va, pāragū ti.

2. Guhaṭṭhakasutta

1. Satto guhāyaṁ bahunâbhichanno [772]
tiṭṭhaṁ naro mohanasmiṁ pagāḷho
dūre vivekā hi tathāvidho so;
kāmā hi loke na hi suppahāyā.

2. Icchānidānā bhavasātabaddhā [773]
te duppamuñcā, na hi aññamokkhā,
pacchā pure vā pi apekkhamānā
ime va kāme purime va jappaṁ.

3. Kāmesu giddhā pasutā pamūḷhā [774]
avadāniyā te visame niviṭṭhā
dukkhûpanītā paridevayanti:—
Kiṁ su bhavissāma ito cutāse?

IV. THE BOOK OF OCTADS

Sutta 1. Desires

The man whose heart's desires are gratified [766]
is glad indeed to see success secured.

But, if his heart's desires and aims be foiled, [767]
he smarts as if a dart had wounded him.

Yet, should he shun desires as he would shun [768]
a snake's head underfoot, by vigilance
he overcomes the world's seductive lures.

Whoso with boundless appetite desires [769]
fields, lands, or gold, herds, horses, women, serfs,
and kinsfolk,—him tumultuous desires

(weak though they seem) o'ercome at last; they crush [770]
their victim. Hereon Ills come surging in,
like waves that flood some wrecked ship's crazy hold.

Therefore by watchfulness discard desires; [771]
expel them; bale your ship; and cross the Flood
to safety's haven on the Further Shore.

Sutta 2. The Octad of the Den

Cooped in a den of clay [772]
o'ergrown with growths and bogged
in crassness dense, a man
is far from inward peace.
For, hard indeed it is
to give up pleasures here.

The creatures of desire, [773]
mere slaves of mundane joys,
shall scarce be saved,—since none
by others can be saved,
who ask to live To-day
or Yesterday afresh.

Through pleasure's hot pursuit, [774]
its frenzied votaries
close-fisted grow and base,
till, plunged in Ills, they cry:—
'What shall we be, when dead?'

4. Tasmā hi sikkhetha idh' eva jantu: [775]
yaṁ kiñci jaññā 'visaman' ti loke
na tassa hetu visamaṁ careyya;
—appaṁ h' idaṁ jīvitam āhu dhīrā.

5. Passāmi loke pariphandamānaṁ [776]
pajaṁ imaṁ taṇhagataṁ bhavesu;
hīnā narā maccumukhe lapanti
avītataṇhāse bhavâbhavesu.

6. Mamāyite passatha phandamāne, [777]
macche va appodake khīṇasote;
etam pi disvā amamo careyya
bhavesu āsattim akubbamāno.

7. Ubhosu antesu vineyya chandaṁ, [778]
phassaṁ pariññāya anānugiddho,
yad attagarahī tad akubbamāno
na lippatī diṭṭhasutesu dhīro.

8. Saññaṁ pariññā vitareyya oghaṁ [779]
pariggahesu muni nôpalitto
abbūḷhasallo caraṁ appamatto
nâsiṁsatī lokam imaṁ parañ ca.

3. Duṭṭhaṭṭhakasutta

1. Vadanti ve duṭṭhamanā pi eke, [780]
aññe pi ve saccamanā vadanti;
vādañ ca jātaṁ muni no upeti,
tasmā munī na 'tthi khilo kuhiñci.

2. Sakaṁ hi diṭṭhiṁ katham accayeyya [781]
chandânunīto ruciyā niviṭṭho
sayaṁ samattāni pakubbamāno?
—Yathā hi jāneyya, tathā vadeyya.

So learn betimes, learn here [775]
and now. Let nothing base
tempt thee to baseness here.
—This life is brief, say seers.

I see distracted folk [776]
agog for lives to come,
—abjects who howl in face
of death, through lust to live.

Parting from cherished things [777]
others distracts,—like fish
stranded when streams give out.
Mark this and self-less walk,
nor pine for lives to come.

When feelings tempt no more [778]
—at start or close—because
all taste for them is dead,
—then, doing nothing which
his heart condemns, the sage
is proof 'gainst things of sense.

Aware of senses' scope, [779]
and safe across the Flood,
unstained by hankerings,
the sage—his barb plucked out—
strides bravely on, nor craves
life here, or anywhere.

Sutta 3. The Octad of Malice

From spite, or honestly, [780]
are charges spread abroad;
but, as all fail to hit
the sage, his heart is light.

When inclination prompts [781]
and self-will reigns, shall men
desert their cherished views?
—Their outlook shapes their speech.

3. Yo attano sīlavatāni jantu [782]
anānupuṭṭho ca paresa' pāvā,
'anariyadhammaṁ' kusalā tam āhu
yo ātumānaṁ sayam eva pāvā.

4. Santo ca bhikkhu abhinibbutatto, [783]
'iti 'han' ti sīlesu akatthamāno,
tam 'ariyadhammaṁ' kusalā vadanti,
yass' ussadā na 'tthi kuhiñci loke.

5. Pakappitā saṁkhatā yassa dhammā [784]
purakkhatā santi avīvadātā;
yad attani passati ānisaṁsaṁ,
tan nissito kuppa-paṭicca-santiṁ.

6. Diṭṭhīnivesā na hi svâtivattā, [785]
dhammesu niccheyya samuggahītaṁ.
Tasmā naro tesu nivesanesu
nirassati ādiyati-cca dhammaṁ.

7. Dhonassa hi na 'tthi kuhiñci loke [786]
pakappitā diṭṭhi bhavâbhavesu;
māyañ ca mānañ ca pahāya dhono
sa kena gaccheyya?—Anūpayo so.

8. Upayo hi dhammesu upeti vādaṁ; [787]
anūpayaṁ kena kathaṁ vadeyya?
Attaṁ nirattaṁ na hi tassa atthi;
—adhosi so diṭṭhim idh' eva sabbaṁ.

4. Suddhaṭṭhakasutta

1. 'Passāmi suddhaṁ paramaṁ arogaṁ; [788]
diṭṭhena saṁsuddhi narassa hoti!'
—evâbhijānaṁ 'paramaṇ' ti ñatvā,
suddhânupassîti pacceti ñāṇaṁ.

The man who sings, unasked, [782]
his virtue's praise, is styled
'ignoble' by adepts
for talking of himself.

The Almsman true, at peace, [783]
not vaunting virtues rare,
adepts as 'noble' hail,
because he 's not puffed up.

When wrong conceptions fill [784]
the mind with prejudice,
the man who looks to find
a blessing there, builds hopes
of Peace on shifting sands.

As rooted prejudice [785]
is hard to quell, a man
should test ideas he holds,
discarding freely, till
he holds the Doctrine's truth.

The inly-washen saint, [786]
now freed from fancies fond
of life hereafter, stripped
of pride and error,—how
place him? He stands apart!

Their mental states define [787]
men with propensities.
But how define the man
with none?—who nought asserts
and naught denies, but waves
all theories aside?

Sutta 4. The Octad of Purity

'Lo! man pure, perfect, hale, [788]
made pure by views he holds!'
—Convinced 'perfection 's found'
through such imaginings,
'experts in purity'
expect to come to *know*!

2. Diṭṭhena ce suddhi narassa hoti, [789]
ñāṇena vā so pajahāti dukkhaṁ,
aññena so sujjhati sôpadhīko;
—diṭṭhī hi naṁ pāva tathā vadānaṁ.

3. Na Brāhmaṇo aññato suddhim āha, [790]
—diṭṭhe sute sīlavate mute vā;
puññe ca pāpe ca anūpalitto
attañjaho na-y-idha pakubbamāno.

4. Purimaṁ pahāya aparaṁ sitāse [791]
ejânugā te na taranti sangaṁ;
te uggahāyanti nirassajanti
kapîva sākhaṁ pamukhaṁ gahāya.

5. Sayaṁ samādāya vatāni jantu [792]
uccâvacaṁ gacchati saññasatto;
vidvā ca vedehi samecca Dhammaṁ
na uccâvacaṁ gacchati bhūripañño.

6. Sa sabbadhammesu visenibhūto, [793]
yaṁ kiñci diṭṭhaṁ va sutaṁ mutaṁ vā,
tam eva' dassiṁ vivaṭaṁ carantaṁ,—
kenîdha lokasmiṁ vikappayeyya?

7. Na kappayanti, na purekkharonti, [794]
'accantasuddhîti' na te vadanti;
ādānaganthaṁ gathitaṁ visajja
āsaṁ na kubbanti kuhiñci loke.

8. Sīmātigo Brāhmaṇo; tassa na 'tthi [795]
ñatvā ca disvā ca samuggahītaṁ;
na rāgarāgī, na virāgaratto;
tassîdaṁ na 'tthi param uggahītaṁ.

If dogma makes men pure, [789]
or if such lore ends Ill,
then something not the Path
makes pure an earthy man
whose views give him the lie.

'The Path—not things of sense— [790]
alone brings purity,'
our self-less 'Brahmin' says,
by 'merit's' quest unsmirched,
aloof from mundane ends.

Chopping and changing fails [791]
to calm distracted folk,
—who now hold fast to this,
and now to that, like apes
that skip from bough to bough.

Self-prompted, slaves of Sense [792]
pursue austerities.
Not so the wise, who *know*,
who grasp the Doctrine's truth.

When once man's thought transcends [793]
what sense-impressions bring,
when, thus inspired, he goes
his clear-eyed way,—what lure
can now unsettle him?

No idols these set up, [794]
no 'final purity'
do they affirm, who burst
the chains of hankering
and yearn for nothing more.

Sinless, the Brahmin true, [795]
through ken and vision, grasps
at nothing; passion-free,
he does not plume himself
on being passionless.
No more has he to learn.

5. Paramaṭṭhakasutta

1. 'Paraman' ti diṭṭhīsu paribbasāno [796]
yad uttariṁkurute jantu loke,
'hīnā' ti aññe tato sabba-m-āha.
Tasmā vivādāni avītivatto.

2. Yad attanī passati ānisaṁsaṁ [797]
diṭṭhe sute sīlavate mute vā,
tad eva so tattha samuggahāya
nihīnato passati sabbam aññaṁ.

3. Taṁ vâpi 'ganthaṁ' kusalā vadanti [798]
yaṁ nissito passati: Hīnam aññaṁ.
Tasmā hi diṭṭhaṁ va sutaṁ mutaṁ vā
sīlabbataṁ bhikkhu na nissayeyya.

4. Diṭṭhim pi lokasmiṁ na kappayeyya [799]
ñāṇena vā sīlavatena vā pi;
'samo' ti attānaṁ anūpaneyya,
'hīno' na maññetha 'visesi' vā pi.

5. Attaṁ pahāya anupādiyāno [800]
ñāṇe pi so nissayaṁ no karoti;
sa ve viyattesu na vaggasārī,
diṭṭhim pi so na pacceti kiñci.

6. Yassûbhayante paṇidhîdha na 'tthi [801]
bhavâbhavāya idha vā huraṁ vā,
nivesanā tassa na santi keci,
dhammesu niccheyya samuggahītaṁ;

7. tassîdha diṭṭhe va sute mute vā [802]
pakappitā na 'tthi aṇū pi saññā;
—taṁ Brāhmaṇaṁ diṭṭhim anādiyānaṁ
kenîdha lokasmiṁ vikappayeyya?

8. Na kappayanti na purekkharonti; [803]
dhammā pi tesaṁ na paṭicchitāse;
na Brāhmaṇo sīlavatena neyyo;
pāraṁgato na pacceti tādī.

6. Jarāsutta

1. Appaṁ vata jīvitaṁ idaṁ; [804]
oraṁ vassasatā pi miyyati;
yo ce pi aticca jīvati,
atha kho so jarasā pi miyyati.

Sutta 5. The Octad of Perfection

The partisan who hugs [796]
the creed he fancies most,
brands rival creeds as 'stuff'.
And so strife dogs his days.

Whatever good he finds [797]
in works or things of sense,
on that he fastens, set
on scouting all things else.

Adepts dismiss as 'clogs' [798]
his claims and arrogance.
So, Almsman, do not build
on works and things of sense;

nor rear on lore or works [799]
a speculative view;
nor claim to be 'as good'
or 'worse' or 'better far'.

Unprejudiced and free, [800]
not based on learning's stores,
owning no sect or school,
holding no theories;

when pray'rs for future life [801]
—on earth, or elsewhere—cease,
when scrutiny of 'creeds'
no dogmas leaves behind;

when things of sense all fail [802]
to wake a conscious thought,
—how place this Brahmin true,
who holds no theories?

Such frame, approve, adopt [803]
no theories at all.
Works prove no 'Brahmin true',
who—saved—returns no more.

Sutta 6. Vita Brevis

Man's years are few, [804]
less than a hundred;
should he drag on,
th' end still is certain.

2. Socanti janā mamāyite; [805]
na hi santi niccā pariggahā;
vinābhāvasantam ev' idaṁ;
iti disvā nâgāram āvase.

3. Maraṇena pi taṁ pahīyati [806]
yaṁ puriso: Mama-y-idan ti maññati.
Evam pi viditvā paṇḍito
na mamattāya nametha māmako.

4. Supinena yathā pi sangataṁ [807]
paṭibuddho puriso na passati,
evam pi piyāyitaṁ janaṁ
petaṁ kālakataṁ na passati.

5. Diṭṭhā pi sutā pi te janā [808]
yesaṁ nāmam idaṁ pavuccati;
nāmam evâvasissati
akkheyyaṁ petassa jantuno.

6. Sokaparidevamaccharaṁ [809]
na jahanti giddhā mamāyite;
tasmā munayo, pariggahaṁ
hitvā, acariṁsu khemadassino.

7. Patilīnacarassa bhikkhuno [810]
bhajamānassa vivittam āsanaṁ
sāmaggiyam āhu tassa taṁ,
yo attānaṁ bhavane na dassaye.

8. Sabbattha muni anissito [811]
na piyaṁ kubbati, no pi appiyaṁ;
tasmiṁ paridevamaccharaṁ,
paṇṇe vāri yathā, na lippati.

9. Udabindu yathā pi pokkhare [812]
padume vāri yathā na lippati,
evaṁ muni nôpalippati
yadidaṁ diṭṭhasutaṁmutesu vā.

10. Dhono na hi tena maññati [813]
yadidaṁ diṭṭhasutaṁmutesu vā,
nâññena visuddhim icchati;
na hi so rajjati no virajjati.

Owning is grief; [805]
belongings last not
but pass away.
Quit house and home then!

Death takes what men [806]
deem their possessions.
Disciple mine,
lay claim to nothing.

As, when we wake, [807]
dream faces vanish,
so pass from view
ghosts of man's dear ones.

We see and hear [808]
friends, by their names known;
but, when they pass,
only their names stay.

Grief, grudging, wails [809]
dog th' itch for owning,
sages find Peace
by owning nothing.

To live aloof [810]
in contemplation,
befits the leal
whose journeys are done.

Detached, the sage [811]
keeps down affections;
—grief, grudging, wails,
like raindrops, are shed.

Just as no splash [812]
sullies the lotus,
so senses leave
sages unsullied;

Cleans'd, they build hopes [813]
neither on senses
nor aught besides;
they're past all passion.

7. Tissametteyyasutta

1. Methunam anuyuttassa vighātaṁ brūhi, mārisa; [814]
(*icc-āyasmā Tisso Metteyyo*)
sutvāna tava sāsanaṁ viveke sikkhisāmase.

2. Methunam anuyuttassa mussat' evâpi sāsanaṁ, [815]
(*Metteyyâti Bhagavā*)
micchā ca paṭipajjati;—etaṁ tasmiṁ anāriyaṁ.

3. Eko pubbe caritvāna methunaṁ yo nisevati, [816]
yānaṁ bhantaṁ va, taṁ loke 'hīnam' āhu 'puthujjanaṁ'.

4. Yaso kittī ca yā pubbe hāyat' evâpi tassa sā; [817]
etam pi disvā sikkhetha methunaṁ vippahātave.

5. Saṁkappehi pareto so kapaṇo viya jhāyati; [818]
sutvā paresaṁ nigghosaṁ manku hoti tathāvidho.

6. Atha satthāni kurute paravādehi codito; [819]
esa khvassa mahāgedho, mosavajjaṁ pagāhati.

7. Paṇḍito ti samaññāto ekacariyaṁ adhiṭṭhito, [820]
athâpi methune yutto mando va parikissati.

8. Etam ādīnavaṁ ñatvā muni pubbâpare idha [821]
ekacariyaṁ daḷhaṁ kayirā, na nisevetha methunaṁ.

9. Vivekaṁ yeva sikkhetha; etad ariyānam uttamaṁ; [822]
tena seṭṭho na maññetha; sa ve nibbānasantike.

10. Rittassa munino carato kāmesu anapekhino [823]
oghatiṇṇassa pihayanti kāmesu gadhitā pajā ti.

8. Pasūrasutta

1. 'Idh' eva suddhiṁ' iti vādiyanti, [824]
nâññesu dhammesu visuddhim āhu;
yaṁ nissitā, tattha subhā vadānā
paccekasaccesu puthū niviṭṭhā.

Sutta 7. Lechery

Tissa Metteyya: Tell us what harm befalls a lecher, sir, [814]
that we, thus schooled by thee, in privacy
may put in practice what thou shalt enjoin.

The Lord: In wickedness, outside my Doctrine's pale, [815]
the lecher lives a base, ignoble life.

'Low, headlong renegade!' is what they call [816]
an anchorite who stoops to lechery.

His old repute is gone; his fame departs. [817]
Be warned; with all your might shun lechery!

Lewd thoughts engross his abject 'reveries', [818]
—whom others' censure leaves morose and glum,

until, to arm his wrath when thus reproached, [819]
(his itch is such!) to lying he resorts.

Reputed wise—whilst upright anchorite— [820]
he's scouted as a dolt for lechery.

These perils known, a sage should straitly walk [821]
alone, aloof, eschewing lechery.

Live then aloof (no nobler life exists!) [822]
yet not puffed up.—Nirvāna's well-nigh won!

Emancipate, from passion freed, the sage [823]
in safety stands upon the Further Shore,
—envied by all whom passion's bonds enslave.

Sutta 8. Warring Sects

Each claims that Purity [824]
abides with him alone,
—but not in rival creeds;
and, though no two agree,
each vaunts his nostrum sound.

2. Te vādakāmā parisaṁ vigayha [825]
bālaṁ dahanti mithu aññamaññaṁ;
vadanti te aññasitā kathojjaṁ
pasaṁsakāmā kusalā vadānā.

3. Yutto kathāyaṁ parisāya majjhe [826]
pasaṁsam icchaṁ vinighāti hoti;
apāhatasmiṁ pana manku hoti,
nindāya so kuppati randhamesī.

4. Yam assa vādaṁ 'parihīnam' āhu [827]
apāhataṁ pañhavimaṁsakāse,
paridevati socati hīnavādo;
'upaccagā man' ti anutthunāti.

5. Ete vivādā 'samaṇesu' jātā; [828]
etesu ugghātinighāti hoti;
etam pi disvā virame kathojjaṁ;
na h' aññadatth' atthi pasaṁsalābhā.

6. Pasaṁsito vā pana tattha hoti [829]
akkhāya vādaṁ parisāya majjhe,
so hassati uṇṇamati-cca tena
pappuyya tam atthaṁ yathā mano ahu.

7. Yā uṇṇati sā 'ssa vighātabhūmi, [830]
mānâtimānaṁ vadate pan' eso;
etam pi disvā na vivādayetha,
na hi tena suddhiṁ kusalā vadanti.

8. Sūro yathā rājakhadāya puṭṭho [831]
abhigajjam eti paṭisūram icchaṁ,
yen' eva so, tena palehi, sūra;
pubb' eva na 'tthī yadidaṁ yudhāya.

9. Ye diṭṭhim uggayha vivādiyanti, [832]
idam eva saccan ti ca vādiyanti,
te tvam vadassu: Na hi te 'dha atthi
vādamhi jāte paṭisenikattā.

10. Visenikatvā pana ye caranti [833]
diṭṭhīhi diṭṭhiṁ avirujjhamānā,
tesu tvaṁ kiṁ labhetho, Pasūra,
yesîdha na 'tthi param uggahītaṁ?

Hot for debate, they meet; [825]
each dubs the other 'fool';
with party arguments
these 'experts' wrangle on,
posing for public praise.

Eager to win the day, [826]
debaters dread defeat,
sit glum when posers come,
and writhe in shame when floored.

And if the judges find [827]
against him and he fails,
in anguish and with tears
he sobs: 'He 's beaten me!'

Let outside anchorites [828]
wage suchlike wordy wars,
to win or lose the day!
—Shun strife; scorn empty praise.

But should he win the day, [829]
and praise be his, loud rings
his laugh; he swells with pride
to gain the prize he sought.

His triumph lays him low; [830]
since pride now fills his talk.
—Learn then to shun debate;
not thence comes Purity.

As with defiant shout [831]
the king's trained champion
goes forth to find his match,
so seek thy foe,—though thou
hast nothing left to quell!

But as for partisans [832]
who deem truth theirs alone,
tell them, if wrangling starts,
you enter not their lists.

To Pasūra, a Wanderer: With saints whose fight is won, [833]
who pit no theory
against your theories,
—how can you cope with minds
withdrawn from earthly things?

11\. Atha tvaṁ pavitakkam āgamā [834]
manasā diṭṭhigatāni cintayanto,
dhonena yugaṁ samāgamā,
na hi tvaṁ sakkhasi sampayātave.

9. Māgandiyasutta

1\. Disvāna Taṇhaṁ Aratiñ ca Rāgaṁ [835]
nâhosi chando api methunasmiṁ.
Kim ev' idaṁ muttakarīsapuṇṇaṁ?
Pādā pi naṁ samphusituṁ na icche.

2\. Etādisañ ce ratanaṁ na icchasi [836]
—nāriṁ narindehi bahūhi patthitaṁ—,
diṭṭhigataṁ sīlavatânujīvitaṁ
bhavûpapattiñ ca vadesi kīdisaṁ?

3\. Idaṁ vadāmîti na tassa hoti (*Māgandiyâti Bhagavā*) [837]
dhammesu niccheyya samuggahītaṁ,
passañ ca diṭṭhīsu anuggahāya
ajjhattasantiṁ pacinaṁ adassaṁ.

4\. Vinicchayā yāni pakappitāni (*iti Māgandiyo*) [838]
te ve, muni, brūsi anuggahāya,
'ajjhattasantîti' yam etam atthaṁ
kathaṁ nu dhīrehi paveditaṁ taṁ?

5\. Na diṭṭhiyā na sutiyā na ñāṇena (*Māgandiyâti Bhagavā*) [839]
sīlabbatenâpi na suddhim āha,
adiṭṭhiyā assutiyā aññāṇā
asīlatā abbatā no pi tena;
ete ca nissajja anuggahāya
santo anissāya bhavaṁ na jappe.

6\. No ce kira diṭṭhiyā na sutiyā na ñāṇena (*iti Māgandiyo*) [840]
sīlabbatenâpi visuddhim āha,
adiṭṭhiyā assutiyā aññāṇā
asīlatā abbatā no pi tena;
—maññām' ahaṁ momuham eva dhammaṁ.
Diṭṭhiyā eke paccenti suddhiṁ.

Inspired by theories, [834]
you came to controvert;
you sought to match the Cleansed,
but cannot compass it!

Sutta 9. Beauty Scorned

The Lord: If Māra's daughters three [835]
could wake no carnal thought,
—what bag of excrements
is this?—I would not touch
her even with my foot!

Māgandiya: If you refuse this pearl [836]
(a maid whom princes court),
declare your creed and rule,
your practices and life;
declare what stage you 've reached.

The Lord: I preach no dogmas drawn [837]
from all the divers 'views'.
Study rejected these,
and Thought found Inward Peace.

Māgandiya: Scouting concocted views, [838]
you speak of Inward Peace.
How would that form of Weal
by experts be described?

The Lord: Not 'views' or hearsay, lore [839]
or works, give Purity;
—nor does the lack of them.
Discard all this; win calm;
be free; crave no rebirth.

Māgandiya: If you say Purity [840]
proceeds from none of these,
nor from the lack of them,
'tis nonsense what you say.
—From 'views' some men get Light.

7. Diṭṭhīsu nissāya anupucchamāno, (*Māgandiyâti Bhagavā*) [841]
samuggahītesu pamoham āgā;
ito ca nâdakkhi aṇum pi saññaṁ;
tasmā tuvaṁ momuhato dahāsi.

8. 'Samo visesī uda vā nihīno' [842]
yo maññati, so vivadetha tena;
tīsu vidhāsu avikampamāno—
'samo, visesîti' na tassa hoti.

9. 'Saccan' ti so Brāhmaṇo kiṁ vadeyya? [843]
'Musā ti' vā so vivadetha kena?
Yasmiṁ samaṁ visamañ câpi na 'tthi,
sa kena vādaṁ paṭisaṁyujeyya?

10. Okam pahāya aniketasārī, [844]
gāme akubbaṁ muni santhavāni,
kāmehi ritto, apurakkharāno,
kathaṁ na viggayha janena kayirā.

11. Yehi vivitto vicareyya loke, [845]
na tāni uggayha vadeyya Nāgo.
Elambujaṁ kaṇṭakavārijaṁ yathā
jalena pankena c' anūpalittaṁ,
evaṁ munī santivado agiddho
kāme ca loke ca anūpalitto.

12. Na vedagū diṭṭhiyā na mutiyā [846]
sa mānam eti, na hi tammayo so;
na kammunā no pi sutena neyyo;
anūpanīto so nivesanesu.

13. Saññāvirattassa na santi ganthā; [847]
paññāvimuttassa na santi mohā;
saññañ ca diṭṭhiñ ca ye aggahesuṁ
te ghaṭṭayantā vicaranti loke.

10. Purābhedasutta

1. Kathaṁdassī kathaṁsīlo 'upasanto' ti vuccati? [848]
Tam me, Gotama, pabrūhi pucchito uttamaṁ naraṁ.

The Lord: Pet views your questions prompt. [841]
By prejudice misled,
you so mistake my point
that nonsense it appears.

'He's my inferior', [842]
'my better' or 'as good',
—such thoughts breed strife. No strife
is his who knows no grades.

When this is meaningless, [843]
how can a Brahmin true
dub this thing 'true', that 'false'?
or start a wordy war?

The homeless wanderer, [844]
who makes no intimates
and scorns delights and grades,
steers clear of bickerings.

Nor will the sage profess [845]
that which his life disowns.
As mud and water leave
unsoiled their denizen,
the lotus,—so the world
and pleasures cannot soil
the want-less sage's Peace.

No 'views', no things of sense, [846]
inflate a sage with pride;
—'tis not his nature. Works
and lore are not his guides;
no errors cabin him.

When sense-impressions cease, [847]
chains snap. Illusions pass
when comprehension brings
Release. But those who cling
to 'views' and things of sense,
spread discord all around.

Sutta 10. Ere Dissolution Comes

An Enquirer: What insight and what conduct make 'a saint'? [848]
Pray, Gotama, portray the perfect man.

2. Vītataṇho purā bhedā, pubbam antam anissito [849]
(*ti Bhagavā*)
vemajjhe n' upasaṁkheyyo, tassa na 'tthi purakkhataṁ;

3. akkodhano asantāsī avikatthī akukkuco [850]
mantābhāṇī anuddhato,—sa ve vācāyato munī;

4. nirāsattī anāgate atītaṁ nânusocati, [851]
vivekadassī phassesu diṭṭhīsu ca na niyyati,

5. patilīno akuhako apihālu amaccharī [852]
appagabbho ajeguccho pesuṇeyye ca no yuto,

6. sātiyesu anassāvī atimāne ca no yuto [853]
saṇho ca paṭibhāṇavā na saddho, na virajjati,

7. lābhakamyā na sikkhati, alābhe ca na kuppati, [854]
aviruddho ca taṇhāya rase ca nânugijjhati;

8. upekkhako sadā sato na loke maññati samam, [855]
na visesī na nīceyyo,—tassa no santi ussadā;

9. yassa nissayatā na 'tthi, ñatvā Dhammaṁ anissito, [856]
bhavāya vibhavāya ca taṇhā yassa na vijjati,

10. —taṁ brūmi 'upasanto' ti kāmesu anapekkhinaṁ; [857]
ganthā tassa na vijjanti; atāri so visattikaṁ.

11. Na tassa puttā pasavo khettaṁ vatthuñ ca vijjati [858]
attaṁ vā pi nirattaṁ vā na tasmiṁ upalabbhati.

12. Yena vajjuṁ puthujjanā atho samaṇabrāhmaṇā, [859]
taṁ tassa apurakkhataṁ, tasmā vādesu n' ejati.

13. Vītagedho amaccharī na ussesu vadate muni [860]
na samesu na omesu, kappaṁ n' eti akappiyo.

14. Yassa loke sakaṁ na 'tthi, asatā ca na socati, [861]
dhammesu ca na gacchati, sa ve 'santo' ti vuccati.

11. Kalahavivādasutta

1. Kuto pahūtā kalahā vivādā [862]
paridevasokā sahamaccharā ca
mānâtimānā sahapesuṇā ca?
Kuto pahūtā te? Tad ingha brūhi.

The Lord: Ere dissolution comes, all cravings cease; [849]
he recks not how of old the world began;
he finds no present place in time to-day;
he has no preference for which he sighs;

devoid of wrath and dread, remorse and vaunts, [850]
a preacher sane, a 'saint' controls his words;

no future hopes has he, no past regrets; [851]
no sense-impressions mar his inward life;

aloof and guileless, freed from hankerings [852]
and envy, meek, he scorns and slanders none;

no joys allure him; pride is far away; [853]
courtly, he shines; detached, not credulous;

at gifts he aims not,—nor resents their lack; [854]
he nothing craves; no dainty fare allures;

poised, vigilant, he never ranks himself [855]
as 'high', or 'low', or 'equal to the best';
since self-assertion finds no place in 'saints';

an independent man, whom grasp of Truth [856]
makes independent, who gives harbourage
to no desire to be or not to be;

—him do I style the 'Saint at peace'; no chains [857]
are his; he 's safe beyond entanglements.

No sons has he, no herds or fields or lands; [858]
no 'yes' or 'no' has he for views on 'Self'.

Ignoring what the world (nay, holy men!) [859]
impute to them, 'saints' reck not what folk say.

Grasping not, grudging not, the saint, unmoved, [860]
to 'high', or 'low', or 'equal' lays no claim;
timeless, he whirls down grooves of time no more.

Whoso owns nothing in the world, nor grieves [861]
o'er what is transient, nor wanders off
to sense-impressions,—*he* is hailed as 'saint'.

Sutta 11. Contentions

An Enquirer: Whence springs the seething mass [862]
of bickerings and strife,
tears, grief, and selfishness,
conceit, pride, calumny?
Explain whence these proceed.

2. Piyappahūtā kalahā vivādā [863]
paridevasokā sahamaccharā ca
mānâtimānā sahapesuṇā ca;
maccherayuttā kalahā vivādā,
vivādajātesu ca pesuṇāni.

3. Piyā su lokasmiṁ kutonidānā, [864]
ye vā pi lobhā vicaranti loke?
Āsā ca niṭṭhā ca kutonidānā
ye samparāyāya narassa honti?

4. Chandānidānāni piyāni loke [865]
ye vā pi lobhā vicaranti loke;
āsā ca niṭṭhā ca itonidānā
ye samparāyāya narassa honti.

5. Chando nu lokasmiṁ kutonidāno? [866]
Vinicchayā vā pi kuto pahūtā,
kodho mosavajjañ ca kathaṁkathā ca
ye vā pi dhammā Samaṇena vuttā?

6. Sātaṁ, asātan ti yam āhu loke, [867]
tam upanissāya pahoti chando;
rūpesu disvā vibhavaṁ bhavañ ca
vinicchayaṁ kūrute jantu loke.

7. Kodho mosavajjañ ca kathaṁkathā ca [868]
ete pi dhammā dvaya-m-eva sante;
kathaṁkathī ñāṇapathāya sikkhe,
ñatvā pavuttā Samaṇena dhammā.

8. Sātaṁ asātañ ca kutonidānā? [869]
Kismiṁ asante na bhavanti h' ete?
Vibhavaṁ bhavañ câpi, yam etam atthaṁ,
etam me pabrūhi yatonidānaṁ.

9. Phassanidānaṁ sātaṁ asātaṁ; [870]
phasse asante na bhavanti h' ete,
vibhavaṁ bhavañ câpi, yam etam atthaṁ,
etaṁ te pabrūmi itonidānaṁ.

The Lord: Affections breed the mass [863]
of bickerings and strife,
tears, grief, and selfishness,
conceit, pride, calumny.
With selfishness there come
all bickerings and strife,
—which lead to calumny.

The Enquirer: Say whence affections spring? [864]
What makes ambitions grow?
What fosters hopes and fears
in man for future life?

The Lord: Affections spring from wants, [865]
which make ambitions grow
and foster hopes and fears
in men for future life.

The Enquirer: Whence spring man's wants? Whence come [866]
all hard and fast beliefs?
Whence wrath, lies, doubts, and all
things else th' Recluse denounced?

The Lord: Things viewed as 'good' or 'bad' [867]
originate man's wants.
Seeing things wax and wane
brought hard and fast beliefs.

Wrath, doubts, and lies arose [868]
when things seemed 'good' or 'bad'.
Let doubters plant their feet
where knowledge guides;—th' Recluse
denounced defects he knew.

The Enquirer: Whence spring things 'good' or 'bad'? [869]
What, being absent, checks
their rise? And tell me too
why things must wax and wane?

The Lord: Things 'good' or 'bad' are bred [870]
of Contact. Contact must
be there, or they're not bred,
nor would things wax and wane.

10. Phasso nu lokasmiṁ kutonidāno? [871]
Pariggahā vā pi kuto pahūtā?
Kismiṁ asante na mamattam atthi?
Kismiṁ vibhūte na phusanti phassā?

11. Nāmañ ca rūpañ ca paṭicca phasso; [872]
icchānidānāni pariggahāni;
icchāy' asantyā na mamattam atthi;
rūpe vibhūte na phusanti phassā.

12. Kathaṁsametassa vibhoti rūpaṁ? [873]
Sukhaṁ dukkhaṁ vā pi kathaṁ vibhoti?
Etam me pabrūhi yathā vibhoti;
taṁ jāniyāma, iti me mano ahu.

13. Na saññasaññī, na visaññasaññī, [874]
no pi asaññī, na vibhūtasaññī,
—evaṁsametassa vibhoti rūpaṁ;
saññānidānā hi papañcasaṁkhā.

14. Yan tam apucchimha akittayī no; [875]
—aññaṁ taṁ pucchāma; tad ingha brūhi:—
Ettāvat' aggaṁ nu vadanti h' eke
yakkhassa suddhiṁ idha paṇḍitāse?
Udāhu aññam pi vadanti etto?

15. Ettāvat' aggam pi vadanti h' eke [876]
yakkhassa suddhiṁ idha paṇḍitāse;
tesaṁ pun' eke samayaṁ vadanti
anupādisese kusalā vadānā.

16. Ete ca ñatvā 'upanissitā' ti, [877]
ñatvā munī nissaye so vimaṁsī,
ñatvā vimutto na vivādam eti,
bhavâbhavāya na sameti dhīro.

The Enquirer: From what does Contact spring? [871]
Whence comes the itch to own?
What, being absent, checks
the craze to deem things 'mine'?
And what must disappear
if Contacts are to end?

The Lord: Matter and Mind result [872]
in Contact. Yearnings breed
the itch to have and hold;
without them is no 'mine'.—
End 'matter',—Contacts end.

The Enquirer: What stage is his for whom [873]
'matter' has disappeared?
Fain would I hear how pain
and pleasure disappear.

The Lord: Matter will disappear [874]
when consciousness (from which
obsessions all arise)
is neither usual,
nor crazed, nor numbed, nor lost.

The Enquirer: Though thou hast answer'd all [875]
we asked, one question more
we raise for thy reply:—
Do thinkers hold this life
perfects man's Purity?
Or is there more to come?

The Lord: Some thinkers hold this life [876]
perfects man's Purity;
but other 'experts' hold
the view that death ends all.

The sage knows such as 'thralls'; [877]
he knows their thraldom. Freed
by knowledge, he avoids
debate and wisely holds
no truck with theories
about an 'after-life'.

12. Cūlaviyūhasutta

1. Sakaṁ sakaṁ diṭṭhiparibbasānā [878]
viggayha nānā kusalā vadanti:—
Yo evaṁ jānāti, sa vedi dhammaṁ;
idaṁ paṭikkosaṁ akevalī so.

2. Evam pi viggayha vivādiyanti, [879]
'bālo paro akusalo' ti câhu.
Sacco nu vādo katamo imesaṁ?
Sabb' eva hîme kusalā vadānā.

3. Parassa ce dhammaṁ anānujānaṁ [880]
bālômako hoti nihīnapañño,
sabb' eva bālā sunihīnapaññā,
sabb' ev' ime diṭṭhiparibbasānā.

4. Sandiṭṭhiyā ce pana vīvadātā [881]
saṁsuddhapaññā kusalā mutīmā,
na tesaṁ koci parihīnapañño;
—diṭṭhī hi tesam pi tathā samattā.

5. Na vâham etaṁ 'tathivan' ti brūmi [882]
yam āhu bālā mithu aññamaññam;
sakaṁ sakaṁ diṭṭhiṁ akaṁsu saccaṁ;
—tasmā hi 'bālo' ti paraṁ dahanti.

6. Yam āhu 'saccaṁ tathivan' ti eke, [883]
tam āhu aññe pi 'tucchaṁ musā' ti;
—evam pi viggayha vivādiyanti.
Kasmā na ekaṁ samaṇā vadanti?

7. Ekaṁ hi saccaṁ na dutīyam atthi [884]
yasmiṁ pajā no vivade pajānaṁ;
nānā te saccāni sayaṁ thunanti;
tasmā na ekaṁ samaṇā vadanti.

8. Kasmā nu saccāni vadanti nānā [885]
pavādiyāse kusalā vadānā?
Saccāni suttāni bahūni nānā?
Udāhu te takkam anussaranti?

Sutta 12. Rejoinders

The Enquirer: Fixed in their pet beliefs, [878]
these divers wranglers bawl—
'Hold this, and truth is yours;'
'Reject it, and you're lost'.

Thus they contend, and dub [879]
opponents 'dolts' and 'fools'.
Which of the lot is right,
when all as experts pose?

The Lord: Well, if dissent denotes [880]
a 'fool' and stupid 'dolt',
then all are fools and dolts,
—since each has his own view.

Or, if each rival creed [881]
proves lore and brains and wit,
no 'dolts' exist,—since all
alike are on a par.

I count not that as true [882]
which those affirm, who call
each other 'fools'.—They call
each other so, because
each deems his own view 'Truth'.

The Enquirer: What some style 'truth', the rest [883]
call empty lies;—strife reigns.
Pray, why do anchorites
not speak in unison?

The Lord: There's one sole 'Truth' (not two), [884]
to know which bars men's strife.
But such a motley crowd
of 'truths' have they evolved,
that anchorites, perforce,
speak not in full accord.

The Enquirer: What makes these 'experts' preach [885]
'truths' so diverse? Is each
inherited? or just
a view they've framed themselves?

9. Na h' eva saccāni bahūni nānā [886]
aññatra saññāya niccāni loke,
takkañ ca diṭṭhīsu pakappayitvā
saccaṁ musā ti dvayadhammam āhu.

10. Diṭṭhe sute sīlavate mute vā [887]
ete ca nissāya vimānadassī
vinicchaye ṭhatvā pahassamāno
'bālo paro, akusalo' ti c' āha.

11. Yen' eva 'bālo' ti paraṁ dahāti, [888]
ten' ātumānaṁ 'kusalo' ti c' āha;
sayam attanā so kusalo vadāno
aññaṁ vimāneti, tath' eva pāvā.

12. Atīsaraṁdiṭṭhiyā so samatto [889]
mānena matto paripuṇṇamānī,
sayam eva sāmaṁ manasâbhisitto,
diṭṭhī hi sā tassa tathā samattā.

13. Parassa ce hi vacasā nihīno, [890]
tumo sahā hoti nihīnapañño;
athavā sayaṁ vedagū hoti dhīro,
na koci bālo samaṇesu atthi.

14. Aññaṁ ito yâbhivadanti dhammaṁ, [891]
aparaddhā suddhim akevalī te;
evam pi titthyā puthuso vadanti,
sandiṭṭhirāgena hi tyâbhirattā.

15. 'Idh' eva suddhiṁ' iti vādiyanti, [892]
nâññesu dhammesu visuddhim āhu,
evam pi titthyā puthuso niviṭṭhā
sakâyane tattha daḷhaṁ vadānā.

16. Sakâyane câpi daḷhaṁ vadāno [893]
kam ettha 'bālo' ti paraṁ daheyya?
Sayam eva so medhagaṁ āvaheyya
paraṁ vadaṁ 'bālam asuddhidhammaṁ'.

The Lord: Apart from consciousness, [886]
no diverse Truths exist.
—Mere sophistry declares
this 'true', and that view 'false'.

The senses' evidence, [887]
and works, inspire such scorn
for others, and such smug
conviction *he* is right,
that all his rivals rank
as 'sorry, brainless fools'.

When he admits himself [888]
to 'expert's' rank and style;
—this fires his scorn anew
and off he starts again.

Chock-full of error, drunk [889]
with pride and arrogance,
he inly consecrates
himself a 'sage',—so grand
is his perfected 'view'.

When scorned opponents dub [890]
him 'low' in turn, he too
joins the 'low intellects'.
If each can make himself
a 'sage', then anchorites
include no 'fools' at all.

Delight in their dear views [891]
makes sectaries assert
that all who disagree
'miss Purity and err'.

These divers sectaries [892]
—these sturdy advocates
of private paths to bliss—
claim Purity as theirs
alone, not found elsewhere.

Whom should the sturdiest [893]
venture to call a 'fool',
when this invites the like
retort upon himself?

17. Vinicchaye ṭhatvā sayaṁ pamāya [894]
uddhaṁ so lokasmiṁ vivādam eti.
Hitvāna sabbāni vinicchayāni
na medhagaṁ kurute jantu loke.

13. Mahāviyūhasutta

1. Ye kec' ime diṭṭhiparibbasānā [895]
'idam eva saccan' ti pavādiyanti,
sabb' eva te nindam anvānayanti?
Atho pasaṁsam pi labhanti tattha?

2. Appaṁ hi etaṁ, na alaṁ samāya; [896]
duve vivādassa phalāni brūmi;
evam pi disvā na vivādiyetha
khemâbhipassaṁ avivādabhummaṁ.

3. Yā kāc' imā sammutiyo puthujjā, [897]
sabbā va etā na upeti vidvā.
Anûpayo so upayaṁ kim eyya
diṭṭhe sute khantim akubbamāno?

4. Sīluttamā saṁyamen' āhu suddhiṁ [898]
vataṁ samādāya upaṭṭhitāse,
—idh' eva sikkhema, ath' assa suddhiṁ,
bhavûpanītā kusalā vadānā.

5. Sace cuto sīlavatāto hoti, [899]
sa vedhati kamma' virādhayitvā,
sa jappati patthayatī ca suddhiṁ,
—satthā va hīno, pavasaṁ gharamhā.

6. Sīlabbataṁ vâpi pahāya sabbaṁ [900]
kammañ ca sāvajjanavajjam etaṁ
suddhiṁ asuddhin ti apatthayāno
virato care 'santim' anuggahāya.

Stubborn in theories [894]
which they themselves devised,
these wrangle on through life.
—Leave then dogmatic views
and their attendant strife!

Sutta 13. More Rejoinders

The Enquirer: Take those who dogmatize [895]
and lay sole claim to Truth;
—is blame their constant fate?
Are they not praised as well?

The Lord: Yes;—though a trifling thing [896]
is all of this (I speak
of both results of strife)
and does not lead to Peace.
Wherefore shun strife and aim
at Peace,—which knows no strife.

No vulgar theories [897]
engage the wise. Why should
the free seek bondage, when
phenomena of sense
appeal to them no more?

They that place practice first, [898]
deeming that regimen
wins Purity, take vows
to practise only what
their 'master taught as pure',
—experts self-styled, who cling
to mere phenomena!

Should one depart from 'Rule', [899]
he quakes, and frets, and pines,
like travellers astray
who lose their caravan.

Scout then all formal codes [900]
of things 'unmeet' and 'meet';
heed not their 'purity',
—nor their impurity;
but walk aloof; ensue
no 'peace' they advocate.

7. Tamūpanissāya jigucchitaṁ vā, [901]
athavā pi diṭṭhaṁ va sutaṁ mutaṁ vā,
uddhaṁsarā suddhim anutthunanti
avītataṇhāse bhavâbhavesu.

8. Patthayamānassa hi jappitāni [902]
saṁvedhitaṁ vâpi pakappitesu.
Cutûpapāto idha yassa na 'tthi,
sa kena vedheyya? kuhiṁ pajappe?

9. Yam āhu 'dhammaṁ paraman' ti eke, [903]
tam eva 'hīnan' ti pan' āhu aññe.
Sacco nu vādo katamo imesaṁ?
—Sabb' eva hîme kusalā vadānā.

10. Sakaṁ hi dhammaṁ paripuṇṇam āhu; [904]
aññassa dhammaṁ pana hīnam āhu.
Evam pi viggayha vivādiyanti,
sakaṁ sakaṁ sammutim āhu saccaṁ.

11. Parassa ce vambhayitena hīno, [905]
na koci dhammesu visesi assa.
Puthū hi aññassa vadanti dhammaṁ
'nihīnato', samhi daḷhaṁ vadānā.

12. Sadhammapūjā ca panā tath' eva; [906]
yathā pasaṁsanti sakâyanāni
sabbe pavādā tathivā bhaveyyuṁ;
suddhī hi nesaṁ paccattam eva.

13. Na Brāhmaṇassa paraneyyam atthi, [907]
dhammesu niccheyya samuggahītaṁ.
Tasmā vivādāni upātivatto;
na hi seṭṭhato passati dhammam aññaṁ.

14. 'Jānāmi, passāmi, tath' eva etaṁ', [908]
diṭṭhiyā eke paccenti suddhiṁ.
Addakkhi ce, kim hi tumassa tena?
—Atisitvā aññena vadanti suddhiṁ.

Penance, and loathliness, [901]
and things of sense, evoke
shrill shrieks for 'purity'
from men who hanker still
to be reborn—somewhere.

Desires breed hopes; and fears [902]
spring from imaginings.
—But he who ne'er shall see
rebirth, pray, what shall make
him quake? or yearn—for what?

The Enquirer: The doctrine some vaunt 'best', [903]
others term 'low'. Which states
the fact?—They 're all 'adepts'.

The Lord: Ah! 'tis his own dear creed [904]
which each proclaims as 'rare'!
His rival's creed is 'low'!
And so they squabble on,
each claiming truth as *his*!

If others' criticisms [905]
could make a doctrine 'low',
then none is excellent;
for all unite to damn
all doctrines—save their own.

As they extol their 'Way', [906]
so they revere their creeds.
Their tune is still the same:
'Our Purity' 's its theme.

The 'Brahmin true' adopts [907]
nothing from others, owes
nothing to others' views;
immune from strife, he deems
no theory 'the Truth'.

' 'Tis so; I see and know' [908]
—say some, who seek by views
to garner 'Purity'.
Yet, should they 'see', what good
is that when rivals urge
a view rebutting theirs?

15. Passaṁ naro dakkhati nāmarūpaṁ, [909]
disvāna vâññassati tāni-m-eva.
Kāmaṁ bahuṁ passatu appakaṁ vā;
na hi tena suddhiṁ kusalā vadanti.

16. Nivissavādī na hi subbināyo [910]
pakappitaṁ diṭṭhi' purekkharāno;
yaṁ nissito, tattha subhaṁ vadāno
suddhiṁvado tattha tath' addasā so.

17. Na Brāhmaṇo kappam upeti sankhaṁ [911]
na diṭṭhisārī na pi ñāṇabandhu;
ñatvā ca so sammutiyo puthujjā,
upekkhatī;—uggahaṇanti-m-aññe.

18. Visajja ganthāni munîdha loke [912]
vivādajātesu na vaggasārī,
santo asantesu upekkhako so
anuggaho;—uggahaṇanti-m-aññe.

19. Pubbâsave hitvā, nave akubbaṁ, [913]
na chandagū, no pi nivissavādī,
sa vippamutto diṭṭhigatehi dhīro
na lippati loke anattagarahī.

20. Sa sabbadhammesu visenibhūto, [914]
yaṁ kiñci diṭṭhaṁ va sutaṁ mutaṁ vā,
sa pannabhāro muni vippamutto
na kappiyo, nûparato, na patthiyo ti. (*Bhagavā ti*)

Through 'seeing', men just 'see' [909]
things and their attributes;
or, having 'seen', can 'know'
just that—and nothing more.
But, 'see' they much, or 'see'
they little, wise men say:—
'Not thus comes "Purity".'

No dogmatist can win, [910]
by self-concocted views,
the way to Purity.
Mere prepossessions point
his road to 'Light'; he 'sees'
his old-time 'Purity'.

No 'Brahmin true' attains [911]
the goal by mere research;
no partisan is he,
nor brother-sectary;
all vulgar theories
—which others toil to learn—
he knows, but heeds them not.

From earthly trammels freed, [912]
aloof from party broils,
at peace where peace has fled,
th' unheeding sage ignores
what others toil to learn.

From whilom Cankers purged, [913]
with no fresh growths afoot,
from lusts and dogmas free,
quit too of theories,
he goes his stainless way,
devoid of self-reproach.

By overcoming all [914]
the theories that start
from things of sense, the sage
—Released, his burthen gone—
has done with conduct 'meet',
with abstinence, and pray'rs.

14. Tuvaṭakasutta

1. Pucchāmi taṁ Ādiccabandhuṁ [915]
vivekaṁ santipadañ ca mahesiṁ:
Kathaṁ disvā nibbāti bhikkhu
anupādiyāno lokasmiṁ kiñci?

2. Mūlaṁ papañcasaṁkhāyâ (*ti Bhagavā*) [916]
mantā 'asmîti' sabbam uparuddhe;
yā kāci taṇhā ajjhattaṁ,
tāsaṁ vinayā sadā sato sikkhe.

3. Yaṁ kiñci dhammaṁ abhijaññā, [917]
ajjhattaṁ atha vā pi bahiddhā,
na tena thāmaṁ kubbetha;
na hi sā nibbuti sataṁ vuttā.

4. Seyyo na tena maññeyya [918]
nīceyyo atha vā pi sarikkho;
phuṭṭho anekarūpehi
nâtumānaṁ vikappayaṁ tiṭṭhe.

5. Ajjhattam eva upasame, [919]
nâññato bhikkhu santim eseyya;
ajjhattaṁ upasantassa
na 'tthi attaṁ,—kuto nirattaṁ vā?

6. Majjhe yathā samuddassa [920]
ūmi no jāyatī, ṭhito hoti,
evaṁ ṭhito anej' assa;
ussadaṁ bhikkhu na kareyya kuhiñci.

7. Akittayi vivaṭacakkhu [921]
sakkhidhammaṁ parissayavinayaṁ;
paṭipadaṁ vadehi—bhaddan te—
pātimokkhaṁ atha vā pi samādhiṁ.

8. Cakkhūhi n' eva lol' assa, [922]
gāmakathāya āvaraye sotaṁ,
rase ca nânugijjheyya,
na ca mamāyetha kiñci lokasmiṁ.

Sutta 14. Without Delay

The Enquirer: Sun's kinsman! Sage! [915]
Expound aloofness and
the way of Peace.
What outlook leaves man calm,
with life's stuff spent?

The Lord: Let him pluck out [916]
obsession's root,—the craze:
'I am'; let him
in constant watchfulness
abide, with all
his inward cravings gone.

Should he observe [917]
a mental state arise
(from in or out),
let it not puff him up,
—since none term this
the calm which good men win.

Nor let him feel [918]
'better' or 'worse' for this,
or build a 'Self'
on such phenomena.

For inward Peace [919]
let Almsmen seek, nor look
for calm elsewhere.
With inward Peace, no Self—
no non-Self—dwells.

As no waves break [920]
the calm of ocean's depths,
unruffled be
the Almsman's tranquil breast.

The Enquirer: Thou hast proclaimed [921]
thy saving Doctrine, seer.
Expound thy Rule—
Confession—Rapt Resolve.

The Lord: No prying eye! [922]
No ear for village talk!
No taste for cates!
No itch to get or have!

9. Phassena yadā phuṭṭh' assa, [923]
paridevaṁ bhikkhu na kareyya kuhiñci,
bhavañ ca nâbhijappeyya,
bheravesu ca na sampavedheyya.

10. Annānam, atho pānānaṁ, [924]
khādanīyānaṁ, atho pi vatthānaṁ
laddhā na sannidhiṁ kayirā,
na ca parittase tāni alabbhamāno.

11. Jhāyī, na pādalol' assa, [925]
virame kukkuccā, na-ppamajjeyya;
ath' āsanesu sayanesu
appasaddesu bhikkhu vihareyya.

12. Niddaṁ na bahulīkareyya; [926]
jāgariyaṁ bhajeyya ātāpī;
tandiṁ māyaṁ hasaṁ khiḍḍaṁ
methunaṁ vippajahe savibhūsaṁ.

13. Āthabbaṇaṁ supinaṁ lakkhaṇaṁ [927]
no vidahe, atho pi nakkhattaṁ,
virudañ ca gabbhakaraṇaṁ,
tikicchaṁ māmako na seveyya.

14. Nindāya na-ppavedheyya, [928]
na uṇṇameyya pasaṁsito bhikkhu,
lobham saha macchariyena
kodhaṁ pesuṇiyañ ca panūdeyya.

15. Kayavikkaye na tiṭṭheyya, [929]
upavādaṁ bhikkhu na kareyya kuhiñci,
gāme ca nâbhisajjeyya,
lābhakamyā janaṁ na lāpayeyya.

16. Na ca katthitā siyā bhikkhu, [930]
na ca vācaṁ payuttaṁ bhāseyya,
pāgabbhiyaṁ na sikkheyya,
kathaṁ viggāhikaṁ na kathayeyya.

When illness comes, [923]
let th' Almsman not lament,
or yearn for life,
or quake with abject dread.

Let him not hoard [924]
the food and drink, the meats,
and clothes he gets;
—nor grieve if he gets none.

Let Reverie [925]
be his, not gadding round,
not vice or sloth.
Sitting or lying down,
let silence reign.

Let him not sleep [926]
o'ermuch, but keep awake,
ban indolence,
deceit, mirth, frolics, pride,
and lechery.

Let him abjure [927]
spells, and interpretings
of dreams and signs;
nor let my follower
prognosticate
from stars or wild-things' notes,
cure barrenness,
or ply the trade of leech.

Let neither blame [928]
depress, nor praise inflate;
let him discard
greed,—with close-fistedness,
slander, and wrath.

Let him not buy [929]
and sell, or cry folk down;
let him not scold
his villagers, or speak
them fair—for gifts.

Let him not boast [930]
or talk for private ends;
or forward be;
or start a wordy war.

17. Mosavajje na niyyetha, [931]
sampajāno saṭhāni na kayirā,
atha jīvitena paññāya
sīlabbatena nâññam atimaññe.

18. Sutvā dūsito bahuṁ vācaṁ [932]
samaṇānaṁ vā puthuvacanānam
pharusena ne na pativajjā;
na hi santo paṭisenikaronti.

19. Etañ ca dhammam aññāya [933]
vicinaṁ bhikkhu sadā sato sikkhe,
santîti nibbutiṁ ñatvā
sāsane Gotamassa na-ppamajjeyya.

20. Abhibhū hi so anabhibhūto [934]
sakkhidhammaṁ anītiham adassī;
tasmā hi tassa Bhagavato
sāsane appamatto sadā namassaṁ anusikkhe ti.

(*Bhagavā ti*)

15. Attadaṇḍasutta

1. Attadaṇḍā bhayaṁ jātaṁ; janaṁ passatha medhagaṁ. [935]
Saṁvegaṁ kittayissāmi yathā saṁvijitaṁ mayā:—

2. Phandamānaṁ pajaṁ disvā—macche appodake yathā— [936]
aññamaññehi byāruddhe disvā, maṁ bhayam āvisi.

3. Samantaṁ asāro loko; disā sabbā sameritā; [937]
icchaṁ bhavanam attano nâddasāsiṁ anositaṁ.

4. Osāne tveva byāruddhe disvā me aratī ahu; [938]
ath' ettha sallaṁ addakkhiṁ duddasaṁ hadayanissitaṁ.

5. Yena sallena otiṇṇo disā sabbā vidhāvati, [939]
tam eva sallaṁ abbūyha na dhāvati, na sīdati.

Let him not lie, [931]
or wittingly defraud,
or look with scorn
on others from proud heights
of way of life,
or lore, or sanctity.

Let him not vent [932]
his spleen by sharp retort
when anchorites
flow on in vapid talk.
—Saints ne'er rejoin.

Let him learn, test, [933]
and hold the Doctrine fast
with watchful care,
convinced that Peace consists
in passions quenched;
let him make Gotama
his constant guide.

For, vision showed [934]
th' unconquer'd Conqueror
the Truth none saw.
Wherefore, with ceaseless praise
let Almsmen cleave
to what the Lord ordained,
—and never flag.

Sutta 15. The Armed Hand

As broils reveal, the armèd hand breeds fear. [935]
Hear now what agitated me so sore:—

Men floundering like fish when ponds go dry; [936]
man's strife with man;—these sights affrighted me.

The world was void of substance; flux held sway; [937]
nor could I shelter find where Ills were not.

Man's doom appalled me, till—within man's heart— [938]
my gaze discerned a secret, rankling barb.

Transfix'd, the victim runs astray; but when [939]
'tis out, he strays no more nor sinks in sloughs.

(*Tattha sikkhânugīyanti*)

6. Yāni loke gathitāni, na tesu pasuto siyā; [940]
nibbijjha sabbaso kāme sikkhe nibbānam attano.

7. Sacco siyā, appagabbho amāyo rittapesuṇo [941]
akkodhano; lobhapāpakaṁ vevicchaṁ vitare muni.

8. Niddaṁ tandiṁ sahe thīnaṁ, pamādena na saṁvase, [942]
atimāne na tiṭṭheyya nibbānamanaso naro.

9. Mosavajje na niyyetha, rūpe snehaṁ na kubbaye, [943]
mānañ ca parijāneyya, sāhasā virato care.

10. Purāṇaṁ nâbhinandeyya, nave khantiṁ na kubbaye, [944]
hīyamāne na soceyya, ākāsaṁ na sito siyā.

11. Gedhaṁ brūmi 'mahogho' ti, ācamaṁ brūmi jappanaṁ, [945]
ārammaṇaṁ pakappanaṁ, kāmapanko duraccayo.

12. Saccā avokkamma muni thale tiṭṭhati Brāhmaṇo; [946]
sabbaṁ so paṭinissajja sa ve 'santo' ti vuccati.

13. Sa ve vidvā, sa vedagū, ñatvā dhammaṁ anissito, [947]
sammā so loke iriyāno na-ppihetīdha kassaci.

14. Yo ca kāme accatari sangaṁ loke duraccayaṁ, [948]
na so socati nâjjheti chinnasoto abandhano.

15. Yaṁ pubbe taṁ visosehi, pacchā te mâhu kiñcanaṁ, [949]
majjhe ce no gahessasi, 'upasanto' carissasi.

16. Sabbaso nāmarūpasmiṁ yassa na 'tthi mamāyitaṁ [950]
asatā ca na socati, sa ve loke na jiyyati.

17. Yassa na 'tthi 'idam me' ti, paresaṁ vā pi, kiñcanaṁ, [951]
mamattaṁ so asaṁvindaṁ 'na 'tthi me' ti na socati.

18. Aniṭṭhurī anānugiddho anejo sabbadhī samo [952]
taṁ ānisaṁsaṁ pabrūmi pucchito avikampinaṁ.

(*Here come the Precepts.*)

Steer clear of worldly trammels; stab to death [940]
pleasures of sense; Nirvāna be thy goal;

let truth, humility, an honest heart, [941]
lips slander-free, and tolerance, be thine;
let greed's discomfiture proclaim the sage;

farewell to slumb'ring on, to torpid sloth; [942]
let indolence be banned, and pride forsworn,
by minds intent upon Nirvāna's bliss;

shun lying; keep thy heart from things of sense; [943]
see through all pride; from license purge thy life;

hug not the past or what to-day brings forth; [944]
bewail not loss; nor sigh for bliss 'Above'.

I call such yearning 'th' all-devouring flood'; [945]
I call it being swallowed up by greed,
—a shifting base, 'the bog of appetites'.

The sage, the Brahmin true, who never strays [946]
from truth, on solid ground has set his foot;
all things forsaking, he 'to Peace has come';

wisdom is his and lore; by Doctrine taught, [947]
he goes his independent, perfect way
along life's path, nor envies any man.

He that has triumphed over appetites [948]
and burst all worldly shackles here on earth,
knows neither grief o'er loss, nor haunting dread.

Consume to ashes past iniquities; [949]
thereafter let no fresh defilement grow;
if—meantime—thou contract no current guilt,
thy feet shall tread the tranquil path of Peace.

Whoso prefers no claim to ownership [950]
of 'personality', and so grieves not
o'er what exists not,—never suffers loss.

Whoso is marred by no such thoughts as —'This [951]
is mine!' or 'That is theirs!' conceives no sense
of ownership, nor grieves to go without.

Neither to grudge nor covet nor to crave, [952]
but still to keep one equal poise through all,
—these blessings, I aver, await the leal.

19\. Anejassa vijānato na 'tthi kāci nisaṁkhiti; [953]
virato so viyārambhā khemaṁ passati sabbadhi.

20\. Na samesu na omesu na ussesu vadate muni, [954]
santo so vītamaccharo nâdeti na nirassatī. (*ti Bhagavā*)

16. Sāriputtasutta

1\. Na me diṭṭho ito pubbe na suto uda kassaci [955]
(*icc-āyasmā Sāriputto*)
evaṁ vagguvado satthā Tusitā gaṇi-m-āgato

2\. sadevakassa lokassa yathā dissati Cakkhumā [956]
sabbaṁ tamaṁ vinodetvā eko ca ratim ajjhagā.

3\. Taṁ Buddhaṁ asitaṁ tādiṁ akuhaṁ gaṇim āgataṁ [957]
bahunnam idha baddhānaṁ atthi pañhena āgamaṁ:—

4\. Bhikkhuno vijigucchato bhajato rittam āsanaṁ [958]
rukkhamūlaṁ susānaṁ vā pabbatānaṁ guhāsu vā

5\. uccâvacesu sayanesu, kīvanto tattha bheravā [959]
yehi bhikkhu na vedheyya nigghose sayanâsane?

6\. Katī parissayā loke gacchato agataṁ disaṁ [960]
ye bhikkhu abhisambhave pantamhi sayanāsane?

7\. Kyâssa byappathayo assu? Kyâssa assu idha gocarā? [961]
Kāni sīlabbatān' assu pahitattassa bhikkhuno?

8\. Kaṁ so sikkhaṁ samādāya ekodi nipako sato, [962]
kammāro rajatassêva, niddhame malam attano?

9\. Vijigucchamānassa yad idaṁ phāsu [963]
(*Sāriputtâti Bhagavā*)
rittāsanaṁ sayanaṁ sevato ce
sambodhikāmassa yathânudhammaṁ
tan te pavakkhāmi yathā pajānaṁ.

When cravings die, the clear-eyed sage stores up [953]
no merit nor demerit; interest
in suchlike quests is merged in perfect calm.

The sage contrasts himself with none, nor claims [954]
equality or inequality.
At peace within, immune from covetise,
the saint has nought to gain and naught to lose.

Sutta 16. What Sāriputta Asked

Sāriputta : I ne'er have seen nor ever yet heard tell [955]
of such a sweet-tongued Master coming down
from Túsitá on high to teach the world

of gods and men,—as stands reveal'd in Him, [956]
th' all-seeing Lord, who swept all mists away
and compassed bliss, unaided and alone.

To Buddha—so endowed, so free, so sure [957]
a guide, a question lo! I bring, to help
the multitudes condemned to bondage here.

If, now, an Almsman who abhors the world [958]
seeks out a lonely lodging,—under trees,
in charnel grounds, or in a mountain cave,

—there grisly noises haunt his lone abode, [959]
which he must stoutly brave in solitude.

What dangers bar his still untrodden road, [960]
which he must vanquish in his loneliness?

How should he shape his speech?—whither resort? [961]
—what pious works should mark him, resolute?

What vows of conduct help the fixèd mind [962]
(with wisdom stored and high collectedness)
foulness to purge, as silversmiths the dross?

The Lord: Hear then from me—who know— [963]
what boons lone aspirants
enjoy, who loathe the world,
and how their life conforms.

10. Pañcanna' dhīro bhayānaṁ na bhāye [964]
bhikkhu sato sa pariyantacārī,
—ḍaṁsâdhipātānaṁ siriṁsapānaṁ
manussaphassānaṁ catuppadānaṁ;

11. paradhammikānaṁ pi na santaseyya [965]
disvā pi tesaṁ bahubheravāni;
athâparāni abhisambhaveyya
parissayāni kusalânuesī.

12. Ātankaphassena khudāya phuṭṭho [966]
sītaṁ accuṇhaṁ adhivāsayeyya;
sa tehi phuṭṭho bahudhā anoko
viriyaṁ parakkamaṁ daḷhaṁ kareyya.

13. Theyyaṁ na kāre, na musā bhaṇeyya, [967]
mettāya phasse tasathāvarāni,
yad āvilattaṁ manaso vijaññā
'Kaṇhassa pakkho' ti vinodayeyya.

14 Kodhâtimānassa vasaṁ na gacche, [968]
mūlam pi tesaṁ palikhañña tiṭṭhe,
atha-ppiyaṁ vā pana appiyaṁ vā
addhâbhavanto abhisambhaveyya.

15. Paññaṁ purakkhatvā kalyāṇapīti [969]
vikkhambhaye tāni parissayāni,
aratiṁ sahetha sayanamhi pante.
caturo sahetha paridevadhamme:—

16. Kiṁ sū asissāmi? Kuvaṁ vā asissaṁ? [970]
Dukkhaṁ vata settha; kuv' ajja sessaṁ?
—ete vitakke paridevaneyye
vinayetha sekho aniketasārī.

Let th' Almsman stoutly brave [964]
with watchful discipline,
the dangers five,—to wit,
mosquitos, gadflies, snakes,
assaults of men, and beasts.

Let not the aspirant [965]
dread—though he sees them all—
onslaughts from sectaries,
but turn to overcome
perils confronting him.

Though sick and hungry, still [966]
let him brave cold and heat,
and (though they press him hard)
let th' homeless wanderer
bear up and struggle on.

Let him not steal or lie; [967]
let him be kind alike
to weak and strong, and, when
disorders plague his mind,
rout them as—'Māra's gang'!

Resisting ire and pride, [968]
let him extirpate them,
and make an end of likes
and dislikes, once for all.

With noble zest, by lore [969]
inspired, let him o'ercome
his perils and dispel
dislike of solitude
and all those four complaints:—

'What fare will come my way? [970]
—and where? Poor lodging this!
—where shall I lodge to-night?'
Let th' homeless aspirant
have done with such complaints.

17. Annañ ca laddhā vasanañ ca kāle [971]
mattaṁ so jaññā idha tosanatthaṁ,
so tesu gutto yatacāri gāme
rusito pi vācaṁ pharusaṁ na vajjā.

18. Okkhittacakkhu na ca pādalolo [972]
jhānânuyutto bahujāgar' assa;
upekkham ārabbha samāhitatto
takkâsayaṁ kukkucciy' ūpacchinde.

19. Cudito vacībhi satimā 'bhinande, [973]
sabrahmacārīsu khilaṁ pabhinde,
vācaṁ pamuñce kusalaṁ nâtivelaṁ,
janavādadhammāya na cetayeyya.

20. Athâparaṁ pañca rajāni loke [974]
yesaṁ satimā vinayāya sikkhe;
—rūpesu, saddesu, atho rasesu,
gandhesu, phassesu sahetha rāgaṁ.

21. Etesu dhammesu vineyya chandaṁ [975]
bhikkhu satimā suvimuttacitto
kālena so sammā dhammaṁ parivīmaṁsamāno
ekodibhūto vihane tamam so ti. *(Bhagavā ti)*

ATṬHAKAVAGGO CATUTTHO

When in due season food [971]
and clothes are given him,
let him just meet his needs
and, in such temperance,
with guarded mien, about
his village go; nor e'er
be stung to sharp retorts.

With steps that loiter not [972]
and eyes downcast, let him,
though plunged in reverie,
keep wide awake. Serene
through equal poise of mind,
let him check lurking doubts
and all malpractices.

In mindfulness let him [973]
welcome reproof, break up
his brethren's fallows, speak
succinctly to the point,
and heed no vulgar creed.

Then come the world's five stains, [974]
which he must set himself
to shed by discipline,
till he subdues the lusts
of eye, ear, taste, smell, touch.

Quit of these things of sense, [975]
let th' Almsman—mindfully,
with heart now freed—betimes
the Doctrine search till clouds
have left his fixèd mind.

END OF THE BOOK OF OCTADS

V. PĀRĀYANAVAGGA

(i) Vatthugāthā

1. Kosalānaṁ purā rammā agamā Dakkhiṇāpathaṁ [976]
ākiñcaññaṁ patthayāno brāhmaṇo mantapāragū.

2. So Assakassa visaye Muḷakassa samāsane [977]
vasī Godhāvarīkūle uñchena ca phalena ca.

3. Tass' eva upanissāya gāmo ca vipulo ahu, [978]
tato jātena āyena mahāyaññam akappayi;

4. mahāyaññaṁ yajitvāna puna pāvisi assamaṁ. [979]
Tasmiṁ patipaviṭṭhamhi añño āgañchi brāhmaṇo

5. ugghaṭṭapādo tasito pankadanto rajassiro; [980]
—so ca naṁ upasaṁkamma satāni pañca yācati.

6. Tam enaṁ Bāvarī disvā āsanena nimantayi, [981]
sukhañ ca kusalaṁ pucchi, idaṁ vacanam abravi:—

7. Yaṁ kho mamaṁ deyyadhammaṁ sabbaṁ vissajjitaṁ mayā; [982]
anujānāhi me, brahme; na 'tthi pañca satāni me.

8. Sace me yācamānassa bhavaṁ nânupadassati, [983]
sattame divase tuyhaṁ muddhā phalatu sattadhā.

9. Abhisaṁkharitvā kuhako bheravaṁ so akittayi. [984]
Tassa taṁ vacanaṁ sutvā Bāvarī dukkhito ahu,

10. ussussati anāhāro sokasallasamappito, [985]
atho pi evaṁcittassa jhāne na ramatī mano.

11. Utrastaṁ dukkhitaṁ disvā devatā atthakāminī [986]
Bāvariṁ upasaṁkamma idaṁ vacanam abravi:

12. Na so muddhaṁ pajānāti kuhako so dhanatthiko, [987]
muddhani muddhapāte vā ñāṇaṁ tassa na vijjati.

13. Bhotī carahi jānāti? Tam me akkhāhi pucchitā [988]
muddhaṁ muddhâdhipātañ ca, taṁ suṇoma vaco tava.

14. Aham p' etaṁ na jānāmi; ñāṇam me 'ttha na vijjati; [989]
muddham muddhâdhipāto ca Jinānaṁ h' eta' dassanaṁ.

15. Atha ko carahi jānāti asmiṁ puthavimaṇḍale [990]
muddhaṁ muddhâdhipātañ ca? Tam me akkhāhi, devate.

BOOK V. THE WAY ACROSS

Prologue

Southwards from Sāvatthī, fair capital [976]
of Kosala, a learned brahmin came
in aspiration for the Plane of Naught.

Near Assaka and hard by Muḷaka, [977]
beside Godhāvarī's fork'd stream, he lived
on wilding fruits and sustenance he culled.

Hard by, he held a thriving village-fief; [978]
its yield he lavish'd on a pious feast;

this done, he sought his hermitage once more. [979]
On his return, another brahmin came

—footsore, athirst, with muddied teeth, dust-stain'd— [980]
who asked him for five hundred pieces down!

First, begging him be seated, Bāvarī [981]
asked how he inly fared, and then replied:—

'Nothing is left of what I had to give. [982]
Forgive me, brahmin;—no such sum have I.'

'If you refuse me, may your head be split [983]
in seven bits upon the seventh day!'

With due formalities, the rascal laid [984]
this curse on Bāvarī,—who quaked with fear,

and took no food, but pined in anguish sore; [985]
and Reverie's delights were his no more.

To help him in his dread and woe, there came [986]
his homestead's deity, who spoke these words:—

'That greedy rascal nothing knows of heads! [987]
Of heads and riving heads he 's ignorant!'

'If you know, madam, let me hear you speak [988]
of heads and riving heads; I yearn to know.'

'I too know nothing, and am ignorant; [989]
'tis only "Conquerors" who know these things.'

'Who then in all the wide, wide world does know [990]
of heads and riving heads? Sprite, tell me this.'

16. 'Purā Kapilavatthumhā nikkhanto lokanāyako [991]
apacco Okkākarājassa Sakyaputto pabhaṁkaro.

17. So hi, brāhmaṇa, Sambuddho sabbadhammāna' pāragū [992]
sabbâbhiññābalappatto sabbadhammesu cakkhumā
sabbadhammakkhayaṁ patto vimutto upadhikkhaye;

18. Buddho so Bhagavā loke dhammaṁ deseti cakkhumā. [993]
Taṁ tvaṁ gantvāna pucchassu; so te taṁ byākarissati.'

19. 'Sambuddho' ti vaco sutvā udaggo Bāvarī ahu; [994]
sok' assa tanuko āsi, pītiñ ca vipulaṁ labhi.

20. So Bāvarī attamano udaggo [995]
taṁ devataṁ pucchati vedajāto:
Katamamhi gāme nigamamhi vā puna
katamamhi vā janapade lokanātho
yattha gantvā namassemu Sambuddhaṁ dipaduttamaṁ.

21. Sāvatthiyaṁ Kosalamandire Jino [996]
pahūtapañño varabhūrimedhaso
so Sakyaputto vidhuro anāsavo
muddhâdhipātassa vidū narâsabho.

22. Tato āmantayi sisse brāhmaṇe mantapārage:— [997]
Etha, māṇavā; akkhissaṁ; suṇotha vacanaṁ mama.

23. Yass' eso dullabho loke pātubhāvo abhiṇhaso [998]
sv' ajja lokamhi uppanno Sambuddho iti vissuto.
—Khippaṁ gantvāna Sāvatthiṁ passavho dipaduttamaṁ.

24. Kathañ carahi jānemu disvā 'Buddho' ti, brāhmaṇa? [999]
Ajānataṁ no pabrūhi yathā jānemu taṁ mayaṁ.

25. Āgatāni hi mantesu mahāpurisalakkhaṇā [1000]
dvattiṁsā ca vyākhyātā samattā anupubbaso.

'A Sákyán of King Okkāka's line [991]
has left their capital to spread the Light.

The Lord of All-Enlightenment is he, [992]
in ev'ry outlook versed; all ken and might
is his; his gaze all outlooks penetrates;
by subjugating all phenomena
life's stuff is spent, and he has won Release.

Th' Enlighten'd and All-seeing Lord is he, [993]
who here on earth proclaims his Doctrine's truth.
Go, ask of him; and he will make all clear'.

'The All-Enlighten'd'—At that name's mere sound, [994]
elation seized on Bāvarī; his grief
abated; joy abounding filled his breast.

Then Bāvarī, elate [995]
with joy, excitedly
besought the sprite to name
the village, town, or realm
where dwelt this Lord of Lords,
that they might go and render homage due
to th' All-Enlighten'd, prince of all mankind.

'At Sāvatthī, beneath [996]
a roof in Kosala,
the Victor dwells, profound
in lore, of searching wit.
This matchless Sákyán,
from Cankers wholly free,
—this paragon of men—
knows well how heads are split.

Then Bāvarī addressed his following [997]
of brahmins, masters of the runes, and said:—
'Draw near, young brahmins; list to what I say!

Lo! One whose advent in the world is rare, [998]
to-day is here on earth,—famed far and wide
as "th' All-Enlighten'd". Speed to Sāvatthī,
and there behold mankind's unchallenged best.'

'But, brahmin, how can we feel sure we see [999]
a very Buddha? Teach our ignorance'.

'The runes detail the marks of Supermen, [1000]
and of those marks the tale is thirty-two.

26. Yass' ete honti gattesu mahāpurisalakkhaṇā [1001]
duve va tassa gatiyo, tatiyā hi na vijjati:—

27. Sace agāraṁ āvasati, vijeyya paṭhaviṁ imaṁ [1002]
adaṇḍena asatthena dhammena-m-anusāsati.

28. Sace ca so pabbajati agārā anagāriyaṁ, [1003]
vivaṭacchado Sambuddho arahā bhavati anuttaro.

29. Jātiṁ gottañ ca lakkhaṇaṁ mante sisse punâpare [1004]
muddhaṁ muddhâdhipātañ ca manasā yeva pucchatha.

30. Anāvaraṇadassāvī yadi Buddho bhavissati, [1005]
manasā pucchite pañhe vācāya vissajessati.

31. Bāvarissa vaco sutvā sissā soḷasa brāhmaṇā [1006]
—Ajito Tissa-Metteyyo Puṇṇako atha Mettagū

32. Dhotako Upasīvo ca Nando ca atha Hemako [1007]
Todeyya-Kappā dubhayo Jatukaṇṇī ca paṇḍito

33. Bhadrāvudho Udayo ca Posālo câpi brāhmaṇo [1008]
Mogharājā ca medhāvī Pingiyo ca mahā isi—

34. paccekagaṇino sabbe sabbalokassa vissutā [1009]
jhāyī jhānaratā dhīrā pubbavāsanavāsitā.

35. Bāvariṁ abhivādetvā katvā ca naṁ padakkhiṇaṁ [1010]
jaṭâjinadharā sabbe pakkāmuṁ uttarāmukhā,

36. —Muḷakassa Patiṭṭhānaṁ purimaṁ Māhissatiṁ tadā [1011]
Ujjeniñ câpi Gonaddhaṁ Vedisaṁ Vanasavhayaṁ.

37. Kosambiṁ câpi Sāketaṁ Sāvatthiñ ca puruttamaṁ [1012]
Setavyaṁ Kapilavatthuṁ Kusinārañ ca mandiraṁ.

38. Pāvañ ca bhoganagaraṁ Vesāliṁ Māgadhaṁ puraṁ [1013]
Pāsāṇakañ cetiyañ ca ramaṇīyaṁ manoramaṁ.

39. Tasito v' udakaṁ sītaṁ, mahālābham va vāṇijo, [1014]
chāyaṁ ghammâbhitatto va, turitā pabbataṁ āruhuṁ.

To one who bears those two and thirty marks, [1001]
two walks of life are open,—and no third.

If house and home be his, the whole wide world [1002]
shall own his sway. On righteousness shall rest
his rule, and not on cudgel or on sword.

But if from home to homelessness he goes, [1003]
he strips the veil from things, and so becomes
the peerless All-Enlighten'd Arahat.

Frame questions mentally about my birth, [1004]
and clan, and marks, and runes, and pupils taught,
—and heads and riving heads. Your questions frame,

and, if he Buddha be of boundless ken, [1005]
his lips will answer what your minds have asked.'

At Bāvarī's behest went sixteen youths, [1006]
—named Ájitá and Tissa Métteyyá,
and Púṇṇaká and kindly Méttagū

—with Úpasīva, Nanda, Dhótaká, [1007]
and Hémaká, Todéyya, Kappa too,
and learned Jatukannī, Údaya,

Bhadrāvudha, the brahmin Pósālá, [1008]
quick Mogharāja, and sage Pingiya.

Each led his train of pupils; each was famed [1009]
throughout the world; they all loved Reverie;
they all could conjure up their former lives.

Of Bāvarī these took devout farewell, [1010]
then northwards went, hide-clad, with matted hair,

through Pátiṭṭhān in Múḷaká, through Old [1011]
Mahíssatí, Ujjéni, Gónaddhá,

then Védisá 'the Weald', Kosámbī next, [1012]
Sākéta, Sāvatthī (of cities queen),
then Sétavyá, and Kápilávatthú,

past Kúsinārā town, past Pāvā too, [1013]
that home of opulence, past Vésālī,
thence on to Mágadhá's proud capital,
and so to Rock-Shrine, fair, delectable.

As thirsty folk to cooling waters haste, [1014]
as merchants wealth pursue, as men forspent
with heat seek shade, these scaled the mountain-side.

40. Bhagavā ca tamhi samaye bhikkhusaṁghapurakkhato [1015]
bhikkhūnaṁ Dhammaṁ deseti, sīho va nadatī vane.

41. Ajito addasa Sambuddhaṁ vītaraṁsi' va bhānumaṁ, [1016]
candaṁ yathā pannarase pāripūriṁ upāgataṁ.

42. Ath' assa gatte disvāna paripūrañ ca vyañjanaṁ [1017]
ekamantaṁ ṭhito haṭṭho manopañhe apucchatha:—

43. Ādissa jammanaṁ brūhi, gottaṁ brūhi salakkhaṇaṁ, [1018]
mantesu pāramiṁ brūhi; kati vāceti brāhmaṇo?

44. Vīsaṁvassasataṁ āyu; so ca gottena Bāvarī; [1019]
tīṇ' assa lakkhaṇā gatte; tiṇṇaṁ vedāna' pāragū;

45. lakkhaṇe itihāse ca sanighaṇḍusakeṭubhe; [1020]
pañca satāni vāceti; sadhamme pāramiṁ gato.

46. Lakkhaṇānaṁ pavicayaṁ Bāvarissa, naruttama [1021]
taṇhacchida, pakāsehi. Mā no kankhāyitaṁ ahu.

47. Mukhaṁ jivhāya chādeti; uṇṇ' assa bhamukantare; [1022]
kosohitaṁ vatthaguyhaṁ;—evaṁ jānāhi, māṇava.

48. (Pucchaṁ hi kiñci asuṇanto sutvā pañhe viyākate [1023]
vicinteti jano sabbo vedajāto katañjali:—

49. Ko nu devo va Brahmā vā Indo vā pi Sujampati [1024]
manasā pucchi te pañhe? Kam etaṁ paṭibhāsati?)

50. Muddhaṁ muddhâdhipātañ ca Bāvarī paripucchati. [1025]
Taṁ vyākarohi, Bhagavā; kankhaṁ vinaya no, ise.

51. 'Avijjā muddhā ti jānāhi; vijjā muddhâdhipātinī, [1026]
saddhāsatisamādhīhi chandaviriyena saṁyutā.'

---

52. Tato vedena mahatā santhambhitvāna māṇavo [1027]
ekaṁsaṁ ajinaṁ katvā pādesu sirasā pati:—

53. Bāvarī brāhmaṇo bhoto saha sissehi, mārisa, [1028]
udaggacitto sumano pāde vandati, cakkhuma.

54. Sukhito Bāvarī hotu saha sissehi brāhmaṇo; [1029]
tvañ câpi sukkhito hohi;—ciraṁ jīvāhi, māṇava.

In conclave, by his Almsmen girt around, [1015]
the Lord was teaching them the Doctrine's truths
and like a lion's roar his voice rang out.

To Ájitá the All-Enlighten'd seemed [1016]
the radiant sun, or mid-month's moon at full!

A survey of his frame—with marks complete— [1017]
filled Ájitá with joy; in reverence
he stood and framed these questions in his mind:—

'Declare our teacher's birth, and clan, and marks, [1018]
what runes he knows, what pupils learn of him.'

The Lord: Six-score years old, a Bāvarī by clan, [1019]
he bears three marks; he knows the Vedas three;

is versed in marks and scholarship; instructs [1020]
five hundred youths; is perfect in his creed.

Ajita: Detail the marks he bears, thou matchless man. [1021]
Cravings' uprooter! Leave us not in doubt.

The Lord: His tongue can hide his face; a downy tuft [1022]
divides his brows; his privities are sheathed.

(Hearing replies to questions heard by none, [1023]
all present raised their folded palms in awe,

wond'ring what godhead—Indra?—or Brahmā?— [1024]
was thinking questions; who received replies.)

Ajita: Of heads and riving heads, asks Bāvarī. [1025]
Explain this, Lord; dispel our doubts, o sage.

The Lord: The head is Ignorance,—which Knowledge rives, [1026]
Knowledge informed by faith and mindfulness,
by earnest heart and mind, by eager zeal.

With deep emotion thrilled, the brahmin youth [1027]
his shoulder bared in homage to the Lord,
and bowed his head before the Master's feet.

Ajita: O sir (he cried), the brahmin Bāvarī, [1028]
with all his pupils, here adores thy feet
in heartfelt thankfulness, All-seeing Lord!

The Lord: May all go well with Bāvarī and train, [1029]
—and thee, young brahmin! Length of days be thine!

55. Bāvarissa ca tuyhaṁ vā sabbesaṁ sabbasaṁsayaṁ [1030]
katâvakāsā pucchavho, yaṁ kiñci manas' icchatha.

56. Sambuddhena katokāso nisīditvāna pañjalī [1031]
Ajito paṭhamaṁ pañhaṁ tattha pucchi Tathāgataṁ.

Ajitamāṇava-pucchā (i)

1. Kena-ssu nivuto loko? Kena-ssu na-ppakāsati? [1032]
(*icc-āyasmā Ajito*)
Ki' 'ssâbhilepanaṁ brūsi? Kiṁ-su tassa mahabbhayaṁ?

2. Avijjāya nivuto loko, vevicchā pamādā na-ppakāsati. [1033]
(*Ajitâti Bhagavā*)
Jappâbhilepanaṁ brūmi. Dukkham assa mahabbhayaṁ.

3. Savanti sabbadhī sotā; sotānaṁ kiṁ nivāraṇaṁ? [1034]
(*icc-āyasmā Ajito*)
Sotānaṁ saṁvaraṁ brūhi. Kena sotā pithiyyare?

4. Yāni sotāni lokasmiṁ, sati tesaṁ nivāraṇaṁ, [1035]
(*Ajitâti Bhagavā*)
sotānaṁ saṁvaraṁ brūmi,—paññāy' ete pithiyyare.

5. Paññā c' eva satī câpi nāmarūpañ ca, mārisa, [1036]
(*icc-āyasmā Ajito*)
etaṁ me puṭṭho pabrūhi: Katth' etaṁ uparujjhati?

6. Yam etaṁ pañhaṁ apucchi, Ajita, taṁ vadāmi te: [1037]
yattha nāmañ ca rūpañ ca asesaṁ uparujjhati,
viññāṇassa nirodhena etth' etaṁ uparujjhati.

7. Ye ca saṁkhātadhammâse, ye ca sekhā puthu idha, [1038]
tesaṁ me nipako iriyaṁ puṭṭho pabrūhi, mārisa.

8. Kāmesu nâbhigijjheyya, manasânāvilo siyā, [1039]
kusalo sabbadhammānaṁ sato bhikkhu paribbaje ti.

Seize now this opportunity and raise [1030]
your difficulties,—yours, or Bāvarī's,
or anyone's. Ask whatsoe'er you will.

The All-Enlighten'd having granted leave, [1031]
first Ájitá took seat and folded palms
of humble supplication, as he asked
his question of the Lord who Found the Truth:—

Ajita's Question (i)

Ajita: What shrouds the world? What stops its being seen? [1032]
And what defiles, what threatens it, say you?

The Lord: 'Tis Ignorance which shrouds the world; 'tis wants [1033]
and sloth which stop its being clearly seen.
Cravings (say I) defile, Ills threaten it.

Ajita: The tides of evil surge around. What force [1034]
can dam them? Say what curb have they? what bar?

The Lord: 'Tis mindfulness dams evil's tides. They have [1035]
a curb (say I);—'tis Knowledge bars their flow.

Ajita: Prithee, take knowledge, and take mindfulness, [1036]
and with them Individuality.
I pray you say what lays this last to rest?

The Lord: Your question, Ájitá, I answer thus:— [1037]
Ere Individuality can cease,
th' informing mind must first be laid to rest.

Ajita: Take experts now, and aspirants, and men [1038]
at large. What way of life do you prescribe?

The Lord: To pleasure deaf, with undistracted mind, [1039]
above phenomena, leave house and home
to be an Almsman watchful and alert.

TISSAMETTEYYAMĀṆAVAPUCCHĀ (ii)

1. Ko 'dha santusito loke? Kassa no santi iñjitā? [1040]
(*icc-āyasmā Tisso Metteyyo*)
Ko ubhanta-m-abhiññāya majjhe mantā na lippati?
Kaṁ brūsi 'mahāpuriso' ti? Ko idha sibbanim accagā?

2. Kāmesu brahmacariyavā vītataṇho sadā sato [1041]
(*Metteyyâti Bhagavā*)
saṁkhāya nibbuto bhikkhu, tassa no santi iñjitā;

3. so ubhanta-m-abhiññāya majjhe mantā na lippati; [1042]
taṁ brūmi 'mahāpuriso' ti; so idha sibbanim accagā ti.

PUṆṆAKAMĀṆAVAPUCCHĀ (iii)

1. Anejaṁ mūladassāviṁ (*icc-āyasmā Puṇṇako*) [1043]
atthi pañhena āgamaṁ:—
Kiṁ nissitā isayo manujā
khattiyā brāhmaṇā devatānaṁ
yaññam akappayiṁsu puthū 'dha loke?
—Pucchāmi taṁ, Bhagavā; brūhi me taṁ.

2. Ye kec' ime isayo manujā (*Puṇṇakâti Bhagavā*) [1044]
khattiyā brāhmaṇā devatānaṁ
yaññam akappayimsu puthū 'dha loke,
āsiṁsamānā, Puṇṇaka, itthabhāvaṁ
jaraṁ sitā yaññam akappayiṁsu.

3. Ye kec' ime isayo manujā (*icc-āyasmā Puṇṇako*) [1045]
khattiyā brāhmaṇā devatānaṁ
yaññam akappayiṁsu puthū 'dha loke,
kacci-ssu te, Bhagavā, yaññapathe appamattā
atāru' jātiñ ca jarañ ca, mārisa?
—Pucchāmi taṁ, Bhagavā; brūhi me taṁ.

4. Āsiṁsanti thomayanti abhijappanti juhanti [1046]
(*Puṇṇakâti Bhagavā*)
kāmâbhijappanti paṭicca lābhaṁ.
Te yājayogā bhavarāgarattā
nâtariṁsu jātijaran ti brūmi.

Tissa Metteyya's Question (ii)

Tissa Metteyya: Who lives content? Who feels no waverings? [1040]
Who, seeing both extremes, has wit to tread
a middle path between them, undefiled?
Who ranks as Superman? Who conquers Wants?

The Lord: The man 'mid pleasures virtuous, devoid [1041]
of Cravings, watchful, always on his guard,
the Almsman who has thought his way to bliss,
—*his* fixèd mind no waverings beset.

He, seeing both extremes, has wit to tread [1042]
a middle path between them, undefiled.
—Him I call 'Superman'; he conquers Wants.

Puṇṇaka's Question (iii)

Puṇṇaka: O thou who cravest nought, whose eye can see [1043]
the roots of things, a question here I bring.
Tell me why hosts of sages—nobly born,
or brahmins—sacrificed on earth to gods?
Vouchsafe an answer, Lord.

The Lord: Because—when old—these hosts [1044]
of sages cherished hopes
by sacrifice to gods
to win some earthy bliss.

Puṇṇaka: But did their tireless zeal [1045]
for sacrificing save
these men from birth and eld?
Vouchsafe an answer, Lord.

The Lord: They crave, they laud, they pray, they sacrifice! [1046]
Praying to be repaid
in pleasures sensory,
these sacrificing folk
who pine for future life
—have *not* 'scaped birth and eld.

5. Te ce nâtarimsu yājayogā (*icc-āyasmā Puṇṇako*) [1047]
yaññehi jātiñ ca jarañ ca, mārisa,
atha ko carahi devamanussaloke
atāri jātiñ ca jarañ ca, mārisa?
—Pucchāmi taṁ, Bhagavā; brūhi me taṁ.

6. Saṁkhāya lokasmiṁ parôparāni [1048]
(*Puṇṇakâti Bhagavā*)
yass' iñjitaṁ na 'tthi kuhiñci loke,
santo vidhūmo anigho nirāso
atāri so jātijaran ti brūmîti.

METTAGŪMĀṆAVAPUCCHĀ (iv)

1. Pucchāmi taṁ, Bhagavā; brūhi me tam. [1049]
(*icc-āyasmā Mettagū*)
maññāmi taṁ vedaguṁ bhāvitattaṁ:
Kuto nu dukkhā samudāgatā ime
ye keci lokasmiṁ anekarūpā?

2. Dukkhassa ve maṁ pabhavaṁ apucchasi; [1050]
(*Mettagûti Bhagavā*)
taṁ te pavakkhāmi yathā pajānaṁ:—
Upadhinidānā pabhavanti dukkhā
ye keci lokasmiṁ anekarūpā.

3. Yo ve avidvā upadhiṁ karoti, [1051]
punappunaṁ dukkham upeti mando.
Tasmā pajānaṁ upadhiṁ na kayirā
dukkhassa jātippabhavânupassī.

4. Yan taṁ apucchimha, akittayi no. [1052]
Aññaṁ taṁ pucchāma; tad ingha brūhi.
Kathan nu dhīrā vitaranti oghaṁ
jātijaraṁ sokapariddavañ ca?
Tam me, muni, sādhu viyākarohi;
tathā hi te vidito esa dhammo.

Puṇṇaka: If sacrifices fail [1047]
to save their votaries
from birth and eld, say who
of men and gods is saved?
Vouchsafe an answer, Lord.

The Lord: The man whose thought has scanned [1048]
the universe entire,
who knows no waverings,
who, good without a trace
of smould'ring vice, is free
from tremors or desires,
—*he* 's saved from birth and eld.

Mettagū's Question (iv)

Mettagū: I ask thee, Lord, to say [1049]
(for, versed in lore and schooled
I deem thee) whence arise
life's teeming, varied Ills?

The Lord: You ask me whence come Ills; [1050]
that knowledge I'll impart.
—From Transmigration spring
life's teeming varied Ills.

The fool who starts that round, [1051]
through crassness drees a weird
of oft-repeated Ills.
Be warned, then; realize
Ills' birth and origin;
start not that gruesome round.

Mettagū: That answers what I asked. [1052]
Vouchsafe to answer this:—
Pray, how do saints o'ercome
life's welter, birth, and eld,
wailing and sorrow's pangs?
Expound this, sage, for clear
this outlook is to thee.

5. Kittayissāmi te dhammaṁ diṭṭhe dhamme anītihaṁ [1053]
(*Mettagûti Bhagavā*)
yaṁ viditvā sato caraṁ tare loke visattikaṁ.

6. Tañ câhaṁ abhinandāmi, mahesi, dhammam uttamaṁ [1054]
yaṁ viditvā sato caraṁ tare loke visattikaṁ.

7. Yaṁ kiñci sampajānāsi (*Mettagûti Bhagavā*) [1055]
uddhaṁ adho tiriyaṁ câpi majjhe,
etesu nandiñ ca nivesanañ ca
panujja viññāṇaṁ bhave na tiṭṭhe.

8. Evaṁ-vihārī sato appamatto [1056]
bhikkhu caraṁ hitvā mamāyitāni
jātijaraṁ sokapariddavañ ca
idh' eva vidvā pajaheyya dukkhaṁ.

9. Etâbhinandāmi vaco mahesino [1057]
sukittitaṁ, Gotam', anūpadhīkaṁ.
Addhā hi Bhagavā pahāsi dukkhaṁ;
tathā hi te vidito esa dhammo.

10. Te câpi nūna pajaheyyu' dukkhaṁ [1058]
ye tvaṁ, muni, aṭṭhitaṁ ovadeyya.
Taṁ taṁ namassāmi samecca, nāga.
Appeva maṁ [Bhagavā] aṭṭhitaṁ ovadeyya.

11. Yaṁ brāhmaṇaṁ vedaguṁ abhijaññā [1059]
akiñcanaṁ kāmabhave asattaṁ,
addhā hi so oghaṁ imam atāri
tiṇṇo ca pāraṁ akhilo akankho,

The Lord: That outlook I'll expound to thee:—'Tis here [1053]
and now; no hearsay vain. By grasping it,
the man who walks thereby in mindfulness
shall leave the world's entanglements behind.

Mettagū: This matchless outlook, sage, rejoices me, [1054]
—to walk thereby in watchful mindfulness
and leave the world's entanglements behind.

The Lord: Reject then smug delight [1055]
in what—here—anywhere—
senses report. Let not
your nature base its hopes
on mere existences.

Thus minded, vigilant, [1056]
and zealous, Almsman, live
a life with nothing dear,
a life that, here on earth,
has plumbed old-age and birth,
wailing and sorrow's pangs,
and so sheds mortal Ills.

Mettagū: It gladdens me to hear [1057]
sage Gotama extol
a state from life's stuff freed.
Assuredly the Lord
has shed all Ills, so clear
this outlook is to him.

Those too shall shed all Ills [1058]
whom thou dost teach so well.
Wherefore, to thee I come
in adoration meet,
and crave thy teachings, Lord.

The Lord: The man you recognize [1059]
as 'Brahmin rich in lore',
emancipate, unsnared
by appetites or life,
—has crossed the welter here
and reached the shore Beyond,
with open'd mind, doubt-free.

12. vidvā ca so vedagu naro idha [1060]
bhavâbhave sangam imaṁ visajja,
so vītataṇho anigho nirāso
atāri so jātijaran ti brūmîti.

DHOTAKAMĀṆAVAPUCCHĀ (v)

1. Pucchāmi taṁ, Bhagavā; brūhi me taṁ; [1061]
(*icc-āyasmā Dhotako*)
vācâbhikankhāmi, mahesi, tuyhaṁ:
tava sutvāna nigghosaṁ sikkhe nibbānam attano?

2. Tena h' ātappaṁ karohi; idh' eva nipako sato [1062]
(*Dhotakâti Bhagavā*)
ito sutvāna nigghosaṁ sikkhe nibbānam attano.

3. Passām' ahaṁ devamanussaloke [1063]
akiñcanaṁ Brāhmaṇaṁ iriyamānaṁ.
Taṁ taṁ namassāmi, samantacakkhu.
Pamuñca maṁ, Sakka, kathaṁkathāhi.

4. Nâhaṁ samīhāmi pamocanāya [1064]
kathaṁkathiṁ, Dhotaka, kañci loke.
Dhammañ ca seṭṭhaṁ ājānamāno,
evaṁ tuvaṁ ogham imaṁ taresi.

5. Anusāsa, Brahme, karuṇāyamāno [1065]
vivekadhammaṁ, yam ahaṁ vijaññaṁ
yathâhaṁ, ākāso va avyāpajjamāno,
idh' eva santo asito careyyaṁ.

6. Kittayissāmi te santiṁ diṭṭhe dhamme anītihaṁ [1066]
(*Dhotakâti Bhagavā*)
yaṁ viditvā sato caraṁ tare loke visattikaṁ.

7. Tañ câhaṁ abhinandāmi, mahesi, santim uttamaṁ [1067]
yaṁ viditvā sato caraṁ tare loke visattikaṁ.

He knows. His lore rejects [1060]
all lures of future life;
from cravings purged, devoid
of tremors or desires,
he 's saved from birth and eld.

Dhotaka's Question (v)

Dhotaka: I ask thee, Lord, to tell, [1061]
I yearn to hear, how men
who hearken unto thee
can work salvation out.

The Lord: Be ardent! Here and now, [1062]
by hearkening to me,
shall thought and watchfulness
work man's salvation out.

Dhotaka: In thee, 'mong gods and men, [1063]
I find the 'Brahmin true'
who walks emancipate.
Wherefore, to thee I come
in adoration meet.
All-seeing Lord, free me
from doubts, great Sákyán!

The Lord: No doubting heart do I [1064]
essay to free. Grasp first
this best of Doctrines; then
thou 'lt cross the welter here.

Dhotaka: In pity, Holy One, [1065]
teach me to live Aloof,
that I may clearly see
how—calm as th' ether—I
may dwell in freedom's peace.

The Lord: That peace will I expound to thee. 'Tis here [1066]
and now; 'tis based on thought, not hearsay vain.
Walk thou by it with constant watchfulness,
leaving the world's entanglements behind.

Dhotaka: This matchless peace, great sage, rejoices me, [1067]
—to walk thereby with constant watchfulness
and leave the world's entanglements behind!

8. Yaṁ kiñci sampajānāsi (*Dhotakâti Bhagavā*) [1068]
uddhaṁ adho tiriyaṁ câpi majjhe,
etaṁ viditvā 'sango' ti loke
bhavâbhavāya mā 'kāsi taṇhan ti.

UPASĪVAMĀṆAVAPUCCHĀ (vi)

1. Eko ahaṁ, Sakka, mahantam oghaṁ [1069]
(*icc-āyasmā Upasīvo*)
anissito no visahāmi tārituṁ.
Ārammaṇaṁ brūhi, samantacakkhu,
yaṁ nissito ogham imaṁ tareyyaṁ.

2. Ākiñcaññaṁ pekkhamāno satimā [1070]
(*Upasīvâti Bhagavā*)
'Na 'tthîti' nissāya tarassu oghaṁ,
kāme pahāya virato kathāhi
taṇhakkhayaṁ nattamahâbhipassa.

3. Sabbesu kāmesu yo vītarāgo (*icc-āyasmā Upasīvo*) [1071]
ākiñcaññaṁ nissito hitva-m-aññaṁ
saññāvimokhe parame vimutto,
tiṭṭhe nu so tattha anānuyāyi?

4. Sabbesu kāmesu yo vītarāgo (*Upasīvâti Bhagavā*) [1072]
ākincaññaṁ nissito hitva-m-aññaṁ,
saññāvimokkhe parame 'dhimutto,
tiṭṭheyya so tattha anānuyāyi.

5. Tiṭṭhe ce so tattha anānuyāyi, [1073]
pūgam pi vassānaṁ, samantacakkhu,
tatth' eva so sītisiyā vimutto,
cavetha viññāṇaṁ tathāvidhassa?

6. Accī yathā vātavegena khitto (*Upasīvâti Bhagavā*) [1074]
atthaṁ paleti, na upeti sankhaṁ,
—evaṁ munī nāmakāyā vimutto
atthaṁ paleti, na upeti sankhaṁ.

The Lord: Reject then smug delight [1068]
in what—here—anywhere—
senses report, and know
'tis but a worldly snare;
crave not for 'life to come'!

Upasīva's Question (vi)

Upasīva: Alone, without support, [1069]
great Sákyan, I should fail
to win across life's surge.
Seer, what support will bear
a man in safety o'er?

The Lord: Th' inherent Nothingness [1070]
of things discern. Make this
conviction—'Naught abides!'—
support thee safely o'er.
Scorn pleasures; gossip not;
strive day and night—each hour—
cravings to extirpate.

Upasīva: Will he whom pleasures tempt [1071]
no more, who cleaves to nought
save Nothingness alone,
who from Perceptions wins
entire Deliverance,
—will he ne'er fall away?

The Lord: The man whom pleasures tempt [1072]
no more, who cleaves to nought
save Nothingness alone,
who from Perceptions wins
entire Deliverance,
—will never fall away.

Upasīva: If, as the years roll on, [1073]
he never falls away
when Fever's fires are quenched,
—will Personality
be born with him again?

The Lord: As flame blown out by wind [1074]
is lost to cognizance,
e'en so the sage, released
from whilom qualities,
has disappeared from ken.

7. Atthangato so uda vā so na 'tthi [1075]
udāhu ve sassatiyā arogo?
Tam me, muni, sādhu viyākarohi,
tathā hi te vidito esa dhammo.

8. Atthangatassa na pamāṇam atthi; (*Upasīvâti Bhagavā*) [1076]
yena naṁ vajju, taṁ tassa na 'tthi;
sabbesu dhammesu samūhatesu,
samūhatā vādapathā pi sabbe ti.

Nandamāṇavapucchā (vii)

1. 'Santi loke munayo' (*icc-āyasmā Nando*) [1077]
janā vadanti. Ta-y-idaṁ kathaṁ su?
Ñāṇûpapannaṁ no muniṁ vadanti
udāhu ve jīvitenûpapannaṁ?

2. Na diṭṭhiyā na sutiyā na ñāṇena [1078]
munîdha, Nanda, kusalā vadanti.
Visenikatvā anighā nirāsā
caranti ye, te munayo ti brūmi.

3. Ye kec' ime samaṇabrāhmaṇāse (*icc-āyasmā Nando*) [1079]
diṭṭhe sutenâpi vadanti suddhiṁ,
sīlabbatenâpi vadanti suddhiṁ,
anekarūpena vadanti suddhiṁ,
—kacci ssu te [Bhagavā] tattha yatā carantā
atāru' jātiñ ca jarañ ca, mārisa?
Pucchāmi taṁ, Bhagavā; brūhi me taṁ.

4. Ye kec' ime samaṇabrāhmaṇāse (*Nandâti Bhagavā*) [1080]
diṭṭhe sutenâpi vadanti suddhiṁ,
sīlabbatenâpi vadanti suddhiṁ,
anekarūpena vadanti suddhiṁ,
—kiñcâpi te tattha yatā caranti,
nâtariṁsu jātijaran ti brūmi.

Upasiva: Does he who 'disappears' [1075]
quite cease to be? or last
for ever hale and strong?
Explain this, sage; for, clear
to thee this outlook shows.

The Lord: Whoso thus 'disappears' [1076]
is measureless; he keeps
nothing that can be named.
When attributes have gone,
denoting terms go too.

Nanda's Question (vii)

Nanda: Men talk of 'sages here'. [1077]
What mean they? Is it lore
that constitutes a sage?
or is it mode of life?

The Lord: 'Tis not for 'views' he holds, [1078]
insight, or garner'd lore,
that experts style him 'sage'.
Sages, say I, are those
who conquer in the fight
and have no hopes or wants.

Nanda: Brahmins and anchorites [1079]
who say that Purity
resides in views, or lore,
or works, or ritual,
or in what things they will,
—have they 'scaped birth and eld?
Vouchsafe an answer, Lord.

The Lord: Brahmins and anchorites [1080]
who say that 'Purity'
resides in 'views', or lore,
or works, or ritual,
or in what things they will,
—have *not* 'scaped birth and eld.

5. Ye kec' ime samaṇabrāhmaṇāse (*icc-āyasmā Nando*) [1081]
diṭṭhe sutenâpi vadanti suddhiṁ,
sīlabbatenâpi vadanti suddhiṁ,
anekarūpena vadanti suddhiṁ,
te ce, muni, brūsi anoghatiṇṇe,
atha ko carahi devamanussaloke
atāri jātiñ ca jarañ ca, mārisa?
Pucchāmi taṁ, Bhagavā; brūhi me tam.

6. Nâham sabbe samaṇabrāhmaṇāse (*Nandâti Bhagavā*) [1082]
jātijarāya nivutā ti brūmi.
Ye sîdha diṭṭhaṁ va sutaṁ mutaṁ vā,
sīlabbataṁ vā pi pahāya sabbaṁ,
anekarūpam pi pahāya sabbaṁ,
taṇhaṁ pariññāya anāsavāse,
—te ve narā oghatiṇṇā ti brūmi.

7. Etâbhinandāmi vaco mahesino [1083]
sukittitaṁ, Gotam', anūpadhīkaṁ.
Ye sîdha diṭṭhaṁ va sutaṁ mutaṁ vā,
sīlabbataṁ vā pi pahāya sabbaṁ,
anekarūpam pi pahāya sabbaṁ,
taṇhaṁ pariññāya anāsavāse,
—aham pi te oghatiṇṇā ti brūmîti.

Hemakamāṇavapucchā (viii)

1. Ye me pubbe viyākaṁsu—huraṁ Gotamasāsanā: [1084]
(*icc-āyasmā Hemako*)
icc-āsi, iti bhavissati, sabban taṁ itihītihaṁ,
sabban taṁ takkavaḍḍhanaṁ; nâhaṁ tattha abhiramiṁ.

2. Tvañ ca me dhammaṁ akkhāhi taṇhānigghātanaṁ, muni, [1085]
yaṁ viditvā sato caraṁ tare loke visattikaṁ.

3. Idha diṭṭhasutamutaviññātesu piyarūpesu, Hemaka, [1086]
chandarāgavinodanaṁ, Nibbānapadam accutaṁ,

4. —etad aññāya ye satā diṭṭhadhammâbhinibbutā [1087]
upasantā ca te sadā, tiṇṇā loke visattikan ti.

Nanda: If you say all those fail, [1081]
who hold that 'Purity'
resides in 'views' or lore,
or works, or ritual,
or in whatever else,
—what god or man succeeds?
Vouchsafe an answer, Lord.

The Lord: I do not say that all [1082]
brahmins and anchorites
are mewed in birth and eld.
'Safe o'er the Flood' are they
who sense-impressions scout,
scout works and ritual
(and whatsoever else),
plumb Cravings, Cankers shed.

Nanda: It gladdens me to hear [1083]
sage Gotama extol
this state from life's stuff freed.
Yes; 'o'er the Flood' are they
who sense-impressions scout,
scout works and ritual
(and whatsoever else),
plumb Cravings, Cankers shed.

Hemaka's Question (viii)

Hemaka: The only things I learned from those who taught [1084]
me, till I heard what Gotama proclaimed,
were hearsay origins and destinies,
—mere hearsay, fostering perplexities,
which failed to satisfy my heart within.

Expound to me the Doctrine, sage, which roots [1085]
all Cravings out and teaches men to walk
in mindfulness, escaping worldly snares.

The Lord: Nirvāna's Way eternal will dispel [1086]
the hot pursuit on earth of mundane joys;

and they who, grasping this, have 'passed away' [1087]
while yet in mindfulness on earth they dwell,
—these sons of peace have done with worldly snares.

TODEYYAMĀṆAVAPUCCHĀ (ix)

1. Yasmiṁ kāmā na vasanti, taṇhā yassa na vijjati, [1088]
(*icc-āyasmā Todeyyo*)
kathaṁkathā ca yo tiṇṇo, vimokkho tassa kīdiso?

2. Yasmiṁ kāmā na vasanti, taṇhā yassa na vijjati, [1089]
(*Todeyyâti Bhagavā*)
kathaṁkathā ca yo tiṇṇo, vimokkho tassa nâparo.

3. Nirāsaso so uda āsasāno? [1090]
Paññāṇavā so uda paññakappī?
Muniṁ ahaṁ, Sakka, yathā vijaññaṁ,
tam me viyācikkha, samantacakkhu.

4. Nirāsaso so, na so āsasāno, [1091]
paññāṇavā so, na ca paññakappī;
—evam pi, Todeyya, muniṁ vijāna
akiñcanaṁ kāmabhave asattan ti.

KAPPAMĀṆAVAPUCCHĀ (x)

1. Majjhe sarasmiṁ tiṭṭhataṁ (*icc-āyasmā Kappo*) [1092]
oghe jāte mahabbhaye
jarāmaccuparetānaṁ dīpaṁ pabrūhi, mārisa,
tvañ ca me dīpam akkhāhi yatha-y-idaṁ nâparaṁ siyā.

2. Majjhe sarasmiṁ tiṭṭhataṁ (*Kappâti Bhagavā*) [1093]
oghe jāte mahabbhaye
jarāmaccuparetānaṁ dīpaṁ pabrūmi, Kappa, te;

3. —akiñcanaṁ anādānaṁ etaṁ dīpaṁ anâparaṁ; [1094]
'Nibbānam' iti naṁ brūmi jarāmaccuparikkhayaṁ.

Todeyya's Question (ix)

Todeyya: If appetites no longer dwell within, [1088]
if Cravings ne'er arise nor doubts persist,
—say, what Release has such a man attained?

The Lord: If appetites no longer dwell within, [1089]
if Cravings ne'er arise nor doubts persist,
—final Release has such a man attained.

Todeyya: Longs he for anything? [1090]
Or are all longings dead?
Has he won lore? Or must
he still amass fresh lore?
All-seeing Sákyán,
answer me this, that I
may recognize 'a sage'.

The Lord: He longs for nothing now; [1091]
all longings now are dead.
All lore is won, nor need
he still amass fresh lore.
By this too recognize
'a sage',—that what he was
has passed away, and now
he stands beyond the reach
of pleasures and rebirth.

Kappa's Question (x)

Kappa: Reveal to those whom fearsome tides surround, [1092]
reveal to those forspent with eld and death,
an island citadel. Point out to me
an island where all this will be no more.

The Lord: Kappa, for those whom fearsome tides surround, [1093]
for those forspent with eld, forspent with death,
an island citadel exists (say I).

Nirvāna is that island's name; and there [1094]
the old has passed away and nothing fresh
can lodgment find; no more come death and eld.

4. Etad aññāya ye satā diṭṭhadhammâbhinibbutā, [1095]
na te Māravasânugā, na te Mārassa paddhagū ti.

JATUKAṆṆIMĀṆAVAPUCCHĀ (xi)

1. Sutvān' ahaṁ Vīraṁ akāmakāmiṁ [1096]
(*icc-āyasmā Jatukaṇṇī*)
oghâtigaṁ puṭṭhuṁ akāmam āgamaṁ.
Santipadaṁ brūhi, sahājanetta,
yathātacchaṁ, Bhagavā, brūhi me taṁ,

2. Bhagavā hi kāme abhibhuyya iriyati, [1097]
Ādicco va paṭhaviṁ teji tejasā;
parittapaññassa me, bhūripañña,
ācikkha Dhammam yaṁ ahaṁ vijaññaṁ
jātijarāya idha vippahānaṁ.

3. Kāmesu vinaya gedhaṁ, nekkhammaṁ daṭṭhu khemato, [1098]
(*Jatukaṇṇîti Bhagavā*)
uggahītaṁ nirattaṁ vā mā te vijjittha kiñcanaṁ.

4. Yaṁ pubbe taṁ visosehi; pacchā te mâhu kiñcanaṁ; [1099]
majjhe ce no gahessasi, upasanto carissasi.

5. Sabbaso nāmarūpasmiṁ vītagedhassa, brāhmaṇa, [1100]
āsavā 'ssa na vijjanti yehi maccuvasaṁ vaje ti.

BHADRĀVUDHAMĀṆAVAPUCCHĀ (xii)

1. Okañjahaṁ taṇhacchidaṁ anejaṁ [1101]
(*icc-āyasmā Bhadrāvudho*)
nandiñjahaṁ oghatiṇṇaṁ vimuttaṁ
kappañjahaṁ abhiyāce sumedhaṁ;
sutvāna nāgassa apanamissanti ito

And they who, grasping this, have 'passed away' [1095]
while yet in mindfulness on earth they dwell,
are not the thralls of Māra, nor his slaves.

Jatukaṇṇī's Question (xi)

Jatukaṇṇī: News of a 'Victor', dead [1096]
to appetites, and safe
beyond this welter, brings
me here to beg the Lord
(on whom omniscience
flashed sudden and entire)
to shew the way of Peace.

For, as the sunlight dominates [1097]
the earth, so moves the sov'ran Lord
to dominate o'er appetites.
Sage, teach my ignorance
thy Truth, that I on earth
may slough mortality.

The Lord: Get rid of appetite for pleasure's gauds; [1098]
peace in Renunciation find; let nought
find lodgment, nought require to be expelled.

Consume to ashes past iniquities; [1099]
thereafter let no fresh defilement grow;
if—meantime—thou contract no current guilt,
thy feet shall tread the tranquil path of Peace.

If, brahmin, Personality has lost [1100]
its fascination, Cankers never rise
to bind man thrall and vassal unto Death.

Bhadrāvudha's Question (xii)

Bhadrāvudha: I pray the Lord who left [1101]
his home and Cravings quenched,
who scorned delights, who crossed
the Flood, and in Release
shed Time, and wisdom found!
We wait an utterance,
great saint, ere we depart

2. nānā janā janapadehi sangatā, [1102]
tava, Vīra, vākyaṁ abhikaṁkhamānā.
Tesaṁ tuvaṁ sādhu viyākarohi,
tathā hi te vidito esa dhammo.

3. Ādānataṇhaṁ vinayetha sabbaṁ [1103]
(*Bhadrāvudhâti Bhagavā*)
uddhaṁ adho tiriyañ câpi majjhe.
Yaṁ yaṁ hi lokasmiṁ upādiyanti,
ten' eva Māro anveti jantuṁ.

4. Tasmā pajānaṁ na upādiyetha [1104]
bhikkhu sato kiñcanaṁ sabbaloke,
ādānasatte iti pekkhamāno
pajaṁ imaṁ maccudheyye visattan ti.

Udayamāṇavapucchā (xiii)

1. Jhāyiṁ virajaṁ āsīnaṁ katakiccaṁ anāsavaṁ [1105]
(*icc-āyasmā Udayo*)
pāraguṁ sabbadhammānaṁ atthi pañhena āgamaṁ:
aññāvimokkhaṁ pabrūhi, avijjāya pabhedanaṁ.

2. Pahānaṁ kāmacchandānaṁ domanassāna' cûbhayaṁ, [1106]
(*Udayâti Bhagavā*)
thīnassa ca panūdanaṁ, kukkuccānaṁ nivāraṇaṁ,

3. upekkhāsatisaṁsuddhaṁ dhammatakkapurejavaṁ, [1107]
—aññāvimokkhaṁ pabrūmi avijjāya pabhedanaṁ.

4. Kiṁ-su-saṁyojano loko? Kiṁ su tassa vicāraṇaṁ? [1108]
Ki' ss' assa vippahānena nibbānaṁ iti vuccati?

5. Nandīsaṁyojano loko; vitakk' assa vicāraṇā; [1109]
taṇhāya vippahānena nibbānaṁ iti vuccati.

6. Kathaṁ satassa carato viññāṇaṁ uparujjhati? [1110]
Bhagavantam puṭṭhuṁ āgamma taṁ suṇoma vaco tava.

7. Ajjhattañ ca bahiddhā ca vedanaṁ nâbhinandato [1111]
evaṁ satassa carato viññāṇaṁ uparujjhatîti.

who come from divers lands [1102]
to hear the Victor's words.
Make all things clear; since clear
this Doctrine is to thee.

The Lord: Shed Cravings to acquire [1103]
aught here, or anywhere;
what men assimilate
brings Māra close at heel.

So, realizing this, [1104]
let mindful Almsmen cleave
to nothing in this world,
but view as "Cravings' slaves"
mankind in Māra's toils.

Udaya's Question (xiii)

Udaya: To him who stainless sits in Reverie, [1105]
with task fulfilled, with Cankers gone, and versed
in ev'ry mental state, I come to ask
this question:—Tell me how can ignorance
be quenched, till Knowledge brings Deliverance.

The Lord: It comes from shedding appetite for joys [1106]
and griefs, from quelling Crassness of the mind,
from stoutly keeping evil deeds at bay;

it comes (say I) with poise and watchfulness; [1107]
it follows in the train of thinking right.

Udaya: What fetters, what explores, the world around? [1108]
What must be dropped before 'Nirvāna' comes?

The Lord: Joys fetter, thought explores, the world around; [1109]
Cravings must cease before 'Nirvāna' comes.

Udaya: How must man walk in watchful mindfulness [1110]
to dissipate the heritage of mind?
—We come to ask the Lord to tell us that.

The Lord: Till feelings—inly bred, or from without— [1111]
have ceased to fill the heart with wonted joy,
—on must man walk in watchful mindfulness
to dissipate the heritage of mind.

POSĀLAMĀṆAVAPUCCHĀ (xiv)

1. Yo atītaṁ ādisati anejo chinnasaṁsayo, [1112]
(*icc-āyasmā Posālo*)
pāraguṁ sabbadhammānaṁ atthi pañhena āgamaṁ:—

2. Vibhūtarūpasaññissa sabbakāyappahāyino [1113]
ajjhattañ ca bahiddhā ca 'Na 'tthi kiñcîti' passato,
ñāṇaṁ Sakkânupucchāmi: Kathaṁ neyyo tathāvidho?

3. Viññāṇaṭṭhitiyo sabbā (*Posālâti Bhagavā*) [1114]
abhijānaṁ, Tathāgato
tiṭṭhantaṁ enaṁ jānāti: Vimuttaṁ tapparāyanaṁ.

4. Ākiñcaññasambhavaṁ ñatvā: Nandī saṁyojanaṁ iti, [1115]
evam etaṁ abhiññāya tato tattha vipassati:
Etaṁ ñāṇaṁ tathaṁ tassa Brāhmaṇassa vusīmato ti.

MOGHARĀJAMĀṆAVAPUCCHĀ (xv)

1. Dvâhaṁ Sakkaṁ apucchissaṁ, na me vyākāsi cakkhumā. [1116]
(*icc-āyasmā Mogharājā*)
Yāvatatiyañ ca devîsi vyākarotîti me sutaṁ.

2. Ayaṁ loko paro loko brahmaloko sadevako; [1117]
diṭṭhin te nâbhijānāmi Gotamassa yasassino.

3. Evaṁ abhikkantadassāviṁ atthi pañhena āgamaṁ:— [1118]
Kathaṁ lokaṁ avekkhantaṁ Maccurājā na passati?

4. Suññato lokaṁ avekkhassu, Mogharāja, sadā sato [1119]
attânudiṭṭhiṁ ūhacca;—evaṁ maccutaro siyā,
evaṁ lokaṁ avekkhantaṁ Maccurājā na passatîti.

Posāla's Question (xiv)

Posāla: I come to question him who reads the past, [1112]
who yearns for nothing, entertains no doubts,
and sounds the depths of ev'ry mental state.

I ask thee, Sákyán, what lore is his [1113]
who scans the Formless, disregards mere Form,
and finds—within, without—just Nothingness.
I ask:—Can such a man go further still?

The Lord: Through comprehending each and ev'ry stage [1114]
which mind's accumulations reach, He knows
(who 'found the Truth'), the stage attained by him
you cite and what Release his stage ensures.

Your Brahmin who has greatly lived, has grasped [1115]
from whence proceeds the sense of Nothingness,
and comprehended joys as 'binding chains',
—Such knowledge true your Brahmin has achieved.

Mogharāja's Question (xv)

Mogharāja: Twice have I asked thee, Sákyán, yet got [1116]
no answer. 'But the third time' (rumour says)
'the godlike sage at last vouchsafes reply.'

Thy views of this and other worlds and skies [1117]
I know not, Gotama, but hither come

to ask of thee, thou sage supreme, the way [1118]
to view the world, to be unseen by Death.

The Lord: Then never cease to view the world as void, [1119]
abjuring 'Personality', till Death
be overthrown, and thou by him unseen.

PINGIYAMĀṆAVAPUCCHĀ (xvi)

1. Jiṇṇo 'ham asmi abalo vītavaṇṇo, [1120]
(*icc-āyasmā Pingiyo*)
nettā na suddhā, savanaṁ na phāsu;
māhaṁ nassaṁ momuho antarāya;
ācikkha Dhammaṁ yam ahaṁ vijaññaṁ
jātijarāya idha vippahānaṁ.

2. Disvāna rūpesu vihaññamāne, [1121]
(*Pingiyâti Bhagavā*)
—ruppanti rūpesu janā pamattā—
tasmā tuvaṁ, Pingiya, appamatto
jahassu rūpaṁ apunabbhavāya.

3. Disā catasso, vidisā catasso, [1122]
uddhaṁ, adho,—dasa disā imāyo.
na tuyhaṁ adiṭṭhaṁ asutaṁ mutaṁ vā
atho aviññātaṁ kiñci na 'tthi loke.
Ācikkha Dhammaṁ yam ahaṁ vijaññaṁ
jātijarāya idha vippahānaṁ.

4. Taṇhâdhipanne manuje pekkhamāno [1123]
(*Pingiyâti Bhagavā*)
santāpajāte jarasā parete
tasmā tuvaṁ, Pingiya, appamatto
jahassu taṇhaṁ apunabbhavāyâti.

Idam avoca Bhagavā Magadhesu viharanto Pāsāṇake cetiye paricāraka-soḷasānaṁ brāhmaṇānaṁ ajjhiṭṭho puṭṭho puṭṭho pañhe vyākasi. Ekamekassa ce pi pañhassa attham aññāya dhammam aññāya dhammânudhammaṁ paṭipajjeyya, gaccheyy' eva jarāmaraṇassa pāraṁ; 'Pārangamanīyā ime dhammā' ti, tasmā imassa dhammapariyāyassa 'Pārāyanan' t' eva adhivacanaṁ.

---

1. Ajito, Tissa-Metteyyo, Puṇṇako, atha Mettagū, [1124]
Dhotako, Upasīvo ca, Nando ca, atha Hemako,

Pingiya's Question (xvi)

Pingiya: Worn out am I and frail, [1120]
squalid to view, purblind,
and hard my hearing grows.
Lest I in folly die,
teach me on earth to learn
how birth and eld to end.

The Lord: In view of th' havoc wrought [1121]
in men by things of sense
(senses plague heedless men!),
take heed to scout them all
and so escape rebirth.

Pingiya: Ten realms there are in all:—— [1122]
above, beneath; north, south,
east, west, and four between;
in none of these has aught
escaped thy mind or ken!
Teach me on earth to learn
how birth and eld to end.

The Lord: Observing Craving's slaves [1123]
harassed and spent with eld,
take heed, O Pingiya,
and diligently seek
to root all Craving out
and so escape rebirth.

Thus spoke the Lord as he was dwelling among the people of Magadha at Rock-Shrine, when, in response to the train of sixteen brahmins, he answered all their successive questions. Anyone who, comprehending the import of each several question and the Doctrine involved, walks conformably to the plenitude of the Doctrine, will assuredly pass beyond death and eld. For such states of mind 'conduct to the shore beyond'; and therefore this exposition of Doctrine is styled—'The Way Across'.

Came Ájitá and Tissa Métteyyá [1124]
and Púṇṇaká and kindly Méttagú,
with Úpasīva, Nanda, Dhótaká,

2. Todeyya-Kappā dubhayo, Jatukaṇṇī ca paṇḍito, [1125]
Bhadrāvudho, Udayo ca, Posālo câpi brāhmaṇo,
Mogharājā ca medhāvī, Pingiyo ca mahā isi,

3. —ete Buddhaṁ upāgañchuṁ sampannacaraṇaṁ isiṁ, [1126]
pucchantā nipuṇe pañhe Buddhaseṭṭhaṁ upāgamuṁ.

4. Tesaṁ Buddho vyākāsi pañhe puṭṭho yathātathaṁ; [1127]
pañhānaṁ veyyākaraṇena tosesi brāhmaṇe Muni.

5. Te tositā cakkhumatā Buddhen' Ādiccabandhunā [1128]
brahmacariyam acariṁsu varapaññassa santike.

6. Ekamekassa pañhassa yathā Buddhena desitaṁ [1129]
tathā yo paṭipajjeyya, gacche pāraṁ apārato,

7. apārā pāraṁ gaccheyya bhāvento maggam uttamaṁ. [1130]
Maggo so pārangamanāya; tasmā 'Pārāyanaṁ' iti.

---

8. Pārāyanaṁ anugāyissaṁ; *(icc-āyasmā Pingiyo)* [1131]
yathā addakkhi tathā akkhāsi vimalo bhūrimedhaso
nikkāmo nibbano Nāgo. Kissa hetu musā bhaṇe?

9. Pahīnamalamohassa mānamakkhappahāyino [1132]
handâhaṁ kittayissāmi giraṁ vaṇṇûpasaṁhitaṁ:—

10. Tamonudo Buddho samantacakkhu [1133]
lokantagū sabbabhavâtivatto
anāsavo sabbadukkhappahīno
Saccavhayo, brahme, upāsito me.

11. Dijo yathā kubbanakaṁ pahāya [1134]
bahupphalaṁ kānanaṁ āvaseyya,
evam p' ahaṁ appadasse pahāya
mahodadhiṁ haṁsor iv' ajjhapatto.

and Hémaká, Todéyya, Káppa too, [1125]
the learned Jatukaṇṇī, Údayá,
Bhadrā́vudhá, the brahmin Pósālá,
quick Mógharājā, Píngiyá the sage.

These came to Buddha, blameless sage, and asked [1126]
their searching questions of the matchless Lord,

who answer'd all they asked with words of truth [1127]
which satisfied those brahmins in their quest.

And, being satisfied, they all embraced [1128]
the higher life as followers convinced
of that all-seeing Kinsman of the Sun,
Lord of Enlightenment, supreme in Lore.

Now, whoso walks as Buddha's answers teach, [1129]
shall win Across and gain the Shore Beyond,

—shall win across, along that Way of Ways [1130]
which guides men safely o'er the surge of life
and so is rightly styled 'the Way Across'.

[*Pingiya to Bāvarī* (*on return*).]

'The Way Across' my lips shall now proclaim. [1131]
As he discerned it, so he set it forth,
—that spotless, wisest Lord, above delights
and yearnings. Wherefore should he publish lies?

Come, let me tell the lovely utterance [1132]
of him whom crassness smirches not, nor pride
besets, nor foul hypocrisy invades:—

The darkness he dispels, [1133]
—the Buddha, who sees all,
who plumbs the universe,
and overcomes rebirth,
in whom no Cankers dwell,
who triumphs o'er all Ill.
Brahmin, I serve 'Truth's Lord'.

As birds desert the brake [1134]
for woodlands bountiful,
so I quit teachers blind
and, like the swan, have gained
the ocean's amplitude.

12. Ye 'me pubbe viyākaṁsu huraṁ Gotamasāsanā [1135]
—icc-āsi, iti bhavissati—sabban taṁ itihītihaṁ,
sabban taṁ takkavaḍḍhanaṁ.

13. Eko tamanudâsīno jātimā so pabhaṁkaro [1136]
Gotamo bhūripaññāṇo, Gotamo bhūrimedhaso,

14. yo me dhammam adesesi sandiṭṭhikaṁ akālikaṁ [1137]
taṇhakkhayam anītikaṁ yassa na 'tthi upamā kvaci.

15. Kin nu tamhā vippavasasi muhuttam api, Pingiya, [1138]
Gotamā bhūripaññāṇā, Gotamā bhūrimedhasā,

16. yo te dhammaṁ adesesi sandiṭṭhikaṁ akālikaṁ [1139]
taṇhakkhayam anītikaṁ yassa na 'tthi upamā kvaci?

17. Nâhaṁ tamhā vippavasāmi muhattam api, brāhmaṇa, [1140]
Gotamā bhūripaññāṇā, Gotamā bhūrimedhasā,

18. yo me dhammam adesesi sandiṭṭhikaṁ akālikaṁ [1141]
taṇhakkhayam anītikaṁ yassa na 'tthi upamā kvaci.

19. Passāmi naṁ manasā cakkhunā va [1142]
rattindivaṁ, brāhmaṇa, appamatto;
namassamāno vivasemi rattiṁ;
—ten' eva maññāmi avippavāsaṁ.

20. Saddhā ca pītī ca mano satī ca [1143]
nâpenti me Gotamasāsanamhā;
yaṁ yaṁ disaṁ vajati bhūripañño,
sa tena ten' eva nato 'ham asmi.

21. Jiṇṇassa me dubbalathāmakassa [1144]
ten' eva kāyo na pareti tattha.
Saṁkappayattāya vajāmi niccaṁ.
Mano hi me, brāhmaṇa, tena yutto.

The only things I learned from those who taught [1135]
me, ere I heard what Gotama proclaimed,
were hearsay origins and destinies,
—mere hearsay, fostering perplexities.

As in lone splendour shines a matchless gem, [1136]
dispelling darkness, spreading light around,
—so shines th' abounding lore of Gotama
and his abounding wit to comprehend.

From him I learn'd his Doctrine,—potent here [1137]
and now, yet outside time—which, utterly
destroying Cravings, brings man saving health,
—that peerless Doctrine without counterpart.

Bāvarī: Why then absent yourself one moment's space [1138]
from Gotama's abounding wit and lore,

from whom you learn'd his Doctrine,—potent here [1139]
and now, yet outside time—which, utterly
destroying Cravings, brings man saving health,
—that peerless Doctrine, without counterpart?

Pingiyā: I am not absent, sir, one moment's space [1140]
from Gotama's abounding wit and lore,

from whom I learn'd his Doctrine,—potent here [1141]
and now, yet outside time—which, utterly
destroying Cravings, brings man saving health,
—that peerless Doctrine, without counterpart.

My mind has eyes to see [1142]
him, brahmin, night and day;
in lauding him I spend
my nights, and never seem
from him to be away.

His teachings still engage [1143]
faith, zest, mind, vigilance;
and wheresoe'er he turns,
I too am thither drawn.

Worn out and frail am I, [1144]
so that my body fails
to hasten thither where
my thoughts consort with him
to whom my mind cleaves fast.

22. Panke sayāno pariphandamāno [1145]
dīpā dīpaṁ upallaviṁ.
Ath' addasāsiṁ Sambuddhaṁ oghatiṇṇaṁ anāsavaṁ.

---

23. Yathā ahu Vakkali muttasaddho [1146]
Bhadrāvudho Āḷavi-Gotamo ca,
evam eva tvam pi pamuñcassu saddhaṁ
gamissasi tvaṁ, Pingiya, maccudheyyapāraṁ.

24. Esa bhiyyo pasīdāmi sutvāna munino vaco. [1147]
Vivaṭacchado Sambuddho akhilo paṭibhānavā

25. adhideve abhiññāya sabbaṁ vedi parovaraṁ, [1148]
pañhān' antakaro Satthā kankhīnaṁ paṭijānataṁ.

26. Asaṁhīraṁ asaṁkuppaṁ yassa na 'tthi upamā kvaci [1149]
addhā gamissāmi; na m' ettha kankhā.
—Evaṁ maṁ dhārehi adhimuttacittan ti.

NIṬṬHITO SUTTANIPĀTO

AṬṬHABHĀṆAVĀRAPARIMĀṆĀYA PĀḶIYĀ

As through life's sloughs from knoll [1145]
to knoll I flounder'd on,
mine eyes beheld the Lord
of All-Enlightenment,
in whom no Cankers dwell,
who found the 'Way Across'.

The Lord: As trust saved Vakkali, [1146]
and saved Bhadrāvudha,
as trust saved Āḷavi,
so Pingiya, evince
an equal trust, and thou
shalt pass beyond the grisly realms of Death.

Pingiya: My gladness grows the greater as I hear [1147]
the sage's words. The All-Enlighten'd Lord
has stripped away the veil from things; his mind
is all-embracing, ready-witted, sure.

Clear vision into things sublime has brought [1148]
things great and small within the Master's ken.
He solves all doubts, till doubters doubt no more.

To th' unsurpassable, th' unchangeable, [1149]
which has no counterpart, assuredly
I shall attain; no doubt of this have I.
Account me, Lord, as winning this Release.

THE END

I
PALI INDEX

(The references are to the gāthās in Fausböll's numerical order, unless the reference is preceded by the italicized letter *p.*, which indicates a page of the text of the present volume.

This index does not attempt to cover the whole lexicographical field, for which see Helmer Smith's *Vocabulary of Sutta-Nipāta* at pp. 645–791 of his P.T.S. edition of the Paramatthajotikā II. As a rule, only those words are here included which have reference to the *thought* of the Sutta-Nipāta.)

---

akankha 477, 1059
akālika 567, 1137, 1139, 1141
akiñcana 176, 455, 490, 501, 620, 645, 1059, 1091, 1094
akkhātar 167
Aggāḷava 342
Aggika-Bhāradvāja *p.* 30
Aggika-Bhāradvāja-sutta (=Vasala-s°) *p.* 30.
Anguttar-āpana *p.*132
accanta-suddhi 794
Ajita Kesakambali *p.*120
Ajita (māṇava) 1006, 1033 &c.
ajjhattaṁ 7, 203, 516, 521, 526, 527, 530, 532, 738, 916, 917, 919, 1111, 1113
ajjhatta-cintī 174, 388
ajjhatta-santi 837, 838
aññā-vimokha 1105, 1107
Aṭaṭa *p.* 158
Aṭṭhaka-vagga *p.* 184
attatthapaññā 75
attañjaha 790
attadattha 284
Attadaṇḍa-sutta *p.* 224
attânudiṭṭhi 1119
atthangata 1075, 1076
adukkhamasukha 738
adhamma 310, 312, 450
adhideva 1148
anangaṇa 517, 662
an-aññaneyya 55, 364
anarahā 135
anariya-dhamma 782
anassāvin 853
an-ālamba 173
anāvila 160, 161, 483, 515, 637, 1039
anāsava 178, 212, 219, 765, 996, 1082–3, 1105, 1133, 1145
anāsasāna 369
aniketasārin 844, 970
anissita 66, 363, 364, 748, 752, 753, 811, 849, 856, 947, 1069
anukampin 693
anuṇṇata 702
anuttara 179, 330, 345, 478, 486, 554, 557, 560, 690, 1003
anuddhata 850
anudhamma-cārin 69
anupādāna 546, 572, 753
anupādiyati 470, 800, 915
anupādisesa 876
anubuddha 384
anuyutta 553, 663, 814, 972
anurodha-virodha-vippahīna 362
anuvidita 528, 530

18*

anusaya 14, 342, 369, 545, 571
anusuyyaka 325
anusotagāmin 319
anussada 624
anūpalitta 211, 392, 468, 790, 845
aneja 87, 372, 477, 638, 646, 751, 920, 952, 953, 1043, 1101, 1112
antakara 32, 337, 510, 511, 539, 1148
antagū 401, 458, 463, 539, 1133
apihālu 852
a-ppagabbha 852, 941
a-ppaṭigha 42
appiccha 628, 707
Ababa *and* Abbuda *p.* 158
abhiññā(ya) 534, 743, 992, 1040, 1042, 1115, 1148
abhisamaya 342, 737, 758
amaccharin 852, 860
amata 80, 204, 453, 635, 960
amama 220, 469, 494, 495, 777
amosa-dhamma 758
arati 270, 271, 436, 642, 835, 938, 969
arahat 403, 539, 590, 644, 1003
ariya 90, 115, 177, 330, 353, 533, 535, 660, 758, 761, 762, 765, 782, 783, 822
alasa 96
alippamāna 71, 213, 456
alīnacitta 68, 717
alola 22, 65, 165, 707
avijjā 199, 277, 729, 730, 1026
aviddasu 762
avidvā 728
aviruddha 365, 630, 704, 854
avihiṁsā 292
avītataṇha 776, 901
avītivatta 796
avedhadhamma 322
Asita 679, 686, 698, 699
asuci 75, 197, 205, 243
asuddhi 893, 900
asura 310, 681
asoka 593
Ahaha *p.* 158
ahirika 133

ākiñcañña 976, 1070–2, 1115
ājīva 407, 617
ājīvika 381
ātappa 1062
ātāpin 926
ātura 331
Āthabbaṇa 927 (the Atharva-Veda)
ādāna 364, 620, 794, 1103–4
ādicca 550, 569, 1097
Ādicca 54, 423, 540, 915, 1128
ānisaṁsa 256, 784, 797, 952
Āpaṇa *p.* 132, 137
āmagandha 240–2, 248, 251
Āmagandha-sutta *p.* 58
āyatana 373, 399, 406
āyāga 486
āraddha 68, 344
ārammaṇa 474, 506, 945, 1069
ālaya 177, 535, 635
Āḷavaka-sutta *p.* 44
Āḷavi 191; *p.* 82; 1146
āvila 160, 967
āsaya 56, 972
āsava 82, 162–3, 178, 370, 374, 535, 546, 572, 749
āsasāna 1090–1
āsā 474, 634, 794, 864–5
āsiṁsati 779, 1044, 1046
āhāra 747–8
āhuti 249, 458

icchā 133, 306, 311, 706–7, 872; *p.* 156
Icchānankala *p.* 146
iñjita 750–1, 1048
itibhavābhavatā 6
itihāsa 1020
itihītiha 1084, 1135

ito-ja 271
ito-nidāna 271, 865, 870
itthabhāva 729, 740, 752, 1044
iddhâbhisaṁkhāra *p.* 138
iddhimant 179
Inda 310, 316, 679, 1024
indriya 63, 214, 250, 340, 516, 697
iriyāpatha 385
isi 82, 284, 356, 458, 679, 684, 689, 691, 698, 1008, 1025, 1043–5, 1116

ukkā-dhāra 335–6
ukkhitta-paligha 622
ujju-gata 350, 477
Ujjeni 1011
uṭṭhātar 96, 187
Uṭṭhāna-sutta *p.* 78
uṇṇamati 206, 366, 829, 928
utûpasevanā 249
utuveramaṇi 291
Udaya 1008, 1105, 1125
uddhaṁ (adho, &c.) 537, 1055, 1068, 1103, 1122
upakkilesa 66
upadhi 33–4, 364, 374, 546, 572, 728, 1050
upadhīka 789, 1057
upanāhin 116
upanissita 877
upaya 786–7, 897
uparujjhati 724, 726, 1036–7, 1110–11
uparodhana 732, 761
upalippati 211, 547, 779, 812
upavāda 389, 929
upavutth-uposatha 403
upasanta 342, 848, 857, 919, 949, 1087, 1099
upasama 257, 737
Upasīva 1007, 1069–70, 1124
upādā 168–9, 363
upādāna 170, 358, 475, 546, 742–3
upādiyati 470, 752, 1103–4
upādi-sesa 354, 876
upekhaka 515, 855, 912
upekhā 67, 73, 972, 1107
uposatha 153, 401–3
Uppalaka *p.* 158
ubhantaṁ 1040, 1042
ubhay-anta 801
uraga 1–17, 604
Uraga-vagga *p.* 2; Uraga-sutta *p.* 2
usabha 26–7, 29, 416, 646, 684, 996
ussada 515, 624, 783, 855, 920
ussukka 43, 298
ūhacca 1119

ejā 87, 751, 791
ettāvat' (aggaṁ) 875–6; 478
Erāvaṇa 379
ereti 325, 350
elamūga 70

oka 628, 844, 966, 1101
Okkāka 302, 306, 991
okkhitta-cakkhu 63, 411, 972
ogha 4, 21, 173–4, 178, 183–4, 219, 273, 471, 495, 538, 771, 779, 823, 1052, 1059, 1064, 1069, 1070, 1081–3, 1092–3, 1096, 1101
ottāpin 133
oma 153, 177, 343, 860, 954
ora(ṁ) 1–17, 804

kankhā 58, 477, 514, 541, 1025, 1149
kankhati 516 (kālaṁ), 540, 1021
kankhin 510, 1148
Kaccāyana (Pakudha) *p.* 120
Kaṇha (= Māra) 355, 439, 967
Kaṇhasirivhayo (isi) 689
katakicca 1105
kathaṁjīvin 181
kathaṁdassin *and* kathaṁsīla 848
kadariya 133, 362
Kapilavatthu 991, 1012

Kapila-sutta (=Dhammacariya-s°) *p*. 68
kappa 373, 517, 521, 535, 860, 911, 1101
Kappa 344, 349, 354
Kappa (māṇava) 1007, 1092–3, 1125
kappiya 521, 860, 914
kappeti 283, 794, 799, 803
kamma 127, 136, 140, 142, 163 A *and* B, 164, 215, 253, 324, 330, 365, 407, 537, 587, 596, 599, 650–4, 661, 666, 846, 899, 900
Kalaha-vivāda-sutta *p*. 204
Kasi-Bhāradvāja-sutta *p*. 20
kāma 50–1, 60, 92, 139, 160–1, 166, 175–6, 239, 243, 272, 284, 315, 337, 359, 361, 423–4, 435–6, 445, 461, 464, 467, 497, 639, 685, 766–9, 771–4, 823, 825, 844, 857, 940, 945, 963, 1039, 1041, 1046, 1070–2, 1088–9, 1096–7, 1106, 1131
Kāma-sutta *p*. 184
kāya 78, 193–4, 198, 203, 206, 340, 407, 548–9, 669, 1074, 1113, 1144
Kāyavicchandanika-sutta (=Vijaya-s°) *p*. 46
kāla 73, 130, 326, 343, 386–7, 463–6, 490–503, 567, 971, 975
kiccâkicca 298, 715
kiñcana 645, 949, 951, 1098–9, 1104, 1122 (*and see* a-k°)
kiṁnissita 458, 1043
Kiṁsīla-sutta *p*. 78
kibbisa 246, 665–6, 671–2, 676
kiṁpattin 513, 518, 528, 533
kilesa 348
kukkuc(c)a 82, 481, 850, 925, 972, 1106
kutoja 270
kutonidāna 270, 864, 866, 869, 871
kuppa 784
Kumuda *p*. 158
kumbhadūhana 309
kuladūsaka 89
Kuvera (=Vessavaṇa) 380
kusala 14, 321, 372, 523, 525, 536, 591, 686, 712, 782–3, 798, 825, 830, 876, 878–9, 881, 885, 888, 898, 903, 909, 1078
kusalânuesin 965
Kusinārā 1012
kusīta 68
kuha(ka) 56, 328, 852, 957, 984, 987
Keniya (a jaṭila) *p*. 132, 134, 136, 140, 142
kevala 393, 517, 524–5, 529, 759
kevalin 82, 481, 490, 519, 595, 878
Kesa-kambalin (Ajita) *p*. 120
Kokāliya *p*. 156, 158
Kokāliya-sutta *p*. 156
kodha 1, 96, 245, 362, 469, 537, 866, 868, 928, 968
kodhana 19, 116
komāra-brahmacariya 289
kovida 484, 627, 653, 763
kosa *p*. 136, 138; 525, 1022
Kosambī 1012
Kosala *p*. 158; 422, 976, 996

Khaggavisāṇakappa 35–75; sutta *p*. 10
khaṇa 325, 333
khattiya 114, 138, 314–15, 417–18, 420, 458, 553, 1043–5
khanti 189, 292, 294, 623, 897
khaya 70, 209, 475, 598, 732, 736, 739, 992
khara 249, 472
khila 19, 212, 477, 540, 780, 973, 1059, 1147
khīṇa 82, 158–9, 162–3, 370, 481, 493, 514, 539, 644, 656, 777
khuppipāsā 436
khetta 82, 473, 481, 486, 524, 769, 858

khema 424–5, 454, 809, 896, 953, 1098

Gangā *p*. 44
gantha 219, 347, 794, 847, 857, 912
Gandhabba 644
gambhīro 173, 175–6, 627
garaha(ti) 141, 313, 660, 665, 778
gahaṭṭha 43, 90, 134, 393, 398, 487–9, 628
-gahaṇika *p*. 146
gāthâbhigīta 81, 480
giddha 210, 243, 248, 328, 809
giha 456, 464, 487, 497
gihin 44, 64, 220–1, 404
guṇa 50–1, 171, 284, 337, 663, 678, 714
gutta 63, 78, 250, 413, 971
guyha *p*. 138; 1022
Guhaṭṭhaka-sutta *p*. 184
gedha 65, 210, 819, 945, 1098
gocara 39, 280, 605, 961
Gotama 91, 1136–8, 1140
Gotama (Āḷavi) 1146
Gotama-sāsana 1084, 1135, 1143
gotta 104, 315, 423, 455–6, 648, 1004, 1018–19
Godhāvarī 977

ghara 43, 188, 337, 359, 406
ghāteti 309, 394, 629, 705

cakka 552, 554–7, 684, 698
cakkhumant 31, 160–1, 405, 541, 562, 570, 596, 706, 956, 992–3, 1028, 1116
Caṁkī (brāhmaṇa) *p*. 146
caṇḍālaputta (=Mātanga) 137
catuvīsatakkhara (=Sāvittī) 457 (cf. 568)
canda 465, 498, 569, 598, 637, 1016
cāga 188–9, 719
citta 23, 37, 50, 65, 68, 160–1, 163 A *and* B, 164, 341, 390, 434–5, 483, 507, 689, 975, 985, 1149
cutûpapāta 517, 902
Cunda (kammāraputta) 83–5
Cunda-sutta *p*. 24
Cūla-vagga *p*. 54
Cūla-viyūha-sutta *p*. 210
cetasa 66, 584, 593
cetovimutti 725, 727

chanda 171, 203–4, 364, 387, 767, 778, 781, 835, 865–7, 913, 975, 1026, 1086
chinna- 219, 711, 715, 948, 111

jaṭā 249, 689, 1010
Jatukaṇṇin 1007, 1096, 1125
janavādadhamma 973
jap(p)a 328, 595
jappati 773, 839, 899, 902, 945
Jambusaṇḍa 552
jaras *and* jarā 311, 575, 581, 725, 804, 1044–8, 1079, 1092–4
Jarā-sutta *p*. 192
jahāti 1, 211, 362, 500, 506, 589, 790, 809, 1101, 1121
jāti 104, 136, 139, 141–2, 209, 275, 294, 351, 355, 421, 462, 467, 476, 484, 500, 517, 596, 599, 600–1, 610, 647, 650, 725, 727–9, 1004, 1045–8, 1052, 1056, 1060, 1079, 1081–2, 1097, 1120, 1122; *p*. 146
jāla 62, 71, 213, 357, 527, 669
jigiṁsa- 690, 700
jiguccha- 215, 852, 901
jina 84, 372, 379, 523, 697–8, 989, 996
jivhā *p*. 136, 138; 1022
jīva 432
jīvati 84, 88, 427, 440, 589, 615, 618, 804, 1029

jīvita 74, 275, 427, 574, 577, 589, 676, 775, 804, 931, 1077
jutimant 508, 539
juhati 428, 1046
jotimant 348

jhāna 69, 156–7, 212, 503, 709, 972, 985, 1009
jhāyati[1] 165, 221, 425, 709
jhāyati[2] 818
jhāyin 638, 719, 925, 1009, 1105

ñāṇa 55, 372, 378, *p.* 172, 789, 799, 800, 839, 840, 868, 911, 987, 989, 1077–8, 1113, 1115
ñāti 104, 123, 579, 580, 589

Ṭaṁkitamañca *p.* 66

ṭhita 215, 250, 327–8, 359, 370, 381, 477, 519, 920, 1017

takka 209, 885–6, 972, 1084, 1107, 1135
taṇhā 3, 70, 83, 114, 306, 339, 355, 495–6, 640, 740–1, 746, 776, 854, 856, 916, 1068, 1085, 1101, 1103, 1109, 1123, 1137, 1139, 1141
tatha 9–13, 172, 1115
tathāgata xix–xx, *p.* 22; 236–8, 252, 347, 351, 467–78, 557, 1031, 1114
tapa 77, 249, 284, 292, 655, 901
tama 248, 278, 348, 763, 956, 975, 1133, 1136
tarati 17, 21, 173–4, 178, 183–4, 273, 319, 321, 333, 367, 515, 545, 571, 706, 771, 791, 1045, 1053–4, 1059, 1064, 1066–7, 1069, 1070, 1085, 1087–9
tasara 215, 464, 497
tādin 86, 154–5, 219, 488, 509, 519, 520, 524–6, 530–2, 697, 712, 803, 957
Tārukkha (brāhmaṇa) *p.* 146; 594

titthakara *pp.* 120, 122
titthiya 381
tiriyaṁ 537, 1055, 1068, 1103
Tissa 814, 1006, 1040, 1124
Tissa-metteyya-sutta *p.* 196
tuma 890, 908
Tuvaṭaka-sutta *p.* 220
Tusita 955
tevijja 594–5
Todeyya 1007, 1088–9, 1091, 1125

thaddha 104
thambha 214, 245, 326, 437
thāvara-tasa 394, 629
thīna 437, 483, 942, 1106
Thera-pañha-sutta (= Sāriputta-s°) *p.* 228

-dakkhiṇa 1010; *pp.* 106, 156
dakkhiṇā 482, 485
Dakkhiṇāpatha 976
dakkhiṇeyya 488–9, 504, 509
daṇḍa 35, 312, 394, 629, 630, 688
danta 23, 370, 375, 463, 491–2, 513, 516, 570, 624
dama 189, 463, 542, 655
dayā 117
daḷha 68, 293, 321, 332, 344, 357, 701, 821, 892–3, 905, 966
dassāvin 1005, 1043, 1118
dassin 57, 176, 209, 219, 344, 371, 385, 474, 478, 693, 793, 809, 848, 887,
diṭṭha 141, 178, 250, 343, 508, 761, 778, 788, 790, 793, 797–8, 802, 808, 812, 887, 897, 901, 914, 955, 1053, 1066, 1079, 1080–3, 1086–7, 1095, 1122
diṭṭhi 55, 116, 243, 471, 474, 781, 785, 787, 796, 799, 800, 802, 832–4, 836–7, 839, 840–1, 846–7, 851, 878, 880, 882, 895 908, 910–11, 913, 1117, 1119

disā 42, 507, 719, 937, 939, 960, 1122, 1143
dipad-uttama 83, 690, 995, 998
dīpa[1] 501 (attadīpa)
dīpa[2] 1092–4, 1145
dukkha 32, 36, 61, 67, 80, 170–2, 183–4, 250, 278, 337, 401, 454, 473, 531, 539, 574, 586, 626, 666, 678, 724, 726, 728, 731–2, 734–5, 738–9, 741–2, 744–5, 747–8, 750–1, 760, 762, 770, 774, 873, 970, 1033, 1049, 1050–1, 1056–8
deva 18–30, 139, 310, 333, 346, 384, 404, 521, 527, 543, 679, 680, 1047, 1063, 1081, 1148
devatā *p.* 26; 316, 986, 990, 995, 1043–5
dvayadhamma 886
Dvayatânupassanā-sutta *p.* 172

dhañña 60, 285, 302, 305
dhana 60, 104, 122, 185, 187, 285, 302–3, 305–7, 422, 659, 987
Dhaniya-sutta *p.* 4
dhamma 58, 69, 81, 83, 87–8, 92, 94, 141, 160–1, 163 A *and* B, 167, 180, 186, 188, 192, 211, 239, 250, 257, 274, 276, 288, 291, 293, 295, 298, 312–14, 316–18, 320, 322–3, 326–7, 330, 343, 351, 353, 361, 365, 368, 378, 380, 383–5, 387, 389, 391–3, 398, 404, 450, 453, 461, 471, 478, 480, 504, 527, 534, 536, 554–7, 575, 693–6, 699, 704, 749, 759, 763–4, 784–5, 787, 801, 803, 824, 837, 840, 861, 866, 868, 880, 886, 891–3, 903–7, 914, 917, 963, 965, 969, 973, 975, 1015, 1020, 1039, 1052–4, 1057, 1064–6, 1075–6, 1085, 1087, 1095, 1097, 1102, 1105, 1107, 1112, 1120, 1122, 1137, 1139, 1141; *pp.* 24, 30, 34, 114, 132, 134, 154, 172, 266
Dhammacariya-sutta *p.* 68
Dhamma-sutta (= Nāvā-sutta) *p.* 76
Dhammika-sutta *p.* 90
dhāreti 401, 478, 688, 1149; *p.* 146
dhi-r-atthu 440
dhitimant 462, 542
dhīra 45–6, 165, 211–19, 250, 317, 349, 371, 380, 531, 581, 591, 709, 719, 775, 778, 838, 877, 890, 913, 964, 1009, 1052
Dhotaka 1007, 1061–8
dhona 351, 786, 813, 834

Nanda 1007, 1077–83, 1124
nandī 175, 637, 1055, 1101, 1109, 1115
nāga 29, 53, 166, 379, 421, 518, 522, 543, 573, 845, 1058, 1101
Nātaputta *p.* 120
Nālaka-sutta *p.* 164
nāma 153, 344, 648, 808, 872, 1037
nāma-kāya 1074
nāma-rūpa 355, 530, 537, 756, 909, 950, 1036, 1100
Nārada-Pabbatā(ubho) 543
Nāvā-sutta (= Dhamma-sutta) *p.* 76
nikati 242
niketa 207, 844
nikkama 68, 542
Nigaṇṭha *p.* 120; 381
Nigrodha-Kappa *p.* 82; 344
Nigrodha-Kappa-sutta(= Vangīsa-s°) *p.* 82
-nighaṇḍu 1020; *p.* 134
nicchāta 707, 735, 758
nidahati 35, 394, 629
nidāna 270–1, 273, 728, 773, 865, 870, 874
niddhamati 56, 281–2, 962
nidhi 285
nindati 658
nindā 213, 826, 895, 928

nipaka 45–6, 144, 283, 962, 1038, 1062
nipaccavādin 217
nipuṇa 176–7, 317, 377, 383
nibbāna 86, 186, 204, 365, 454, 758, 822, 940, 942, 1061–2, 1086, 1094, 1108–9
nibbuta 19, 593, 630, 638, 707, 1041
nimitta 341–2
niyāma 55, 371
niyyāna *p.* 172; 170, 172
niratta 787, 858, 919, 1098
Nirabbuda (niraya) *p.* 158; 660
niraya 248, 277, 531, 660–1, 677–8
nirāmagandha 251–2, 717
nirāsa 460, 469, 491–2, 494, 1048, 1060, 1078
nirāsaya 56, 369, 634, 1090–1
nirūpadhi 33–4, 642
nirodha *pp.* 172, 174, 176, 178, 180; 372, 731–2, 735, 744, 747, 750, 754–5, 1037
nivāta 265, 326
niviṭṭha 57, 324, 756, 774, 781, 824, 892
nivissavādin 910, 913
nivuta 348, 763, 1032–3, 1082
nivesana *p.* 30; 210, 300, 305, 470, 785, 801, 846, 1055
nisaṁkhiti 953
nissita 66, 280, 458, 538, 752, 784, 798, 824, 910, 938, 1069, 1071–2
nihīna 132, 661, 797, 842, 880, 890, 905
nīvaraṇa 17, 541
nekkhamma 424, 1098
Nerañjarā 425
nhātaka 518, 521, 646

pakappita 648, 784, 786, 802, 838, 886, 902
Pakudha (Kaccāyana) *p.* 120
panka 535, 845, 945, 980, 1145
paccaya 15, 339
pajā *p.* 22; 298, 545, 571, 684, 823, 936, 1104
pajahāti 586, 789, 806, 1056, 1058
paññā 77, 83, 90, 182, 184–6, 329–30, 343, 346, 352, 373, 381, 390–1, 432, 434, 443, 468, 591, 847, 880–1, 931, 969, 1036, 1090–1
paṭigha 42, 371, 536
paṭiccasamuppādadasa 653
paṭibaddhacitta 37, 65
paṭisena 390, 832, 932
Paṇḍava 414, 416–17
paṇḍita 115, 254, 335–6, 523, 526, 578, 653, 721, 733, 743, 820, 875–6, 1007, 1125
Patiṭṭhāna 1011
pattheti 18–29, 70, 114, 900, 902, 914, 976
patha 139, 176–7, 370, 385, 476, 540, 868, 976, 1045, 1076
pada *p.* 106; 88, 204, 208, 252, 374, 446, 603, 700, 765, 768
padaka 595
Paduma (niraya) *p.* 158; 677
padhāna 70, 424–5, 428–9, 531
Padhāna-sutta *p.* 100
panudati 81, 359, 469, 480, 483, 535, 928, 1055
papañca 530, 874, 916
pabbajati 405–7, 564–5, 1003
pabbajita *p.* 122; 43, 274, 385, 423
pabbajjā *p.* 122; 252, 405–6, 567
Pabbajjā-sutta *p.* 98
pabhankara 991, 1136
pamatta 57, 70, 329, 332, 399, 430, 1121
pamāda 156–7, 184, 218, 334, 942, 1033
pamutta 212, 465, 498, 524–5, 530, 532

pamocana 78, 166, 1064
parama 68, 87, 138, 219, 293, 296, 347, 471, 693, 697, 788, 796, 903, 1071–2
Paramaṭṭhaka-sutta *p.* 192
parābhava 91–2, 114–15
Parābhava-sutta *p.* 26
parāyana 377, 578, 717, 1114
pariggaha 393, 470, 779, 805, 809, 872
parijānāti 202, 254, 455, 473, 537, 737, 748, 755, 778–9, 1082–3
parideva- 328, 582–3, 585, 590, 592, 774, 809, 811, 862–3, 923, 969, 970
parinibbāti 591, 765
parinibbānagata 514
parinibbuta 346, 359, 370, 467, 735, 737, 739, 758
paribbajati 359–75, 639, 640, 741, 751, 753, 1039
paribbāja- *p.* 120; 134, 533, 537
pariyanta *p.* 136; 214, 537, 577, 964
parivajjeti 57, 341, 395–7, 768, 771
parissaya 42, 45, 770, 921, 960, 965, 969
parovara 353, 475, 704, 1048, 1148
pasaṁsā 213, 256, 825–6, 895
pasanna 316, 402–3, 550, 690
pasīdati 356, 434, 563, 1147
Pasūra 833
Pasūra-sutta *p.* 196
passati *p.* 22; 76, 153, 164–5, 176–7, 229, 313, 435, 580, 587–8, 647, 653, 666, 676, 739, 761, 763, 784, 797–8, 907–9, 935, 953, 998, 1063, 1113, 1118–19, 1142
pahāya (pajahāti) 17, 46, 66, 74, 209, 493, 520, 771–2, 786, 791, 800, 844, 900, 1070, 1082–3, 1134
pahāyin 1113, 1132
pahitatta 425, 432–3, 445, 961
pahīna 250, 351, 370, 546, 558, 572, 715, 1132
pahūtapañña 83, 359, 539, 996
pāgabbhiya 930
pāṇa 117, 156–7, 220, 242, 247, 394, 400
pāṇin 201, 220, 307, 575, 587
pātimokkha 340, 921
pāpa 22–4, 57, 116, 133, 140, 216, 246, 257, 280, 282, 399, 407, 452, 520, 547, 636, 662, 674, 790; *p.* 156
pāpaka 127, 215, 519, 664
pāpimant 33, 430
pāpiyo 275
pāragata 21, 210, 359, 638, 803
pāragū 167, 251, 539, 699, 771, 1019, 1105, 1112
pāramī 1018, 1020
Pārāyana 1130–1
pāva 782, 789, 888
Pāvā 1013
Pāsāṇaka (cetiya) 1013; *p.* 266
Pingiya 1008, 1120–1, 1123, 1125, 1138, 1146
pīti 257, 687, 695, 766, 969, 994, 1143
puggala 544, 684
puñña 82, 427–8, 431, 463–6, 481, 486–9, 503, 505, 520, 547, 569, 636, 697, 790
Puṇḍarīka (niraya) *p.* 158
Puṇṇaka 1006, 1043–8, 1124
putta 24, 33–4, 38, 41, 43, 48, 60, 137, 255, 579, 686, 858
puthujja 897, 911
puthujjana 351, 455, 706, 816, 859
puthuso 891–2
punabbhava 162–3, 273, 502, 514, 730, 733, 743, 746, 754
puppha 2, 5
pubbavāsanavāsita 1009
pubbenivāsa 647
pura 192, 695, 976, 1012–13
purakkharoti 199, 277, 421, 784, 794 803, 844, 849, 969, 1015

purisa 91, 102, 112, 181–2, 303, 316, 323, 348, 544, 657, 664, 806–7
Pūraṇa (Kassapa) *p*. 120
pūraḷāsa 459, 467–79, 486
pekkhati 36–7, 39, 49, 580, 1070, 1104, 1123
pecca 185, 188, 248, 278, 598, 661
peta 585, 590, 807–8
peyya 303
pesala *p*. 156; 678
pesuṇa- 362, 389, 663, 852, 862–3, 928, 941
Pokkharasāti *p*. 146; 594
porisa 256, 769
porohicca 618
posa 110, 662
Posāla 1008, 1112, 1114, 1125
posin 65, 220

phandati 587, 777, 936
pharusa 247, 932, 971
phala 80, 191, 239, 256, 576, 896, 977, 1134
phassa 387, 506, 736–7, 759, 778, 851, 870–2, 923, 964, 966, 974
phassati 54, 393, 967
phusati 693, 739, 871–2, 918, 923, 966

bandhana 29, 44, 242, 367, 491, 522, 524, 532, 948
bandhava 60, 140
bandhu 54, 241, 430, 769, 911
bala 4, 68, 212, 297, 623, 770, 992
bahiddhā 203, 388, 516, 521, 526–7, 530, 532, 738, 917, 1111, 1113
bahussuta 58, 316, 320, 322–3
bāla 199, 318, 399, 578, 657, 662, 721, 825, 879, 880, 882, 887–8, 890, 893
Bāvarī 981, 984, 986, 994–5, 1006, 1019, 1021, 1025, 1028–9–30
Bimbisāra *p*. 134; 409
bīja 77, 209
buddha 81, 83, 85–6, 134, 157, 161, 167, 202, 252, 276, 357, 377, 383, 386, 401, 408, 429, 454, 486, 513, 517, 523, 545, 558, 571, 622, 643, 646, 696, 993, 999, 1005, 1126–9, 1133
Belaṭṭhiputta (Sañjaya) *p*. 120
Bodhisatta 683
brahmă 241, 285, 293, 315, 479, 508, 519, 524–5, 656, 982, 1024, 1065, 1133
brahmacariya 32, 274, 289, 292, 294, 326, 354, 396, 428, 463, 566–7, 655, 693, 696, 1128
brahmacārin 695, 973
Brahmaloka 139, 508–9, 1117
brāhmaṇa 81, 100, 129, 130, 136, 138, 140, 142, 189, 285, 291, 298, 301, 303, 305, 308, 344, 356, 382, 455–60, 463–6, 469, 480, 490–503, 518, 529, 560, 566, 596, 599, 612–20, 649–50, 655, 790, 802–3, 843, 911, 946, 976, 979, 992, 997, 999, 1006, 1008, 1018, 1029, 1043–5, 1063, 1079, 1080–2, 1115, 1125, 1127, 1144; *pp*. 30, 70, &c.

bhakuṭi 485
Bhagavant 19, 31, *et passim*. Te bhagavanto *p*. 136
Bhadrāvudha 1008, 1101, 1103, 1125, 1146
bhaya 37, 49, 51, 167, 207, 546, 561, 576, 753, 935–6
bhava 5–6, 16, 69, 175–6, 361, 367, 472, 514, 639, 640, 736, 746, 764, 773, 776–7, 836, 839, 856, 867, 869, 870, 923, 1046, 1055, 1133
bhavâbhava 6, 496, 776, 786, 801, 877, 901, 1060, 1068
Bhāradvāja (Aggika-) *pp*. 30, 34

Bhāradvāja (Kasi-) *p.* 20
Bhāradvāja (māṇava) *p.* 146; 596
Bhāradvāja (Sundarika-) *p.* 106
bhāveti 256, 277, 322, 341–2, 507, 558, 1049, 1130
bhikkhācariyā 700
bhikkhu 1–17, 87–8, 202, 204, 221, 276, 280, 343, 359, 361–2, 366–8, 384–6, 388–9, 392–3, 411–12, 416, 513–14, 551, 735, 739, 741, 751, 753, 783, 798, 915, 919, 920, 923, 925, 928–30, 933, 958–9, 960–1, 964, 975, 1015, 1039, 1056, 1104.
bhīru 437
bhūta 35, 146–7, 154–5, 194, 321, 394, 542, 629, 742, 793, 975
bhūnahu 664
bhūripañña 346, 376, 538, 792, 1097, 1136, 1138, 1140, 1143
bhūrimedhasa 996, 1131, 1136, 1138, 1140
bhedāsankin 255
bherava 546, 923, 959, 965, 984
bhoganagara 1013
bhovādin 620

maṁsika 244
makkha 56, 437, 631, 1132
Makkhali (Gosāla) *p.* 120
makkhin 116
maga 275, 763, 880
Magadha 408; *pp.* 20, 266
magga 55, 84–9, 277, 347, 429, 441, 582, 627, 724, 726, 736, 1130
mangala 360
macca 249, 574, 576–7, 580, 766
maccu 332, 357–8, 578–9, 581, 587, 755, 776, 1092, 1094, 1100, 1104, 1118–9, 1146
macchara 811, 862–3, 954
maccharin 133, 663, 852
macchariya 863, 928
maññati 199, 206, 349, 382, 539, 588, 756–7, 799, 806, 813, 822, 840, 842, 855, 918, 1049, 1142
mada 218, 245, 328, 399
manas 77, 154–5, 252, 270–1, 330, 365, 388, 449, 470 512, 659, 660, 678, 680, 689, 692, 697, 766, 780, 829, 834, 873, 889, 942, 967, 985, 1004–5, 1024, 1039, 1142, 1144
manuja 458, 553, 661, 1043–5, 1123
manussa 75, 333, 335–6, 521, 568, 607, 612–19, 683, 964
mano-chaṭṭha 171
mano-pañha 1017
manopadosa 702
manta 249, 302, 306, 850, 1000, 1004, 1018
mantā *and* mantar 140, 159, 251, 455, 690, 916, 1040, 1042
manteti 126, 379; *p.* 136
manda 666, 674, 728, 820, 1051
mamatta 806, 871–2, 951
mamāyati 119, 466, 777, 805, 809, 922, 950, 1056
maraṇa 32, 318, 426–7, 575–6, 742
mahāpurisa 549, 1000–1, 1040, 1042; *pp.* 134, 136, 138
mahāvīra 543, 562
mahiddhika *p.* 122
mahesi 82, 176–7, 208, 646, 915, 1054, 1057, 1061, 1067, 1083
Māgadha 1013
Māgandiya 837–41
Māgha (māṇava) 487–9
Māgha-sutta *p.* 114
Mātanga 137–8
māna 4, 132, 245, 328, 342, 370, 469, 473, 631, 756, 786, 830, 846, 862–3, 889, 943, 1132
māmaka 719, 806, 927
māyā 89, 116, 245, 357, 469, 494, 537, 786, 926, 941

Māra 33, 429–31, 442, 545, 561, 563, 571, 733, 764, 1095, 1103
Māhissati 1011
micchā 438, 815
Migāra-mātar *p.* 172
mitta 37, 58, 75, 185, 187, 244, 254–5, 296, 338
mithu 825, 882
mukha 91, 93–114, 198, 275, 550, 568–9, 608, 657–8, 664, 686, 1010, 1022; *p.* 140
muñja 28, 440
muṇḍa(ka) *pp.* 30, 106
muṇḍiya 249
muta 714, 790, 793, 797–8, 802, 812–13, 887, 1086, 1122
muti 344, 846
mutimant 61, 321, 385, 539, 881
mutta-saddha 1146
muddhā 682, 689, 983, 987–90, 996, 1004, 1025–6
muni 31, 83, 87, 163A–165, 207–21, 251, 359, 414, 462, 508, 523, 527, 540–1, 545, 571, 698, 700, 703, 708, 711, 723, 779–80, 809, 811–12, 821, 823, 838, 844–5, 850, 860, 877, 912, 914, 941, 946, 1052, 1074–5, 1077–8, 1081, 1090–1, 1127, 1147
Muni-sutta *p.* 48
musā- 100, 122, 129, 158–9, 242, 397, 400, 757, 843, 883, 886, 967, 1131
mūga 70, 713
mūla 14, 239, 369, 524–5, 530, 532, 916, 968, 1043
Mettagū 1006, 1049, 1124
mettā 73, 967
Metteyya (Tissa) 814–15, 1006
methuna 218, 291, 293, 400, 609, 704, 814–17, 820–1, 835, 926
medha 303
medhaga 893–4, 935
medhāvin 323, 627, 1008, 1125
Moggallāna *p.* 156
Mogharājā 1008, 1116, 1119, 1125
mona 540, 718, 723
moneyya 484, 698, 700–1, 716
momuha 840–1, 1120
mosa-dhamma 739, 757–8
mosa-vajja 819, 866, 868, 931, 943
moha-dhamma 276
moh-antara 478
moha-magga 347
moheti 332, 352, 1076

yakkha 153–63, 168, 179, 273, 449, 478, 875–6; *pp.* 44, 66
yajati 302–3, 307, 463–6, 487–503, 505–6, 509, 569; *p.* 114
yañña 249, 295, 308, 458, 461, 482, 484, 505, 509, 568, 1043–5, 1047
yata 78, 216, 220, 490, 723, 850, 971
yathākammûpaga 587
yathātaccha 1096
yathātathaṁ 172, 600, 699, 732, 1127
yathātathiya 368
yathābhūtaṁ 194, 202, 653
yasa 138, 438, 817
yasassin 179, 298, 343, 1117
yācayoga (*or* yājay°) 487–9, 509, 1046–7; *p.* 114
yogakkhema 79, 425

rakkhasa 310
raja 139, 207, 275, 334, 391–2, 406, 517, 662, 665, 974, 980
rasa 65, 181–2, 243, 257, 387, 759, 854, 922, 974
rāga 2, 11, 74, 139, 204, 270–1, 341, 361, 364, 370, 476, 493, 631, 764, 795, 891, 974, 1046
Rāga 835
Rājagaha 408

rājā 46, 72, 299, 303, 308–9, 332, 379–80, 411–12, 415–16, 419, 422–3, 455, 552–5, 568, 619, 652, 831, 991
Rāhu 465, 498
riñcati (ritta) 69, 156–7, 823, 844, 941, 958, 963
rūpa 387, 530, 754–5, 759, 872–4 &c.
roga 24, 51, 311, 530
roseti 125, 130, 216

lakkhaṇa 360, 408–9, 690, 927, 1004, 1018–21
lābhā 31, 438, 828, 854, 929, 1014, 1046
linga 601–7, 610
lippati (limpati) 71, 250, 547, 625, 778, 811–12, 913, 1040, 1042
līna 68, 717
ludda 247
Lumbineyya 683
lūkhasa 244
loka 9, 25, 59, 73, 83, 86, 115, 135, 139, 168–72, 185, 219, 249, 298, 339, 359–75, 394, 443, 455, 458, 466, 490, 496, 501, 522, 534, 560, 579, 581, 598–9, 633–4, 648, 683, 728, 768, 772, 775–6, 783, 786, 793–4, 796, 816, 845, 847, 855, 861, 864–7, 871, 894, 912–13, 915, 922, 940, 947–8, 950, 960, 974, 991, 993, 995, 998, 1035, 1040, 1043–5, 1047–9, 1053–4, 1064, 1066–8, 1077, 1087, 1103, 1122, 1133
lobha 10, 367, 371, 537, 663, 706, 864–5, 928, 941
lolo 22, 63, 922
lolupa 56, 165, 707
lohita 196, 433–4, 671; *p.* 156

Vakkali 1146
vagga 371, 800, 912
vaggu 350, 668, 955
Vangīsa *p.* 82
Vangīsa-sutta *p.* 82
vaco 54, 330, 356, 365, 663, 890, 988, 994, 1006, 1057, 1083, 1110, 1147
vacana 202, 417, 699, 932, 981, 984, 986, 997
vacī 78, 407, 472, 973
vañceti 100, 129, 356
vata (*or* -bata) 89, 624, 782, 792, 798, 839, 898
Vanasavhaya 1011
vambhayita 905
vara 301, 391, 408, 564–5, 683, 698, 996, 1128
vasa *p.* 156; 274, 297, 315, 332, 444, 561, 578, 586–7, 968
vācā 49, 125, 130, 214, 254, 353, 426, 451–4, 660, 678, 711, 850, 930, 971, 973, 1005, 1061
vāda 100, 315, 327, 381–2, 390, 780, 787, 819, 827, 829, 832, 859, 906, 913, 973, 1076
vādin 59, 217, 357, 382, 430, 620, 661, 910
vādiyati 824, 832, 892
vādayati 682
Vāsavassa (deva) 384
Vāseṭṭha (māṇava) 612–19, 656; *pp.* 146, 154
Vāseṭṭha-sutta *p.* 146
vikappeti 7, 793, 802, 918
vikkhambheti 969
vigāhati 2, 825
vigganhati (viggayha) 844, 878–9, 883, 904
vighāta 814, 830
vicāraṇa 1108–9
vicikicchā 343, 346–7, 437, 540
vicināti 5, 517, 524–6, 529, 658, 933
vijānāti 93–113, 253, 316, 482, 656, 720, 739, 763, 953, 967, 1065, 1090–1, 1097, 1120, 1122
vijigucchati 41, 253, 958, 963

vijjati 20–1, 23, 189, 431–2, 611, 634–5, 715, 856–7, 987, 989, 1001, 1088–9, 1098, 1100
vijjā 162–4, 289, 334, 594, 656, 730
viññāṇa 323, 329, 734–5, 1037, 1055, 1073, 1086, 1110–1, 1114, 1122
viññu 39, 294, 313, 317, 396, 403
vitakka 7, 270–1, 970, 1109
vitatha 9–13
vitarati 495, 514, 746, 779
vitta 102, 181–2, 302, 307
vidita 504, 1052, 1057, 1075, 1102
vidu 758, 762
vidhūpita 7, 472, 475
vidhūma 460, 1048
vippamutta 176, 218, 363, 373, 472, 483, 492, 501, 913–14
vibhava 514, 856, 867, 869, 870
vibhavati 871–4, 1113
vibhāveti 230, 318
vibhūsā 59
vimala 378, 384, 476, 519, 637, 1131
vimāna 887–8
vimuccati 23, 211, 354, 475, 491–2, 522, 534, 536, 755, 847, 975, 992, 1071–4, 1101, 1114
vimutti 54, 73, 725, 727
vimokha 1071, 1088–9, 1105
viyatta 800
viyāpanna 314
viramati 59, 175, 218, 367, 400, 531, 704, 828, 900, 925, 943, 953, 1070
virāgaratta 795
viriya 68, 79, 184, 353, 422, 432, 528, 531, 548, 966, 1026
viruddha 73, 248, 365, 630
vivajjeti 53, 399, 407
vivaṭa 19, 374, 763, 793, 921, 1003, 1147
vivattacchadda 372, 378
vivadati 830, 832, 842–3, 879, 883–4, 895–6
vivāda 596, 796, 828, 862–3, 896, 907, 912
vivitta 221, 338, 810, 845
viveka 474, 772, 814, 822, 851, 915, 1065
visaṁyutta 621, 626, 634, 641
visatta 38, 272, 1104
visattikā 333, 768, 857, 1053–4, 1067, 1085, 1087
visama 57, 215, 243, 468, 774–5, 843
visalla 17, 86, 367
visuddha 67, 517, 687, 693
visuddhi 813, 824, 840, 892
visūka 55
viseni 793, 833, 914, 1078
visesin 799, 842, 855, 905
visoseti 3, 433, 949, 1099
vissuta 137, 597, 998, 1009
vihanati 168–70, 673, 975, 1121
vihāra 220, 391, 679
vihārin 45, 375
vihiṁsati 117, 451
vihesā 247, 275, 277
vītivatto 6, 375, 796
vīmaṁsati 215, 405
vīra 44, 543, 573, 642, 646, 1096, 1102
vīvadāta 784, 881
vutti(r) 68, 81, 220, 326, 676
vusita 463, 493, 514
Vetaraṇī 674
veda 462, 529, 792, 995, 1019, 1023, 1027
vedagū 322, 458–9, 463, 472, 479, 503, 528–9, 749, 846, 890, 947, 1049, 1059–60
vedeti 211–19, 251, 346, 467, 643, 647, 758, 762, 878, 1148
vedanā 435, 529, 739, 1111
Vedisā 1011
vevicchā 941, 1033
Vesālī 1013

vesiyā 108
Vessavaṇa 380
vyappatha 158, 163A–4, 961
vyāruddha 936, 938

saṁyata 88–9, 156–7, 216, 284, 464, 716
saṁyama 264, 326, 655, 898
saṁyuta 574, 1026
saṁyutta 194, 300, 304
saṁyojana 62, 74, 175, 363, 375, 476, 491–2, 621, 736, 1109
saṁvara 1034–5
saṁvuta 340, 413
saṁsaya 682, 1030, 1112
saṁsarati 730, 740
saṁsāra 517, 519, 638, 729, 740, 746, 752
saṁsuddha 162–3, 372, 881, 1107
sakāyana 892–3, 906
Sakka (= Indra) 346, 656, 679
Sakka (= Sākyan) 345, 1063, 1069, 1090, 1113
sakkhi 84, 122, 479, 508, 921, 934
Sakya (= Sākyan) 225, 683, 685–6, 690–2, 991, 996
saṁkappa 154–5, 280, 444, 818, 1144
saṁkhata 21, 784
saṁkhaya 74
saṁkhā 209, 874, 911, 916, 1074
saṁkhāyati 70, 209, 351, 391, 749, 1038, 1041, 1048; *p.* 158
saṁkhāra 372, 731–2, 751
sanga 61, 212, 250, 386, 390, 473, 527, 532, 621, 636, 791, 948, 1060
saṁgha 421, 550, 569, 589, 680, 1015; *p.* 24
saṁghāṭī 391–2, 456
sacca 59, 78, 182, 187–9, 450, 453, 463, 479, 508, 632, 756, 758, 824, 832, 843, 882–6, 895, 903–4, 941, 946, 1133
saññā 175, 535, 732, 779, 841, 847, 874, 886, 1071–2, 1113
saṭha 133, 931
sata 466, 741, 751, 753, 768, 771, 855, 916, 933, 962, 964, 1041, 1053–4, 1056, 1066–7, 1087, 1095, 1104, 1110–1
sati 77, 340, 434, 444, 1026, 1035–6, 1107, 1143
satimant 45, 70, 88, 174, 212, 411, 446, 503, 515, 973–5, 1070
satta 248, 378, 387, 435, 643, 654, 683–4, 730, 754
satthar 31, 153, 179, 343, 345, 545, 547, 556, 571, 573, 955, 1148
sadda 71, 213, 387, 685, 759, 974; *pp.* 106, 136
saddahati 186
saddha 188, 371, 663, 853
saddhā 77, 90, 182, 184, 286, 337, 432, 1026, 1143, 1146
sa-dhamma 906, 1020
santa (sammati) 460, 475, 656, 702, 721, 746, 783, 839, 861, 912, 946, 954, 1048, 1065
santi 204, 208, 330, 332, 584, 593, 784, 837, 845, 900, 915, 919, 1066–7, 1096
santhava 37, 168–9, 207, 245, 844
sandiṭṭhi 567, 881, 891, 1137, 1139, 1141
sannidhi 306, 924
sapadānaṁ 65, 413
sabbadhamma 167, 534, 699, 793, 914, 992, 1039, 1105, 1112
sabbaloka 25, 56, 348, 378, 486, 515–16, 521, 527, 642, 761, 1009, 1104
Sabhiya (paribbājaka) 510–14, 547; *pp.* 120, 122, ...132
Sabhiya-sutta *p.* 120
sama[1], 896

sama[2] 47, 57, 90, 215, 220, 468, 508, 661, 668, 670, 672, 799, 842–3, 860, 952, 954
samaṇa 83–4, 100, 129–30, 282, 515, 518, 520, 529, 550, 714, 722, 828, 866, 868, 883–4, 890, 932
samaṇa-brāhmaṇā 189, 190, 441, 859, 1079–82
samatta 402, 781, 881, 889, 1000
samatha 67, 732
samantacakkhu 345–6, 378, 1063, 1069, 1073, 1090
samādhi 329, 330, 434, 921, 1026
samāhita 174, 212, 214, 471, 477, 519, 972
samitāvin 499, 520
samuggaṇhāti 352, 785, 795, 797, 801, 837, 841, 907
samuppāda 653
samūhata 14, 360, 369, 1076
samecca 361, 374, 475, 792, 1058
sampajāna 413, 931, 1055, 1068
sampadā 47, 505
samparāya 141, 190, 864–5
sampassati 81, 480, 582
sambuddha 178, 180, 192, 446, 541, 555, 559–60, 597, 994–5, 998, 1003, 1016, 1031, 1145, 1147
-sambudha 764
sambodhi 478, 503, 693, 696, 963
sambhava 620, 724, 726, 731, 734, 741–2, 744, 747, 750, 1115
sambhavati 272, 731, 734, 744, 747, 750
sammata 713, 760
sammasitar 69
Sammāsambuddha 565
sammuti 648, 897, 904, 911
Sayampabha (deva) 404
saraṇa 31, 179, 570, 591; *pp.* 24, 34, 74, 114, 132
sarīra 478, 584, 611
salla 17, 51, 331, 334, 592–3, 767, 938–9, 985
sallakatto 560, 562
savana 265, 345, 1120
sahati 20, 253, 942, 969, 974
sahassanetta 346
sahājanetta 1096
sahāya 35, 40–1, 45–7, 57
Sākiya 423, 695
Sāketa 1012
sāta 773, 867, 869–70
Sātāgira 153, 155, 157, 159, 161, 163
Sātāgira-sutta (=Hemavata-s°) *p.* 38
sādhu 45–6, 376, 379, 393, 482, 519, 678, 712, 1052, 1075, 1102; *p.* 134 &c.
sārathi 83; *p.* 132 &c.
Sāriputta 557, 955, 963
Sāriputta-sutta *p.* 228
Sāriputta-Moggallānā *p.* 156–8
sāvaka 90, 134, 345, 357, 376, 389, 391, 393, 395, 444; *p.* 22 &c.
Sāvatthī 996, 998, 1012; *p.* 26 &c.
sāvittī 457, 568
sāsana 445, 482, 565, 570, 698, 815, 933–4, 1084
s(i)neha 36, 66, 209, 272, 943
siva 115, 478
sissa 997, 1004, 1006, 1028–9
sīta 52, 467, 642, 966, 1014, 1073
sīmanta 484
sīmâtigo 795
sīla 244, 246–7, 292, 294, 324, 381, 783, 839, 840, 848
sīlabbata (sīlavata) 174, 212, 624, 782, 790, 797–9, 803, 836, 839–40, 887, 898, 900, 961, 1079–83
sukha 59, 67, 181–2, 256, 297–8, 323, 383, 439, 592, 658, 683, 738, 760–2, 873, 981
Sugata 32, 391, 643, 659
suci 75, 128, 205, 243, 410, 678–9

Sujampati 1024
sujjhati 487, 508, 789
sutavant 70, 90, 371
suti 839–40, 1078
suddha 90, 283, 435, 476, 636–7, 662, 788, 1120
suddhi 373, 478, 526, 789–90, 794, 824, 830, 839–40, 875–6, 891, 898–901, 906, 908–10, 1079–81
Suddhodana 685
sudhammatā 180, 192
subbata 89, 220, 441
Sundarika-Bhāradvāja (brāhmaṇa) *pp*. 106, 114
Sundarika-Bhāradvāja-sutta *p*. 106
Sundarikā (nadi) *p*. 106
subha 199, 341, 633, 824, 910
sura 681
surādhutta 106
Sūciloma *p*. 66
Sūciloma-sutta *p*. 66
sūra 439, 831
sekha 970, 1038
Setavya 1012
senā 436, 439, 443, 556, 561
Seniya (Bimbisāra) *p*. 136
Sela (brāhmaṇa) *p*. 134
Sela-sutta *p*. 132
sevati 47, 57, 72, 75, 88, 385, 391, 927
soka 449, 469, 584, 586, 591, 593, 809, 862, 985, 994, 1052, 1056
Sogandhika (niraya) *p*. 158
socati 34, 79, 185, 188, 333, 445, 581, 805, 827, 861, 944, 948, 950–1
1. sota 322, 345, 461, 922
2. sota 197, 250, 319, 355, 433, 715, 736, 777, 1034–5; *p*. 138
sottiya 533–4
sopadhīka 789
sopāka 137
somanassa 67
soracca 78, 292, 330
sorata 309, 513, 515, 540

haṁsa 221, 350
(loma-)haṁsa 270
(loma-)haṭṭha-jāta 1017; *p*. 24
hadaya-nissita 938
hāpeti 37, 90
hiṁsati 117, 309, 368, 515, 583, 585
hita 233, 665, 683, 692–3, 697
Himavant 422
hiri 77, 133, 253, 462, 719
hīna 725, 776, 796–9, 816, 827, 899, 903–5
huta 459, 461, 479, 487
hutta 249; *p*. 106
huraṁ 468, 470, 496, 801, 1084, 1135
hetu 16, 122, 775, 1131
Hemaka 1007, 1084, 1086, 1124
Hemavata (yakkha) 154, 156, 158, 160, 162, 168–9
Hemavata-sutta *p*. 38

II
ENGLISH INDEX

Abhidhamma-Piṭaka *p.* xiii
Across 539, 1129; *pp.* 235, 267
Adept 143, 528–9, 595, 782–3, 798, 838, 870, 903, 1038
Affection(s) 36, 41, 185, 187, 209, 811, 863–5
Ajita 1006, 1016–17, 1124
Ajita's Question Sutta *p.* 243
Āḷavi 1146
Alert 413, 751, 753, 1039
Almsman 1, 43, 87, 202, 204, 221, 252, 266, 276, 278, 280, 282, 343, 374, 385–6, 389, 392–3, 403, 411–12, 416, 513–14, 573, 700, 715, 735, 739, 741, 745, 751, 753, 783, 919, 920, 923, 975, 1039, 1041, 1104; *pp.* xiii, xix, 105, 133, 135, 175, 183
Almsman's Life and Householder's, Sutta *p.* 91
Almswomen *p.* xix
Alone 35–75, 388, 718, 821; *pp.* 25, 143
Aloof(ness) 213, 257, 718, 810, 821–2, 852, 900, 915, 1065; *pp.* xxi, 25, 143
Anāthapiṇḍika *pp.* 27, 31, 65, 71, 91
Anchorite 83, 99–100, 129–30, 189, 375, 385, 441, 515, 518, 520, 529, 533, 537, 551, 689, 718, 722, 816, 820, 828, 883–4, 890, 932, 1079, 1080, 1082; *pp.* 31, 45, 67, 121, 123, 133, 135, 137
Anchorite's Ideal Sutta *p.* 87
Anga *p.* 133
Anger *see* Wrath
Anguttara Nikāya *pp.* xiii, xv
Apt Words Sutta *p.* 105
Arahat(s) 186, 539, 644, 1003; *pp.* 25, 133, 135, 137, 139, 143, 147
Arise! Sutta *p.* 79
Armed Hand Sutta *p.* 225
Arrow 331, 335
Asita's *Nunc Dimittis* Sutta *p.* 165
Asoka xiv, xviii
Augustine, St. *pp.* xxii
Austerity 77, 249, 267, 284, 292, 792; *pp.* xix, xxi

Barbs 367
Bāvarī 981, 984, 994–5, 997, 1006, 1010, 1019, 1025, 1028–9, 1030; *p.* xviii
Beauty Scorned Sutta *p.* 201
Beliefs, outworn 1
Bewilderment 347
Beyond 1059, 1129; *p.* 267
Bhadrāvudha 1008, 1125, 1146
Bhadrāvudha's Question Sutta *pp.* xviii, 261
Bhāradvāja 595; *pp.* 147, 155
Bhāradvāja (Aggika) *p.* 31, 35
Bhāradvāja (Kasi) *p.* 21, 25
Bhāradvāja (Sundarika) *pp.* 107, 115
Bhāradvāja Sutta *p.* 21
Bimbisāra *p.* 135
Birth 136, 139, 141–2, 456, 462, 476, 596, 599, 620, 650, 733, 1045–8, 1052, 1056, 1060, 1079, 1080, 1082; *p.* 107
Birth and Death 32, 351, 467, 484, 500, 517, 520, 725, 727, 729, 1122
Blameless 1126
Blamelessness 88

Bliss 5, 228, 249, 323, 399, 478, 525–6, 561, 709, 892, 1044
Bliss, final 78, 86, 115, 139
Body, last 471, 478
Bonds 29, 375, 476, 491–2, 522, 532
Bondages 347
Boon of Boons Sutta *p.* 65
Brahmā(s) 310, 315, 479, 508–9, 656, 1024; *p.* 135
Brahmin(s) 129, 136, 138, 140–42, 286–93, 301, 303, 308, 382, 441, 455, 458, 460, 462–3, 469, 518, 529, 596, 599, 612–21, 647, 649–50, 655, 790, 795, 802–3, 843, 907, 911, 946, 1059, 1063, 1079, 1080, 1082, 1115; *pp.* 31, 67, 107, 135, 147
Brahminism's Golden Age Sutta *p.* 71
Buddhaghosa *p.* xiv *n.*
Buddha(s) 202, 204, 224, 226, 233–4, 236, 276, 330, 401, 429, 446, 454, 468, 559, 683, 696, 957, 999, 1005, 1126, 1129, 1133; *pp.* xix–xx, 135, 137
Buddhahood 558; *p.* xx
Butler, Dom Cuthbert *p.* xxii

Calm, Calmly 67, 82, 322, 341–3, 434, 460, 467, 491–2, 519, 534, 630, 642, 707, 721, 839, 915, 917, 953
Cankers 162–3, 178, 219, 367, 374, 471, 481, 535, 539, 546, 572, 644, 749, 765, 913, 996, 1082–3, 1100, 1105, 1133, 1145; *p.* 183. *See* Uncankered
Cankī *p.* 147
Canon *pp.* xiii–xviii
Carrion Sutta *p.* 59
Cause(s) 209, 473–4
Certitude 55, 70
Cessation 754–5; *p.* 181
Charpentier, J. *p.* xvii *n.*
Chastity 396; *p.* xx
Cleanse 279, 351, 435, 476, 508, 636, 739, 834; *p.* xxi
Commentary *pp.* xiv *and n.*, xvi, xviii
Companionship 36–7, 40–41, 45, 47, 54, 57–8
Comprehension 329, 352, 537, 847; *pp.* xix, 183
Conceit 4, 245
Concentration 329, 434; *pp.* xxi, xxii
Conduct 136, 142, 145, 263, 324, 376, 393, 650, 848, 898, 914, 962; *p.* 79
Confession 921
Conscience (fear to err) 77, 133
Consciousness 734–5, 874, 886; *pp.* xxi, 177
Constancy 531
Contact 736–7, 870–2; *p.* 177
Contemplation 226, 810; *pp.* xxi, xxii
Contentions Sutta *p.* 205
Control 154–5, 250, 340, 850
Conversion 227
Cool 467
Council, First *p.* xiv; Asoka's *pp.* xiv, xviii
Covetise 367, 371, 663, 706, 954
Crassness 13, 212, 772, 1051, 1106, 1132
Craving(s) 3, 70, 82–3, 211, 272, 306, 339, 436, 474, 495, 592, 635, 640, 715, 740–1, 746, 854, 916, 953, 1021, 1033, 1041, 1060, 1070, 1082–3, 1085, 1088–9, 1101, 1103–4, 1109, 1123, 1137, 1139, 1141; *p.* 177
Cunda 83, 85
Cunda Sutta *p.* 25

Death 576, 578–9, 581, 587, 590, 629, 755, 776, 806, 876, 1100, 1118–19, 1146
Deathlessness 80, 204, 225, 635

Deceit 56, 116, 242, 328, 926
Defile 1032–3
Defilement 334, 949, 1099
Deliverance *see* Release
Detached 811, 853
Desire(s) 367, 706–7, 766–9, 771, 773, 856, 902, 1048, 1051; *p.* 185
Desires Sutta *p.* 185
Dhammapada *pp.* xv, xvii
Dhammika *p.* 91
Dhaniya 30
Dhaniya Sutta *p.* 5
Dhotaka 1007, 1124
Dhotaka's Question Sutta *p.* 251
Dīgha Nikāya *pp.* xiii, xxi
Discipline 7, 23, 898, 964, 974
Disillusion Sutta *p.* 47
Doctrine 69, 70, 81, 83, 87, 182, 186, 188, 225, 257, 265, 276, 316, 326–7, 374, 389, 450, 453, 461, 480, 570, 694–6, 763, 785, 792, 905, 921, 933, 947, 975, 993, 1015, 1085, 1102, 1122, 1137, 1139, 1141; *pp.* xx, 25, 35, 75, 105, 133, 135, 267
Donor 458
Doubt(s) 58, 86–7, 231, 249, 318, 320, 343, 346–7, 367, 477, 500, 510, 514, 534, 540–1, 559, 635, 638, 682, 866, 868, 972, 1059, 1063–4, 1088–9, 1112, 1148–9
Dread 231, 257, 270–1, 546, 572, 850, 923, 948
Dyads Sutta *p.* 173

Effort 79, 184; *p.* xxi
Eightfold 401–2
Elephant 166
Ender 467
Energy 432
Enlightened 81, 83, 85, 134, 180, 192, 408, 523, 541, 545, 555, 560, 565, 571, 643, 696, 993–5, 998, 1003, 1016, 1031, 1147; *pp.* 135, 137, 139, 417
Enlightenment 139, 167, 178, 191–2, 478, 503, 513, 517, 597, 622, 646, 693, 992, 1128, 1145; *pp.* xix
'Ere Dissolution comes' Sutta *p.* 203
Errors, 470, 493, 638, 786, 846, 889
Erudite 533–4
Evil 519, 521, 1034–5
Existence(s) 742, 1055

Faculty 63, 340
Failure 91–115
Failures Sutta *p.* 27
Faith 77, 182, 184, 286, 337, 371, 432, 719, 749, 1026, 1143
Fausböll, V. *p.* vii, xvi
Fear(s) 167, 546, 561, 572, 902
Feelings 738–9; *p.* 177
Fetters 62, 74, 175
Fire-worshipper *pp.* 133, 135, 141, 143
Fires 19
Flood 21, 173–4, 178, 183–4, 210, 219, 273, 471, 495, 515, 771, 779, 1082–3, 1101
Fool(s) 61, 259, 399, 662, 706, 721, 825, 879, 880, 882, 890, 893, 1051
Forbearance 294
Form 754–5; *p.* 181
Formless 754–5; *p.* 181
Franciscan Exhortation *p.* xx
Free, freed 473, 475, 490–2, 501, 508, 536, 546, 572, 593, 626, 643, 715, 758, 823, 839, 852, 877, 897, 975, 1057. *See* Release
Friendship Sutta *p.* 63
Fruit(s) 227, 486
Further Shore 771, 823

Gayā *p*. 67
Gem 224–35
Gem Sutta *p*. 55
Generosity 187–8
Goal 68, 228, 318, 377, 627, 725, 727, 911, 940
God(s) 333, 346, 377, 443, 521, 527, 543, 680–1, 756, 956, 1043; *p*. 135
Godhāvarī 977
Good 94, 152, 219, 229, 239, 274, 324, 450, 460, 662, 1048
Good Life Sutta *p*. 69
Good Ship Sutta *p*. 77
Goodwill 73, 223, 507
Goodwill Sutta *p*. 37
Gotama 91, 153, 164, 167, 448, 461, 487, 848, 933, 1117, 1135–6, 1138, 1140; *pp*. xiii, xiv, xix, xx, xxii, 23, 25, 31, 35, 71, 75, 115, 121, 123, 133, 135, 137, 155
Gotama's Pilgrimage Sutta *p*. 99
Gotama's Temptation Sutta *p*. 101
Greed 328, 928, 941, 945
Grief(s) 805, 809, 811, 948, 1106
Growth(s) 14, 208, 235, 272, 329, 731, 913
Growths Sutta *p*. 67
Grudging 809, 811, 860
Grumbling 43

Hankerings 470, 758, 852
Harm, Injury 35, 117, 148, 156–7, 200, 223, 288, 368, 513
Hatred 12, 74, 150, 371, 493, 631
Heart(s) 6, 23, 63, 75, 160–1, 183–4, 203, 228, 259, 269, 282, 341, 402–3, 435, 437, 482, 506, 531, 659, 725, 727, 746, 766, 778, 943, 975, 1026, 1111; *pp*. 135, 183
Hemaka 1007, 1124
Hemaka's Question Sutta *p*. 257
Here and Now 343, 567, 626, 775, 1062, 1066, 1137, 1139, 1141; *pp*. 25, 143, 173, 183
Hereafter 730, 786
Hero(es) 439, 642, 646, 684
Higher Life 326, 354, 566, 695–6, 717, 1128; *pp*. 135, 143
Himālayan Sprite Sutta *p*. 39
Hindrances, the Five 17, 66
Holiness 285, 288, 487, 693, 697
Holy Life 267, 274, 289, 292, 294, 463, 493, 655; *p*. xxi
Homeless(ness) 274, 376, 406, 487, 497, 741, 751, 753, 844, 966, 970, 1003; *pp*. 25, 133, 143
Hooker, Richard, xx
Horner, I. B., *p*. xi *and* xix *n*.
Household Life 43–4, 64
Humility 326
Hunger 436
Hurrying and Lagging 8–13

Ignorance 277, 347, 729, 730, 1026, 1033, 1105; *p*. 175
Ill(s) 32, 36, 80, 170–2, 183–4, 250, 252, 283, 337, 454, 473, 537, 539, 626, 724, 726, 728, 731–2, 734–5, 739, 741–2, 744–5, 747–8, 750–1, 753, 760, 762, 770, 774, 789, 937, 1033, 1049, 1050–1, 1056–8, 1133; *pp*. 173, 175, 183
Illumination *pp*. 173, 183
Illusion 56, 74, 160–1, 847
Ill-will 270–1, 507
Inda 310, 316, 679
Indifference 67, 73
Individuality 1036–7
Insight 55, 152, 163 A *and* B, 184–6, 323, 373, 425, 539, 706, 743, 837, 848
Island 1092–4

Jains 381
Jānussoṇi *p.* 147
Jātaka *p.* xvii *n.*
Jatukaṇṇī 1007, 1125; *pp.* xviii, 261
Jealousy 56, 109–10
Jewels, the Seven *p.* 137
Joy(s) 33, 67, 327, 330, 853, 1106, 1109, 1111

Kaccāyana *p.* 121
Kapilavatthu 1012
Kappa 344, 349, 354, 356, 358, 1007, 1093, 1125; *p.* 83
Kappa's Destiny Sutta *p.* 83
Kassapa (Buddha) 242
Kassapa, Pūraṇa *p.* 121
Khandhakas *p.* xiv *n.*
Khuddaka-Nikāya *p.* xiii
Khuddaka Pāṭha *p.* xv
King 553–4
Know 317, 504, 527, 528, 530, 723, 730, 733, 737, 788, 792, 908–9, 1060
Knowledge 322, 334, 378, 722–3, 868, 877, 1026, 1035–6, 1105; *pp.* xx, 135
Kosala 976, 996

Lanman, C. R. *p.* xvi *n.*
Largesse Sutta *p.* 114
Layman 44, 64, 220–1
Lecher 107–8, 814–15
Lechery 816–17, 820–21, 926; *p.* 197
Lechery Sutta *p.* 197
Lévi, S. *p.* xvi *n.*
Lie(s) 397, 400, 1131
Life 5, 175–6, 235, 243, 278, 746, 752, 764, 775, 779, 801, 875–7, 923, 1046, 1059, 1060, 1068
Life's fuel 742–3; *p.* 179
Life, last 502, 624
Light 378, 501, 910, 991
Lion 166, 546, 562, 684, 1015; *p.* 137
Long Book *p.* 98
Lore 70, 83, 261, 432, 434, 443, 463, 468, 503, 528–9, 539, 627, 733, 749, 789, 799, 846, 947, 969, 996, 1059, 1079, 1080, 1090–1, 1136, 1138, 1140
Love 150, 162–3, 678
Loyalty Sutta *p.* 63
Lust(s) 176–7, 228, 243, 247, 270–2, 315, 367, 445, 467, 472, 483, 631, 913, 974

Magadha 408, 1013; *pp.* 21, 267
Māgha *pp.* 115, 121
Mahā-pajāpatī *p.* xix
Majjhima Nikāya *pp.* xiii, xv, xix, xxi
Makkhali Gosāla *p.* 121
Man *and* Men 324, 333, 364, 377, 435, 443, 508, 521, 527, 558, 607, 610–19, 654, 740, 756, 792, 806–7, 936, 938
Māra 33, 355, 357–8, 429, 430–1, 435, 439, 442, 545, 561, 563, 571, 733, 764, 835, 967, 1095, 1103–4; *pp.* 67, 135
Matter 872–4
Meditation *p.* xxi
Meek 499, 513, 515, 623–4, 662, 719, 852
Mendicants 381
Mental State(s) 69, 264, 372, 478, 699, 787, 917, 1105, 1112
Merit 82, 427–8, 431, 463, 481, 486–7, 490, 503, 505, 569, 697, 744–5, 953; *pp.* 115, 179
Mettagū 1006, 1124
Mettagū's Question Sutta *p.* 247
Migāra's Mother *p.* 173
Mind 14, 19, 58, 154–5, 171, 203, 270–1, 388, 434, 470, 478, 558,

699, 717, 725, 727, 783, 872, 1026, 1037, 1039, 1110–11, 1143–4; *pp*. xx–xxii
Mindful 413, 975, 1104; *p*. xxi
Mindfulness 45, 70, 77, 88, 973, 1026, 1036, 1053–4, 1085, 1087, 1110–11; *p*. xxi
Moggallāna *pp*. 157, 159
Mogharāja 1008, 1125
Mogharāja's Question Sutta *p*. 265
More Rejoinders Sutta *p*. 215
Müller, Max *p*. xvii

Nālaka 697, 699
Nanda 1007, 1124
Nanda's Question Sutta *pp*. xviii, 255.
Nāta-putta *p*. 121
Nerañjarā 425
Niddesa *pp*. xiv *n*., xv, xvi, xviii
Nikāyas *pp*. xiii, xv
Nirvāna 86, 204, 233, 267, 365, 453–4, 514, 758, 822, 940, 942, 1086, 1094, 1108–9
Noble 533, 535, 758, 761–2, 765, 783; *pp*. xix, 181, 183

Obey, 340
Obsession 916
Octad of the Den Sutta *p*. 185
Octad of Malice Sutta *p*. 187
Octad of Purity Sutta *p*. 189
Octad of Perfection Sutta *p*. 193
Octads, Book of *pp*. xvii, 185
Offerings Sutta *p*. 107
Okkāka 302, 306, 991
Open-handed(ness) 505, 509
Order 227, 232, 235, 238
Owning 805, 809

Pack 626
Pangs of Grief Sutta *p*. 145
Paragon 518, 522, 543
Paramatthajotikā *p*. xiii
Parivāra *p*. xiv *n*.
Passion 2, 11, 74, 139, 204, 341, 370, 465, 476, 493, 498–9, 507, 751, 795, 813, 823, 933
Path(s) 227, 323, 374, 441, 514, 696, 714, 789, 790, 947, 949, 1040, 1042, 1086, 1099, 1130
Pātimokkha *p*. xiii
Patna *pp*. xiv, xviii
Peace 79, 143, 146, 204, 208, 225, 257, 268, 332, 424–5, 454, 465, 481, 499, 519, 593, 683, 707, 714, 735, 737, 739, 746, 753, 765, 772, 783–4, 809, 837–8, 857, 896, 900, 912, 915, 919, 933, 946, 949, 954, 1065–7, 1087, 1096, 1099
Perception(s) 732, 1071–2
Perfect 376, 393, 788, 848, 947, 953, 1020
Perfection 87, 788; *p*. 193
Perplexity 510
Personality 231, 530, 537, 756, 761, 950, 1073, 1100, 1119
Pilgrim(s) 407, 456, 639, 640; *pp*. 25, 133, 137, 143
Pilgrimage 405, 564–5, 567
Pingiya 1008, 1125, 1146
Pingiya's Question Sutta *pp*. xviii, 267
Piṭakas *pp*. xiii, xiv
Plastic Force 372, 731–2, 751; *p*. 175
Pleasure(s) 50–1, 59–60, 152, 160–1, 166, 171, 175, 243, 284, 337, 435–6, 464, 497, 625, 639, 704, 719, 738, 772, 774, 845, 873, 940, 1039, 1041, 1046, 1070–2, 1091, 1098; *pp*. xxi, 121
Poise, Poised 67, 73, 328, 515, 855, 952, 972, 1107; *p*. xxi
Pokkharasāti 594; *p*. 147
Posāla 1008, 1125

Posāla's Question Sutta *p.* 265
Power(s) 498
Pride 203–4, 244–5, 328, 342, 370, 438, 469, 473, 493, 537, 631, 756, 786, 830, 853, 862–3, 889, 926, 942–3, 968, 1132
Psychic Power *p.* 137
Puṇṇaka *p.* xviii, 1006, 1124
Puṇṇaka's Question Sutta *pp.* xviii, 245
Pure, Purity 90, 162–3, 283, 372–3, 476, 517, 526, 636–7, 662, 678, 788–9, 790, 794, 824, 830, 839, 840, 875–6, 891–2, 898, 900–901, 906, 908–9, 910, 1079, 1080; *pp.* xxi, 135, 189

Quaking 752, 902, 923; *p.* 181

Rāhula Sutta *p.* 81
Rājagaha *p.* 115
Rancour 6
Reality 9–13, 759
Rebirth 16, 147, 152, 162–3, 209, 230, 273, 278, 339, 474, 496, 499, 514, 519, 535, 546, 572, 638, 647, 656, 740, 743, 746, 754, 839, 901–2, 1091, 1121, 1123, 1133; *pp.* 25, 143
Rejoinders Sutta *p.* 211
Release 10–13, 54, 66, 73, 166, 170, 172, 176–7, 211–12, 231, 344, 354, 373, 465, 472, 498, 522, 534, 725, 727, 746, 755, 847, 914, 992, 1071–2, 1088–9, 1101, 1105, 1114, 1149
Renunciation 424, 1098; *p.* xix
Resolve 187, 444, 921
Return *p.* 173
Reverie 69, 156–7, 165, 221, 425, 503, 638, 709, 719, 925, 972, 985, 1009, 1105
Rhinoceros 35
Rhinoceros Sutta *pp.* xv, 11
Rhys Davids, T. W. *p.* xvi *n.*
Right 215
Right Conduct Sutta *p.* 79
Righteousness 554, 1002
Rites 231, 249, 1079, 1080
Ruth 189, 292, 378

Sabhiya *pp.* 121, 123, 125, 127, 129, 131, 133
Sabhiya's Questions Sutta *p.* 121
Sage(s) 39, 82–3, 87, 115, 177, 209, 210–11, 213, 216, 218–19, 220–1, 225, 252, 284, 343, 460, 481, 484, 523, 538, 540–1, 545, 591, 646, 691–2, 695, 698, 700, 703, 721, 723, 749, 778–9, 780, 809, 811–12, 821, 823, 845–6, 850, 860, 877, 889, 890, 912, 914–15, 941, 946, 953–4, 1074, 1077–8, 1090–1
Sage Sutta *p.* 49
Saint(s) 90, 135, 235, 250, 277, 441, 453, 458–9, 490, 518, 521, 573, 590, 656, 659, 775, 786, 848, 857, 861, 932, 954, 1052
Sāketa 1012
Sakka 346, 656, 679
Sakyan 423, 683, 685–6, 691–2, 695, 991, 996, 1069; *pp.* 133, 137
Salvation 371, 545, 571, 1061–2
Saṁyutta Nikāya *pp.* xv, xviii
Sāriputta 557; *pp.* 157, 159
Sāvatthī 976, 996, 998, 1012; *pp.* 27, 31, 65, 71, 91, 105, 157, 173
Schooled 513, 516
Scion 528, 532
Scornful 335–6
See 317, 346, 374, 504, 908–9, 910
Sela 554; *pp.* 135, 137, 139, 141, 143
Self 271–2, 425, 432–3, 445, 477, 756, 790, 858, 918–19, 961; *pp.* 25, 143, 173, 183
Self-bred 516, 527

Self-denial 655
Self-mastery, -restraint, -control 189, 216, 284, 326, 413, 463, 490, 497, 624, 723
Self-poised 328
Self-will 329
Sense(s) 144, 214, 250, 373, 413, 436, 526, 529, 535, 538, 697, 714, 719, 778–9, 790, 792–3, 797–8, 802, 812–13, 846–7, 851, 861, 887, 897, 901, 914, 940, 943, 975, 1055, 1068, 1082–3, 1121; *p.* xxi
Serene 174, 328, 342, 972
Short Book *p.* 54
Sin 399
Sinless 795
Slander's Doom Sutta *p.* 157
Slokas *p.* xvii
Sloth 157, 334, 430, 436, 942, 1033
Snake-book *p.* 2
Snakes 1
Solitude 718, 959, 969; *p.* xxii
Souls 284
Speech 450–1, 453, 961
Stainless 176, 468, 515, 517, 624, 913, 1105
Steadfast 228–9, 519, 591, 719; *p.* xxi
Steadfastness *pp.* xx–i
Stream 173
Stuff of Existence, of Life 728, 915, 992, 1057, 1083; *pp.* 173, 175, 183
Suddhodana 685
Sumangala Vilāsinī *pp.* xiv *and n.*, xx *n.*
Superman 165, 548, 1000, 1040, 1042; *pp.* 135, 137
Superman Sutta *p.* 133
Sure 17, 324, 370, 477, 536
Sustenance 747–8; *p.* 179
Sutta *pp.* xiii, xiv, xviii
Sutta-Nipāta *p.* xiii, *et seqq.*
Sutta-Piṭaka *p.* xiii
Sutta-Vibhanga *p.* xiii–iv *and n.*

Tamer *p.* 135
Tathāgata *pp.* xiv *n.*, xix
Taylor, Jeremy *p.* xx
Theft 395
Thirst 436
Thought(s) 7, 63, 69, 149, 154–5, 211–12, 270–1, 330, 444, 506, 516, 524–6, 717, 793, 1048, 1062, 1066, 1109, 1144
Threefold Lore 594–5, 656
Tie(s) 473, 522, 527, 634, 717
Time 535, 567, 860, 1101, 1137, 1139, 1141
Tissa Metteyya 1006, 1124
Tissa Metteyya's Question *p.* 245
Todeyya 1007, 1124; *p.* 147
Todeyya's Question *pp.* xviii, 259
Toiling and Moiling *p.* 179
Tranquillity *p.* xxi
Transmigration 69, 1050
Trenckner, V. *p.* xvii
Truth 182, 187–9, 224–38, 267, 318, 320, 323, 327, 351, 353, 365, 368, 378, 383, 397, 450, 453, 463, 467, 471, 478, 536, 543, 554, 632, 684, 693, 698, 756, 758, 763–4, 785, 792, 856, 882–6, 895, 907, 934, 946, 993, 1015, 1031, 1097, 1133; *pp.* xix, xx, 105, 181
Truth-finder *p.* 23

Udāna *p.* xvi *n.*
Udaya 1007, 1125
Udaya's Question Sutta *p.* 263
Unburdened 495, 501
Uncankered 493
Undefiled 1040
Unfettered 68

Unfevered 542, 642
Upasīva 1007, 1124
Upasīva's Question Sutta *p.* 253
Upright 533, 536

Vakkali 1146
Vangīsa *pp.* 83, 105
Vāseṭṭha *pp.* 147, 155
Vedas 1019; *pp.* xvii *and n.*, 135
Veil 372, 378, 763, 1147; *p.* 137
Vesālī 1013
Vice 348
Vigilance 466, 768, 1143
Vigilant 855, 1056
Vinaya-Piṭaka *pp.* xiii, xiv et seqq.
Violence 394
Virtue 226, 294, 509, 665, 678, 717, 763, 783
Vision 231, 290, 471, 635, 647, 795, 934, 1115, 1148
Vita brevis Sutta *p.* 193

Wanderer *p.* 133
Want(s) 10, 56, 210, 280, 372, 460, 491–2, 537, 865–7, 1033, 1040, 1042, 1078
Warring Sects Sutta *p.* 197
Wastrel 116–36, 142
Wastrel Sutta *p.* 31
Watchful 446, 515, 751, 753, 933, 964, 1039, 1110–11
Watchfulness 434, 771, 916, 1062, 1066–67, 1107, 1119
Waverings 750–1, 1040, 1048; *p.* 179
Way 55, 84–9, 176–7, 454, 701, 716, 724, 726, 906, 1096; *pp.* 235, 267
Way Across 1130–1, 1145; *p.* xiii
Way-across Book *pp.* 235, 267
Weal 53, 146, 181–2, 258, 269, 326, 377, 385, 439, 453, 460, 592, 683, 760–2, 838; *p.* 183
'What is a brahmin?' Sutta *p.* 147
What Sāriputta asked, Sutta *p.* 229
Wheel 554–7, 684, 693, 698
Wisdom 77, 182, 565, 718, 723, 947, 962, 1101
Wise 259, 349, 581, 653, 733, 743, 792
Woe(s) 34, 61, 273, 574, 658, 666, 694
Women 703; *p.* xix
Woodland Sprite Sutta *p.* 45
Words 254, 454, 850; *p.* 105
Works 790, 803, 846, 887, 961, 1079, 1080, 1082–3
World(s) xviii, 1, 9–13, 25, 56, 71, 73, 86, 135, 150, 168–70, 219, 340, 378, 441, 516, 520, 581, 666, 759, 845, 963, 1032–3, 1104, 1108–9, 1117–19; *pp.* 135, 137
Worth 58, 488–9, 509; *pp.* 135, 137
Wrath 1, 216, 245, 469, 537, 850, 866, 868, 928
Wrong 14, 22–24, 57, 215–16, 369, 400, 531, 627, 757

Yoke 641

Zeal 88, 156, 184, 334, 344, 528, 531, 1026
Zealous 445, 1056
Zest 1143; *p.* xxi

DESCRIPTIVE LIST

OF THE

HARVARD ORIENTAL SERIES

Advertising Pages, giving the titles of the volumes of the Series, and of some other works concerning India which are published by
The Harvard University Press.

PREFATORY NOTE

THE HARVARD ORIENTAL SERIES was founded in 1891. It aims to make available for us people of the West the incomparable lessons which (if we be wise enough to maintain the teachable habit of mind) the Wise Men of the East can teach us. These lessons concern mutual good will as between persons and nations, repose of spirit by the overcoming of ill will and worry and hurry, moderation of our desires, the simple life, and above all, the search after God, and the realization — whether by reasoning or by faith — of the divine immanence.

Buddha (563–483 B.C.) was the greatest teacher of pre-Christian Asia. His precepts and example have been or are an untold blessing to India and Ceylon and the Far East. The West and the Far East have now become near neighbors. From the responsibilities and the consequent results of such neighborhood there is no escape. Already, across the Pacific, there is at work an interchange of mighty influences that will affect profoundly, for better, for worse, the politics and literature and philosophy and religion and morals of both East and West, in short, the habits of mind of both hemispheres.

The first league of nations, we are told, was the International Telegraphic Union (1865); and the second was the Universal Postal Union. A concrete example, say of a universal tariff truce, if strikingly successful, might prove to be the most effective possible world-lesson. Such agencies of world-progress, involving for each member a partial surrender of individual freedom, are now many and various. Their logical outcome is a League of All Nations and a World Court and the outlawry of war. To make such outlawry effective, mutual distrust and fear must give way to a pervading spirit of good will.

For working out this miracle, we need everywhere, as leaders, men of action who can command the sympathies and enthusiasm of great masses. And behind these leaders must stand scholars who know what the best and noblest achievements of the East and of the West are, and who can bring them to bear upon the life and ways of thought of the West and of the East. The work of the scholar is in vital relation with the practical needs of today.

The volumes of this Series may be roughly grouped as follows:

VEDAS, BRAHMANAS, UPANISHADS — 16 VOLUMES

The Veda of Praise or Rig-Veda, volumes 33*, 34*, 35*
The Veda of the Sacrifice or Yajur-Veda, volumes 18, 19
The Veda of Magic Charms or Atharva-Veda, volumes 7, 8
Vedic Concordance, volume 10
Rig-Veda Repetitions, volumes 20, 24
Rig-Veda Brahmanas (Aitareya, Kaushitaki), volume 25
Brhad-Devata, deities and myths of the Rig-Veda, volumes 5, 6
Religion and Philosophy of the Veda and Upanishads, volumes 31, 32
Rig-Veda Index, volume 36*

BUDDHISM — 8 VOLUMES

Buddhism in Translations, volume 3
Buddha's Teachings or Sutta-Nipata, Pali and English, volume 37
Buddhist Legends, volumes 28, 29, 30
Buddha's Former Births or Jataka-Mala, Sanskrit, volume 1
Buddha-ghosa's Way of Holiness or Visuddhi-magga, Pali, volumes 39*, 40*

PHILOSOPHY — 2 VOLUMES

Sankhya System, by Vijnana-Bhikshu, Sanskrit text, volume 2
Yoga System of Patanjali, Sanskrit text, volume 17

STORIES, COURT EPIC, PROVERBS — 8 VOLUMES

Pancha-tantra, oldest recension, Sanskrit text of Kashmir, volume 14
Pancha-tantra of Purna-bhadra, Sanskrit text, volumes 11, 12, 13
Vikrama's Adventures, Sanskrit (four texts) and English, volumes 26, 27
Bharavi's Arjuna and the mountaineer, German, volume 15
Indian Epigrams, done out of Sanskrit into English verse, volume 38*

DRAMA — 6 VOLUMES

Kalidasa's Çakuntala, Sanskrit and Prakrit text, volume 16
Shudraka's Little Clay Cart, English, volume 9
Raja-çekhara's Karpura-manjari, Prakrit text and English, volume 4
Bhava-bhuti's Later Rama-history, Part 1, English, volume 21
Bhava-bhuti's Later Rama-history, Part 2, Sanskrit, Prakrit, volume 22*
Bhava-bhuti's, Later Rama-history, Part 3, text-criticism etc., volume 23*

* Of the above-listed forty volumes, nine are marked with a star to show that they are not yet actually issued. But of those nine, not less than seven have a good chance of being soon issued; for each of the seven is all, or nearly all, in type or printed. The seven volumes are: three of Rig-Veda, two of Buddha-ghosa, one of Indian Epigrams, and one (Part 2, text) of the Rama-play. — Thus, happily, there remain only two volumes of less assured future: they are Part 3 of the Rama-play, and the Rig-Veda Index.

Foreign Governments and various Learned Corporations, during the forty-odd years in which the volumes of the Harvard Oriental Series have been appearing, have intimated their confidence in the value and trustworthiness of these works by conferring upon the responsible editor such titles as Honorary Fellow or Correspondent or the like. — Of these public marks of confidence in the Series, the Harvard University Press, as its official Publisher and in these advertising-pages, would mention the following:

From the Government of India, Hon. Correspondent (1912) of the Archæological Department; from the Gov't of French Indo-China, Hon. Life-member of the École Française d'Extrême Orient; from the University of Aberdeen on her Four-hundredth Anniversary (1906), and from Yale University (in 1902), Honorary Doctor of Laws;

Honorary Fellow (1896: now Senior) of the Asiatic Society of Bengal (founded, Calcutta, 1784); Honorary Member of the Société Asiatique (Paris, 1822), of the Royal Asiatic Society (London, 1823) and of its North-China Branch (Shanghai), and of the Deutsche Morgenländische Gesellschaft (Leipzig, 1845);

Member of the American Philosophical Society (1727); Fellow of the American Academy of Arts and Sciences (1780); Member of the Colonial Society of Massachusetts; President (1889) of the American Philological Association (1869); President (1907, 1919) of the American Oriental Society (1842);

From the Academy of Sciences of the Institute of Bologna (1712), the Imperial Russian Academy of Sciences (1725), the Royal Society of Sciences at Göttingen, Prussia (1751), the Royal Bohemian Society of Sciences (Prague, 1759), the Oriental Institute (Czecho-Slovakia), the Finnish-Ugrian Society (Helsingfors), the British Academy, the Academy of Inscriptions and Belles-Lettres (1663) of the Institute of France, — Correspondent.

HARVARD ORIENTAL SERIES

Founded in 1891 by CHARLES ROCKWELL LANMAN and HENRY CLARKE WARREN.

Edited, with the coöperation of various scholars (from volume 1), by C. R. LANMAN, and continued (from volume 41) by WALTER EUGENE CLARK, Wales Professor of Sanskrit at Harvard University.

Published by the HARVARD UNIVERSITY PRESS, Cambridge, Massachusetts, U.S. of America.

Agent of the Press in Great Britain is HUMPHREY MILFORD, Oxford University Press, Amen House, Warwick Square, London, E.C. 4, England.

Direct application for books of this Series may be made, with remittance, to the Harvard University Press at Cambridge, Massachusetts. The volumes will then be sent by post direct to the buyer.

The List-prices are subject to a trade-discount. No extra charge is made for postage. This list is here revised up to date of 1932. Prices of previous revisions are cancelled.

Descriptive List. A substantial pamphlet, containing a list of the volumes of this Series, and a brief Memorial of HENRY CLARKE WARREN, joint-founder, will be sent free upon application to the Harvard University Press, Cambridge, Massachusetts. — The List tells the general nature and contents of these works, and the uses which they are designed to serve.

Externals of the volumes. The books of this Series are all printed on paper of high quality and tensile strength, and durably bound in full buckram. The edges are cut, but the margins are ample; and the tops are gilded, not for ornament, but to make cleaning easy. The backs are properly lettered. No work is issued until it is complete. Volume 10 is royal quarto (32 cm.); volumes 7 and 8 are super-royal octavo (28 cm.); and the rest are royal octavo (26 cm.).

LIST OF THE HARVARD ORIENTAL SERIES

REVISED TO DECEMBER, 1932

Volume 1. Jâtaka-Mālā. Stories of Buddha's former incarnations, by Ārya Çūra. Edited in Sanskrit [Nāgarī letters] by Professor HENDRIK KERN, University of Leiden, Netherlands. 1891. Second issue, 1914. Pages, 270. Royal 8°. *Out of print.*

A masterpiece, as to language and style and metrical form, of Buddhist literature of the Northern Canon. By the Honorable (ārya) Çūra. Stories used as homilies in old Buddhist monasteries. Editio princeps. Kern (1833-1917), long the honored Dean of the Dutch Orientalists, thought that Çūra flourished not far from 600 A.D., or earlier. English translation by Speyer, London, 1895, Frowde.

Volume 2. Sānkhya-Pravachana-Bhāshya, or Commentary on the Exposition of the Sānkhya philosophy. By Vijñāna-Bhikshu. Edited in Sanskrit [Roman letters] by Professor RICHARD GARBE, University of Tübingen, Germany. 1895. Pages, 210. Royal 8°. *Out of print.*

Sānkhya is dualistic. It recognizes souls and primeval matter, but not God. Vijñāna, however, is a pronounced theist. But in spite of his distortions of the original system, his Commentary (about 1550 A.D.) is the fullest source that we have for a knowledge of the Sānkhya system, and one of the most important (Garbe's Preface). Garbe studied the whole work with Bhāgavata Āchārya in Benares. German translation by Garbe, Leipzig, 1889, Brockhaus. Partial English version in J. R. Ballantyne's The Sānkhya Aphorisms of Kapila, London, 1885, Trübner.

Volume 3. Buddhism in Translations. Passages selected from the Buddhist sacred books, and translated from the original Pāli into English, by HENRY CLARKE WARREN, late of Cambridge, Massachusetts. 1896. Eighth issue, 1922. Pages, 522. Royal 8°. Price, $3. Of Warren's Buddhism, a seventh issue, abridged, giving the Life of Buddha, for circulation in India, was published in 1922. Pages, 173. Strong paper covers. Royal 8°. Price, $1. — The Warren Memorial (see below) was also reprinted in both the seventh and eighth issues.

Buddhism portrayed in the words of the Buddhists themselves. The life of Buddha (a beautiful narrative), his teachings, and his monastic order form the substance of this work. The Pāli passages, done into vigorous English and accurately rendered, are chosen with such broad and learned circumspection that they make a systematically complete presentation of their difficult subject. Warren's material is drawn straight from the fountain-head. It is this fact that has given to his work an abiding importance and value. It has been highly praised by competent judges. Moreover, it has enjoyed a very wide circulation in America and Europe and the Orient. And nearly half of the work was included by President Eliot in *The Harvard Classics* (New York, P. F. Collier and Son), of which a quarter of a million sets and more have been sold. The usefulness of Warren's work has thus been incalculably enhanced.

The life of Henry Warren as a scholar is memorable in the annals of American learning. A brief memorial of his life and public services is appended to volume 30 of this Series, of which he was joint-founder. It is also issued with the Descriptive List of this Series (see above, page 1). The List may be had, free, upon application to the Harvard University Press.

Volume 4. Karpūra-Mañjarī. A drama by the Indian poet Rāja-çekhara (900 A.D.). Critically edited in the original Prākrit [Nāgarī letters], with a glossarial index, and an essay on the life and writings of the poet, by STEN KONOW, Professor of Indic Philology at the University of Christiania, Norway, and Epigraphist to the Government of India. — And translated into English with introduction and notes, by C. R. LANMAN. 1901. Pages, 318. Royal 8°. Price, $5.

A play of court-intrigue, and the only extant drama written entirely in Prākrit. It presents interesting parallels with the Braggart Soldier of Plautus.

Volumes 5 and 6. Brhad-Devatā (attributed to Çāunaka), a summary of the deities and myths of the Rig-Veda. Critically edited in the original Sanskrit [Nāgarī letters], with an introduction and seven appendices [volume 5], and translated into English with critical and illustrative notes [volume 6], by Professor ARTHUR ANTHONY MACDONELL, University of Oxford. 1904. Pages, 234 + 350 = 584. Royal 8°. Not sold separately. Price, $7.50.

The Great-Deity (-book), "hardly later than 400 B.C.," is one of the oldest books ancillary to the Rig-Veda. It includes very ancient epic material: so the story of Urvaçī, the nymph that loved a mortal (whence Kālidāsa's great drama, Urvaçī). The text is edited in a way that meets the most rigorous demands of exact philological criticism. The typographic presentation of text, version, and notes (critical and expository) is a model of convenience.

Volumes 7 and 8. Atharva-Veda. Translated, with a critical and exegetical commentary, by WILLIAM DWIGHT WHITNEY, late Professor of Sanskrit in Yale University, Editor-in-Chief of *The Century Dictionary*, an Encyclopedic Lexicon of the English Language. — Revised and brought nearer to completion and edited by C. R. LANMAN. 1905. Pages, 1212. Super-royal 8°. Not sold separately. Price, $15.

The Atharva-Veda is, next after the Rig-Veda, the most important of the oldest texts of India. Whitney (1827–1894) was the most eminent American philologist of his century, and these monumental volumes form the crowning achievement of his life-long labors as an Indianist. For his translation, he expressly disclaims finality; but his austere self-restraint, resisting all allurements of fanciful interpretation, makes of his version, when taken with his critical and exegetical commentary, the sure point of departure for future study of this Veda and for its final comprehension.

The text-critical notes form the most important single item of the work. These give the various readings of the "authorities." The term "authorities" includes not only manuscripts (of Europe, India, Kashmir), but also living reciters (the Hindu equivalents, and in some respects the superiors, of manuscripts); and, in addition, the corresponding (and often variant) passages of the other Vedas. Whitney gives also the data of the scholiast as to authorship and divinity and meter of each stanza; extracts from the ancillary literature concerning ritual and exegesis; and a literal translation. Version and Comment proceed *pari passu*. Prefixed is an elaborate historical and critical introduction, and a sketch of Whitney's life, with a noble medallion portrait. A leaf of the birch-bark ms. from Kashmir is beautifully reproduced in color. The typography is strikingly clear.

Few texts of antiquity have been issued with appurtenant critical material of so large scope. And never before or since has the material for the critical study of an extensive Vedic text been so comprehensively and systematically gathered from so multifarious sources, and presented with masterly accuracy in so well-digested form.

Volume 9. The Little Clay Cart (Mṛc-chakaṭika). A Hindu drama attributed to King Shūdraka. Translated from the original Sanskrit and Prākrits into English prose and verse by ARTHUR WILLIAM RYDER, Instructor in Sanskrit in Harvard University. 1905. Pages, 207. Royal 8°. Price, $3.

A play of such variety, humor, and swift-moving action, that it has often been produced on the modern stage. Version, true and spirited. "The champagne has been decanted, and has not lost its fizz." Noble typography (Merrymount Press). Most books of this Series are technical. This one, like Warren's *Buddhism*, may be happily chosen as a gift-book.

Volume 10. Vedic Concordance: being an alphabetic index to every line of every stanza of the published Vedic literature and to the liturgical formulas thereof, that is, an index [in Roman letters] to the Vedic mantras, together with an account of their variations in the different Vedic books. By Professor Maurice Bloomfield, of the Johns Hopkins University, Baltimore. 1906. Pages, 1102. Royal 4°. Price, $25.

The Vedas are, in general, the oldest extant records of the antiquity of India, and indeed of Indo-European antiquity. They are the sacred books of the oldest religion of the Hindus. They represent parts of a mass of traditional material, current in the various schools of Vedic learning, and handed down from teacher to pupil by word of mouth. What was originally one and the same stanza, appears in the texts of the various schools in more or less varying forms. The variations are often such as appear in the varying forms of popular ballads or of church hymns. Thus it happens that the texts of these different Vedic schools are often virtually related to each other and to their presumable original, as are the several kindred manuscripts of (let us say) a Greek play to each other and to the archetype from which they are descended. The comparison of these variant forms of a given text is often indispensable for ascertaining its original form and true meaning. This comparison is just what the Concordance enables us easily to effect. It is a tool of the very first importance for future editors and revisers and translators of Vedic texts.

The Concordance covers nearly all the important published texts, and is in one single alphabetic arrangement and one single volume. It is a royal quarto of over 1100 pages, of double columns, containing 125,000 lines or more. For the lines of the Rig-Veda alone, about 40,000 entries are required. The lines of the Atharva-Veda by themselves would require over 18,000 entries, but are often merged with those of their Rig-Veda correspondents. No less than 119 texts have been drawn upon for contributions to the work.

The book was printed (in the early years of the century) in a limited edition of 1000 copies, now half exhausted; and was printed, not from electrotype plates, but from type. The expense in money alone, to say nothing of scholarly labor, was about seven thousand dollars. It is not likely that any publisher or scholar will soon undertake a new edition. For many decades, doubtless, the work will maintain its value unimpaired, an enduring monument to the industry and learning and resolute will of Professor Bloomfield.

Volume 11. The Pañcha-tantra: a collection of ancient Hindu tales, in the recension (called **Pañchākhyānaka**, and dated 1199 A.D.) of the Jaina monk, **Pūrna-bhadra**, critically edited in the original Sanskrit [in Nāgarī letters; and, for the sake of beginners, with word-division] by Dr. Johannes Hertel, Professor am königlichen Realgymnasium, Doebeln, Saxony. 1908. Pages, 344. Royal 8°.

Volume 12. The Pañchatantra-text of Pūrnabhadra: critical introduction and list of variants. By Professor Hertel. 1912. Pages, 246. Royal 8°.

Volume 13. The Pañchatantra-text of Pūrnabhadra, and its relation to texts of allied recensions, as shown in **Parallel Specimens**. By Professor Hertel. 1912. Pages, 10: and 19 sheets, mounted on guards and issued in atlas-form. Royal 8°. Vols. 11-13 not sold separately. Price of all three together, $5.

Volume 14. The Pañchatantra: a collection of ancient Hindu tales, in its oldest recension, the Kashmirian, entitled **Tantrākhyāyika**. The original Sanskrit text [in Nāgarī letters], editio minor, reprinted from the critical editio major which was made for the Königliche Gesellschaft der Wissenschaften zu Göttingen, by Professor HERTEL. 1915. Pages, 160. Royal 8°. Price, $4.

For two thousand years and more, the tales of the Panchatantra have instructed and delighted the Hindus. The Panchatantra has exercised a greater influence than any other work of India upon the literature of the world. It was the Panchatantra that formed the basis of the studies of the immortal pioneer in the field of comparative literature, Theodor Benfey. His Pantschatantra laid the foundation of the scientific treatment of the history of the fable. From the Panchatantra there came the lost Pahlavi translation, among whose effluxes are some of the most famous books of southwestern Asia and of Europe, the Arabic Kalilah and Dimnah, the Directorium of John of Capua (1270), the Buch der Beispiele (1483) in German of great vigor and beauty, — and so on, down to that gem of racy Tudor English, Sir Thomas North's translation of Doni (1570), reprinted by Joseph Jacobs, London, 1888.

Hertel gives us here one recension of known authorship and date (1199), and another, the Kashmirian, many centuries older. To volume 11, Lanman adds an essay on The Externals of Indian Books. Of the Kashmirian recension, Hertel made a German version (Berlin, 1909, Teubner). The typography of both editions is clear and beautiful. The confusing emboxments of the stories (a second in the first, a third in the second, and so on) are disentangled in a most ingenious and simple way.

Volume 15. Bhāravi's poem Kirātārjunīya, or Arjuna's combat with the Kirāta. Translated from the original Sanskrit into German, and explained, by CARL CAPPELLER, Professor at the University of Jena. 1912. Pages, 232. Royal 8°. Price, $3.50.

The subject-matter is taken from the great epic of India, the Mahā-Bhārata. Like the Ajax of Sophocles as compared with the Ajax of Homer, this poem is an instructive example for the student of literary evolution or literary genetics. For centuries it has been acknowledged in India as one of the six Mahā-kāvyas or most distinguished specimens of artificial poetry, a masterpiece of its kind.

Volume 16. Çakuntalā, a Hindu drama by Kālidāsa: the Bengālī recension, critically edited in the original Sanskrit and Prākrits by RICHARD PISCHEL, late Professor of Sanskrit at the University of Berlin. 1922. Pages, 280. Royal 8°. Price, $5.

As descendants of Bharata, the Hindus are called Bhāratans. Their "continent" is called Bhārata-varsha, and their great epic is called the Great Bhāratan (Story or Fight), Mahā-Bhārata. Çakuntalā is the mother of Bharata, and the beautiful story of her birth and life is told in the Great Epic. This play is a dramatization of that story, and is the masterpiece of the literature of India.

In 1898, Pischel wrote: "Es ist der sehnlichste Wunsch meines Lebens eine korrekte Ausgabe zu machen." His Prākrit Grammar was off his hands in 1900. In 1902 he was called to the Berlin professorship. The six years of his tenancy were crowded with toil (finds from Chinese Turkestan, etc.). Then came the call to Calcutta, and, in 1908, his death at the threshold of India. Under many difficulties, the book (all but a couple of sheets) was printed at Stuttgart (Kohlhammer). Then came the world-conflagration. . . . The printed sheets reached America November 28, 1923.

Volume 17. The Yoga-system of Patañjali, or the ancient Hindu doctrine of concentration of mind. Embracing the Mnemonic Rules, called Yoga-sūtras, of Patañjali; and the Comment, called Yoga-bhāshya, attributed to Veda-Vyāsa; and the Explanation, called Tattva-vāiçāradī, of Vāchaspati-Miçra. Translated from the original Sanskrit by JAMES HAUGHTON WOODS, Professor of Philosophy in Harvard University. 1914. Second issue, 1927. Pages, 422. Royal 8°. Price $5.

Three works in one pair of covers. The Rules are a set of mental pegs on which to hang the principles and precepts of a system which you must learn from the living teacher of your "school." The Comment is a reinvestiture of the skeleton of the Rules with the flesh and blood of comprehensible details. And the Explanation is of course a commentary on the Comment. The Comment is the oldest written systematic exposition of Yoga-doctrine in Sanskrit that we possess.

Of the Hindu philosophies, by far the most important are the ancient dualism called Sānkhya, the monism of the Vedānta, and the Yoga-system. Kāuṭilya, prime-minister of Chandragupta (300 B.C.), mentions Sānkhya and Yoga as current in his day. But the elements of Yoga, rigorous austerities and control of the senses, are indefinitely antique, and are one of the oldest and most striking products of the Hindu mind and character.

When one considers the floods of pseudo-scientific writing with which the propagandists of Indian "isms" in America have deluged us, one is the better prepared to appreciate the self-restraint of Dr. Woods in keeping all that pertains to miracle-mongering and sensationalism in the background, and in devoting himself to the exposition of the spiritual and intellectual aspects of Yoga. His work "continues the tradition of austere scholarship" which has, from the beginning, characterized the Harvard Oriental Series.

Volumes 18 and 19. The Veda of the Black Yajus School, entitled Tāittirīya Samhitā. Translated from the original Sanskrit prose and verse, with a running commentary. By Arthur Berriedale Keith, D.C.L. (Oxford), of the Inner Temple, Barrister-at-law, and of His Majesty's Colonial Office, sometime Acting Professor of Sanskrit at the University of Oxford, Author of 'Responsible Government in the Dominions.' Volume 18, kāṇḍas I–III; volume 19, kāṇḍas IV–VII. 1914. Pages, 464 + 374 = 838. Royal 8°. Price, $10. Not sold separately.

The Rig-Veda holds unquestioned primacy in the sacred literature of the Hindus; but their greatest mediæval scholiast on the Vedas, Sāyaṇa, did not write his commentary on the Rig-Veda until after his commentary on the Yajur-Veda, because (as he expressly tells us) of the transcendent importance of the Yajur-Veda for the sacrifice. The Yajur-Veda is the Veda of sacrificial formulas. An accurate edition of the Tāittirīya-Samhitā was published in 1871–2 by Weber. It waited nigh fifty years for a translator.

For the difficult task of translation, no English or American Sanskritist was so well qualified by previous studies as Keith. To it he has brought his wide and varied learning, and with such effectiveness as to produce a work, which, in spite of its large extent, is notable for its well-rounded completeness. The entire text is translated. The commentary runs *pari passu* with the version, embodies the gist of Sāyaṇa's scholia, and is presented with the utmost typographical perspicuity. An elaborate introduction is given, treating of the relation of this text to kindred texts, its contents, language, style, and date ('about 600 B.C.'), and the religious ritual of ancient India.

Volumes 20 and 24. Rig-Veda Repetitions. The repeated verses and distichs and stanzas of the Rig-Veda in systematic presentation and with critical discussion. By Maurice Bloomfield, Professor of Sanskrit and Comparative Philology in the Johns Hopkins University, Baltimore. 1916. Pages, 508 + 206 = 714. Royal 8°. Not sold separately. Price, $10.

Volume 20 contains Part 1: The repeated passages of the Rig-Veda, systematically presented in the order of the Rig-Veda, with critical comments and notes. Volume 24 contains Part 2: Comments and classifications from metrical and lexical and grammatical points of view, and from the point of view of the themes and divinities of the repeated passages. Also Part 3: Lists and indexes.

The aim of this work is to help us to understand the oldest religious document of Indo-European antiquity. The arrangement of Part 1 enables the student to bring under his eye at one time all the passages that he needs to compare, and to do so with utmost ease and speed. The material of this work was, from a typographical point of view, exceedingly intractable. The result as a whole is a marvel of clarity and convenience.

This work is the first of the natural sequels to the late Professor Bloomfield's Vedic Concordance (see above, volume 10). Others, begun or planned by him, are in course of publication by Professor EDGERTON of Yale University. They are issued, under the title "Vedic Variants," by the University of Pennsylvania, Philadelphia.

Volumes 21 and 22 and 23. Rāma's Later History, or Uttara-Rāma-Charita, an ancient Hindu drama by Bhavabhūti. Critically edited in the original Sanskrit and Prākrit, with an introduction and English translation and notes and variants, etc. By SHRIPAD KRISHNA BELVALKAR, Graduate Student of Harvard University. (Now, 1920, Professor of Sanskrit at Deccan College, Poona, India.)

Dr. Belvalkar, when returning to India in 1914 from his studies at Harvard, shipped his manuscript-collations and other papers and his books by the German freighter, Fangturm. In August, 1914, the Fangturm was interned at the port of Palma, Balearic Islands. In 1919, she was released. In May, 1920, Dr. Belvalkar recovered his papers.

Volume 21 was issued in 1915, complete.

Of volume 22, the first 92 pages, containing the text of the whole play, have been in print since January, 1915, awaiting for nigh eighteen years the recovery of the material for the rest of the book.

Of volume 23, the material included collation-sheets giving the readings of manuscripts from widely-separated parts of India, from Nepal to Madras, from Calcutta to Bombay. In spite of the generous assistance of His Majesty's Secretary of State for India in Council, the work of getting the loan of these mss. was so great that it seemed best not to try to do it again, but to await the release of the Fangturm. — There is hope now that volumes 22 and 23 may be issued.

Volume 21. Rāma's Later History. Part 1. Introduction and translation. (Prefixed is a convenient synoptic analysis of the play. The introduction treats of Bhavabhūti's life and date and works, and includes a summary of the Rāma-story as given by the Rāmāyaṇa. Lanman adds an essay entitled 'A method for citing Sanskrit dramas.' The method is very simple and practical.) 1915. Royal 8°. Pages 190. Price, $3.

Volume 22. Rāma's Later History. Part 2. The text, with index, glossaries, etc. (This was printed at Bombay, with the exquisitely beautiful type, newly cast for this work, of Jāvajī's Nirṇaya Sāgara Press, and upon paper made expressly for this edition at the Wolvercote Mill of Oxford. Each Prākrit speech is followed by the Sanskrit version in immediate sequence.) See above.

Volume 23. Rāma's Later History. Part 3. Explanatory and critical epilogue. (Critical account of the manuscripts. Running expository comment. The variant readings of the mss. The typographical 'make-up' of Comment and Variants into pages is such that they go *pari passu*. These epilegomena close with an essay on the two text-traditions of the play, a time-analysis, a note on the Hindu stage, etc.) See above.

Volume 24. Rig-Veda Repetitions. Parts 2 and 3. By Professor BLOOMFIELD. Described above, with volume 20.

Volume 25. Rig-Veda Brāhmaṇas: The Aitareya and Kauṣītaki Brāhmaṇas of the Rig-Veda. Translated from the original Sanskrit. By ARTHUR BERRIEDALE KEITH, D.C.L., D.Litt., of the Inner Temple, Barrister-at-law, Regius Professor of Sanskrit and Comparative Philology at the University of Edinburgh. 1920. Pages, 567. Royal 8°. Price $7.50.

In August, 1915, this work was ready for printing. In August, 1916, it was delivered to the Controller of the Oxford University Press. In 1918, the Press had nigh 350 men at the war. Of the older men who were left, many were busy with urgent war-work, such as a Report on Trench-fever for the American Expeditionary Force. And when, after the armistice, the printing was resumed, the author was engrossed in the work of Lord Crewe's Committee on the Home Administration of Indian Affairs.

The Vedic literature falls into three clearly sundered groups: the Vedic hymns or Mantras; the Brāhmaṇas, 'the priestlies' or 'priestly (discourses)'; and the Sūtras. Keith thinks that the Aitareya is not later than 600 B.C. The plan of the work is like that of volumes 18–19: elaborate introduction; translation; running comment on the same page. The skill of the priestly story-tellers is at its best in the splendid legend of Çunaḥçepa (threatened sacrifice of son by father: cf. Isaac, Iphigeneia, Phrixos). Despite the pseudo-profundity and puerility of the Brāhmaṇas, they are of genuine significance to the student of Hindu antiquity, social and religious. And they are in fact the oldest Indo-European prose extant.

Volumes 26 and 27. Vikrama's Adventures, or The Thirty-two Tales of the Throne. A collection of stories about King Vikrama, as told by the Thirty-two Statuettes that supported his throne. Edited in four different recensions of the Sanskrit original (Vikrama-charita or Sinhāsana-dvātrinçakā) and translated into English with an introduction, by FRANKLIN EDGERTON, Professor of Sanskrit at the University of Pennsylvania. 1926. Pages, 372 + 384 = 756. Royal 8°. Not sold separately. Price, $10.

Vikrama's Adventures is one of the most famous story-books of mediæval India. Vikrama is one of the most noted quasi-historical heroes of his times. His magic throne, hidden upon his death, is discovered by a later king, Bhoja. Each of the thirty-two (dvā-trinçat) statuettes that support his throne (sinhāsana) tells one story to Bhoja. Hence the alternative title. The theme of the tales is Vikrama, who is meant to serve as a kind of Hindu King Arthur, an example for real kings.

Edgerton hopes that his work may prove suggestive as a model for students of comparative literature. The text of each of the recensions (Southern, Metrical, Brief, Jain) is printed in horizontally parallel arrangement, so that the stories which correspond to each other in substance are given, each story in all four recensions, in immediate juxtapositon. And the translation is treated in like manner. Comparisons are thus facilitated to a degree never before attained in a work of this kind.

From all this, Edgerton reconstructs, with some detail, and with reasonable certainty, the original work from which the current versions are derived. This he presents in the form of a Composite Outline, the concrete solution of a problem in literary genetics.

Volumes 28 and 29 and 30. Buddhist Legends. Translated from the original Pāli text of the Dhammapada Commentary, by EUGENE WATSON BURLINGAME, Fellow of the American Academy of Arts and Sciences, sometime Harrison Fellow for Research at the University of Pennsylvania, and Johnston Scholar in Sanskrit at the Johns Hopkins University, and Lecturer on Pāli in Yale University. 1921. Pages, 366 + 370 + 378 = 1114. Royal 8°. Not sold separately. Price $20.

Dhámma-pada, or Way of Righteousness, is the name of one of the canonical books of the Buddhist Sacred Scriptures. It consists of 423 stanzas. These are reputed to be the very words of the Buddha himself. The Dhammapada Commentary, composed by an unknown author in Ceylon about 450 A.D., purports to tell the circumstances under which Buddha uttered each one of these stanzas. In telling them, it narrates 299 stories or legends. These stories are the preponderating element of the Commentary, and it is these which are here translated.

In style and substance the tales resemble those of the famous Jātaka Book, the Buddhist Acta Sanctorum, a counterpart of the Legends of the Christian Saints. And they present many parallels to well-known stories of mediæval literature, Oriental and European. For the comparative study of such parallels, Dr. Burlingame's Synopses, clear and brief, will prove a very great convenience. His vigorous diction suggests familiarity with such "wells of English undefyled" as the Bible and the Book of Common Prayer. The work gives a vivid picture of the every-day life of the ancient Buddhists — monks, nuns, lay disciples. It is thus, incidentally, an admirable preparative for the study of the more difficult Buddhist books in the original. As especially attractive stories may be cited: Lean Gotamī seeks mustard-seed to cure her dead child; Murder of Great Moggallāna; Buddha falsely accused by Chinchā; Visākhā; the Hell-pot. A critical and historical introduction is prefixed. At the end is an *intelligent* index, modeled after that of George Foot Moore's *History of Religions*.

In September, 1909, Mr. Burlingame came to Harvard University to pursue his studies with Mr. Lanman. It was at the suggestion of the latter that Mr. Burlingame undertook the task of translating into English the Dhammapada Commentary. He first made a table of contents of the work, giving the title of each story and the place of its occurrence in the Burmese text and also in the Cingalese text. He added an index to the titles, and an extremely good analysis of Books 1 to 4. This most useful preliminary work was formally presented to the American Academy of Arts and Sciences on December 8, 1909, by Mr. Lanman. The manuscript of the article was delivered February 5, 1910, and published soon after as pages 467–550 of volume 45 of the Proceedings of the Academy. The admirably elaborated manuscript of the entire translation of the Dhammapada Commentary was delivered by its author on January 10, 1917, just before the War.

Volumes 31 and 32. The Religion and Philosophy of the Veda and Upanishads. By ARTHUR BERRIEDALE KEITH, D.C.L., D.Litt., of the Inner Temple, Barrister-at-Law, and of the Scottish Bar; Regius Professor of Sanskrit and Comparative Philology at the University of Edinburgh; formerly of the Colonial Office. 1925. Pages 332 + 380 = 712. Not sold separately. Royal 8°. Price $10.

This work aims to deal objectively with Vedic religion and philosophy as distinctive manifestations *of the Indian genius*. Free use has indeed here been made of the light thrown on the development of Indian religion by modern studies of other religious origins and types. But the fundamental fact has been constantly borne in mind that the Vedic religion is a system *sui generis*; and that (no matter what it may share with other religions) the *character of this Vedic religion*, as revealed in the elaborate Vedic literature itself, is, and for us should be, throughout the whole exposition, the feature of prime importance.

Of all classes among the people of India, it was the Brahman class of whose genius the Vedic literature is the manifestation. From earlier and simpler beliefs, the Vedas have evolved a definite and strikingly individual system of deities and a unique conception of the relations of men with their gods. — Doubtless in other, non-Brahmanic, elements of the people of India, there existed beliefs and practices quite different from those recorded in the Vedas, and more in keeping with what modern study rates as marks of a low order of civilization. — But India is entitled to have her religion judged by the essential product of her highest intellects. Accordingly, in this work, the Vedic religion is presented essentially as it appears in the Vedas, and as it was no doubt felt by those responsible for these texts.

The philosophy of Vedic India, likewise, has been presented objectively, with full recognition of the fact that the Upanishads are the work of many minds, often in discord upon essentials, upon such final problems as being and non-being, birth and death, good and evil. To later thinkers of India, the Upanishads became sacred texts whose messages had to be brought into harmony. No attempt has been made to do this here. The author does not try to disguise the primitive character of much of this early thought; but on the other hand, fails not to point out the remarkable glimpses of a deep intuition into the problems of reality which the Upanishads do present. It is easy to overestimate these evidences of insight; but it is wrong to depreciate the intellectual achievement of some of these early Indian sages, or to deny their right to be set beside the great names of the pre-Socratic philosophy of Greece. — Due regard has also been had to the evolution, from the unsystematic Upanishads, of the Indian philosophical systems.

Keith's treatise is disposed under five main parts: 1. the sources; 2. the gods and demons of the Veda; 3. the Vedic ritual; 4. the spirits of the dead; 5. the philosophy of the Veda. — The references to the great mass of modern books appurtenant to the Veda are so ample that this treatise may well serve as an adequate bibliography of its vast themes. The usefulness of the work is enhanced by two indexes (they fill about 100 columns), a General index and a Sanskrit index. — Of the whole, Professor Frederick William Thomas of Oxford (*Journal of Theological Studies*, 31.250) writes: "A treatise of such character and compass as in the case of an ordinary scholar might well be the crown of a life's work."

Volumes 33 and 34 and 35. The Veda of Praise, or Rig-Veda. Translated from the original Sanskrit into German, with a complete running Commentary. By Karl Friedrich Geldner, late Professor of Sanskrit at the University of Marburg in Hesse, Editor of the Avesta or Sacred Books of the Parsees. — Part One, Books 1 to 4, revised edition, Pages, about 500; Part Two, Books 5 to 8, Pages, 444; Part Three, Books 9 and 10, Pages, 412. Pages in all three Parts, about 1356. Royal 8°. Not sold separately. Price, $20.

Geldner was born December 17, 1852 (not 1853!), and died, a little over 76 years old, early in 1929. In his twenty-first year, in 1873, he came to Tuebingen to be a pupil of Rudolph Roth, the greatest Occidental master of Vedic learning. Geldner's first book was Siebenzig Lieder des Rigveda, uebersetzt von Karl Geldner und Adolf Kaegi. Mit Beitraegen von R. Roth, 1875. Forty-eight years later, in 1923, Part One of Geldner's Der Rigveda, uebersetzt und erlaeutert, was issued. It was published under the auspices of the Gesellschaft der Wissenschaften zu Göttingen, and contains Books 1 to 4, pages 442.

In consequence of the World-war, the completion of this work seemed uncertain. The Göttingen Society graciously accepted the proposal that the Harvard Oriental Series should carry it through to the end. By 1928, the printing of Part Two, Books 5 to 8, and that of Part Three, Books 9 and 10, was finished. It remained to print a revised edition of Part One, Books 1 to 4. In spite of discouragements and obstacles, the printing of this revision was going on, when, early in 1929, Geldner suddenly died.

Whitney, the translator of the Atharva-Veda, as well as Geldner, were pupils of Roth. Both pupils devoted over fifty years of a busy life to the study and interpretation of the

Vedas. The life of each was proved otherwise fruitful: Whitney's, notably by The Century Dictionary, an Encyclopedic Lexicon of the English Language; and Geldner's, notably by his edition of the Avesta. Both Vedic works, the Atharva-Veda and the Rig-Veda, may truly be said to have been on the stocks for over half a century. The issue of each was postponed by the author's death, — Whitney's for about a decade. It is reasonable to hope that Geldner's may appear in 1933.

Volume 36. Index to Geldner's Rig-Veda translated. The plans of author and editor included a Historical and Critical Epilogue, to be issued, with an Index to Parts One and Two and Three, and as Part Four, volume 36 of this Series. To avoid further delay in the distribution of the translation, the Index will be treated as a Supplement to the translation, and completed as soon as is feasible.

Volume 37. Buddha's Teachings. Being the Sutta-Nipāta or Discourse-Collection. Edited in the original Pali text, with an English version facing it. By Lord Chalmers, G. C. B., Hon. D. Litt., Oxford. Sometime Governor of Ceylon. Sometime Master of Peterhouse, Cambridge University. 1932. Pages 326. Royal 8°. Price, $5.

A word as to the English title of this volume from the publisher's point of view. For students of Pali and Buddhism, the traditional name, Sutta-Nipāta, is doubtless the best name by which to call the Pali work itself. But for the general reader, the title Discourse-Collection is far too vague to be useful. Accordingly, since the suttas or discourses are mostly didactic and pronounced by the Buddha, the difficulty is perhaps best met by calling the volume "Buddha's Teachings, being the Sutta-Nipāta or Discourse-Collection."

The Jātaka or stories of the Buddha's former births, translated from the Pali by various hands (complete in six vol's, 1895–1907), marks an epoch in Occidental studies of Buddhist literature. The first volume (stories 1–150) was done by Robert Chalmers of Oriel College, Oxford, a friend and pupil of Rhys Davids. — Three years later, continuing and completing Trenckner's edition of the Pali text of the Majjhima-Nikāya (vol. 1, 1888), Chalmers issued, in quick succession, in 1898, vol. 2, and, in 1899, vol. 3.

After long and distinguished public service, begun (1882) in Her Majesty's Treasury and covering some years as Governor of Ceylon, Lord Chalmers became, in 1924, Master of Peterhouse, the oldest of Cambridge Colleges (founded in 1284 by Hugo de Balsham, Bishop of Ely). The Master's experience in translating and editing Pali texts (Jātaka, Majjhima), his residence in Ceylon (where Buddhism is a living religion), and his command of the outcome of the work of his colleagues (notably the work of Rhys Davids, and "the illuminating labours of Mrs. Rhys Davids in interpreting philosophical terms and ideas"), — these are some of the elements of a rare equipment for the exceedingly hard and important task of translating Buddha's teachings as set forth in the Suttas or Discourses or Dialogues of the Majjhima. And for that task, the years of relative leisure in Peterhouse (1924–1931) offered the occasion. Lord Chalmers made those years signally fruitful by issuing, promptly, and again in quick succession (1926, 1927), the two volumes of his translation. To us moderns, the teachings of the Majjhima are strange in form and alien in substance. That substance is so *thoroughly done into genuine English* that the version has become a true rendering. We can understand it without comments and without knowing the original Pali. By cutting out the profuse and tiresome repetitions, the three volumes of the Pali have become two in the English. With Hesiod, we may say, The half is more than the whole, πλέον ἥμισυ παντός.

His Majjhima work ended, with unabated vigor Lord Chalmers turned to the editing and translating of Sutta-Nipāta. In his *Introduction* thereto, he states and weighs the facts that bear upon the age of certain parts of Sutta-Nipāta, to wit, The Way-across (book 5) and The Octads (book 4) and The Rhinoceros (Sutta 3 of book 1). These he deems "the earliest elements of our present canonical Sutta-Nipāta." For there exists a commentary, actually named Nid-desa or Ex-position, upon these "certain parts," which commentary was admitted into the Canon. And a commented text must be prior to its commentary, and is usually long prior. — Again, he holds that the narrative Suttas (1-2 of book 3), which tell of Gotama's renouncing the world and of his struggle with the Tempter, are clearly marked as primitive records by their straightforward simplicity and austere avoidance of fanciful embellishment. — Or again, for the age of some Suttas (1.12; 3.11; 4.16), he adduces the fact that they are cited in the Emperor Asoka's rock-inscriptions, of about 250 B.C.

But apart from their venerable antiquity, the Suttas of Sutta-Nipāta are of import also as Pali poetry. Take for example the dramatic scene (1.2) on some Indian Rio Grande (Mahī-tīre), where Gotama, now a Buddha, meets and converts the brahmin herdsman named Wealthy. — The herdsman has worked hard and likes to tell that he is prosperous. The first two items of his boasting are that he's well-fed and well-housed. The first he expresses by the phrase 'Done is my rice,' *pakk-odano.* The Pali word *pakka,* 'cooked, done,' Anglo-Indian pucka, is common to this day in the senses 'well-done, substantial.' His meaning is 'Substantial is my food.' And for 'well-housed' he says 'My hut is snug with rain-tight thatch and cozy fire.' And adds, in smug defiance, 'So, if the heavens will, the storm may burst amain.' — Gotama gives the herdsman a Roland for his Oliver, and answers in quiet dignity, but with a pun of age-long fame, *a-kkodhano,* 'Without anger am I. My roof's aleak. The fires [of lust] are quenched. Let the storm burst.'

Herdsman: Pakk-odano, Done is my broth = My food is drest.
Gotama: A-kkodhano, None am I wroth = My mood is blest.

And so on to the end, Gotama matches each wholesome joy of the layman's life with a higher joy of the spiritual quest. The storm bursts amain. The herdsman sees a new light.

The Sutta-Nipāta, taken on the whole, is the clearest extant picture of primitive Buddhism. The most practical of Buddha's Teachings is his doctrine of Goodwill. In one century or another this has proved an incalculable blessing to one people or another. So may it do again! Goodwill, beyond all else, is what the world needs just now.

Volume 38. Indian Epigrams, done out of Sanskrit into English Verse. By CHARLES ROCKWELL LANMAN, Professor at Harvard University.

This is a small collection of Sanskrit epigrams, mostly done into English many years ago. They are such as the translator hoped and thought might prove acceptable as gifts to his friends. The Series, as a whole, consists mainly of books which are hard to study or even to read, and yet harder to write or even to edit. For the maker of a gift-book, near the end of his eighty-third year, — it is "Now or never."

Volumes 39 and 40. Budda-ghosa's Visuddhi-magga or Way of Salvation. Edited, in the original Pali, by the late Henry Clarke Warren, and revised by Dharma-ananda Kosambi. Pages 638. Royal 8°.

Buddha-ghosa flourished about 400 A.D. His *Way of Salvation* is an encyclopedia *raisonnée* of Buddhist Doctrine. There is a certain fitness in calling him the Saint

Augustine of India. Both were men of majestic intellect and wide learning. Both were authors of works which for fifteen hundred years have maintained for themselves, each in its sphere, a place of surpassing influence. It is highly probable that Buddha-ghosa, at Great Minster in Ceylon, was composing the Visuddhi-magga at about the same time as that in which (413–428) Saint Augustine was writing *The City of God*.

Warren (1854–1899) planned to publish a scholarly edition of the Pali text of the Visuddhi-magga, in English letters, with English translation, index of names, and so on. — Accordingly, he had the text of the entire Visuddhi-magga copied out four times just as it stands in his four chief palm-leaf manuscripts, two Burmese and two Cingalese. These copies were made on the type-writer, and in Roman characters. The text of each manuscript was copied from beginning to end, in bits, each bit as long as the width of the paper would conveniently allow, the four corresponding bits of each manuscript in four horizontally parallel lines, and in the order B1, B2, C1, C2; and so on with the next bit. Thus the readings of any given word form a short four-line *vertical* column. This makes it very easy to collate the readings of the four different manuscripts and to note the points of agreement and disagreement. — Moreover, he had prepared a type-written manuscript of the whole work which he hoped might serve as final copy for the printer. And of the English translation he had made about one third, considerable portions having already appeared in his *Buddhism*. — Buddha-ghosa makes constant reference to the Sacred Texts of Buddhism, quite after the manner of the Fathers of the Christian Church. And of these quotations about one half had been identified by Warren in the extensive literature from which Buddha-ghosa drew.

Shortly before Warren died, Lanman told him that he, Lanman, hoped and expected to take up the work on Buddha-ghosa's *Way of Salvation* and finish it. "But," he added, "the obligation to Professor Whitney is the prior one." To "revise, bring nearer to completion, and edit" and issue Whitney's *Atharva-Veda* took much of Lanman's best working years, from Warren's death to the issue of the Whitney volumes in 1905. The general editorial conduct of the Harvard Oriental Series on the one hand, and on the other hand the work of finishing Buddha-ghosa's *Way*, — both these were for Lanman conflicting duties, too heavy perhaps for any one pair of shoulders.

Meantime, Buddhist scholars of Siam and Burma and Ceylon had not been idle. Their editions of Visuddhi-magga and appurtenant commentaries are in Asiatic letters. The first edition of the text of Visuddhi-magga in English letters is that of Mrs. C. A. F. Rhys Davids. On page ix of her *Foreword*, dated 1920, Mrs. Davids, with the modesty and unselfishness of a nobly true scholar, speaks of all these works as "error-clearing helps" for "the great edition to which my collaborators and I shall have served as stepping-stones." And now, in his turn, Henry Warren, no less true and noble, would be the first to welcome as a stepping-stone this long-delayed issue of his own work, in the same spirit of unselfish and practical devotion to the ideals of the scholar.

THE HARVARD UNIVERSITY PRESS

publishes other works relating to India, as follows:

Sanskrit Reader: Text and Vocabulary and Notes. By CHARLES ROCKWELL LANMAN, Wales Professor of Sanskrit at Harvard University. Seventh issue, 1920. Royal 8°. Pages, 430. Price, $3.

The Reader furnishes the text for 60 or 80 lessons, and with it the needed lexicon and notes. The notes make constant reference to Whitney's Sanskrit Grammar: see below. These two volumes supply all that is strictly indispensable for the beginner. The text is in the Oriental (Nāgarī) letters; but a transliteration of the first four pages in Roman letters is added. The Reader is designed especially to meet the needs of those who have not the aid of a teacher.

The text is chosen: 1. from Classical Sanskrit works (Nala-story, fables of Hitopadeça, "Manu's Laws"); and 2. from the Vedic literature (Rig-Veda hymns, Brāhmaṇas, Sūtras for wedding and burial). A literary-historical introduction is given for each kind of text. The vocabulary is in Roman letters, and is elaborated with the utmost care. Special heed is given to the development of the meanings (semantics: pāda, foot, leg, leg of lamb, quarter, quarter of a four-lined stanza, line, line of a three-lined stanza), and also to the etymological cognates in English, Greek, and so on (ta-d, τό, ðæ-t. tha-t, is-tu-d).

Parts of Nala and Hitopadesha in English letters. Prepared by C. R. LANMAN. 1889. Royal 8°. Pages, 50. Price, 50 cents.

A reprint of the first 44 pages of the Reader (see above), transliterated from the Oriental characters into English letters. It corresponds page for page and line for line with its original, so that the references of the Vocabulary and Notes of the Reader apply exactly to this reprint. With the Grammar and Reader and this reprint, the student is enabled to acquire a knowledge of the structure of the Sanskrit and to do some reading, without first learning the Oriental letters.

Sanskrit Grammar: including both the Classical language, and the older dialects of Veda and Brāhmaṇa. By WILLIAM DWIGHT WHITNEY, late Professor of Sanskrit at Yale University. Fifth issue, 1923, of second edition, 1889. 8°. Pages, 578. Price, $4.50.

The greatest extant repository of the grammatical facts concerning the Sanskrit language. A masterpiece of orderly arrangement. Prefixed is a brief account of the literature of India.

Vedanta Philosophy. Outline of the Vedanta system of philosophy according to Shankara. By PAUL DEUSSEN. Translated by JAMES H. WOODS, Professor of Philosophy at Harvard University, and CATHARINE B. RUNKLE of Cambridge, Massachusetts. Second edition. 1915. 8°. Pages, 56. Price, $1.

This book, a translation of the summary given by Deussen at the end of his monumental work, Das System des Vedanta, was first published in 1906. Since then, thanks to the learning and enthusiasm of Charles Johnston, the whole great work has been made accessible in an English version (Chicago, 1912, The Open Court Publishing Company). Nevertheless, the small book was so inexpensive and practical that a new edition was made in 1915. The summary, although brief and compact, is yet so lucid and adequate, — in short, so altogether admirable, that it is not likely soon to be superseded by a better exposition of what has been to untold millions at once a philosophy and a religion.

IN PREPARATION

Sanskrit Grammar. The essentials, in briefest form and for beginners, as to sounds and sound-changes and inflection. With an appendix of linguistic Comment, entirely separate from the Grammar, and drawn from English and Greek and Latin. By C. R. Lanman. 1924. Royal 8°. Pages, about 50 + 50.

Of all the Indo-European languages, Sanskrit is incomparably well adapted as an elementary study for the purposes of mental discipline in general and of rigorous linguistic training in particular. The transparency of its structure is absolutely unique. The various elements — prefix, root, derivative suffix, inflectional ending — which in synthesis constitute the word, are easily made the subject of quick and certain analysis by the veriest beginner. Thus Sanskrit serves best to reveal the fundamental principles which underlie the structure of English, Greek, Latin, etc. For these have suffered linguistic erosion to such a degree that their original structural features are often no longer recognizable. The habit and power of alert observation and of linguistic reflection (such, for example, as shows you without reference to any book, the connection of *batch* with *bake*, of *fil-th* with *foul*, of *gris-t* with *gri*ⁿ*d*) are best won by the study of some foreign language. One single year of Sanskrit may, with proper books, be made so fruitful, that any intending Anglicist or Hellenist or Latinist may well hesitate to forego the unmatched opportunity which it offers for winning a habit and a power that shall enable him to tackle his English or his Greek or his Latin more vigorously and effectively.

For this purpose, the mastery of Oriental alphabets is of no use whatever. The inflections and sound-changes of Sanskrit are far less difficult than is commonly supposed, and are positively easy if you separate the difficulties of the language from those of the writing. Therefore this grammar prints all Sanskrit words in Roman letters. The use of Roman letters makes clear to the eye, instantly and without a word of comment, countless facts as to the structure and analysis of the forms. And by combining ingenious typographic arrangement with the use of Roman letters, it is possible to accomplish wonders for the visualizing memory.

The explanatory or illustrative matter, drawn from English, Greek, and Latin, will be found helpful and often entertaining. Thus palatalization (important in Sanskrit: *k* becomes *ch*, *g* becomes *j*) is illustrated by *drink drench*, *hang hinge*, and so on. The section-numbers of the Comment correspond throughout with those of the Grammar, so that reference from the one to the other is 'automatic.'

Bhāratan Readings. Easy and interesting stories from the Mahā-Bhārata in the original Sanskrit. Printed in Roman letters, with a literal English version. By C. R. Lanman.

These show to the beginner how exceedingly easy the easy epic texts are. They are chosen with common sense and good taste, and are purged of long-winded descriptive passages. They are in simple unstilted language, entertaining, full of swift-moving action and incident. Among them are the story of Çakuntalā (heroine of the masterpiece of the Hindu drama, and mother of Bhārata: see above, page 9), the Flood, the great Gambling-scene, the Night-scene on the Ganges (in which the fallen heroes come forth from the river and talk with the living), Vipula (who restrains Ruchi from a lapse of virtue by hypnotizing her), the Man in the Pit (prototype of the famous mediæval allegory), Nala and Damayantī (cut down from a thousand stanzas to a few hundred), and so on. To make easier and quicker the understanding of the text, each stanza is printed as four lines (not two), and the literal version is given in a parallel column.